SERVICE QUALITY IN LEISURE, EVENTS, TOURISM AND SPORT

2nd Edition

CABI TOURISM TEXTS are an essential resource for students of academic tourism, leisure studies, hospitality, entertainment and events management. The series reflects the growth of tourism-related studies at an academic level and responds to the changes and developments in these rapidly evolving industries, providing up-to-date practical guidance, discussion of the latest theories and concepts, and analysis by world experts. The series is intended to guide students through their academic programmes and remain an essential reference throughout their careers in the tourism sector.

Readers will find the books within the CABI TOURISM TEXTS series to have a uniquely wide scope, covering important elements in leisure and tourism, including management-led topics, practical subject matter and development of conceptual themes and debates. Useful textbook features such as case studies, bullet point summaries and helpful diagrams are employed throughout the series to aid study and encourage understanding of the subject.

Students at all levels of study, workers within tourism and leisure industries, researchers, academics, policy makers and others interested in the field of academic and practical tourism will find these books an invaluable and authoritative resource, useful for academic reference and real world tourism applications.

Titles available

Ecotourism: Principles and Practices
Ralf Buckley

Contemporary Tourist Behaviour: Yourself and Others as Tourists
David Bowen and Jackie Clarke

The Entertainment Industry: an Introduction
Edited by Stuart Moss

Practical Tourism Research
Stephen L.J. Smith

Leisure, Sport and Tourism, Politics, Policy and Planning, 3rd Edition
A.J. Veal

Events Management
Edited by Peter Robinson, Debra Wale and Geoff Dickson

Food and Wine Tourism: Integrating Food, Travel and Territory
Erica Croce and Giovanni Perri

Strategic Management in Tourism, 2nd Edition
Edited by L. Moutinho

SERVICE QUALITY IN LEISURE, EVENTS, TOURISM AND SPORT

2nd Edition

By

John Buswell
Formerly University of Gloucestershire, UK

Christine Williams
University of Central Lancashire, UK

Keith Donne
University of Gloucestershire, UK

and

Carley Sutton
University of Central Lancashire, UK

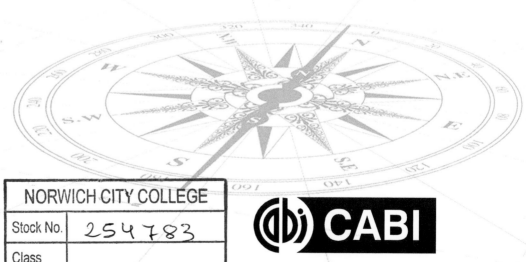

CABI

CABI is a trading name of CAB International

CABI
Nosworthy Way
Wallingford
Oxfordshire OX10 8DE
UK

CABI
745 Atlantic Avenue
8th Floor
Boston, MA 02111
USA

Tel: +44 (0)1491 832111
Fax: +44 (0)1491 833508
E-mail: info@cabi.org
Website: www.cabi.org

Tel: +1 (617)682-9015
E-mail: cabi-nao@cabi.org

A catalogue record for this book is available from the British Library, London, UK.

Library of Congress Cataloging-in-Publication Data

Names: Buswell, John, author. | Williams, Christine, 1951- author. | Donne, Keith, author. | Sutton, Carley, author.
Title: Service quality in leisure, events, tourism and sport / by John Buswell, Formerly University of Gloucestershire, UK, Christine Williams, University of Central Lancashire, UK, Keith Donne, University of Gloucestershire, UK, and Carley Sutton, University of Central Lancashire, UK.
Other titles: Service quality in leisure and tourism
Description: 2nd Edition. | Boston, MA : CAB International, [2016] | Series: CABI Tourism Texts | Christine Williams is the first author listed on the title page of the first edition.
Identifiers: LCCN 2016029186 (print) | LCCN 2016047431 (ebook) | ISBN 9781780645445 (Hardback : alk. paper) | ISBN 9781780645452 (Paperback : alk. paper) | ISBN 9781780645469 (pdf) | ISBN 9781786391087 (ePub)
Subjects: LCSH: Tourism. | Leisure industry. | Quality assurance.
Classification: LCC G155.A1 W488 2016 (print) | LCC G155.A1 (ebook) | DDC 910.68/8—dc23
LC record available at https://lccn.loc.gov/2016029186

ISBN-13: 978 1 78064 544 5 (hbk)
ISBN-13: 978 1 78064 545 2 (pbk)

Commissioning editor: Claire Parfitt
Associate editor: Alexandra Lainsbury
Production editor: Shankari Wilford

Typeset by SPi, Pondicherry, India
Printed and bound in the UK by CPI Group (UK) Ltd, Croydon, CR0 4YY, UK

Contents

Introduction

BACKGROUND TO THE BOOK

> Service always comes with an experience … and all service encounters provide an opportunity for emotional engagement, however mundane the product or service might be (Johnston and Kong 2011: 5)

> Successful organizations in this experience economy understand that they are in the business of producing sensations and memories (Ellis and Rosman 2008: 2)

The first edition was written at a time when the competitive edge and growing voice of the customer were beginning to impact on approaches to service quality and the management of the service encounter with customers. We also suggested that leisure and tourism did not simply involve a product or a service, but were increasingly founded on an experience, which required sensitive design as well as careful management and delivery. The second edition has updated some sections and chapters, particularly in the area of quality tools and methods but also reflects the moves within the business world and especially the leisure, events, tourism and sport (LETS) sector to address the emotional engagement of both customers and staff in the consumption and delivery of services and experiences. As the quotations above indicate, the experiential aspects of a product and a service are now perceived to be widespread and in certain settings, like the LETS industry, to involve feelings and senses as well as more perfunctory requirements.

Indeed, the increasing significance of the experience economy and of customer experience management is a defining feature of many LETS organizations and contexts and permeates most chapters in the book. The book also acknowledges and analyses the considerable development in the last decade of social media and the semantic web and its rapidly growing influence on organizations and the relationships with customers and markets. It has created a mutual responsiveness on both sides so that there is immediate commentary and feedback on instruments like TripAdvisor, and the imperative for organizations to listen and respond where necessary.

This also signifies an increasingly complex relationship between organizations and their customers and other stakeholders as we see in Chapters 2 and 3. Outsourcing and the delivery of events and other activities through a tripartite mix of clients, suppliers or partners and external customers provide particular challenges for the design and delivery of service quality, and a number of chapters reflect this.

Conceptually, service quality and customer satisfaction remain complex and their symbiotic relationship is an area for discussion and debate within the service management literature, as we see in Chapters 3 and 4 especially. Design and capacity management have also moved on with more sophisticated approaches to service design and to managing queuing and fluctuations in demand and supply. Indeed, as we see in Chapters 1 and 5, the experiential properties of the LETS service and product also shape approaches to service design and how customer engagement, emotional and motivational elements and value creation add an extra dimension to this process.

The developments in customer experience management, experience design and the emotional dimensions of consumption across the LETS sector also have implications for the monitoring and measuring of customer satisfaction as we see in Chapters 9 and 10. There is still the demand, and indeed the need, for numbers in customer satisfaction measurement and organizations are pragmatically often more comfortable with this, but the message of the book is that the need to understand the nature of the customer experience and the emotional bond that the customer has with the organization transcend straightforward quantitative measures and require a mix of methods and approaches that can capture the richness and the real meaning of the experience to the customer (see the sections on Human Sigma theory in Chapters 4 and 8).

The book also emphasizes the involvement and engagement of staff in the creation of value for the customer. The first edition acknowledged the importance of employees and their genuine commitment to the organization, as encapsulated in Deming's principles and the philosophy of total quality management, but empirically we can see more clearly the need for thoughtful and sensitive management of staff to connect more closely and effectively with the customer's emotions and senses. The monitoring of employee engagement is now part of that process.

Finally, the strategic challenges facing LETS organizations are also perhaps more intense and multi-faceted than when the first edition was published in 2003. We are conscious that students of service quality, as well as practitioners, are faced with a growing body of theories, principles and practices and need some guidance in selecting and adapting the appropriate ones in particular contexts as we offer in Chapter 11.

THE BOOK'S APPROACH

The book's approach is to offer an understanding of the underpinning theory of service quality as well as informing the reader of the practical application of service quality management tools and techniques in the context of the LETS industry and its specific demands. The book sets out to theorize practice and to provide illustrative examples of approaches to service quality and customer experience management. Case studies and focus boxes offer extended exemplars throughout the book and draw on a range of contexts and organizations in the LETS industry. A key challenge for the student or the practitioner is to connect theory with practice and to apply or adapt ideas, methods and solutions to particular settings. The case studies and focus boxes set out to offer insights into the approaches to the enhancement of service quality or to highlight mistakes made and lessons learned. Each chapter concludes with some questions for further enquiry and selected readings to underpin this. An extensive list of references at the end of each chapter is a reminder to the reader of the scope and extent of background reading in the service quality literature and the key references are sources that the co-authors have identified as having particular importance to the topic.

The first edition contained several important elements:

1. It attempted to present a structured and ordered overview of the study of service quality in its specific application to leisure and tourism.
2. Its essence lay in the nature of the leisure and tourism product and, particularly, the consumption experience.
3. It emphasized the human dimension and the characteristics of both consumer behaviour and organizational response.
4. A distinctive feature was a synthesis of the human and social elements with the more mechanistic aspects of service quality.

These features also apply to the second edition, but the second edition has been updated and revised to acknowledge and reflect key developments in both the industry and the academic literature since the early 2000s. In particular, it should be noted that:

- The industry addressed by the book has been widened to formally embrace leisure, events, sport and tourism (referred to as 'LETS' throughout the book for the sake of brevity) and acknowledges the increasing significance of the events sector and the developments in recent years in approaches to both event and sports management;
- The established context in recent years of the 'experience economy' in the service sector, and particularly the LETS industry, has had a considerable impact on approaches to customer experience management;
- The emotional and motivational dimensions of consumer behaviour have influenced both the design of the experience and its delivery through approaches to service quality;
- There is a continued emphasis on the human dimension of service quality but with more attention paid to the emotional engagement of both consumers and employees, and particularly the importance attached to Human Sigma theory;

- The co-creation of value-in-use is a concomitant development;
- The developments in technology and social media have had a profound impact on the immediacy and significance of feedback;
- The industry and the literature have a responsibility to promote sustainable practices and experiences;
- The imperative for managers to make informed decisions about approaches to service quality is underpinned by the final chapter on Business Improvement Strategies.

The book further acknowledges the growing literature that enables the practitioner, the academic and the student to develop their knowledge and understanding of developments in management in the LETS industry, and the very concepts and theories that help to define the fields of enquiry in service quality. The subjects of service management, service operations management and service quality have matured and expanded significantly since the first edition was published as the extensive references at the end of each chapter demonstrate. The book's content is cognisant of the strides made by both the literature and the LETS sector, but it also highlights the challenges continuing to face many LETS organizations, as they grapple with rapid developments in technology and social media and the competitive edge of a dynamic industry.

THE BOOK'S STRUCTURE

The book is divided into three parts:

1. Understanding the LETS Product.
2. Designing and Delivering Quality in the LETS Product.
3. Monitoring and Enhancing Quality in the LETS Product.

It is expected that practitioners and students will access the various sections as and when required rather than reading them in their entirety. The three parts link with other aspects of management including service operations management/services management, marketing and human resource management. They reflect the importance of a deep knowledge and understanding of both consumers and their requirements and the principles and methods of service quality, and particularly the skills of experience design and customer experience management.

Part 1 sets out to establish the background to service quality in the LETS industry, and particularly the context of the experience economy with its emphasis on emotional and motivational dimensions. It is concerned with developing an understanding of the concepts and theories that underpin the application of quality management methods, tools and philosophies.

While Part 1 establishes the context to the challenges facing LETS managers in achieving service quality, Part 2 examines the skills and techniques of translating the understanding of consumers, stakeholders, quality and the nature of the LETS experiences into appropriate designs and delivery systems. This part will enable the reader to understand the complexity of designing a service package to meet customers' expectations and to deal with the challenges of queuing and matching demand and supply. It enables the reader to examine and weigh up the various ways in which design can then be translated into delivery of service quality through the creation of an appropriate service culture and the use of effective quality tools and systems. Part 3 takes the management of service quality beyond the design and delivery of services and experiences and considers the monitoring and measuring of service quality and how this can be used to enhance the design and delivery of service quality.

Part 1: Understanding the LETS Product

Chapter 1 examines the rapid growth in the notion of the experience economy and the place of the LETS industry within it. Chapter 2 contextualizes the development and diversity of the LETS product, and shows how it is increasingly driven by consumer requirements and particularly experiential consumption.

It examines the nature of services and evaluates the distinctiveness of LETS products and services, with their complex mix of motives and attributes, and the challenges posed by this for the management of service quality. Chapter 3 outlines the theoretical developments in service quality that have influenced the thinking behind such customer-led strategies. Chapter 3 also outlines the typology of consumer characteristics and motives, which needs to be understood in order to appreciate fully the complex nature of LETS service quality and explores the relationship between consumers and the increasingly complex mix of providers and other stakeholders. Chapter 4 extends this understanding by examining the concept of quality and the core theories that shape our understanding of service quality and customer satisfaction, including the relationship between expectations and perceptions and between service quality and customer satisfaction.

Part 2: Designing and Delivering Quality in the LETS Product

An important prerequisite for achieving service quality is understanding its conceptual underpinnings in the first place, as the chapters in Part 1 attempted to explain. The logical extension of the understanding of service quality and the experience economy is the application of concepts and principles to the design and delivery of the LETS product and service and the shaping of the LETS experience.

We have established that service quality is concerned with 'doing the right thing' as well as 'doing things right' and that incremental improvements to both underpin the symbiotic relationship between design and delivery – between intended and actual outcomes.

The characteristics of services such as perishability and heterogeneity and the experiential nature of the LETS service encounter, with its emotional engagement of both customers and employees in co-creating value pose challenges for the design of the experience and the management of service quality. The service design process is complicated for the reasons outlined in Part 1 and Chapter 5 considers how its principles can be extended into experience design. Service and experience design raises questions about the flow of people through the service process and its relationship with the deployment of resources. Chapter 6 therefore considers some fundamental issues of managing capacity in LETS operations and their implications for service quality. The uneven demand for, and usage of, facilities and services require an understanding of aspects such as yield management and queuing and how they can be managed to achieve both productivity and customer satisfaction.

Chapter 7 highlights the importance of service culture to the achievement of quality and the crucial role of staff in this process. It highlights how staff and their interaction with customers (which is central to many contexts) can be managed and enhanced and links clearly to the analyses of the service encounter in Chapters 4 and 5. The notions of emotional labour and emotional engagement of staff are explored in depth and build on the application of Human Sigma theory in Chapter 4. Finally, Chapter 8 investigates the introduction and implementation of specific service quality management systems, tools and techniques in all sectors of the LETS industry for delivery and improvement of service quality. A diverse range of quality systems and awards, both accredited and non-accredited, are evaluated for their application to developing business strategies for improvement and contain very recently updated systems such as BS ENISO 9001:2015.

Part 3: Monitoring and Enhancing Quality in the LETS Product

The first edition contained one chapter on the measurement of service quality, but it was felt by the authors that this aspect should be covered more extensively in the second edition, partly because of the growing impact of social media and the increased capacity organizations have for collecting and analysing data about their customers. The continuous improvement cycle involves a loop from the conceptualization of service quality and the customer experience, through the underpinnings to the design and delivery of quality experiences and to the collection and analysis of feedback. Without appropriate and constant monitoring of customer satisfaction, it is difficult to make informed judgements on what improvements to make to both the product and the process, i.e. the design features of the service and experience and the way it is managed and delivered to the customer. While earlier chapters demonstrated the complexity of customer requirements and expectations, Chapters 9 and 10 examine the challenges in monitoring and measuring them and the levels of customer satisfaction. They distinguish between qualitative and quantitative methods and offer insights into the choice of methods for tracking and for understanding consumer behaviour and customer satisfaction. Finally, Chapter 11 addresses the need to make strategic decisions about service quality and provides some signposting and the options to consider for implementing business improvement strategies.

Part 1

Understanding
the LETS Product

INTRODUCTION

The first four chapters examine the context of managing quality in the LETS industry and establish a conceptual framework that reflects the challenges facing organizations in a post-digital age in which the relationship between them and their customers and other stakeholders is increasingly dynamic and complex. Part 1 is concerned with establishing the distinctiveness of LETS products and services and Chapter 1 explores the experiential properties of LETS products and services and how they have assumed much greater significance since the publication of the first edition of this book. In particular, the emotional and motivational aspects of an experience that may be co-created between the consumer and the organization raise a number of issues and questions that are explored throughout Part 1 and, indeed, the entire book.

First, the nature of the experience economy and the role and place of LETS organizations within it is now a key aspect of any examination of service quality in the LETS industry, and Chapter 1 explores the background to this and how the literature has moved on considerably during the 21st century. We see how the three main drivers of the experience economy – technology, more demanding consumers and increasing competition – are encouraging organizations to promote differentiation and customer loyalty by designing and delivering products and services to customers that contain experiential properties.

Second, this highlights the importance of a conceptual understanding of service quality and related aspects, including the centrality of expectations and perceptions to this, particularly where they are now rooted in the emotions and stimuli of experiences. Chapter 3 shows how expectations are linked to brand and image and uses Lovelock and Wirtz's Model of Consumption Experience to illustrate its argument. Chapter 4 builds on this and examines the concepts of satisfaction and zones of tolerance and, with Chapter 1, highlights the principles of 'guestology' in the Disney context, which are concerned with performance and satisfaction from creating and then meeting expectations.

Third, a further conceptual aspect relates to the nature of the LETS product and service and the set of service characteristics that apply to the LETS sector. Chapter 2 highlights the importance of tangible elements, particularly around the setting or servicescape, and the impact of this on the customer experience. One significant strand of the recent literature has been the examination of what service quality really means to the customer and has provided an important paradigmatic development in the subject. The terms 'service quality' and 'customer satisfaction' are central to such an emerging theoretical framework and, although there is an aetiological dimension to the debate, it has pragmatic implications for the work of the practitioner as well as the discourse of the academic. The meaning of each term is important, but so too is the relationship, perhaps symbiotic, between the two terms, and the chapter offers some pragmatic viewpoints on the nature of service quality.

Fourth, a typology of service characteristics in Chapter 2 and the content of Chapters 1 and 3 emphasize the importance of the service encounter to much of the discussion about service quality in the LETS industry. This involves tangible and intangible aspects as well as the increasingly significant dimension of online contact and processes, and shows how the experiential properties of the LETS product and service are now shaping approaches to the management of service quality and the expectations that consumers have of such experiences.

Finally, the management of the customer experience is now more explicitly related to the creation of value, especially through engagement by customers and staff, and the interaction between them and other stakeholders. Chapters 1 and 2 both examine the nature of value-in-use and co-created value, whilst Chapters 1 and 3 consider the benefits of the LETS customer experience and the aspects of consumer behaviour. Chapter 3 provides a wide-ranging framework for understanding the LETS consumer as well as other stakeholders involved. The LETS industry contains a wide range of interested groups, and their interrelationships are an important factor in understanding the dynamics of managing service quality. The place and role of volunteers is highlighted in both Chapters 3 and 4 and the concept of engagement, through Human Sigma Management, is examined in Chapter 4. The Cycles of Service Failure and Success are examined in Chapter 3 and demonstrate how human resource strategies can have a profound impact on customer experience management and the engagement of both staff and customers in the process of achieving service quality.

Therefore, Part 1 provides the opportunity to connect theory with practice and to demonstrate that the successful management of quality in LETS organizations demands an informed knowledge and understanding of key concepts and theories. On completion of Part 1, the reader will have an in-depth understanding of the nature of the LETS experience economy, LETS products and services and the conceptual underpinnings to customer satisfaction and service quality; this will provide an awareness of the implications for customer experience management and the ability to theorize service quality practice, and to apply such knowledge and understanding to various contexts in the LETS industry.

The LETS Experience Economy

LEARNING OBJECTIVES

- To appreciate the growing significance of the experience economy;
- To understand the nature of the experience economy and the experiential properties of the LETS product and service;
- To understand the importance and meaning of the LETS experience to the consumer as value is co-created;
- To examine the relationship between the LETS experience and the management of service quality; and
- To consider the ways in which the consumer experience can be facilitated and enhanced by appropriate management.

INTRODUCTION

Cinema manager? No, I'm in the guest experience business (Goodman, 2014: 6).

The first edition of this book pointed out how the product and service across the LETS industry was gradually being supplemented by an additional dimension, the consumer experience, in the way it could be perceived, although not all practitioners, perhaps, at that time managed as if it were. The quotation in Goodman's newspaper article in 2014 is perhaps more representative of how LETS professionals view the nature of their business and how it is managed, although, empirically, there are different views on this, as we discuss later. At the cutting edge of the LETS industry, the product, in the guise of an activity and a setting, and the service processes underpinning the delivery of the product, are now increasingly subsumed by their experiential properties, where the emotional engagement of the consumer is paramount and the professional is involved in customer experience management. The purpose of this chapter is to examine the growth in the importance of the experience economy and the nature of the LETS consumer experience and to consider their implications for the management of service quality.

GROWING IMPORTANCE OF THE EXPERIENCE ECONOMY

We have seen an increase in recent years in the literature examining the experience economy, hedonic consumption and experiential marketing, with implications for the management of the customer experience and service quality (Hirschman and Holbrook, 1982; Pine and Gilmore, 1998; Arnould and Thompson, 2005; Carú and Cova, 2007). Some theorists identified the origins, perhaps in the 18th-century notion of romanticism (Holbrook, 1999; Carú and Cova, 2007), but it was Hirschman and Holbrook (1982) who really suggested consumers were looking to integrate their lifestyle with the symbolic meaning of the products they purchased. Indeed, they suggest that it led to the notion of 'hedonic consumption', which they defined as 'those facets of consumer behaviour that relate to the multi-sensory, fantasy and emotive aspects of one's experience with products' (Hirschman and Holbrook, 1982: 92).

However, Pine and Gilmore's book published in 1999, and their article of the previous year, on the experience economy are seen by many as the key influence in this aspect of services management (Ferreira and Teixeira, 2013). The results of their research confirmed the broad scope of influence of the concept of 'customer experience' and also coined the term 'experience economy'. They contended that the 'experience economy' represents a fourth stage in the development of economies after the agrarian, industrial and service stages. They suggested that organizations in many contexts were increasingly staging experiences, a fourth level of adding economic value and achieving competitive advantage. There may be some uncertainty about the status of the service in such cases – whether it is the core offering or the means to experiencing the core offering – but there is still value created in the process (Chen et al., 2012; Grönroos, 2012; Pareigis et al., 2012). Indeed, in the USA, experiences have supplanted service as the predominant economic offering, in terms of GDP, employment and actual value (Pine and Gilmore, 2014), and across the service sector and the LETS industry in many countries the experience economy has assumed great significance. The spectacular natural beauty of Milford Sound in New Zealand's South Island has become one of the world's most attractive tourist destinations and represents one of the early initiatives to market a natural resource as a tourist experience (Fig. 1.1). Another key influence, of course, was the Walt Disney Company, which coined the term 'guestology' to represent their customer-focused approach; indeed, this phrase was introduced at the time that they were developing Epcot and gathered much feedback from customers in the design of the park and they would argue that guestology is the science of continuous improvement in their customer care.

Fig. 1.1. Milford Sound, New Zealand: an early mass consumer experience.

Emergence of the experience economy

Table 1.1 shows how an experience economy offers more than goods, commodities and services. In a service economy, organizations deliver intangible benefits to the customer which are seen as rational and functional. In an experience economy there are many benefits, of course, but there is much more emphasis on emotions and feelings, as we see later in this chapter. In such an experience economy, people readily exchange valued resources (time, money, physical, social and psychological safety) for motivational and emotional experiences that are staged by organizations that have traditionally been thought of as 'service' organizations, as well as organizations that offer products and commodities (Ellis and Rosman, 2008: 4).

The customer experience, in this context, assumes much greater importance and complexity for organizations to manage and raises questions about exactly what it is.

THE IMPORTANCE OF THE CUSTOMER EXPERIENCE

There are a number of factors that explain why there is increasing attention to the experience economy and the customer experience:

- There is growing support for the view that spending discretionary money on experiential rather than material purchases leads to greater happiness (Howell *et al.*, 2012; Howell and

Table 1.1. The nature of experience economy: comparison with goods and services (Adapted from Pine and Gilmore, 2008: 5; Ellis and Rosman, 2008: 5).

	Goods industry	**Service industry**	**Experience economy**
Economic function	Manufacturing	Service delivery	Staged encounter
Characteristics of offering	Tangibility	Intangibility	Experiential
Value creation through	Consumption	Interactive processes	Experience sharing
Consumer	Customer	Customer/ Co-producer	Customer/ co-producer/participant
Nature of offering	Tangible	Intangible (inseparable, perishable, heterogeneous)	Experience encounters that are engaging, memorable and, in some contexts, transformational
Key attribute	Standardized; quality = same valuable product every time produced	Customized to markets	Personalized to individuals

Guevarra, 2013). The concept of people needing fulfilment through creating the lifestyle they want and achieving intrinsic satisfaction through engaging with service and brand experiences was highlighted in the first edition, as was the growing importance attached to the experiential properties of the LETS product and service;

- It is further noted that modern lifestyles including the UK's intense work culture have increased demand for fun, fantasy and escapism through exciting, memorable and enriched customer experiences (Anderson, 2006) that feel 'special'.

As Willis (2015) suggest:

> Delivering a memorable customer experience is the key driver for many companies in the leisure and hospitality industry. As a sector, operators are united by the fact that their product is actually an experience and it is the ability of a company to successfully manage and deliver this experience which can determine its success.

- Providing a good experience is also important because it influences customer expectations and customer satisfaction and can lead to greater customer loyalty (Zomerdijk and Voss, 2010) and support brand awareness (Berry and Carbone, 2007), as we see in Chapter 4.

- It is also argued that competitive dynamics and the impact of technology are now empha-sizing the crucial role of the customer experience (Wikstrom, 2008; Fawcett *et al.*, 2014); indeed, Fawcett *et al.* suggest that, in achieving a competitive edge, organizations must focus on the 'last 100 meters of the supply chain' (Fawcett *et al.*, 2014: 450). The service encounter in the LETS industry of course represents the core elements of the 'supply chain', particularly the face-to-face encounters, to which we will return later in the chapter and in Chapters 5 and 8. Technological advances can also provide the opportunity for LETS providers to innovate and create far more sensory and immersive experiences that further blur the lines between fun and learning (McGrath, 2014).

Thus we can see that the three main drivers of the experience economy – technology, more de-manding consumers, and increasing competition – are encouraging organizations to promote differentiation and customer loyalty (Zomerdijk and Voss, 2010) by delivering products and services to customers that contain experiential properties. This also implies that the meaning of the customer experience and how organizations perceive and understand it also becomes more important. For example, Hilton Hotels are 'passionate about delivering exceptional guest ex-periences' and Sydney Opera House is 'committed to providing outstanding customer service to ensure an enjoyable experience for all customers'.

A number of writers have built on the momentum of Pine and Gilmore's theorizing in 1998 to offer various perspectives on the experience economy and the concept of the customer experience as the literature on these aspects of services management has grown considerably in the last decade.

THE CONCEPT OF CUSTOMER EXPERIENCE

There are different views of what customer experience is. Johnston and Kong (2011) suggest that whereas a product is a thing and service is an activity or a process involving the customer, customer experience is 'their personal interpretation of the service process and their interaction and involvement with it during their journey or flow through a series of touch points and how those things make the customer feel' (Johnston and Kong, 2011: 7). It can also be seen from the perspective of the organization where it is a service experience which is designed, staged and delivered by the organization (Heinonen *et al.*, 2010). It is therefore a planned and controlled process with outcomes defined by the organization and may be termed a 'provider-dominant logic' approach to customer service. This may embrace aspects of customer relationship man-agement in which the customer's perceptions of the overall experience develop over time and perhaps a number of contacts or visits. This, however, ignores those aspects outside the control of the organization and its management of the service process and is more concerned with the cognitive, affective and behavioural elements of the service offering (Klaus and Maklan, 2012) rather than the emotional aspects of the customer experience.

Indeed, Palmer (2010) identifies a move away from utilitarian views of experience towards def-initions based more on the hedonistic properties of a product. This suggests that 'experience' is more than just entertainment or knowledge acquisition and interaction with an activity or a setting, and seems to be relevant to all services. Indeed, Johnston and Kong (2011) suggest that 'service always comes with an experience … and that all service encounters provide an opportunity for emotional engagement, however mundane the product or service might be' (Johnston and Kong, 2011: 5).

A number of specific observations on customer experience focus on its emotional and motivational dimensions and take us into the domain of experiential-phenomenological research (Carú and Cova, 2003; Heinonen *et al.*, 2010; Ziakas and Boukas, 2014) in which consumer experience is seen as internal and emotional and includes the flow of fantasies, feelings and fun where the behaviour is not goal-directed (Heinonen *et al.*, 2010). Such an approach can be seen in the Eden Project's stated approach to customer experience management:

> Our site is an international visitor attraction with a difference, and not only because it's in a hole in the ground. Our mission is to provide a stage on which we entertain and communicate both our work and that of others. Most importantly we want to give you a good day out by taking you on a journey that is memorable and inspiring. Everything links together – from what we grow, to what we cook and what we sell.

Such an example resonates with the views that experience management should encourage the customer to engage as many senses as possible to achieve memorable experiences and the two additional dimensions raised by Pine and Gilmore (1998) of absorption or immersion in the activity and, secondly, active or passive participation are central to this. The Eden Project, perhaps, also embraces the four types of experience also outlined by Pine and Gilmore: entertainment; education; aesthetic; and escapism.

It follows from such analysis that customer experiences can be seen as multi-dimensional and situation-specific (Palmer, 2010; Ferreira and Teixeira, 2013). In the LETS industry the overwhelming evidence from the literature is that its meaning in many managed contexts is shaped by a myriad of complex perceptual constructs and the nature of the setting or context for the activity (Schulz and Watkins, 2007; Martin and Woodside, 2011). Indeed, Martin and Woodside (2011) suggest that tourists' behaviour is governed by many past experiences and a wide range of stimuli, with a complex mix of psychological properties including arousal, sensation and imagery. Berridge (2012) suggests that understanding the nature of an event experience is also complex, particularly given that the relationship between the event provider and the customer is often not straightforward.

Such complex properties also dovetail with leisure theory, which is constructed upon the socio-psychological constraints of perceived freedom and intrinsic motivation as well as various stages of the LETS experience. Manfredo *et al.* (1996) suggested that there are three interrelated approaches to the study of the psychological nature of leisure. One is *definitional* (leisure or non-leisure). The second is the *immediate conscious experience approach*; Manfredo *et al.* (1996) described it as a phenomenological topography of the leisure experience – its meaning, quality, duration, intensity and memorability. The third is *post hoc* satisfaction, related to the notion of expectations, though much service quality literature has emerged from the conceptual framework of 'disconfirmation theory'. This is consistent with more recent literature examining the stages of the customer experience, comprising the total customer experience (Verhoef *et al.*, 2009; Ferreira and Teixeira, 2013). Heinonen *et al.* (2010) also suggest that customer experiences can go beyond direct service encounters and transactions with service transactions and should be seen in the wider context of the customer's way of life and sense of meaning. For example, holidays and attendance at events involve planning and memories of the activity itself. Several authors identified three stages: pre-experience involving any previous experiences or word-of mouth and the creation of expectations; the core consumption or real-time experience; and post-experience representing the customer's perceptions and memories of the experience (Knutson and Beck, 2004; Arnould and Thompson, 2005). Howell and Guevarra (2013) also add another stage just before the consumption experience, that of the purchase experience; it has less resonance with the LETS sector although applies to many retail settings and examples like wine tourism, and is more part of the pre-experience stage as in purchasing holidays.

Chauhan and Manhas' (2014) study of the aviation sector in India also revealed customer experience to be a multi-dimensional construct with a combination of functional and emotional benefits. They identified a significant impact of experiential dimensions on the overall experience in three airlines, particularly hedonism and novelty, manifested in their constructs of escapism, a sense of adventure and excitement. Similarly, a study of a mountain-biking camp identified five dimensions – hedonic pleasure, personal progression, social interaction, efficiency and surreal feeling – with hedonism and personal progression seen by the customers as the two core elements leading to memorable experiences in their evaluations (Klaus and Maklan, 2012).

Value

Klaus and Maklan (2013) suggest that defining and enhancing the customer experience has shifted the emphasis from service quality, where there was too much of a focus on the provider, to the value derived by the customer. Although Grönroos (2008) suggests that value is an elusive concept he eventually suggests that 'value creation is a process through which the customer becomes better off (or worse off) in some respect or which increases the customer's well-being' (Grönroos, 2012: 1521). This highlights Vargo and Lusch's (2008) notion of value-in-use where the value of tangible goods is transformed by the addition of services and, by extension, the addition of experiential values (Palmer, 2010) so that the product and service experienced by the customer is also appreciated by them in particular ways. There is also the view that value is also created through interactive processes (Gummesson, 2011; Grönroos, 2012). Recent literature suggests that there is increasing importance attached to the active customer who co-creates the enhanced value (Vargo and Lusch, 2008; Ferreira and Teixeira, 2013). A topical example of a product in the broadly defined LETS industry is the coffee shop, where there is much more to the offering than simply the coffee. In research in two separate studies, Richelieu and Korai (2014) and Tumanan *et al.* (2012) found that customers at coffee shops in Canada and the Philippines associated the consumption of coffee with ritual, happiness, pleasure and social contexts and relationships.

A similar development can be seen in wine tourism, where the process of sampling and buying wine from producers has become a sophisticated and emotional experience in what are described in some cases as 'boutique wineries'. They are clear examples of tangibles which have been experientialized and where customers play an active role in creating the experience. Carlsen and Boksberger (2015), in their meta-analysis of studies of wine tourism destinations and wineries, show that value-for-money is not an imperative for many visitors; the quality of the service and the setting and the nature of the experience are more influential in determining perceptions of the overall experience. This concurs with one of the authors who experienced a number of Australian wineries in the Hunter Valley, Barossa Valley and Adelaide Hills areas, and the settings and servicescape, undoubtedly, influenced the emotions and feelings throughout the total experience.

Co-creation of value

In such analyses, we begin to see not simply a customer experience that can be designed and controlled by the provider but one that is shaped and influenced by the customer's actions and their active participation in the process. Such a perspective is also beginning to alter our conceptualization of the characteristics of services as we see in Chapter 2. Nysveen and Pedersen (2014) suggest that 'we are moving away from a company-centric value creation to a more customer-centric value creation where customers interact with the company and co-create value' (Nysveen and Pedersen, 2014: 807).

This is becoming more significant in a digital world. Customers can have one to one interactions in near real-time with businesses on social media. Tweets on twitter can go viral (with good or bad sentiment) and these all contribute to the perception, experience and enjoyment of an experience of an event/brand/service (from being stuck on a train, to watching sport on TV at home but participating with an online community, to having a plane cancelled at the start of a holiday). Businesses now need strong social media community managers who almost have to be trained in PR to manage and choreograph the digital part of a typical customer experience.

It can also be seen in the context of sports stadia and other events venues where organizers set out to leverage technology within large crowds to build participation and create more enjoyment from the experience. Baseball in the USA for years has built-in-action on the pitch to real-time promotions in the bars and restaurants – e.g. every time there's a home run, drinks are 50% off for the next 10 minutes. We also see this in Disney's commitment to innovation by involving their customers in co-creating the experience.

It is also referred to as 'experience sharing' (Chen *et al.*, 2012). They suggest that experiences are predicated on the customer participation in the process and often be seen as brand engagement (Hollebeek, 2011) where value is not only co-created between the customer and the provider but influenced by the customer's mood, understanding and frame of interpretation. Palmer (2010) suggests that in these instances the point-of-view is the customer's (outside-in) and not the organization's (inside-out), describing it as 'the customer will get/see/feel rather than the organisation will provide' (Palmer, 2010: 204).

Therefore, value is uniquely, experientially and contextually perceived and determined by the customer (Grönroos and Voima, 2013). It also follows that the provider's view of the experience might be at variance with the realization of the experience by the customer, a challenge to LETS managers we address in Part 2 and particularly Chapter 5, and which is also illustrated in Case Study Box 1.1. Hygiene factors are sometimes significant (i.e. factors which are not part of the core product but which can impact on the overall experience). For example, Fitness First has done much work in acquiring new members for their gyms with marketing efforts, promotions, product innovation (e.g. cheap off-peak rates), but they were losing gym memberships by the dozen for simple hygiene factors (like dirty changing rooms).

THE CHALLENGE TO LETS MANAGERS IN MANAGING SERVICE QUALITY

The Ski Company case study (see Case Study 1.1) also confirms that the customer experience is affected not only by the emotional and hedonistic attributes of the product and service but also the more functional aspects, the hygiene factors, which only become noticeable when they are absent. The setting and the interaction with staff at a winery may create a warm and memorable ambience, but if there is a delay in getting served or the venue needs cleaning, then the overall experience is impaired. Frow and Payne (2007) tell us that the customer experience can involve information-processing and normal day-to-day routine actions as well as more emotional experiences.

Although the LETS manager's skill lies in the ability to analyse and interpret the meaning attached by people to the events and phenomena taking place at a particular time, we are also reminded that customer experience is often created through a longer process of company–customer interaction across multiple channels, generated through both functional and emotional clues as a stream of experiences developed over time (Palmer, 2010). Rawson *et al.* (2013: 90), reporting on incidents of customer satisfaction, found that:

> As company leaders dug further, they uncovered the root of the problem. Most customers weren't fed up with any one phone call, field visit, or other interaction – in fact, they didn't much care about those singular touchpoints. What reduced satisfaction was something few companies manage – cumulative experiences across multiple touchpoints and in multiple channels over time.

Therefore, the perceptions of consumers, their levels of satisfaction and the meanings they ascribe to leisure activities and the impact of management processes upon their perceptions require description of LETS experiences, firstly, followed by explanation and interpretation of their meanings. This can apply to the management of people in the least structured context (e.g. a national park) as well as more directly managed contexts, such as venues for events and theme

Case Study 1.1. Ski company case study

One of the authors was involved in 2015 in a service problem with a UK ski company in St Anton in Austria that not only highlighted issues with service processes and the customer experience but also the company view of what constitutes a good customer experience. The group of eight, including the author, arrived at their catered chalet to be told that there was a problem with the Jacuzzi in the wellness room; there had been a leak, the Jacuzzi was still out of use (it had happened 3 weeks earlier) and there were dehumidifiers throughout the chalet. There was the offer of alternative accommodation in a nearby hotel, which was large and lacking the specification and amenities of the chalet. The hotel therefore did not offer the type of experience the group wanted (having booked up very early) and decided to stay. The matter of compensation was raised with the local resort manager who appeared to have problems receiving an answer from senior management in the UK. It was only when one of the group posted a comment on Facebook that there was a response (almost immediate) from the company. There was the offer of €50 per head compensation and the argument that the terms and conditions of booking suggested that anything deemed to be important for the experience (including presumably the Jacuzzi and a chalet free of dehumidifiers!) should be communicated to the company at the time of booking! This seemed to be taking the concept of value-in-use a little too far and probably represents a very company-centric view of how a customer-focused approach should be adopted.

The customer experience, needless to say, was impaired by:

- Not only the deficiency in the offering;
- The complete lack of communication pre-holiday when the company knew of the problem. The terms and conditions stated that either a full refund could be given when there is a change to the specification or an alternative could be booked by the group before the trip;
- The initial inadequate service recovery on the part of the company, involving a rather impersonal and perfunctory response on the part of the company in the UK, and inadequate offers of compensation;
- The growing lack of trust with the company; and
- The impact on the post-experience stage when memories should be memorable and positive.

However, there was a more positive note on which to end this anecdote. A managing director of the company eventually became aware of the issue when he was contacted by the organizer of the holiday, and his intervention led to a much increased offer of compensation to each member of the group (which was accepted) and some restoration of trust and confidence in the company.

parks. It can apply to superficial, commodified and passive activities or more creative, skilled and challenging activities. It can also explain why emotional attributes of the experience can often outweigh other more functional aspects. An example is the 4 days of frantic race-going during the Cheltenham Horse-Racing Festival in the UK every March when up to 70,000 punters are squeezed together in very cramped conditions with very long queues, both inside and outside the course, at every stage of the process – but they clearly are having a great time. Another example can be seen in the study of a kite-flying festival in Focus Box 1.1.

Yet there are different perceptions of the extent to which experience consumption has been acknowledged by the service sector, including the LETS industry. Fawcett *et al.* (2014) in their research found that few companies they analysed really understood how to use the customer experience to add value to their operations. Indeed, as Frow and Payne (2007) point out, there are over 200 million references to the expression 'customer experience' in cyberspace and yet few companies actually understand what this means, what it actually looks like and how their managers can galvanize the organization to deliver a superior customer experience. Wikstrom (2008: 32) emphasizes 'knowledge is still limited as to how consumer experiences are created. In particular, little is known about the relative roles of providers and consumers in the creation of such experiences'.

Focus Box 1.1. Understanding the meaning of event experiences

Muge *et al.*'s study (2013) examined the experiences of participants at a kite festival in western Turkey. The Kite Festival is an annual 2-day outdoor festival celebrating the coming of the spring, held in the city of Eskisehir. This regional event is organized by Anadolu University Physical Education and Sport Faculty for families and individuals of all ages to gather together to celebrate the coming of the spring through flying a kite and through the performance of traditional dances and songs. There are also concerts and shows, food areas and several sponsor attractions. Their study of the festival set out to conceptualize and examine the experiences of 300 participants because of limited understanding of experiential marketing and consumptions experiences at celebratory events. They found that participants were seeking an enjoyable and memorable experience through engagement and social interactions and were less concerned with the functional attributes of the festival. They were more engaged by the hedonic aspects – particularly an emotional experience; an escapist relaxing experience; and a social and nostalgic experience. This appears to resonate with Muge *et al.*'s view that traditional marketing approaches that see consumers as purely rational decision-makers and the attributes sought as functional and cognitive are no longer appropriate in the experience economy. They suggest that: 'Instead they are in search of experiences that dazzle their senses, engage them personally, touch their hearts, and stimulate their minds … look for affective memories which combine to create a holistic and long-lasting personal experience' (Muge *et al.*, 2013: 17).

Furthermore, Getz (2012) claims that factors contributing to a great event experience have not been fully tested and Ziakas and Boukas (2014) emphasize that the core phenomenon of events is the experiences and the meanings attached to them, and that there is a need for much more management research on the experiential dimensions of events. There is a need for a greater understanding of the leisure experience and its meaning and how it relates to the management of the contexts in which it takes place. The challenge, therefore, for LETS professionals in the management of service quality would appear to lie in their understanding of the experience economy and the customer experience and to apply it to the design, delivery and monitoring of the product and service.

THE EXPERIENTIAL PROPERTIES OF THE LETS PRODUCT

Having examined the nature of the customer experience, we have established that there is increasing recognition of its relationship with co-created value in the services management literature. This synthesis of the theories and concepts of service management with discourse on the customer experience leads us to consider the experiential properties of the LETS product and service.

Motives/pre-conditions

Figure 1.2 focuses on the nature of the LETS experience. It considers the conditions necessary for the attainment of satisfaction and enjoyment and the generic motives of consumers in engaging in LETS activities. Much evidence suggests that the prerequisites for achieving a LETS experience are a sense of freedom of choice, freedom from evaluation and intrinsic motivation or the expectations of preferred experiences. It could be argued that all positive experiences

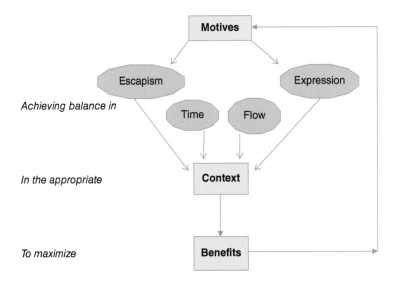

Fig. 1.2. The dialectic nature of the LETS experience.

will contain enjoyment and then will range from a level of relaxation to fun, entertainment, excitement and adventure or escapism, apart from the specific motives of, for example, health and fitness, education or personal development. Whichever applies to particular activities, the model points to the need for balance in the five key factors of time, flow, escapism, expression and context, and emphasizes the dialectical nature of the LETS experience.

Time

It is important to distinguish between the characteristics of the LETS experience and the determinants or causal factors of that experience and to move beyond viewing it as merely residual time or as an activity. Freely chosen time is integral to the LETS customer experience, but the requirement here is the balance between the purposeful use of time and a sense of timelessness, and how acutely providers can appreciate this. The essence of contexts providing relaxation like a health spa or entertainment like a theme park for some people is a sense of timeliness; for others, the goal may be more instrumental and more concerned with a purposeful and effective use of time for achievement and self-actualization as in a game of squash or visiting a museum or an exhibition.

Some leisure theorists (Stebbins, 2005; Kelly, 2009) have demonstrated how the view of leisure changed from one of simply time away from work to perceived freedom, and then to a focus on the psychological attributes (motives and benefits) and the perceptual dimensions of leisure. Others (Ryan, 2010; Stone and Sharpley, 2011), from a tourism perspective, also identified time or the sense of timelessness to be an essential ingredient to a holiday, particularly for older tourists. Quality service delivery involves creating the appropriate conditions for the particular needs or motives of individual customers and perceiving time in a qualitative way. Ryan (1997) showed how holidays are a temporal experience in that they can include: (i) freedom from constraint by the perceived or actual lack of time; (ii) the passing of time (holidays have a chronological sequence); (iii) an experience of time in that, even for some intensive events or activities, time can appear to slow down; and (iv) possessing temporal boundaries beyond the holiday itself with all the stages including anticipation, recall and travel.

Noe *et al.* (2010) even highlighted the cultural differences for tourist experiences of time-bound societies like Germany and Switzerland, with public clocks very prominent, and other parts of the world like Brazil and Polynesia, where time on holiday is perceived to be much more elastic.

Therefore, the notion of time as a social construct in addition to a chronological sequence is relevant to the analysis of service quality and highlights the pivotal role of some professionals in enhancing the quality of the experience. The travel agent can help to shape the planning of time as well as the memories associated with its use; the airline, through its delayed flight, can have a deleterious effect; the tour operator, through schedules, mix of activities and the interaction with holidaymakers, can also contribute greatly to the temporal experience. Queuing and how it is managed at visitor attractions and events is also influential in shaping the customer experience. It can impair the experience if the time lost is perceived as significant, but, as we see in Chapter 6, it can also be used to enhance the experience.

In a different context, one of the authors was involved in some research with a leisure centre that was experiencing some dissatisfaction with its bowls users, most of whom were senior citizens with time-rich, cash-poor lifestyles. The centre was in the middle of the town and was built over a car park that was also used by many shoppers. Everybody paid the normal parking rates, which were in time bands and became quite expensive after a certain period of time. Unfortunately, at that time the centre's users did not have their parking fee refunded, which meant that the bowls players, in an activity and at a stage of life when time should not matter, were constantly looking at the clock. The sense of timelessness, which occurs with many LETS activities, was not present and the overall experience was impaired. After the recommendation to refund the parking fee to users was accepted, usage, income and customer satisfaction were all improved.

Thus, it is possible to move beyond the uncomplicated notion of a LETS experience as simply free time, which can often be regarded as what something is not, rather than what it represents. The sense of absorption, control or detachment is a key precondition for many LETS activities, which can offer intrinsic benefits to the individual.

The flow

Therefore, state of mind is also a factor in the next element of the model, which considers the relationship between the participant and the activity. There is a need to examine the distinction between serious, committed leisure and everyday activities, though perhaps this should be considered less in terms of a dichotomy and more as a continuum. There is a spectrum ranging from Maslow's 'peak experience' theory and Csikszentmihalyi's 'concept of flow' (Csikszentmihalyi, 2012), which describes more sporadic but intense moments of fulfilment and self-actualization particularly in physical outdoor activities, to activities of a more mundane and less memorable nature. It should be noted that the latter represents much managed LETS activities but, perhaps, poses as much of a challenge for the management of service quality as do the less common but distinctive and special moments in a range of contexts: the feeling of magic in a theme park; the feeling of wonder at viewing the Grand Canyon, or Sydney Harbour from the top of the Sydney Bridge guided walk; the sheer exhilaration that some skiers can experience in the mountains; the sense of achievement and absorption that the individual learning a craft or a sporting skill can have; the feeling of utter relaxation quietly reading a book amongst the trees outside the villa at Center Parcs when the rest of the group are chasing from wind surfing to badminton; or the unique atmosphere and sensory stimuli as experienced by spectators at a sporting occasion, pop concert or opera. These and many other activities can be designed and managed by organizations with skill and sensitivity and with Csikszentmihalyi's indicators of flow experience in mind:

1. The perception that personal skills and challenges posed by an activity are in balance (the grading of pistes in skiing is a clear example).

2. The centring of attention where there is focus and the ability and opportunity to switch off.
3. The loss of self-consciousness.
4. Clear feedback from a person's actions.
5. Feelings of control over actions and environment.
6. A momentary loss of anxiety and constraint.
7. Feelings of pleasure and enjoyment.

The characteristics of flow or peak experience illustrate the attraction, and indeed function, of many LETS activities, yet it must not be forgotten that the more regular activities (e.g. the visit to the health club or cinema or urban park) also involve feelings and sensations, as well as the benefits beyond the visit. Indeed, Palmer (2010) highlights the importance of sequencing in maintaining the intensity of people's emotional experiences as they continue to match their skill level with the challenge involved.

Escapism

Feelings of immersion and absorption may also be present in the third element of escapism, which has been recognized as contributing to the recent escalation in experience consumption. The idea that consumers look for escape from their day-to-day routines was introduced by Pine and Gilmore (1998) but it has begun to assume more significance. As we suggested earlier, the UK's demanding work culture has rapidly increased the demand for escapist consumption. Anderson (2006: 73) asserts that 'by leaving the real world behind, consumers also leave behind their real stresses and pressures, which provides the benefit of escapism'. Wikstrom (2008) also found that events which involved 'escapism' provided the highest degree of stimulation for consumers and suggested that 'indulging in daydreams, fantasies, or entertainment provides a break from reality' (Wikstrom, 2008: 41). Many contexts such as mountains and wilderness areas or national parks provide the opportunity for spiritual experiences and escapism from everyday settings, where the key elements appear to be freedom from constraints and responsibilities as well as the spiritual attributes of the setting (Schmidt and Little, 2007; Heintzman, 2012). Heintzman also emphasizes the individual nature of such experience, suggesting that a 'wide variety of nature activities may enhance spirituality and the types of activities that enhance spirituality vary from person to person' (Heintzman, 2012: 293).

However, some studies have also suggested that 'being away' in a setting different than one's everyday environment may be as important as the natural environment itself (Stone and Sharpley, 2011). This highlights another dialectical feature of the LETS experience, where consumers take to a world of hyper-reality created by the provider like the reconstructed Disney parks (Fig. 1.3) or Center Parcs or complex, sophisticated events. An example is provided by Center Parcs' marketing literature, which presents subliminal images of tranquil settings, traffic-free environments and activity breaks detached from the real world. In such cases, the customer leaves behind the reality of normal life and enters a context closely aligned with fantasy and dream worlds pioneered by Hirschman and Holbrook (1982).

Fig. 1.3. The hyperreality of the Disney experience.

Expression

The fourth part of the dialectical process is closely related to the others in that the opportunities for personal identity and self-expression must be balanced against the lack of self-awareness that a sense of timeliness can evoke or the escapism desired. For many people, the LETS experience provides the most natural means to expressing oneself and exploring one's identity and also reinforces the growing need for individuality in self-expression. Wikstrom (2008) suggests that two important factors in the growing demand for such experiences are dissatisfaction with the homogeneity of mass consumption, and liberalization of values resulting in a greater need for freedom of choice and more personal identity in the expression of interests, particularly in Generation Z, those people born between the mid-1990s and the late 2000s (Lauzon, 2010). This generation is predicted to be more sophisticated and to express greater individualism than previous generations. The importance of diversity can be seen in Bond and Falk's theoretical model of identity-related tourism motivations, which contains five categories of tourist:

1. Explorers who have a curiosity in a particular site or destination.
2. Facilitators who are socially motivated in the experiences and learning in others (for example, parents and children).
3. Professionals/hobbyists who are pursuing an interest or pastime like hiking, skiing, bird-watching or visiting art galleries.

4. Experience-seekers who see their destination as important in its own right – it is important to be there and to have memories and images of the trip.

5. Rechargers who are simply seeking a spiritual, relaxing or rejuvenating break – like many tourists (Bond and Falk, 2013: 435).

However, the lifestyle and the pattern of work and leisure for some people mean that LETS activities may be simply cathartic and an escape from the main activities of life. Stebbins (2011) described the essence of serious leisure in which, for some people, the activity becomes a central life interest. For them, leisure as a recreational activity is, perhaps, the greatest opportunity to explore and express identity (Kelly, 2009). The provider's understanding of such motives and satisfactions and how individuals construct and perceive their social world is part of the skill in service design and service delivery, as we see in Chapter 5. For example, the diversity of films offered at multiplex cinemas or the design of a package following the British Lions Rugby Team on an overseas tour or the management of Lake Windermere for various and possibly con-flicting users will cater for different needs and motives. Skilful management will recognize the importance to the customer experience of the expression it provides and the need, in some cases, for an escape from normal everyday life, as well as the influence of the context of the activity.

Context

Whereas the previous four elements can involve a delicate balance between contrasting demands, the impact of the fifth element, perhaps, depends on how it is perceived by the con-sumer. The context in which the activity takes place is particularly important to the quality of the consumer experience (Dillard and Bates, 2011). Weed and Bull (2014) referred to the significance of social settings for many consumer experiences and argued that people perceive and define LETS activities situationally. Many LETS activities therefore have a social element, where friendship or the desire to meet new friends is a strong underlying motive. Additionally, the nature and appropriateness of the physical context (the landscape and servicescape, as we see later in this chapter) are also key variables and explain the motive for some activities.

Benefits and outcomes

Having examined the motives for consumption and the process and context involved, the benefits and psychological outcomes of the LETS experience also need to be considered. As we discussed earlier in this chapter, value is a complex construct when considering customer experiences and service quality, but we can view value, more simplistically, as benefits and out-comes linked to individual motives, and as positive changes in feelings and emotions (Grön-roos, 2012). Ellis and Rosman (2008) point to the staged encounters in many settings where customers exchange resources of time, money and energy for a valued emotional experience. Indeed, Yoshida *et al.* (2013) in the context of the sports sector suggest that perceived value is the benefits relative to what is given up by the customer, with increasing emphasis on hedonic and symbolic benefits in addition to cognitive, functional and utilitarian benefits. For example, consumers attending sporting events assess their benefits and experiences against both extrinsic costs (time, money and effort) and intrinsic costs (feelings of commitment, involvement and expression), particularly when they associate with a team and the symbolic benefits extend to self-image and personal identity. In the tourism context, Bond and Falk (2013) argue that many tourist motivations are identity-related and influenced by factors such as race/ethnicity, cultural heritage, gender, personal interests and preferences as well as relationships – in other words 'who we are and why we are here'. In other contexts like outdoor recreation, heritage interpretation and exercise, there are immediate benefits but also longer term ones which can be transformative through the impact of cherished memories and personal development (Edginton, 2007; Ellis and Rosman, 2008; Godbey and Mowen, 2011).

Indeed, in some early research into the psychological benefits of recreation, Manfredo *et al.* (1996) suggested that recreational activities are behavioural pursuits that are instrumental in attaining psychological and physical goals. They argued that recreation emerges from a problem state, the need for participation in a recreational activity; leisure experience is the bundle of psychological outcomes desired from recreational activities, which influence the choice of activities and settings. In other words, the participant uses leisure time and money to participate in a chosen setting or context with certain outcomes (and long-term benefits) in mind. Similar thoughts led Driver *et al.* (1991) to develop the PAL (Paragraphs About Leisure) model. They argued that leisure experiences result in the satisfaction of some of the psychological needs of the individual. This need gratification helps to maintain physical and mental well-being and life satisfaction, which then helps personal development. The needs being satisfied are regarded as intervening variables. PAL identified: 27 need-gratifying dimensions, including achievement, catharsis, creativity, play and social status, which could be achieved in varying degrees by different activities; and 17 common needs, such as autonomy, relaxation and recognition. More recently, Dillard and Bates (2011) identified four core motivations for recreation around the axes of inner-directed against outer-directed and experience against results, with a number of implications for providers (see Fig. 1.4). The most significant motivation was enhancing relationships, and the smallest was winning, whereas there was no difference, demographically, between the inner and outer sides; the results side of the quadrant was dominated by males (90%) and those in the higher income groups. Certain activities can be linked to each motivation:

- Escape: outdoor activities;
- Enhancing relationships: ten-pin bowling, tennis;
- Mastery: many activities, including skiing and golf;
- Winning: a number of sports involving organized competition.

Interestingly, a number of activities could cater for all four motivations in different people, for example golf, and there are clear implications for managers to differentiate between them and to know their markets. Such a model also identifies with Stebbins' relationships between casual, serious and project leisure (Stebbins, 2007). Apart from the winning motivation, arguably we again can see that a common factor is hedonic consumption, as well as some natural tensions within each motivation and desired outcome.

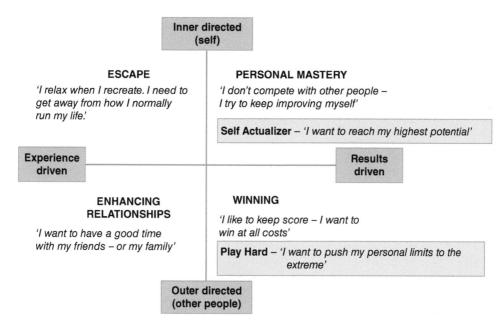

Fig. 1.4. Recreation/leisure perceptual map (Dillard and Bates, 2011: 258).

DIALECTICS OF THE LETS EXPERIENCE

Indeed, what our analysis does reveal is that many LETS experiences involve a dialectical process. There is a clear dichotomy between the desire for relaxation and tranquillity or for stimulus and action; between passivity and creativity; between the search for the new experience and the fear of the unknown; between the common requirement for social interaction and the need for space and solitude; and between escaping to natural landscapes in for example national parks and to those servicescapes, like theme parks, that are designed to blur reality with hyper-reality in the creation of a multifaceted experience. People are different and the same person's moods and needs can vary according to circumstances. The attraction of a superficial, passive entertaining activity can be overwhelming and, indeed, necessary at certain times. At other times, especially for some people, the need for activity or exercise is paramount. The desire for knowledge and personal development (Aristotle's notion of eudaemonia embracing action and citizenship as well) drives some people's motives and, indeed, seems to be increasingly important. As Edginton (2007) pointed out, 'today's cultural, social and economic environment provides enormous opportunities centered on the desire for people to improve their lives through the creation and provision of quality leisure and cultural experiences' (Edginton, 2007: 39).

For the purposes of this book, we have established that the LETS experience is not a unitary concept but a complex and multifaceted phenomenon that can also be multiphasic and transitory. Feelings and emotions can fluctuate according to the stage or circumstances of the activity and are linked to the benefits sought. It is suggested that the psychological benefits of the LETS experience can be seen in a number of ways, which incorporate the dichotomies described earlier but which also represent a hierarchy of needs and motives for LETS experiences:

- Passive – relaxation, peace, tranquillity, solitude, space;
- Stimulating – escape, fantasy, adventure, travel, novelty;
- Lively – fun, excitement, entertainment;
- Competent – health, fitness, sport, crafts and hobbies (DIY);
- Social – family, friendship and esteem, social networks/groups; and
- Personal development – education, cultural awareness, self-expression, personal identity.

As a final dimension it might also be possible to categorize the six groups of motives and the stages of Manfredo *et al.* (1996), Verhoef *et al.* (2009), Ferreira and Teixeira (2013) into four levels of experiences and benefits (Table 1.2):

1. The definitional level, which shapes the participant's expectations and is influenced by needs and wants.

2. The immediate experience, possibly incorporating Csikzentmihalyi's concept of flow, containing fun, relaxation, excitement, entertainment and other attributes, many of which are associated with commodified leisure and tourism.

3. Experiential learning with an impact on skills and knowledge and physical and psychological health and a behaviourally observable condition.

4. More of a concern with personal or self-development and life satisfaction, self-actualization and identity affirmation.

If the definition of a benefit as an improved condition, a gain or an advantageous change (Gronroos, 2012) is accepted, there are some clear questions for the management of LETS activities:

- What do we mean by an improved condition or gain?
- How many managed activities would lead to such an improved condition?
- How are various need satisfactions linked to LETS activities, settings and experiences and how do they contribute to longer-term benefits?
- How far can we differentiate the market to meet and satisfy individual experiences?

From these questions, there are several implications for the management of service quality in LETS organizations and they go to the core of what is distinctive and challenging about the management of LETS experiences:

1. LETS managers must facilitate the consumer experience rather than simply provide the activity, facility or opportunity. Ellis and Rosman (2008: 2) suggest that 'Successful organizations in this experience economy understand that they are in the business of producing sensations and memories'.

2. In order to do this, they need to fully understand the concepts of the experience economy and customer experience in which customer's motivations, emotions and feelings lead to valued outcomes.

Table 1.2. The hierarchy of LETS experiences.

Stage	Level	Related preoccupations	Mode	Domain	Outcomes	Implications for Management
Pre-experience	1. Definitional	Expectations	Functional	Anticipation	The means to participation	Image and word of mouth
Purchase	2. Immediate	State of mind	Transient	Memorability Intensity, senses Feelings/emotions	Enjoyment	Interactive processes
Core consumption	3. Experiential learning	Activity and progress	Cumulative	Skills/knowledge	Achievement	Value co-creation
Post-experience	4. Personal development	Progress and life satisfaction	Holistic	Lifestyle Memories	Well-being	Customer relationship management

3. Value is increasingly viewed as co-created through a customer-centric approach in which the involvement and engagement of the customer enables the achievement of emotional and sensory experiences.

4. The ability to justify particular approaches and methodologies used in service quality is important to the development of firmer theoretical foundations for the study and practice of LETS management, particularly where the customer experience within managed contexts and the application of service delivery principles are emphasized.

It will be seen in Chapter 5 that at a micro-level the LETS system becomes a system of service delivery and focuses on the human dimensions of individual consumption and participation. This chapter is concerned with the relationship between the system of delivery of the product and service and its experiential properties perceived by the customer. This approach embraces the contextual aspects of the setting, environment and activity and the social dimensions of the experience and interface. LETS activities may be viewed not merely as self-centred acts but as experiences that have a particular meaning.

The meaning of the experience and its impact on personal identity, social relations and quality of life is significant and raises many questions and issues for the management of service quality in LETS experiences; in turn, so does the way in which the LETS experience and its meaning and quality are affected by the other elements in the system. Second, the corollary suggests a similar relationship from the perspective of the LETS manager; the actions of the professional may seem to be deterministic but are also shaped by the actions and reactions of the consumer. The human dimension of such interactions provides the rationale for the approaches to managing service quality in LETS management examined in Part 2 and particularly Chapter 7 and underlines the growing significance of engagement and emotional labour in the relationship between the customer experience and service quality in the LETS industry.

FACTORS IN THE RELATIONSHIP BETWEEN SERVICE QUALITY AND THE LETS EXPERIENCE

It could be argued that the study of the relationship between service quality and the LETS experience is based on what might be described as 'interaction analysis' (Williams and Buswell, 2003). Weed and Bull (2014) propose the unique interaction between activity, people and place as the core experience of sports tourism. Gummesson (2011) points to the crucial role the interaction between providers' and customers' networks plays in shaping the customer experience. Sfandla and Björk (2013) built on this perspective to develop their Tourism Experience Network (TEN), which they argue represents the pivotal relationships between customer, provider, professional, resources and systems and procedures. This value-in-network approach is co-created between the various parties involved, but the customer is central to this. In developing our understanding of this process we break down the discrete elements of each topic and focus on particular issues, problems and contexts in a more integrated manner. The conceptual underpinnings to such an approach, as illustrated by Fig. 1.5, provide the basis for the model of the LETS service delivery system outlined in Chapter 5 and have two main domains: contextual and human.

Context

There are, perhaps, two subthemes here. First, there exists an interaction between the customer and the physical setting of the LETS experience. The physical environment plays an important part in determining the outcomes of individual participation in leisure activities and is shaped in turn by the way it is used. Much work has been undertaken into the landscape of natural resources and the psychological and spiritual impact on individuals, particularly in North America (Heintzman, 2012). Management processes in this context are more concerned with environmental issues and with the stewardship of a sensitive resource. However, the design and management of built facilities and surroundings including tourist resorts, leisure complexes, theatres, visitor attraction sites, conference centres, museums and sporting venues have been subject to critical enquiry since Bitner's model of the 'servicescape' first appeared (Bitner, 1992), and Wakefield and Blodgett (1996) examined the effects of sports stadium features such as seating, parking, cleanliness and queuing on spectators' enjoyment and satisfaction.

Since then more specific terms like Sportscape and Dinescape (for restaurants) and Sensescape (tourism) have been applied to certain contexts. Interestingly, Mari and Poggesi (2013), in their overview of studies of the servicescape literature, found that leisure contexts were the most popular. They also highlighted emerging trends and their impact on the customer experience, including reference to the virtualscape, or 'e-servicescape' in which encountering and navigating a website can help shape the overall experience and image of the organization and the growing significance of the relationship between environmental cues and the emotional responses of the customer (like music or lighting) or the assurance provided at events by appropriate signage and sight-lines.

	Human	
	Social setting	Influence of staff
Landscape/ servicescape	Individual perception	Impact of policies Systems and procedures
Activity	Interaction with other consumers	Nature of the service encounter

Contextual

Fig. 1.5. Human and physical dimensions of the LETS experience.

Second, the interaction between the customer and the LETS opportunities provided by the activity also helps to shape the nature of the experience. We have seen how the type of activity engaged in is related to the motivations and behaviour of the customer, with a spectrum of interests from the immediate and long-term benefits of an aerobics session to the hedonism and intrinsic benefits of attending a pop concert. This embraces many aspects of LETS management, including programming, the range and nature of LETS opportunities, sustainability and service and experience design, which represents the creation and maintenance of the service package and the customer experience. The relationship between the goals and motives of the customer and the experiential properties of the LETS product and service package can also be related to the human interaction in the process.

Human

The human dimension of LETS experience management, through the different approaches observed, can be founded, perhaps, on the view that interaction occurs symbolically and that the interaction is dynamic and interdependent. An individual's reality is based on personal perceptions and experiences and interpretations of actions and events or social contexts, and individuals are neither free nor constrained. Typical interaction involves a network in which individuals are linked to others through perceived roles and expectations. They attempt to see themselves from the perspective of others in order to judge the appropriateness of behaviours and actions.

There are also two subthemes to this domain. First, many managed LETS contexts create interaction between the customer and the social setting of the experience; they occur in the presence of other people and, indeed, the need for socialization and enhancing relationships is one of the most significant motives behind LETS experiences. The influence of other people and the meanings and identities ascribed to social settings have been studied through symbolic interaction theory, which provides a phenomenological framework for studying how people interpret activities, events and other people in their lives and act on the basis of that interpretation (Henderson, 2006; Chen *et al.*, 2012). In other words, we behave as we think others expect us to and the role of the customer as a co-producer helps to create and shape the consumer experience in so many contexts. Chen *et al.* (2012) suggest that to deliver co-created experiences leading to value depends on the context and 'experience environment' and requires engagement through deeper experience sharing. They offer four perspectives to underpin this view:

- The actor-to-actor world view in which resource integration and service provision represents all actors doing the same thing;
- Although they also point out that some actors can be sole creators of value;
- However, the co-creation process based on engagement is driven by the motives to be better-off; and
- Value is not delivered but is embedded in the experience.

Second, the nature of the LETS industry also involves considerable interaction between customer and staff. This draws on aspects of human resource management and service quality and, in particular, focuses on the psychological or service encounter that takes place between staff and customers and clearly draws on the emotional labour highlighted in Chapter 7. Grönroos (2012) suggests that the same interactive processes that create value for the customer should also create value for the provider; interactive communication processes between customers and staff, particularly front-line staff, may be dialogical in nature, but to create value for the organization the feedback from customers has to be carefully analysed and acted upon as we see in Chapters 9 and 10.

This approach illustrates the need for a balance between management and leadership abilities. LETS managers require the functions and skills of management such as human resource management, finance, law, information and communication technology, marketing, service operations and strategic planning, but they need to combine them with an in-depth knowledge and understanding of the consumer and their motivations, behaviour and experiences. LETS managers are required to operate in a conventional, bureaucratic, managerialist manner in certain respects, but they also need the softer skills and vision of leaders. Many LETS contexts require the professional to facilitate, enable, motivate, guide, enthuse and animate customers and participants and to understand how they interact with the various referents in the service process to co-create value.

CONCLUSIONS

In moving towards a more coherent approach to the study of service quality and the customer experience in LETS management, a number of points have been established:

1. The LETS sector involves more than a product or a service and their benefits and is now a significant part of the experience economy.
2. The experience of the activity or its context is part of the motivation for the individual consumer and involves multi-dimensional senses and emotional responses.
3. Consumers help to create the very experience itself, whether through their encounter with staff, systems or procedures or in the atmosphere created at large events such as concerts or sports events. This also requires responsive and empathetic management.
4. Experiences are staged by the operator but value is co-created to achieve a range of benefits.
5. Value is not derived from consumption of the activity but is embedded in the experience and the engagement of the customer's emotions.
6. Consumers will experience the activity or context in different ways and a conundrum for operators is to decide how much the market can be differentiated. The greater the differentiation, the more difficult it is to achieve consistency of delivery.

The importance of giving managers and academics a grounded understanding of the differences between individuals and groups, rather than the average consumer based on aggregated results, has been highlighted but it also raises the issue of how far the market can be broken down. The roles of the LETS professional require an understanding of how people define the world around them. Furthermore, they need to understand this reality in order to provide the most appropriate settings, activities and experiences. The approach of this book accepts that the LETS industry, at one level, is engaged in providing activities and services and does this through managing facilities, resources, people, events and programmes. There is a product and a process and they contain particular features or attributes, which are important to the customer, but the significant development since the first edition of this book was published has been the growth in the size and the impact of the experience economy.

The customer experience involves much more than functional and instrumental goals, and increasingly embraces the senses, feelings and memorable moments. The nature of the customer experience is affected by the customer's self-awareness and personal motives as well as the process and system of service delivery and requires a deep understanding by the LETS provider of the interactions that occur in the management of the experience. The deeper the understanding, the more likely it is that the customer experience will be facilitated and service quality enhanced.

QUESTIONS

1. Why has the experience economy become so significant in recent years?
2. Explain why you think there is a need for LETS providers to co-create value.
3. To what extent is the LETS experience dialectical?
4. Choose a LETS activity or event with which you are familiar and identify its experiential dimensions and how you might enhance them.

FURTHER READING

Four core readings which provide a very comprehensive background to the experience economy and customer experience management:

Ellis, G.D. and Rosman, J.R. (2008) Creating value for participants through experience staging: parks, recreation, and tourism in the experience industry. *Journal of Park and Recreation Administration* 26(4), 1–20.

Ferreira, H. and Teixeira, A.C. (2013) 'Welcome to the experience economy': assessing the role of customer experience literature through bibliometric analysis. *FEP Working Paper 481*, University of Porto, Portugal.

Palmer, A. (2010) Customer experience management: a critical review of an emerging idea. *The Journal of Services Marketing* 24(3), 196–208.

Pine, J.B. and Gilmore, J.H. (1999) *The Experience Economy: Work in Theatre and Every Business a Stage.* McGraw-Hill, London.

REFERENCES

Anderson, J. (2006) Entertainment consumption: how entertainment goods give people what they want. *American Marketing Association* 17, 73–74.

Arnould, E.J. and Thompson, C.J. (2005) Consumer Culture Theory (CCT): twenty years of research. *Journal of Consumer Behaviour* 31(4), 868–882.

Berridge, G. (2012) Event experience: a case study of differences in the way in which organisers plan an event experience and the way in which guests receive the experience. *Journal of Park and Recreation Administration* 30(3), 7–23.

Berry, L.L. and Carbone, L.P. (2007) Build loyalty through experience management. *Quality Progress* 40(9), 26–32.

Bitner, M.J. (1992) Servicescapes: the impact of physical surroundings on customers and employees. *Journal of Marketing* 56(2), 57–71.

Bond, N. and Falk, J. (2013) Tourism and identity-related motivations. *International Journal of Tourism Research* 15, 430–442.

Carlsen, J. and Boksberger, P. (2015) Enhancing consumer value in wine tourism. *Journal of Hospitality & Tourism Research* 39(1), 132–144.

Carú, A. and Cova, B. (2003) Revisiting consumption experience: A more humble but complete view of the concept. *Marketing Theory* 3(2), 267–286.

Carú, A. and Cova, B. (2007) *Consuming Experience*. Routledge, Oxford, UK.

Chauhan, V. and Manhas, D. (2014) Dimensional analysis of customer experience in civil aviation sector. *Journal of Services Research* 14(1), 75–98.

Chen, T., Drennan, J. and Andrews, L. (2012) Experience sharing. *Journal of Marketing Management* 28(13–14), 1535–1552.

Csikszentmihalyi, M. (2012) The importance of challenge for the enjoyment of intrinsically motivated, goal-directed activities. *Personality and Social Psychology Bulletin* 38(3), 317–330.

Dillard, J.E. and Bates, D.L. (2011) Leisure motivation revisited: why people recreate. *Managing Leisure* 16, 253–268.

Driver, B.L., Tinsley, H.E.A. and Manfredo, M.J. (1991) Results from two inventories designed to assess the breadth of the perceived psychological benefits of leisure. In: Driver, B.L., Brown, P.J. and Peterson, G.L. (eds) *Benefits of Leisure*. Venture Publishing Inc., State College, Pennsylvania, pp. 263–287.

Edginton, C. (2007) World leisure: promoting social, cultural and economic development in the 21st century. *Australasian Parks and Recreation*, Winter 2007, 39–42.

Ellis, G.D. and Rosman, J.R. (2008) Creating value for participants through experience staging: parks, recreation and tourism in the experience industry. *Journal of Park and Recreation Administration* 26(4), 1–20.

Fawcett, A.M., Fawcett, E., Cooper, M.B. and Daynes, K.S. (2014) Moments of angst: a critical incident approach to designing customer-experience value systems. *Benchmarking: An International Journal* 21(3), 450–480.

Ferreira, H. and Teixeira, A.C. (2013) 'Welcome to the experience economy': assessing the role of customer experience literature through bibliometric analysis. *FEP Working Paper* 481, University of Porto, Portugal.

Frow, P. and Payne, A. (2007) Towards the 'perfect' customer experience. *Journal of Brand Management* 15, 89–101.

Getz, D. (2012) *Event Studies. Theory, Research and Policy for Planned Events*. Routledge, London.

Godbey, G. and Mowen, A. (2011) The benefits of physical activity provided in parks and recreation services: the scientific evidence. *Australasian Parks and Leisure*, 26–30.

Goodman, M. (2014) Cinemas manager? No, I'm in the guest experience business. *Sunday Times*, 6.

Grönroos, C. (2008) Service logic revisited: who creates value? And who co-creates? *European Business Review* 20(4), 298–314.

Grönroos, C. (2012) Conceptualising value co-creation: a journey to the 1970s and back to the future. *Journal of Marketing Management* 28(13–14), 1520–1534.

Grönroos, C. and Voima, P. (2013) Critical service logic: making sense of value creation and co-creation. *Journal of the Academy of Marketing Science* 41, 133–156.

Gummesson, E. (2011) *Total Relationship Marketing*, 3rd edn. Butterworth-Heineman, Oxford, UK.

Heinonen, K., Strandvik, T., Mickelsson, K.-J., Edvardsson, B., Sundstrom, E. and Andersson, P. (2010) A customer-dominant logic of service. *Journal of Service Management* 21(4), 531–548.

Heintzman, P. (2012) The spiritual dimension of campers' park experience: management implications. *Managing Leisure* 17, 291–310.

Henderson, K.A. (2006) *Dimensions of Choice: Qualitative Approaches to Research in Parks. Recreation, Tourism, Sport, and Leisure*. Venture Publishing, College Park, Pennsylvania.

Hirschman, E.C. and Holbrook, M.B. (1982) Hedonic consumption: emerging concepts, methods and propositions. *Journal of Marketing* 46, 92–101.

Holbrook, M.B. (1999) *Consumer Value: A Framework for Analysis and Research*. Routledge, London.

Hollebeek, L. (2011) Exploring customer brand engagement: definitions and themes. *Journal of Strategic Marketing* 19(7), 555–573.

Howell, R.T. and Guevarra, D.A. (2013) Buying happiness: differential consumption experiences for material and experiential purchases. In: Columbus, A.M. (ed.) *Advances in Psychology Research*. Nova Science Publishers, Hauppauge, New York, pp. 57–69.

Howell, R.T., Pchelin, P. and Lyer, R. (2012) The preference for experiences over possessions: measurement and construct validation of the experiential buying tendency scale. *Journal of Positive Psychology* 7(1), 57–71.

Johnston, R. and Kong, X. (2011) The customer experience: a road-map for improvement. *Managing Service Quality* 21(1), 5–24.

Kelly, J. (2009) Work and leisure: a simplified paradigm. *Journal of Leisure Research* 4(3), 439–451.

Klaus, P. and Maklan, S. (2012) Bridging the gap for destination extreme sports: a model of sports tourism customer experience. *Journal of Marketing Management* 27(13/14), 1341–1365.

Klaus, P. and Maklan, S. (2013) Towards a better measure of customer experience. *International Journal of Market Research* 55(2), 227–246.

Knutson, J.B. and Beck, A.J. (2004) Identifying the dimensions of the experience construct: development of the model. *Journal of Quality Assurance in Hospitality & Tourism* 4(3–4), 23–35.

Lauzon, E. (2010) Are you ready for generation Z? *Enterprise Innovation* 6(2), 44–47.

Manfredo, M.J., Driver, B.L. and Tarrant, M.A. (1996) Measuring leisure motivation: a meta-analysis of the recreation experience preference scales. *Journal of Leisure Research* 3, 188–213.

Mari, M. and Poggesi, S. (2013) Servicescape cues and customer behaviour: a systematic literature review and research agenda. *The Service Industries Journal* 33(2), 171–199.

Martin, D. and Woodside, A.G. (2011) Gestalt modeling of international tourism behavior: applying dimensional qualitative research in constructing grounded theory. *Psychology & Marketing* 28(10), 998–1026.

McGrath, R. (2014) Visitor Attractions. *Mintel Report,* December 2014.

Muge, A., Mehpare, T.A., Metin, A. and Tuba, S. (2013) Thematic events as an experiential marketing tool: kite festival on the experience stage. *International Journal of Sport Management Recreation & Tourism* 12, 17–28.

Noe, F.P., Uysal, M. and Magnini, V. (2010) *Tourist Customer Satisfaction: An Encounter Approach*. Routledge, London.

Nysveen, H. and Pedersen, P. (2014) Influence of co-creation and brand experience. *International Journal of Market Research* 56(6), 807–852.

Palmer, A. (2010) Customer experience management: a critical review of an emerging idea. *The Journal of Services Marketing* 24(3), 196–208.

Pareigis, J., Echeverri, P. and Edvardsson, B. (2012) Exploring internal mechanisms forming customer servicescape experiences. *Journal of Service Management* 23 (5), 677–695.

Pine, J.B. and Gilmore, J.H. (1998) Welcome to the experience economy. *Harvard Business Review* 76(4), 97–105.

Pine, J.B. and Gilmore, J.H. (1999) *The Experience Economy: Work in Theatre and Every Business a Stage.* McGraw-Hill, London.

Pine, J.B. and Gilmore, J.H. (2008) Keep it real. *Marketing Management* 17(1), 18–24.

Pine, B.J. and Gilmore, J.H. (2014) A leader's guide to innovation in the experience economy. *Strategy & Leadership* 42(1), 24–29.

Rawson, A., Duncan, E. and Jones, C. (2013) The truth about customer experience. *Harvard Business Review* 91(9), 90–98.

Richelieu, A. and Korai, B. (2014) An expanded servicescape perspective. *Qualitative Market Research: An International Journal* 17(3), 192–208.

Ryan, C. (1997) From motivation to assessment. In: Ryan, C. (ed.) *The Tourist Experience.* Cassell, London.

Ryan, C. (2010) Ways of conceptualizing the tourist experience: A review of literature. *Tourism Recreation Research* 35(1), 37–46.

Schmidt, C. and Little, D.E. (2007) Qualitative insights into leisure as a spiritual experience. *Journal of Leisure Research* 39(2), 222–247.

Schulz, J. and Watkins, M. (2007) The development of the leisure meanings inventory. *Journal of Leisure Research* 39(3), 477.

Sfandla, C. and Björk, P. (2013) Tourism experience network: co-creation of experiences in interactive processes. *International Journal of Tourism Research* 15, 495–506.

Stebbins, R.A. (2005) Project-based leisure: theoretical neglect of a common use of free time. *Leisure Studies* 24, 1–11.

Stebbins, R.A. (2007) *Serious Leisure: A Perspective for Our Time.* Transaction, New Brunswick, New Jersey.

Stebbins, R.A. (2011) The semiotic self and serious leisure. *American Society* 42, 238–248.

Stone, P.R. and Sharpley, R. (2011) *Tourist Experiences: Contemporary Perspectives.* Routledge, London.

Tumanan, M., Lansangan, J. and Ryan, G. (2012) More than just a *cuppa* coffee: a multi-dimensional approach towards analyzing the factors that define place attachment. *International Journal of Hospitality Management* 31(2), 529–534.

Vargo, S.L. and Lusch, R.F. (2008) Service dominant logic: continuing the evolution. *Journal of the Academy of Marketing Science* 36(1), 1–10.

Verhoef, P.C., Lemon, K.N., Parasuraman, A., Roggeveen, A., Tsiros, M. and Shlesinger, L.A. (2009) Customer experience creation: determinants, dynamics and management strategies. *Journal of Retailing* 85(1), 31–41.

Wakefield, K.L. and Blodgett, J.G. (1996) The effect of the servicescape on customers' behavioural intentions in leisure service settings. *Journal of Services Marketing* 10, 45–61.

Weed, M. and Bull, C. (2014) *Sports Tourism: Participants, Policy and Providers.* Routledge, London.

Wikstrom, S.R. (2008) A consumer perspective on experience creation. *Journal of Customer Behaviour* 7(1), 31–50.

Williams, C. and Buswell, J. (2003) *Service Quality in Leisure and Tourism.* CAB International, London.

Willis (2015) The leisure and hospitality risk environment. Available at: http://www.willis.co.uk/Client_Solutions/Industries/Leisure_and_Hospitality (accessed May 2016).

Yoshida, M., Jeffrey, D.J. and Cronin, J. Jr (2013) Value creation: assessing the relationships between quality, consumption value and behavioural intentions at sporting events. *International Journal of Sports Marketing & Sponsorship* 14(2), 126.

Ziakas, V. and Boukas, N. (2014) Contextualizing phenomenology event management research: deciphering the meaning of event experiences. *International Journal of Event & Festival Management* 5(1), 56–73.

Zomerdijk, G.L. and Voss, A.C. (2010) Service design for experience-centric services. *Journal of Service Research* 13(1), 67–82.

chapter 2

Service Characteristics and the Nature of the LETS Product

LEARNING OBJECTIVES

- To explore the convergence of goods and service products when offering experiences to customers;
- To recognize the importance of the physical elements (tangibles) in the service environment and the effect on the employees and customers;
- To understand the effect on customers of social interactions in the servicescape;
- To investigate the traditional and the new approaches to service characteristics;
- To understand the importance of core and peripheral service offerings; and
- To explore whether or not a typology of services is necessary.

INTRODUCTION

The historical debate on the characteristics of service was that they comprise tangibles and intangibles (elements that are illusive, cannot be touched and which are not seen in the production of goods). This characteristic is frequently used to distinguish goods from service. Currently, there is a paradigm shift from the traditional theoretical framework of intangibility, heterogeneity, inseparability and perishability (IHIP) being the characteristics of service due to the use of technology in the production and delivery of services (Edvardsson *et al.*, 2005).

The authors will address both the traditional (IHIP) and the newer approaches to service characteristics such as non-ownership, value creation and value-in-use. The demand to provide core and peripheral services is discussed; the need to categorize services into typologies is also questioned in this chapter.

GOODS VERSUS SERVICE DICHOTOMY

The tangible characteristic of goods versus the intangibility of services was usually the one element that enabled customers to distinguish between goods and services, if they so wished. According to Chandon *et al.* (1997) at the end of the service encounter there is an absence of exchange of tangible goods. This can be seen as an over-simplification of the technology-embedded service environment of today.

Whilst economists reinforce the notion that goods and service are independent of each other, their premise is that the intangibility of services makes them readily identifiable. This is not the case in practice (Greenfield, 2002). Xin *et al.* (2013) in their knowledge-intensive business services research noted that distinguishing between goods and services is increasingly difficult. Goods and services are combined into what Shankar *et al.* (2009, pp. 95) call Hybrid Solutions (e.g. a car rental or football pitch booking) whereby a supplier hands over goods to fulfil a service contract. A characteristic of service which is overlooked according to Lovelock and Gummesson (2004, pp. 23) is the *'absence of ownership'*, which helps to make some distinction between goods and service. In the examples above the customer has temporary rights to use the car or the football pitch, but within a specified timespan.

Gummesson (2007) suggests in his later work that the notion of a goods versus service dichotomy is invalid. A holistic approach is proposed by Daniels (2012), comprising an integrated system of production and consumption with no distinction between goods and service, as the servitization of goods illustrates.

Servitization of goods

Before moving on from the goods versus service dichotomy, it is useful to consider what is happening in the manufacturing arena. A phenomenon known as 'servitization' is being endorsed. Servitization is defined as giving the customers a high level of service to meet their needs when purchasing goods (Looy *et al.*, 2003). The Aston University Centre for Servitization Research and Practice (2014) definition goes further, stating it is 'The process by which a manufacturer changes its business model to provide a holistic solution to the customer, helping the customer to improve its competitiveness, rather than just engaging in a single transaction through the sale of a physical product'. Their impact study of servitization showed that it is a way of developing a long-term relationship with the customer (Aston University Centre for Servitization Research and Practice, 2013). As manufacturers embrace services, this practice is in keeping with Daniels' (2012) notion of holistic integrated systems.

Neely *et al.* (2011) seem to favour the inclusive definition of Looy *et al.* (2003) and state that servitization is finding service solutions that support or complement products, but agrees that it can differentiate a manufacturer from its competition. In practice this manifests itself in acceptable delivery times, installation, after-care and information hotlines. The supplementing of goods with additional services follows closely the concept of core and peripheral services which will be discussed later in this chapter. Additionally, the convergence of goods and services will be explored in the context of whether or not a typology of services is needed.

One characteristic that is prevalent to both goods and services is that of tangibility. A potential customer may not be able to pre-judge a meal before eating it but they are able to assess the 'look' of the restaurant premises even if it is via a website. The use of the tangible elements of the service experience to favourably arouse customers can be seen in Fig. 2.1 and will be discussed next.

Tangible service characteristic

If we consider the previous mainstream thinking that production and consumption of services takes place simultaneously, consumers are therefore exposed to tangible (physical) elements required for the service delivery, referred to as the service factory (Bitner, 1992). For example

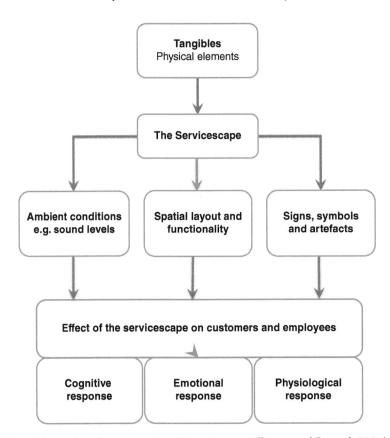

Fig. 2.1. Tangible service characteristics (Bitner, 1992; Williams and Dargel, 2004).

in hotels, sports arenas, restaurants and visitor centres this not only includes the environment the customer instantly sees when they walk into the front of house but in having dress codes for front-line staff and sometimes even the customers.

With high levels of technology within the service delivery processes, the tangible element first exposed to the consumers may be the company's website (train and flight tickets; hotel and holiday bookings). The look and ease of use of a website can give a customer a positive or negative impression of the service providers. Websites can also: provide potential clients with 360° virtual tours of the facilities; stream welcome talks by key personnel; and allow past concerts to be seen via their computers prior to purchase. Previously, organizations looked towards their written literature such as holiday brochures to give clients clues and reduce the risk of engaging with an inappropriate experience or service provider; now, websites have taken their place.

Organizations realize that the tangible elements of the service delivery process are important in influencing their consumers and that it is an area within their control. The Ritz-Carlton Hotels now use experiential service design techniques to attract a younger generation looking for a luxury hotel. Instead of having a corporate colour palette, standardized furniture and artefacts, each hotel is able to furnish and develop services to complement the destination and its guests. Nixon and Rieple (2010) use the term 'scenography', as illustrated by the redesign of the Afternoon Tea specifically for the Ritz-Carlton hotel at South Beach Miami. This consists of acid jazz lounge music and mojito cocktails rather than classical music, scones and earl grey tea.

Bitner, as early as 1992, recognized the importance of the tangible elements of the service setting. She devised the still widely used concept of the 'servicescape', which is discussed next in this chapter.

Tangibles: the servicescape concept

According to Bitner (1992), the servicescape is made up of three component parts:

- Ambient conditions;
- Spatial layout and functionality; and
- Signs, symbols and artefacts (see Fig. 2.1).

Ambient conditions of the servicescape include the level and type of music, lighting levels and temperature. At a rock concert the audience would expect loud music, explosive lighting effects and be disappointed if this did not happen. Equally the audience would require safe levels of lighting in the concert venue's passageways, toilet facilities and food outlets. Visiting the same venue for a classical concert, good sound quality would be expected but not necessarily very loud, and lighting so the audience could see the performers but not a light show. At events the ambient conditions are often the most powerful determinant of customer satisfaction.

Spatial layout and functionality is somewhat dictated by the services to be delivered. Even so service providers still have the ability to decide on the image they wish to portray or the goal they are trying to achieve. For example a budget hotel will have much smaller communal areas than a five-star luxury hotel. Some facilities will have dual functionality in the budget end of the market with the breakfast room being used as the bar and residents lounge in the evenings. Rosenbaum and Massiah (2011) remind us of the 'designscape' of Las Vegas whereby theming has made this city a premier destination not just for the gambling community but for other tourists and conference goers. The themed servicescape, exemplified by The Rainforest Café, Hard Rock cafes and hotels, can create fantasies linked to guests' emotional responses mentioned later in this chapter and also in Chapter 1.

Signs, symbols and artefacts are 'explicit communicators' according to Bitner (1992). She refers to the white tablecloths in restaurants, which gives the customers a clue to it being a fine dining establishment and not a fast food outlet. The yellow arches of McDonald's branches instantly make the potential customer aware of the service offering there (Fig. 2.2).

A more profound example is provided by Magee and Gilmore (2015) who, when researching the servicescape in memorial sites such as World War 2 concentration camps, found that the authenticity of the physical site was fundamental to the visitor experience. Each dark heritage site due to its multitude of symbolic meanings also brings intangible dimensions to the visitor via the servicescape. The way that the curators interpreted the site for each category of visitor, whether they have personal connections or not, is important so that they can all have a

Fig. 2.2. The McDonald's golden arches symbol explicitly communicates the fast food on offer without overseas tourist being able to read the sign.

transformative service experience. Therefore these historic sensitive sites according to Magee and Gilmore (2015) are said to be 'experiencescape' for present-day tourists.

In the tourism industry one of the main symbols that triggers a response from potential customers is the rating systems of national tourist authorities. These ratings indicate to the customer the level of facilities and quality of service they should expect. With the introduction of hotel review websites such as TripAdvisor, additional star ratings and information from past customers can be accessed.

Although many writers have concentrated on Bitner's three servicescape elements, others including Bitner have discussed the impacts of the tangible service characteristic on customers. The responses are said to be cognitive, emotional and physiological, and we need to bear in mind that employees are affected as well customers (Bitner, 1992; Looy *et al.*, 2003; Williams and Dargel, 2004), as illustrated in Fig. 2.1. Furthermore, signage and its associated information is often seen as a critical determinant of service quality, especially at events and unique tourist attractions:

- *A cognitive response* to the servicescape enables the customer to formulate expectations as to the service quality they will receive. Psychology theory suggests that customers assimilate the servicescape not only by thought processes but by feeling it as well.
- *An emotional response* is said to enable the customer to perceive whether or not the servicescape is pleasant and can affect their length of engagement with the experience. Emotional responses can be generated by the degree in which excitement or arousal is generated (Looy *et al.*, 2003). This can be seen put into practice in the Thursford Collection Christmas Spectacular Show and Santa's Magical Journey Case Study (see Case Study 2.1).
- *A physiological response* to tangible elements of the service delivery setting is very much on an individual basis. Customers will be impacted upon at different rates depending on the stimulus. For example, queuing for rides at a theme park or waiting to enter a popular art exhibition, or noise late at night in a hotel or in a wilderness area can all affect the response of a customer.

Demographic factors of the customers, such as age, social class and gender, are also said to influence the impact of a stimulus (Williams and Dargel, 2004).

Williams and Dargel (2004) build on Bitner's notion of servicescape and refer to the tangible element of services accessed by the Internet as the 'cyberscape'. They suggest that this 'enhances their (customers') own search and evaluation capacities' (Williams and Dargel, 2004: 311). They go on to point out that the cyberscape can easily by manipulated by companies to get positive responses from potential clients based on the website design and its content. Unfortunately for the service producer the Internet can be accessed globally and it can be hard therefore to facilitate a positive response from an international audience with one website design. Second, potential customers can have differing IT skills, from beginners to experienced users, which is unknown to the website designer and can lead to customer frustration

Case Study 2.1. Christmas Spectacular Show and Santa's Magical Journey, Thursford, Norfolk

The Servicescape Generating an Emotional Response in Customers

The Thursford Collection in Thursford, Norfolk uses the servicescape to generate an emotional response each year in the approaches to the theatre where the Christmas Spectacular Show is performed. They do this by installing a stunning illuminated walk from the car park with Christmas music playing followed by Santa's Magical Journey, which is comprised of animated traditional Christmas figures, until you arrive at the middle of the journey at the Father Christmas' house. The customer whether young or old reaches the theatre already excited, with high expectations, and cannot wait for the show to begin.

Components of the Thursford's Servicescape

The path from the car park has been landscaped to facilitate an interesting environment for visitors during the remainder of the year, but the large trees have enabled a stunning Christmas light show to be developed.

The route can take visitors to the themed shopping experience and restaurants, cafés etc. The retail outlets are set around an 'olde worlde' village, which includes an all year round Christmas store and a traditional sweet shop (Thursford Shopping, 2015).

Santa's Magical Journey Experience

This is basically a visit to see Father Christmas that is available at any large department store or garden centre, the difference being the setting or servicescape.

'Fantasy land', as Thursford calls it, is an indoor forest setting dotted with original steam engines, Santa's toy factory and house are seen populated by animated elves, the snowman's family (who throw snowballs) and animals associated with the time of year, such as reindeers, penguins and polar bears. Also a short 4D Christmas Story film is shown at the start of the experience and midway through the customer's journey you meet a live Father Christmas with his helpers situated in a beautifully designed house. Throughout the experience you are accompanied by festive music and lighting effects. The length of time you can take over this experience is entirely up to you but it generally takes 45 minutes, however it is so popular that admission is only by pre-booked timed tickets (Thursford Santa's Magical Journey, 2015).

This attraction was devised 8 years ago and attracts over 50,000 people each year paying £9.50 for adults and £15.50 for children including a present from Father Christmas. A recent visitor to this attraction was Prince George with the Duke and Duchess of Cambridge (Fricker, 2014). Staff and other customers were amazed by their presence, but as tickets were purchased in secret and no warning given to Thursford staff no special preparations were made. It was said that Prince George 'gazed in awe' and chatted to Father Christmas (Geraldine Rye General Manager cited in Fricker, 2014). Whilst it is possible to complete

(Continued)

Case Study 2.1. Continued.

your Thursford experience at this point totally satisfied with what you have seen and heard, most adults continue to the theatre for the show.

The Christmas Spectacular Show

This 3-hour Christmas Show is said to be the largest in the UK if not Europe. It started in 1977 as a small carol concert with music played by the Wurlitzer Organ in an old farm building in the middle of the countryside. Presently, the show consists of non-stop singing, dancing and variety acts. Most of the items are of a festive nature but not all, with major variations in the programme year on year. John Cushing CEO said in 2012 'I always try to keep things fresh and bring in more variety to attract new audiences' (cited in Lazzari, 2012).

The show now attracts over 100,000 visitors each year, with over 50 coach-loads of visitors each day during its 2-month run. It is estimated to be worth £10m to the region's yearly economy, especially as visitors and coach companies make a mini-break out of a visit by staying in local accommodation (Lazzari, 2014). The recent organized mini-break of one of the authors consisted of a three-night stay at a four-star hotel on a dinner, bed and breakfast basis, a trip on the Norfolk Broads, a visit to Cromer as well as the Thursford experience. It needs to be remembered that the show is staged during November and December, finishing on the 23rd of the month, the off-peak season for UK holidays.

Why is the show attracting so many people and considered a spectacular? Some of the statistics give a clue to this.

- The show features a cast of 130 dancers, singers and musicians. Some have appeared on the West End stage, auditions are held in London to attract those with recent experience and the most talented. Each year 1200 singers apply, 300 are selected for auditions with only 40 singers required. Again, 300 dancers are auditioned and only 22 spaces are available. Having been selected the year before does not guarantee an automatic place the next, every artist has to re-apply and go through the audition process.
- Thursford has a creative production team of ten, with vast experience;
- The 2015 show had a budget of £4m;
- There are approximately 80 musical numbers;
- Thursford has 30 costume makers and fitters producing 2000 costumes;
- The cast goes through 2 months of rehearsals. Small sequences of the dress rehearsals are made available on YouTube so the audience can see a little of the excitement they will be exposed to prior to their visit;
- During the show the artists perform in the aisle and around the audience;
- Also in the auditorium there are historic steam engines, steam fairground rides and enormous amounts of decorations.

(Price, 2014; Thursford Christmas Spectacular, 2015; Thursford Jobs, 2015)

(Continued)

Case Study 2.1. **Continued.**

The 2015 ticket price range is from £30 to £42 per ticket and, as with Santa's Magical Journey, tickets must be pre-booked. The coach operator the author travelled with pre-books a year in advance.

Conclusion

The concepts and theories associated with utilizing the tangible elements of the service experience to arouse and excite an audience can be seen to be used to full advantage here at Thursford. The small details are not overlooked; for example the author commented on the quality and good design of the costumes that staff wore when meeting and greeting customers walking from the car park. They fulfilled the need to keep staff warm but looked as if they had come straight out of the Christmas Carol film set.

Thursford also understands the effect that the website can have on buyer behaviour, and is easy to use, very exciting and effective. They also place a small amount of film from the dress rehearsal (approximately one and half minutes) on YouTube to give the potential customer a taster of the show, which ends with a ticket sales advertisement.

As previously stated, this is an excellent example of academic concepts and theories operationalized and successfully put into practice.

Fig. 2.3. Thursford Christmas Spectacular Show – even the servicescape of the self-service café is designed to generate an emotional response in the customers.

(Williams and Dargel, 2004). Daniels (2012) reminds us that there are now virtual services companies such as ticket agencies, but this does not allow customers to engage in social interactions in the service setting.

Whilst the above discussion centres on the customer, the importance of the servicescape for employees has been recognized by a number of international organizations. This is not only to enable employees to carry out their work efficiently and effectively but to enhance their well-being. For example, Google UK Head Office have workspaces that look like public houses, and home living spaces allowing staff to be creative and increasing their engagement. Google now commissions bespoke designs for each head office in line with the Ritz-Carlton concept of scenography. For example, Google Tel Aviv is filled with orange trees and the London office has balcony gardens and allotments where staff can grow vegetables (Fairs, 2014). On a smaller scale, some travel organizations have video game booths for staff breaks and event companies have offices with Astroturf floor and snooker tables to enhance the staff's working environment and well-being.

Whilst these additional elements in the servicescape are made available for the well-being of the staff, one aspect of the servicescape that is hard for the service provider to control is the informal and spontaneous social interaction that may take place. Front of house staff can be given training as to how they can appropriately address other employees and customers in the workplace, but unless a script is given there is very little control by the service provider on what is actually said. This can lead to positive or negative responses from the customers as the discussion in Focus Box 2.1 illustrates.

Social interaction in the servicescape

When entering the physical space of a service provider, customers can benefit from the impromptu social interactions that ensue whilst engaged in the service (Lin and Liang, 2011). This can be with front-line staff as well as other consumers; Rosenbaum and Massiah's (2011) research suggests that building a social relationship benefits both parties.

On the other hand there can be negative responses to these interactions, such as noisy restaurant customers, queue jumpers or bad language in a theme park (Lewis and Clacher, 2001) and, in the past, violence at football matches. These negative incidences could be due to an inappropriate density of customers in a service setting (Rosenbaum and Massiah, 2011). High density of customers in a tourist attraction, art exhibition or retail environment can have a negative impact on many customers, but attending a professional football match with a low density of a few thousand spectators could also achieve a similar response. Service providers in some LETS contexts can manage densities by the introduction of timed admission tickets for 'block buster' art exhibitions with individual audio guides to control the flow patterns of the customer. The added advantage of the individual audio guides is that the commentary can be translated into numerous languages to meet the needs of international tourists.

Focus Box 2.1. Guest to Guest Interaction in the Servicescape

Jeremy Clarkson's Fracas in a North Yorkshire Hotel: The Effect on Other Guests

Jeremy Clarkson is a broadcaster who specializes in motoring and is best known for being a presenter on the highly successful BBC TV show *Top Gear* (Jeremy Clarkson Fan Site, 2015).

Top Gear **Programme Statistics**

- 350 million – *Top Gear*'s estimated worldwide audience
- 3 million YouTube subscribers
- 1.7 million global circulation of *Top Gear* magazine

(BBC Entertainment and Arts, 2015)

Unfortunately, a recent fracas in The Simonstone Hall County House Hotel in Hawes in North Yorkshire led to the presenter being dropped from the television show (Sweney, 2015). His Fan Site (2015) quotes the BBC as saying he is 'Not a man given to considered opinion'.

Jeremy Clarkson threatened to have a *Top Gear* producer fired because he had not arranged for hot food to be available at the hotel at the end of the day's filming. According to hotel guests who witnessed the event a physical and verbal attack laden with expletives took place. This incident led to the presenter being suspended from the BBC and after an internal investigation the BBC's Director General would not renew his contract. This decision caused more than a million fans to sign an online petition to have him reinstated (BBC Entertainment and Arts, 2015; Sweney, 2015).

Due to the nature of the attack North Yorkshire Police also had to investigate the incident and this resulted in hotel guests who witnessed the event being interviewed. North Yorkshire Police said that the perspective of other hotel guests who had been affected by the event needed to be taken into consideration (Conlan, 2015). No charges or further action was taken by the police.

Although the hotel advertises itself as the 'ultimate tranquil retreat', the guests may have been excited to hear that television celebrities were staying there. It is stated that some had earlier asked for 'selfies' to be taken with Jeremy Clarkson (Sweney, 2015); this positive interaction would have had the ability to make their stay even more memorable than they were expecting. It is stated by the hotel that they have relaxing lounges, 'a perfect haven to relax and unwind' plus a bar to 'enjoy a drink in convivial company', but no amount of planning could have stopped this unexpected behaviour from disrupting the ambience (Simonstone Hall, 2015).

Unfortunately, the fact that the TV presenter was staying at the same hotel resulted in some of the other guests witnessing inappropriate behaviour, giving them a negative, unsatisfactory

(Continued)

> Focus Box 2.1. **Continued.**
>
> experience, which was similar to Lewis and Clacher's (2001) research findings. Whether or not hotel staff would have been trained to make appropriate interventions is not known.
>
> The hotel would also have no control on the ongoing investigations by the BBC and the North Yorkshire Police and so their guests would have the negative encounter reinforced. The hotel could have offered the affected guests a future stay free of charge, but whilst their reputation may be retained by this goodwill gesture, through no fault of their own they will incur a cost.

One example of a recent negative guest-to-guest interaction in the servicescape can be seen in Focus Box 2.1 above. This was not caused by customer density, but the hotel would find it very difficult to plan for.

As the example in Focus Box 2.1 shows, social interaction with other consumers and employees can influence customers into engaging with, or avoiding, particular service providers, known as 'approach or avoidance decisions' (Rosenbaum and Massiah, 2011: 475). Staff training in appropriate interactions and interventions can to some extent orchestrate this element to achieve a positive outcome.

To summarize, when practitioners create physical and social service environments that meet the needs of their customers, these encounters can result in positive emotional responses of loyalty and increased satisfaction and have the advantage of differentiating one organization's service offerings from another (Miles *et al.*, 2012). Unfortunately for service providers, as the example in Focus Box 2.2 below illustrates, customers do not always conform to expected responses.

Continuing the discussion on the remaining service characteristics, two approaches will be considered: first the traditional and second the newer characteristics of service. The elements of each approach are illustrated in Fig. 2.4.

TRADITIONAL SERVICE CHARACTERISTICS

As illustrated in Fig. 2.4, the traditional theoretical framework of service characteristics suggests that service has four other elements as well as the tangibles:

- Intangibility;
- Heterogeneity;
- Inseparability; and
- Perishability.

These four characteristics are collectively known as IHIP. This framework has been reviewed by many writers and is said to separate services from goods. This next section adds to the current academic debate by critiquing the IHIP model.

Focus Box 2.2. **England versus Germany, Women's International Football Teams, Played at Wembley, London**

The England women's football team played a friendly game against the Germany women's team and for the first time it was held at Wembley Stadium. The game was almost a sell out with 55,000 tickets bought, when a target of 25,000 had been set. Prior to the game taking place the sports websites were stating that it would be a fantastic occasion based on the projected spectator numbers as the quality of the actual game was not known (England lost 0-3) (Topping, 2014). This is a low spectator density for this stadium when compared with the number of tickets available at the same venue for the England men's international football games (90,000). So a negative response could have been expected from the potential spectators to a move to a larger venue than normal for international women's football matches. The opposite happened; the fact that women's football had not been played at Wembley, the prestigious national football stadium, created heightened expectations and increased ticket sales even though the spectator numbers were far lower than a normal Premier Division game. For example, Manchester United regularly achieve 75,000 spectators (Topping, 2014).

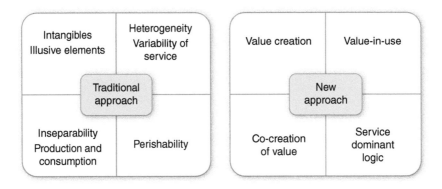

Fig. 2.4. **Service characteristics: traditional and new approaches.**

Intangibles – illusive elements

According to Zeithaml and Bitner (1996), the intangible aspects of a service cannot be seen. However, Berry (1995) and Becker (1996) instructed managers to 'tangibilize' the intangibles if at all possible in order to give clues to service quality. This helps customers to assess the quality of the experience prior to the visit and reduces risk (Buttle, 1993). This strategy is crucial for the LETS organizations to follow, due to the ephemeral nature of many of their services. Taking the example of a takeaway restaurant distributing their menus as printed advertising literature, elements such as the typeface and quality of the paper need to be considered as part of 'tangibilizing' the intangibles strategy. Such details can counteract any misgivings that customers may have about an organization's ability to provide an excellent service.

Another strategy to overcome uncertainty due to the intangible nature of service is for organizations to create an image that customers find reassuring, a service offering they can consistently recognize and service-delivery processes that they can trust (De Chernatony and Segal-Horn, 2001; Villar *et al.*, 2012). Examples of this can be seen throughout the LETS context: Costa and Starbucks coffee shops; Marriott Hotels, Holiday Inn Hotels; Virgin Active and Bannatyne Health and Fitness.

These examples so far are concerned with the pre-purchase of services, but Lovelock and Gummesson (2004) consider that the same uncertainty exists prior to purchasing goods. They cite foodstuffs and medicines, suggesting that only the most seasoned buyers are able to fully evaluate these types of purchase prior to use. Therefore they deem that intangibility is not an exclusive characteristic of service as once thought. As seen in Focus Boxes 2.1 and 2.2, customers do not do what the service provider expects of them, a characteristic of service known as heterogeneity, which can be observed in front-of-house staff as well. This is the next traditional service characteristic to be discussed.

Heterogeneity – variability of service

The characteristic of heterogeneity has a number of aspects. The individuality of both the customer and front-line members of staff and the way they interact with each other is one. A second aspect is what some writers have called *variability* of service, where the adherence to the service specification is compromised. The interaction between customers and employees is one of the most important aspects when managing the service delivery process. To eliminate spontaneity by front-line staff and inconsistency in service provision, some organizations standardize the service delivery (Wright, 1995). This production-line approach is so that employees do not deviate from what has been rehearsed in training. Levitt's (1972) solution is to introduce technology wherever possible into the service production system, which is seen in fast-food outlets such as McDonald's. One advantage of this strategy is that front-line staff are fully informed as to the appropriate level of service they should be delivering. Unfortunately, these strategies possibly counter any initiative that the member of staff may have, which could be detrimental to the organization as social relationships are not formed and unique customized customer needs less likely to be met.

The strategies mentioned above do not remove the heterogeneity or variability characteristic from the customers. One way that this can be achieved is via the information that service organizations provide to potential customers. For example, a number of hotels' and airlines' websites will not allow bookings from large same-sex groups, as hen and stag parties have been known to cause problems in the past. Unfortunately, this can eliminate bookings from other same-sex groups such as sports teams, or Women's Institute holidaymakers who would otherwise be welcomed by the service organization. Therefore this is not a fool-proof method as other tourists may behave in an inappropriate way and cause a disturbance.

Heterogeneity is said to increase when the service delivery process is complex and labour intensive, but a standardized, technology-based delivery system does not fulfil some customers' needs (Lovelock and Gummesson, 2004). Of course, the heterogeneity characteristic is not necessarily exclusive to service; Moeller (2010: 363) points out that artisan baked goods can have variability and can only be eliminated by the introduction of machinery, echoing Levitt's point of view.

The third traditional service characteristic is that of inseparability of production by the service provider and consumption by the consumer. As considered earlier when examining the goods versus services dichotomy this is not always found to be the case.

Inseparability – production and consumption

This is the concept that customers are present when all or part of the service is being performed (for example theatre productions or sports coaching courses). Sometimes the consumer is required to be part of the delivery process (self-service restaurant) (Voss *et al.*, 1985; Buttle, 1993). With the advent of technology the customer when booking a ticket for a concert online is expected to select the performance, then the seat and print off the ticket. In the case of a flight or cruise, not only is the customer expected to make the initial booking and print off the confirmation but to check in prior to travelling. The customer can be penalized for not doing so by having to pay extra if they arrive at the port or airport without the necessary boarding passes.

If the service delivery process requires high levels of customer contact with the service provider, this can have an adverse effect on revenue if they do not turn up. To counteract this, especially at Christmas time, some restaurants require a non-returnable deposit to secure a table. Online hotel booking sites require non-refundable payment in advance, especially if a special deal has been secured, to overcome this dilemma of 'no shows'. Equally, the absence of specialist staff on sick leave can lead to the very same effect on the organization as the cancellation of bookings. Having additional staff to cope with these eventualities is not always a cost-effective solution.

Service setting designers have used the inseparability characteristic of service with the presence of customers during the production as a feature to enhance their experience. The kitchens of pizza restaurants are exposed to the customers with the pizza bases being thrown into the air for their entertainment. Equally the cocktail waiter uses flamboyant movements to add ingredients and mix the cocktail for the same reason. The strategy has the ability to heighten the arousal response of the customers as purported in Bitner's servicescape concept. Lovelock and Gummesson (2004) in their critique of the inseparability characteristic of service point out that many services are delivered without the customer being present, such as house cleaning, pool maintenance, dog walking and gardening services. Inseparability and the last traditional characteristic of service perishability are interrelated as there is a connection between the customers needing to be present at the time of production of the service and the lack of ability to store the service experience for a future sale.

Perishability of the service experience

If the service provider requires the customer to be present when the service is produced and subsequently consumed, then the management of the perishability characteristic comes to the fore. For example, a theatre ticket can only be sold for a particular seat on a specific day, and if it is not then revenue is lost. Hotels and airlines use yield management or capacity planning techniques to minimize the effects of service perishability, selling rooms and aircraft seats below the normal rate (Looy *et al.*, 2003), as we see in Chapter 6. Demand and supply of a service can be difficult to manage when specialist facilities are involved. Usage of squash courts at peak times is generally full but during office hours they lie empty. After years of unsuccessfully trying to fill this specialist facility some providers are reducing the number of courts available. A strategy to overcome the reduced revenue stream of unsold live performances is to transform them so they can be stored and sold later as e-resources, DVDs or CDs (Lovelock and Gummesson, 2004), but this is not possible with every service experience. It would seem that service perishability is a phenomenon that must be managed for organizations to be successful, as having too few customers can lead to low revenue against high fixed costs such as wages and rent.

It was suggested by Moeller (2010), who looked at the transformation that takes place after a service or product has been consumed or used, that the characteristic of perishability can be detected in both scenarios and that it was not exclusively a characteristic of services. Examples of manufactured goods with a use-by date are prescription drugs, paints, adhesives and foodstuffs and can be said to be subject to this characteristic. Although the IHIP characteristics were previously recognized as important features of service, they are not considered as valid or as important as previously thought. In Fig. 2.4 both the traditional and new approach to service characteristics are shown. Value creation and its associated elements are the components that are now considered more appropriate by writers.

NEW APPROACH TO SERVICE CHARACTERISTICS

The new approach to service characteristics focuses on value creation. The value creation framework has a number of aspects to it as Fig. 2.4 illustrates:

- Value-in-use;
- Co-creation of value;
- Service dominant logic.

These concepts are different from the value chain (Zehrer and Raich, 2010) where networks are formed with complementary organizations to facilitate complex offerings to customers such as when a city is hosting a major event, as discussed in Chapter 3.

Value creation

Edvardsson *et al.* (2005: 118) state that the focus of service research has moved to the portrayal of value creation, as we saw in Chapter 1, where customers are not passive receivers of services but are involved. Customers are not buying goods or services but value propositions, which turn into value actualization on usage and consumption. Reliance, to a lesser or greater degree, on customers' cooperation for value creation is more than the self-service elements in a café or retail outlet (Gallouj and Savona, 2008: 155). Edvardsson *et al.* (2005), Gummesson (2007) and Gummesson *et al.* (2014) suggest that networks and multiple stakeholders are required, as value creation is not only about fulfilling the customers' needs but creating a lasting impression on the consumer through the service experience.

The value of events can come from emotional experiences of escapism, relaxation or thrills and is not wholly reliant on the entertainment or spectacle provided (Akyildiz *et al.*, 2013: 25). This type of behavioural response was observed by Birch (2014: 5) when events were held in shopping centres, suggesting that the spectators play a part in the co-creation of a 'hedonistic service drama'. Customers are said to be buying experiences and dreams when engaging with service providers (Gummesson, 2007: 2). This consumer buyer behaviour is considered in Chapter 3.

When designing a service production system the extent of customer involvement must be considered (Edvardsson *et al.*, 2010) and we elaborate in Chapter 5. The co-creation of a service relating to the customers' and other stakeholders' notion of value means that the service offering can deviate but the customer is satisfied. Even a mass standardized service designed to control variability from both customers and front-line staff can be compromised. Vargo and Lusch (2008: 8) are not worried about this situation as they state that the service has been 'uniquely and phenomenologically determined' and it has been rightly 'determined by the beneficiary' (Vargo and Lusch, 2004: 7). This can be difficult in practice as potentially the service provider has no control of the service offering or the standard of delivery.

Experiential consumption is seen in many LETS activities. Chen and Chen's (2010) work in the heritage sector suggests that tourists want social-psychological benefits such as involvement, peace of mind and education. They wish to immerse themselves in the unique attraction and forget time etc. for a total experience.

As the example above illustrates it is difficult to measure the customers' contribution to value creation, 'therefore the less complex customer satisfaction is usually used' (Gummesson, 2007: 2). This is not the case when the economic importance to the local and regional area of major sporting events such as a Formula 1 motor race is concerned. A predictor of customers' experiential responses was devised by Musa and Kassim (2013). This is known as the Sport Event Experiential Value (SEEV) and it is said to enable the service provider to identify the determinants of value creation for these spectators and allow them to offer a service in which a 'total experience' can be achieved (Musa and Kassim, 2013). Vargo and Lusch (2004) take a different approach to value creation, their theory being known as the service dominant logic and is based on the value-in-use concept, as we saw in Chapter 1.

Service dominant logic

Vargo and Lusch (2004) have researched this increasingly significant aspect extensively. Their model is service-centred with value co-creation judged by the customer. This is said to be a collaboration of internal and external resources, such as IT and other outsourced elements, by applying knowledge and skills to co-create a service. Within this dynamic is the role for the customer as a co-creator of the service and it is for them to determine whether or not the service is 'value-in-use' (Lusch *et al.*, 2007; Vargo and Lusch, 2004). They consider that there is no value until the service has been used. Indeed, Grönroos and Voima (2011) have concerns regarding this concept. They argue that if a service only has value at the time of consumption then that implies there is no value creation prior to use and that it would be difficult for customers to be co-creators with others at the end of production.

Vargo and Lusch (2004) seem to disagree and see that co-creation is possible when they consider that customization of a service is achievable due to efficiencies made possible by the co-creation with customers. Lusch *et al.* (2007) suggest one of the main benefits of co-creation is the enjoyment this act can give to the customer, as can be seen in learning a new skill in sport or cooking. Lusch *et al.* (2007) consider that value-in-use is interlinked with 'value in exchange'. Their proposition is that the customer must also feel that the price paid for co-producing and using the service is appropriate. Grönroos and Voima (2011) disagree that there is an exchange as the customers are central to the production of the value.

In conclusion, the benefit to organizations of having customers engaged in service value creation is that there is a possibility of a service provider building an enduring inter-relationship with their customers. Organizations must continue to differentiate their offering, especially in a crowded marketplace, where a customer will only form relationships with a few service providers. Although in some LETS contexts there are customers who require a single transaction rather than a relationship with an organization (for example a hotel or attraction at a faraway destination or a game of golf at a unique course), their recommendations on social media, or via face-to-face conversations known as word of mouth (WOM), can be powerful marketing tools. Memorable service from customer-centred service design is a growing concept in service management (Edvardsson *et al.*, 2011: 554).

Service providers when designing their offerings will not only think about what is expected but what would enhance their customers' experience. For example, airports are expected to have car parking facilities nearby but now many offer valet parking for their customers' convenience at an additional cost. The customer leaves the car at the door to the airport terminal for it to be driven to the car park by a car park employee and it is returned to the same location at the end of their trip.

In conclusion, when a comparison of the traditional with the newer approaches to service characteristics is undertaken it can be seen that the conventional way of thinking (IHIP) does not allow for the innovations in service design that have taken place within the service sector. The introduction of technology that enables easier customization of service and the use of the customer in its production has blurred the lines between service and goods. Although the traditional service characteristics are not considered to be exclusive to services it can be argued that heterogeneity and perishability characteristics have a place in the management of both goods and service experiences. For example, in the LETS service environment the inseparability characteristic can be found in hotels, sports coaching and the arts.

A change in the production of service offerings is that they are coming from multidisciplinary sources to customers via a service provider. Grönroos and Voima (2011) refer to a number of writers when giving examples of this multiple supplier context such as education, IT and production and innovation elements. Disney theme parks are an example of a LETS context that requires high level skills and knowledge from a number of disciplines to evolve and maintain a flexible innovative working environment.

The next section will examine one way of operationalizing a flexible and innovative service experience with the provision of not only the core service but other elements, to provide an enhanced service. This enables the customer to customize their experience to meet their individual needs. These additional services are known as peripheral or augmented services as they are not needed to perform the basic service. This strategy was seen in the servitization of manufactured goods earlier in this chapter.

CORE AND PERIPHERAL SERVICES

Normann (2000) states that services have two distinct components:

- Core services; and
- Peripheral or additional services.

Unlike static service environments, for example parcel delivery, the LETS context enables organizations to differentiate their core offering from their competitors by adding any amount of peripheral or additional services. Lovelock and Wirtz (2011) suggest that some peripheral services are needed to facilitate the core service such as a car park at a leisure facility and some give additional appeal to it, for example regional flights being added to faraway holiday packages.

Core service has been defined by Bruhn and Georgi (2006) as the main value creation elements of a service. It is said that the core service not only determines how satisfied the customers are but also enables them to formulate their expectations prior to purchasing the service. When Hume (2008) researched these principles in the context of performing arts, she considered the core service to be the performance of the actors (the show) but found that the peripheral services offered by the servicescape, for example the venue quality, to be of major importance to customers. Therefore, in the case of performing arts service providers they need to consider both elements to meet their customers' needs. Tsuji *et al.*'s (2007) research into action sports events found that the quality of the teams prior to the game was considered by the customers to be the core service and subsequently enables the organizers to estimate the number of spectators. When teams play in a particular league or competition such as the football World Cup, which teams play against each other is outside of anyone's control and so is 'down to the luck of the draw'.

Peripheral services are also named secondary or augmented. Peripheral services can be provided as an addition to the core service to either satisfy customers' needs or gain an advantage over an organization's competitors. Simple examples are that of a bar providing their customers with a bowl of olives, crisps or peanuts with their drinks order or a café giving a biscuit with a cup of coffee. Although the examples above may increase overall revenue, they are not in themselves income generating (Normann, 2000). The strategy of providing customers with peripheral services to maximize income is seen frequently at pop concerts, where programmes, T-shirts and CDs are sold to facilitate secondary spend opportunities.

Another case in point is the provision of WiFi access. In the UK many hotel groups charge for WiFi access, whilst in other countries, for example Sweden and Chile, it is expected by customers to be part of the core service. On the other hand the guest laundry service in the same establishments would be seen by customers as a peripheral component that they would expect to pay for.

Gummesson (cited by Barnes and Cumby, 1995) considered peripheral services as the 'peanut syndrome', meaning that customers have to pay indirectly for the 'free' peanuts in the bar whether they require them or not. Airlines, not only budget ones, take the opposite approach and have capitalized on offering only the core service and thereby reducing basic fares. Extra legroom seating, food, drinks and baggage going into the aircraft hold are charged extra.

Organizations that place customers' needs central to their decision-making process, especially when considering the service design, will be able to make informed choices as to whether peripheral services should be offered or not. As Hume (2008) states, the combination of the core and peripheral services allows the customer to judge whether or not they have received appropriate value for money and time and have had their needs met, and whether this leads to an intention to repurchase.

Previous service quality management literature suggested that the core service, and in some cases the peripheral elements, allowed services to be classified into a typology and also questioned whether or not there are any differences between goods or services and whether there are specific service characteristics. This leads us to question whether or not a typology of services can or should be devised, and this is examined in the next section of the chapter.

TYPOLOGY OF SERVICES

The people who critique the newer theoretical framework of goods and services merging suggest that a typology of service is neither achievable nor useful. Even if the traditional IHIP service characteristic perspective is taken, Verma (2000: 9), when writing about service classifications, argues that it is difficult to generalize about service categorization.

Bitner's servicescape typology

However, Bitner (1992) proposed a typology of service organizations based on her Servicescape theory, where the tangible elements dictate the classification. She divides the servicescape into two types depending on whether an elaborate or simple design is needed to produce the service and uses three categories depending on who creates the service, such as customers creating the service offering at home with online airline check-in (see Table 2.1). Whilst this model does not always allow for a holistic service classification, it would accommodate

Table 2.1. Service typology (adapted from Bitner, 1992).

Types of service organization	Physical complexity of the servicescape Based on who performs actions within the servicescape	
	Elaborate	Lean
Self-service Customers only	Golf ranges Airlines Airport check-in	Budget hotels
Interpersonal services Both customers and employees	Hotels Restaurants Airlines	Fast food outlets
Remote services Only customers		Ticket bookings Airline check-in Netflix films downloads Amazon retail Airport car parking
Remote services Only employees	Online marketing videos of resorts or cruise ships Online computer support	Call centres

an integrated service system by allowing various processes or core and peripheral service offerings to be classified as separate items.

Self and mass service classification

Services are also classified using self or mass service nomenclature. With developments in technology, service organizations are creating more opportunities for *self service*. This evolved from customers collecting and bagging their own goods in a supermarket to collecting, scanning, paying and bagging the goods themselves without the intervention of, or social interaction with, front-line staff (Lee and Yang, 2013). This can be classified as *mass service* with many customer transactions, little customization and limited interaction with staff (Ng *et al.*, 2007: 475). Ng *et al.* even consider the once-a-day character appearances and parades at Disney theme parks to be mass service. Their classification divides mass services into hedonic services such as theme park visits, spectators at musical performances or sports events, and distinguishes these activities from utilitarian mass service of fast food, libraries and transport.

Goods and services continuum

Another classification not based on either Bitner's Servicescape, or Ng's Self and Mass Service, used the amount of customer and front-line staff interactions as a criterion (Voss *et al.*, 1985; Oakland, 1993). Voss *et al.* (1985) use this criterion to place services at various points along a continuum, known as the goods and services continuum. Their continuum goes from pure service to pure manufacturing and suggests that there are two categories of service: pure service business and service orientated product business (a combination of goods and services). Pure service is generally considered to be one-to-one encounters where specialist knowledge or skill is being offered (e.g. sports coaching). Bhattacharya (2013) also uses the classification of pure service. Examples of pure business services according to Bhattacharya are event management, tour management including ticketing, concierge services and performing arts. Service-oriented businesses include hospitality services, transportation, restaurants and other food outlets, books and storable entertainment media, theme parks and beauty salons. Sport is not included in either classification.

Armistead (1994) followed Bitner's premise and modified the goods and service continuum by adding the proportion of tangibles to intangibles to dictate where a service lies. He considered that there was no such thing as pure manufacturing and therefore finished his continuum at quasi-manufacturing, a combination of goods and services. This is where part of the offering is produced in isolation from the customer.

Current writers would embrace Armistead's notion, as they perceive that hybrid offerings are the norm, whereby goods and services are in combination generally for value-added reasons.

Lovelock (1992) uses the proportion of three inputs to classify services: customers, materials and information (expert knowledge or skill), with all or one involved at any one time. This seems to acknowledge early on that customers create value and that goods are necessary to produce a service. Lovelock's perspective has the advantage of allowing LETS services to move classifications throughout the service process unlike fixed or continuum typologies.

Ulaga and Reinartz (2011: 17), whilst recognizing an integrated approach to goods and services, take a different element of service production for classification purposes as theirs is based on who is the recipient. They have two categories: services oriented towards the supplier's goods and services oriented towards the customer process. A specific service is not specified in their classifications but they use attributes or impacts. For example, one criterion is *orientation services to achieve productivity gains*. This is moving towards the notion of servitization of goods discussed earlier in this chapter.

The present view is that organizations with a variety of stakeholders, especially customers, co-create a unique, individualist service which is hard to categorize. Schmenner (2004 cited in Miles, 2013) acknowledges that restaurants many fit into a number of service classifications in any one typology depending on the type of establishment the service provider created.

Although investigating the nature of service characteristics in order to distinguish goods from service and produce a typology of services may seem to be somewhat of an academic task of no relevance to LETS practitioners, having insights into what elements contribute to the production of a complex service offering can only enhance its management.

Utilizing the current thinking on service characteristics, Table 2.2 illustrates the LETS service attributes. Six service characteristics have been used: the first three columns give examples of whether or not the type of service can be accessed virtually, and if any elements can be owned. The next three columns indicate using low, medium and high to illustrate the extent that interaction with others takes place and the possible social and physiological impacts gained from engaging in LETS activities.

Whilst it is relatively easy to identify the attributes of many LETS activities, there are areas that are of an individualistic nature such as the social and physiological impacts. It is said that the level of these impacts is related to the customers' degree of involvement (Musa and Kassim, 2013). In their research based on these impacts on Formula One spectators, they found that they are an 'indicator of pleasure' (Musa and Kassim, 2013: 110).

If consideration is given to the impact of air travel when going on holiday, both positive and negative effects can be experienced. The positivity of going to a new destination, the anticipation of new activities, freedom and well-being; but if the airport is crowded, the plane delayed and the weather at the resort is not as expected it can lead to negative impacts.

The LETS categories of home-based leisure and volunteering have so many diverse opportunities for participating in that the social and psychological impacts depend on the context, and a number of generalizations may be made. In the first edition of this book it is stated that

Table 2.2. Attributes of leisure, events, tourism and sport services.

	Virtual services	Non-ownership elements	Ownership elements	Interaction with staff	Interaction with other customers	Social physiological impacts
Leisure						
Art and craft workshop	Book place online	Facility Knowledge and Skills of tutor	Development of skills Craft or artist materials	Medium	Medium	Medium
Home-based leisure		None	Facilities Equipment	None	None	Depends on activity
Volunteering		Facility		Depends on context	Depends on context	Depends on context
Parks and gardens	Ticket booking Virtual tours	Facility Knowledge of Guides	Guidebooks Merchandise	Low	Low	Low to medium
Events						
Pop concert	Book tickets online	Venue Skills of performers	Programme Merchandise	Low	High	High
Sporting event	Book tickets online	Venue Skills of the players	Programme Merchandise	Low	High	High
Christmas market		Displays Entertainment	Unique produce and crafts	Medium	Medium	Medium

(Continued)

Table 2.2. Continued.

	Virtual services	Non-ownership elements	Ownership elements	Interaction with staff	Interaction with other customers	Social physiological impacts
Tourism						
Package holiday	Book tickets online	Location, transport, facilities of hotel and resort	Souvenirs	Medium	Medium	Medium to high
Cruise ship holiday		Booking agency Ship and its facilities, ports, locations	Professional Photographs Souvenirs	High	High	Medium to high
Visit to a unique attraction	Entrance ticket booked online	Location, facilities Knowledge and skills of guide	Merchandise Books, postcards	Medium	High	Medium to high
Air travel	Book tickets and check-in online In-flight entertainment	Airport Aircraft	Merchandise Food	High	High	High
Sport						
Team games		Facilities	Individual kit	Low	High	High
Individual games		Facilities	Individual kit	Low	Medium	High
Personal trainer		Facilities	Individual kit Development of skills	High	Low	Medium
Group coaching course		Facilities	Individual kit Development of skills	Medium	Medium	Medium

enjoyment, involvement and intellectual challenge are some of the reasons to engage in these activities. Whilst home-based leisure may not give the participant the opportunity to socialize with likeminded people, this can come about by attending events specifically associated with their home-based activity.

As shown above, the LETS product is diverse as are the impacts on the customers. The service experience can be designed or manipulated to maximize positive impacts on the customers, but as each one has individual needs and responses it requires knowledge and understanding from the service providers. Methodologies for collecting robust data will be discussed later in this book.

CONCLUSIONS

In the past, characteristics of service were said to be composed of tangibles and intangibles and it is the latter that distinguished goods from service. The introduction of technology in the production and delivery of services and the addition of services to enhance goods has not only allowed for diversity but also the convergence of offerings. Newer concepts of customers and other stakeholder being co-creators of value in the production of service and service dominant logic theory are the current debates within the academic community.

QUESTIONS

1. Why are goods and services merging when experiences are offered to LETS customers?
2. Should organizations allocate a large part of their annual budget to the servicescape or staff training?
3. Consider the traditional and new approaches to service characteristics; which will be more appropriate in the future?
4. Is a typology of service experiences necessary?

FURTHER READING

Bitner, M.J. (1992) Servicescapes: the impact of physical surroundings on customers and employees. *Journal of Marketing* 58, 57–71.

Grönroos, C. and Voima, P. (2011) *Making Sense of Value and Value Co-Creation in Service Logic.* Hanken School of Economics Working Paper, Dept of Marketing, Helsinki, Finland.

Looy, B.V., Gemmel, P. and Dierdonck, R.V. (2003) *Services Management – An Integrated Approach*, 2nd edn. Prentice-Hall, Harlow, UK.

Lovelock, C. and Wirtz, J. (2011) *Services Marketing: People, Technology, Strategy*, 7th edn. Pearson, Boston, Massachusetts.

Vargo, S.L. and Lusch, R.F. (2008) Service-dominant logic: continuing the evolution. *Journal of Academic Marketing* 36, 1–10.

REFERENCES

Akyildiz, M., Argan, M.T., Argan, M. and Sevil, T. (2013) Thematic events as an experiential marketing tool: kite festival on the experience stage. *International Journal of Sport Management, Recreation and Tourism* 12, 17–28.

Armistead, C. (1994) The journey to date: lessons from past services management research. In: Armistead, C. (ed.) *The Future of Services Management*. Kogan Page, Cranfield, UK, pp. 27–40.

Aston University Centre for Servitization Research and Practice (2013) Servitization Impact Study. Aston Business School. Available at: https://connect.innovateuk.org/documents/416351/3926914/Servitization+impact+study.pdf (accessed 21 November 2014).

Aston University Centre for Servitization Research and Practice (2014) What is Servitization? Aston Business School. Available at: http://www.aston-servitization.com (accessed 21 November 2014).

Barnes, J.G. and Cumby, J.A. (1995) The cost of service quality. In: Glynn, W.J. and Barnes, J.G. (eds) *Understanding Services Management*. Wiley, Chichester, UK, pp. 178–202.

BBC Entertainment and Arts (2015) Jeremy Clarkson Dropped from Top Gear, BBC Confirms. Available at: http://www.bbc.co.uk/news/entertainment-arts-32052736 (accessed 27 April 2015).

Becker, C. (1996) Implementing the tangibles: a total quality approach for hospitality service provides. In: Olsen, M.E., Teare, R. and Gummeson, E. (eds) *Service Quality In Hospitality Organisations*. Cassell, London, pp. 278–298.

Berry, L.L. (1995) *On Great Service – A Framework for Action*. The Free Press, New York.

Bhattacharya, H. (2013) Service business: some reflections. *International Journal of Economics and Business Studies* 3(1), 11–19.

Birch, D. (2014) Contextualising The Experiential Quality of Shopping Centre Entertainment Events: A Service Drama Approach. Available at: http://eprints.bournemouth.ac.uk (accessed 10 February 2015).

Bitner, M.J. (1992) Servicescapes: the impact of physical surroundings on customers and employees. *Journal of Marketing* 58, 57–71.

Bruhn, M. and Georgi, D. (2006) *Services Marketing – Managing The Service Value Chain*. Prentice-Hall, Harlow, UK.

Buttle, F. (1993) *Quality Management: Theories and Themes*. Working Paper, Manchester Business School, University of Manchester, UK.

Chandon, J., Leo, P. and Philippe, J. (1997) Service encounter dimensions – a dyadic perspective: measuring the dimensions of service encounters as perceived by customers and personnel. *International Journal of Service Industry Management* 1, 65–86.

Chen, C.F. and Chen, F.S. (2010) Experience Quality, Perceived Value, Satisfaction and Behavioral Intentions for Heritage Tourists. *Tourism Management* 31, 29–35.

Conlan, T. (2015) Jeremy Clarkson will face no further action, say Police. *The Guardian*, 7 April 2015. Available at: http://www.theguardian.com/media/2015/apr/07/jeremy-clarkson-police-top-gear-bbc (accessed 27 April 2015).

Daniels, P.W. (2012) Service industries at a crossroads: some fragile assumptions and future challenges. *Service Industries Journal* 12(4), 619–639.

De Chernatony, L. and Segal-Horn, S. (2001) Building on service characteristic to develop successful services brands. *Journal of Marketing Management* 17, 645–669.

Edvardsson, B., Gustafsson, A. and Roos, I. (2005) Service portraits in service research: a critical review. *International Journal of Service Industry Management* 16(1), 107–121.

Edvardsson, B., Ng, G., Min, C.Z., Firth, R. and Yi, D. (2011) Does service-dominant design result in a better service system? *Journal of Service Management* 22(4), 540–556.

Fairs, M. (2014) *Dezeens Book of Interviews – Architect Interios Design*. Dezeen Ltd, London.

Fricker, M. (2014) Kate Middleton and Prince William take baby George to Visit Santa in his Grotto. *The Mirror Newspaper* 21 December 2014. Available at: http://www.mirror.co.uk/news/uk-news/kate-middleton-prince-william-take-4849503 (accessed 16 May 2015).

Gallouj, F. and Savona, M. (2008) Innovation in services: a review of the debate and research agenda. *Journal of Evolutionary Economics* 19(2), 149–172.

Greenfield, H.I. (2002) A note on the goods/service dichotomy. *Service Industries Journal* 22(4), 19–21.

Grönroos, C. and Voima, P. (2011) *Making Sense of Value and Value Co-Creation in Service Logic.* Hanken School of Economics Working Paper, Dept of Marketing, Helsinki, Finland.

Gummesson, E. (2007) Exit services marketing-enter service marketing. *The Journal of Customer Behaviour* 6(2), 113–141.

Gummesson, E., Kuusela, H. and Närvänen, E. (2014) Reinventing marketing strategy by recasting supplier/customer roles. *Journal of Service Management* 25(2), 228–240.

Hume, M. (2008) Understanding core and peripheral service quality in customer repurchase of the performing arts. *Managing Service Quality* 18(4), 349–369.

Jeremy Clarkson Fan Site (2015) Jeremy Clarkson Home Page. Available at: http://www.jeremyclarkson.co.uk (accessed 27 April 2015).

Lazzari, A. (2012) Thursford's Christmas Spectacular Ready To Start. The Norwich Evening News 24, 9 November 2012. Available at: http://www.eveningnews24.co.uk/news/photo_gallery_thursford_christmas_spectacular_ready_to_start_1_1686912 (accessed 16 May 2015).

Lazzari, A. (2014) Thursford's Christmas Spectacular Returns to Dazzle Audiences Again. The Eastern Daily Press Review, 11 November 2014. Available at: http://www.edp24.co.uk/news/review_thursford_s_christmas_spectacular_returns_to_dazzle_audiences_again_1_3843035 (accessed 16 May 2015).

Lee, H.-J. and Yang, K. (2013) Interpersonal service quality, self-service technology (sst) service quality and retail patronage. *Journal of Retailing and Consumer Services* 20, 51–57.

Levitt, T. (1972) Production-line approach to service. *Harvard Business Review* (September–October), 41–52.

Lewis, B.R. and Clacher, E. (2001) Service failure and recovery in UK theme parks: the employees' perspective. *International Journal of Contemporary Hospitality Management* 13(4) 166–175.

Lin, J.-S. and Liang, H.-Y. (2011) The influence of service environments on service emotion and service outcomes. *Managing Service Quality* 21(4), 350–372.

Looy, B.V., Gemmel, P. and Dierdonck, R.V. (2003) *Services Management: An Integrated Approach*, 2nd edn. Prentice-Hall, Harlow, UK.

Lovelock, C. (1992) *Managing Services: Marketing, Operations and Human Resources*, 2nd edn. Prentice-Hall, Hemel Hempstead, UK.

Lovelock, C. and Gummesson, E. (2004) Whither services marketing? In search of a new paradigm and fresh perspectives. *Journal of Service Research* 7(20) 12–38.

Lovelock, C. and Wirtz, J. (2011) *Services Marketing: People, Technology, Strategy*, 7th edn. Pearson, Boston, Massachusetts.

Lusch, R.F., Vargo, S.L. and O'Brien, M. (2007) Competing through service: insights from service-dominant logic. *Journal of Retailing* 83, 5–18.

Magee, R. and Gilmore, A. (2015) Heritage site management: from dark tourism to transformative service experience? *The Service Industries Journal* 35(15–16), 898–917.

Miles, P.C. (2013) Competitive strategy: the link between service characteristics and customer satisfaction. *International Journal of Quality and Service Science* 5(4), 395–414.

Miles, P.C., Miles, G. and Cannon, A. (2012) Linking servicescape to customer satisfaction: exploring the role of competitive strategy. *International Journal of Operations and Production Management* 32(7), 772–795.

Moeller, S. (2010) Characteristics of service – a new approach uncovers their value. *Journal of Service Marketing* 24(5), 359–368.

Musa, R. and Kassim, R.M. (2013) Predictors and outcomes of sport event experiential value: insights from Formula One Petronas Malaysia grand prix. *International Journal of Management and Marketing Research* 6(1), 107–120.

Neely, A., Benedetinni, O. and Visnjic, I. (2011) The servitization of manufacturing: further evidence. In: *Proceedings of 18th European Operations Management Association Conference*, Cambridge, UK. Available at: https://www.researchgate.net/profile/Andy_Neely/publication/265006912_The_

Servitization_of_Manufacturing_Further_Evidence/links/5474eaad0cf29afed60ffc20.pdf (accessed 30 May 2016).

Ng, S., Russell-Bennett, R. and Dagger, T. (2007) A typology of mass services: the role of service delivery and consumption in classifying service experiences. *Journal of Services Marketing* 21(7), 471–480.

Nixon, N. and Rieple, A. (2010) *Luxury Redesigned: How The Ritz-Carlton Uses Experiential Service Design to Position Abundance in Times of Scarcity*. The Design Management Institute, Boston, Massachusetts.

Normann, R. (2000) *Service Management: Strategy and Leadership*, 3rd edn. Wiley, Chichester, UK.

Oakland, J.S. (1993) *Total Quality Management: The Route to Improving Performance*, 2nd edn. Butterworth-Heinemann, Oxford, UK.

Price, N. (2014) Thursford's Christmas Spectacular. BBC Radio Norfolk, 9 November 2012. Available at: http://www.bbc.co.uk.iplayer programme/p02b7fg3 (accessed 16 May 2015).

Rosenbaum, M.S. and Massiah, C. (2011) An expanded servicescape perspective. *Journal of Service Management* 22(4), 471–490.

Shankar, V., Berry, L.L. and Dotzel, T. (2009) A practical guide to combining products and services. *Harvard Business Review* 87(November), 94–99.

Simonstone Hall (2015) Simonstone Hall Yorkshire Dales Hotel. Available at: http://www.simonstone-hall.com (accessed 27 April 2015).

Sweney, M. (2015) Jeremy Clarkson Threatened to Have Top Gear Producer Fired, Witnesses Claim. *The Guardian*, 13 March 2015. Available at: http://www.theguardian.com/media/2015/mar/13/jeremy-clarkson-top-gear-producer-bbc-oisin-tymon (accessed 27 April 2015).

Thursford Christmas Spectacular (2015) Thursford. About Us. Available at: http://www.thursford.com/christmas-spectacular.aspx (accessed 16 May 2015).

Thursford Jobs (2015) Welcome to Thursford Jobs.com. Available at: http://www.thursfordjobs.com (accessed 16 May 2015).

Thursford Santa's Magical Journey (2015) Santa's Magical Journey. Available at: http://www.thursford.com/santas-magical-journey.aspx (accessed 16 May 2015).

Thursford Shopping (2015) Shopping. Available at: http://www.thursford.com/shopping.aspx (accessed 16 May 2015).

Topping, A. (2014) Womens' Football in Britain Comes of Age with Wembley International. *The Guardian Newspaper*, 21 November 2014. Available at: https://www.theguardian.com/football/2014/nov/21/women-football-britain-wembley-england-v-germany (accessed 22 November 2014).

Tsuji, Y., Bennett, G. and Zhang, J. (2007) Consumer satisfaction with an action sport event. *Sport Marketing Quarterly* 16(4), 199–208.

Ulaga, W. and Reinartz, W.J. (2011) Hybrid offerings: how manufacturing firms combine goods and services successfully. *Journal of Marketing* 75, 5–23.

Vargo, S.L. and Lusch, R.F. (2004) Evolving a new logic for marketing. *Journal of Marketing* 68, 1–17.

Vargo, S.L. and Lusch, R.F. (2008) Service-dominant logic: continuing the evolution. *Journal of Academic Marketing* 36, 1–10.

Verma, R. (2000) An empirical analysis of management challenges in service factories, service shops, mass services and professional services. *International Journal of Service Industry Management* 11(1), 8–25.

Villar, C., Pla-Barder, J. and Leon-Darder, F. (2012) Service characteristics as moderators of the entry mode choice: empirical evidence on the hotel industry. *The Service Industries Journal* 32(7), 1137–1148.

Voss, C., Armistead, C., Johnston, B.J. and Morris, B. (1985) *Operations Management in Service Industries and the Public Sector*. Wiley, Chichester, UK.

Williams, R. and Dargel, M. (2004) From servicescape to 'cyberscape'. *Marketing Intelligence and Planning* 22(3), 310–320.

Wright, L. (1995) Avoiding services marketing myopia. In: Glynn, W.J. and Barnes, J.G. (eds) *Understanding Services Management*. Wiley, Chichester, UK, pp. 33–56.

Xin, Y., Chai, K.-H., Ojanen, V. and Brombacher, A. (2013) The moderating effect of service solution characteristics on competitive advantage. *The Service Industries Journal* 33(15–16), 1633–1658.

Zehrer, A. and Raich, F. (2010) Applying a lifecycle perspective to explain tourism network development. *The Services Industry Journal* 30(10), 1683–1705.

Zeithaml, V.A. and Bitner, M.J. (1996) *Services Marketing*. McGraw-Hill, London.

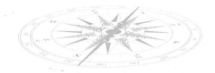

chapter 3

Service Providers and Consumers: a Multidimensional Interface

LEARNING OBJECTIVES

- To explore the difference between consumers and customers as well as external and internal customers;
- To appreciate the importance of volunteers to the LETS operational environment and the ambiguous role of volunteer tourists;
- To be able to comprehend the multitude of stakeholders with which LETS organizations have to develop relationships;
- To understand the benefits of participating in leisure to the consumer and customer;
- To explore consumer buyer behaviour utilizing the Lovelock and Wirtz (2011) three-stage model of service consumption;
- To understand the importance of employees in the delivery of excellent customer service utilizing Schlesinger and Heskett's (1991) cycles of failure and success together with Lovelock's (1995) cycle of mediocrity theories.

INTRODUCTION

In this chapter the wider perspective of LETS stakeholders is addressed rather than the simplistic two-dimensional notion of service providers and customers. Therefore external and internal customers, volunteers and the supply chain will be examined, together with other stakeholders such as shareholders, sport governing bodies and National Lottery Funding bodies. The cooperation and coordination required to facilitate major events will also be considered.

The chapter will continue by considering consumer behaviour and the benefits sought from a specific LETS service provider. This discussion is divided into three sections utilizing Lovelock and Wirtz's (2011) three-stage model of service consumption, which comprises the pre-purchase phase, the service encounter and post encounter phases.

THE DIFFERENCE BETWEEN CONSUMERS, EXTERNAL AND INTERNAL CUSTOMERS

Although LETS practitioners have numerous designations for their customers, such as guests, tourists, visitors, spectators, audience, sportsmen and women, punters and patron of the arts, the most frequently used name is customer. This section will explore the concepts of consumer and customers and how this affects their evaluation of a service and their loyalty to a service provider.

Consumers

Consumers can be defined as those people who actually consume a service, such as diners in a restaurant, or a member of the audience at a concert or event; Figure 3.1 shows heritage

Fig. 3.1. Heritage day out: consumers at Titanic Museum, Belfast, Northern Ireland.

attraction consumers outside the Titanic Museum Belfast, Northern Ireland. This definition is validated by UK legislation and regulations. If a problem arises with a LETS experience the consumer can utilize The Consumer Protection Act 1987 and its amendments to resolve it. Also the Package Travel, Package Holidays and Package Tours Regulations 1992 glossary of interpretations acknowledges this definition by defining holidaymakers as consumers, but confusingly The Football Spectators Act 1989 uses the term spectators for the football fans.

Practitioners acknowledge that consumers are important as they are in a position to make immediate judgements on the quality of the service provided. They are also able to utilize their own recent experiences when deciding whether or not to return to a particular service provider. Consumers are also in a position to post immediate comments or photographs on social media such as Twitter or Facebook. One supermarket that gave away free coffee or tea to loyalty cardholders changed their system so that drinkers of free coffee or tea were not able to sit in the café unless they purchased a meal or snack. A coffee machine was installed just outside the café and users either had to take away the drink or drink it standing up. Anecdotal evidence suggests that regular shoppers were taking pictures with their mobile phones and posting them on Facebook with negative comments and also sending them to the supermarket's head office. This is a good example of unsolicited instant feedback from consumers.

The definition of a consumer may seem to be describing a customer, and whilst consumers can also be customers in some cases (see Table 3.1), a customer is not a consumer. In the next section this phenomenon will be explored together with the concept of internal and external customers.

External customers

The definition of an external customer is one who arranges or purchases services from a provider but who does not necessarily consume them, such as a secretary of an amateur football team or choir booking a pitch or rehearsal room. Whilst the term external customer in practice does encompass consumers, this can be problematic for practitioners to know to whom to market their services or gain feedback from.

This is made even more difficult in the LETS context due to the complex nature of services and experiences on offer. Therefore it is important for organizations to recognize who is actually purchasing the service and understand the difference between consumers and external customers. A number of tourist boards invite coach companies and group-travel organizers to familiarization weekends to show them what the area has to offer in terms of attractions, events, accommodation and restaurants in the hope that they will package a holiday or an away day for their own customers. The example given in Table 3.1 is of a school visit to a heritage attraction, a frequent experience offered to schools to facilitate the teaching of specific parts of the National Schools Curriculum. The complex notion of who customers and consumers are is illustrated.

Table 3.1. A school visit to a heritage attraction.

Service provider	Consumers	Customers
Visit package supplied by the school	The pupils Members of teaching staff Volunteer helpers	The parents are customers of the school
The coach from the school to the attraction	Pupils Members of teaching staff Volunteer helpers	The school is a customer of the coach company
Education services of the heritage attraction	Pupils	The school is a customer of the heritage attraction
Catering facilities at heritage attraction	Pupils Members of teaching staff Volunteer helpers	The school is a customer of the heritage attraction
Shop at heritage attraction	Pupils Members of teaching staff Volunteer helpers	None
Coach parking at the heritage attraction	Coach driver	Coach company is a customer of the heritage attraction

As can be seen from the example above, the service provider needs to be able to understand and recognize the various levels of importance to their organization of the different consumers and external customers to enable them to meet their needs appropriately. The organization must also identify the main decision-makers; in the example above is it the parents or the teaching staff? This knowledge will enable an attraction not only to devise new services but allow them to make the external customers aware of specific services being offered by the organization.

Before moving on to the next part of this section where the concept of internal customers will be considered, it is worth noting that practitioners tend to use the nomenclature of 'customers' to refer to both consumers and external customers.

Internal customers

Although the term internal customer is an alternative name for paid employees, volunteers should be considered in this category as they are a major human resource in the LETS operational environment. This is supported by Stebbins (2013) and Wilks (2014), who question whether short-term volunteering should be considered a leisure activity; their premise is that volunteers need to be considered as unpaid employees of an organization rather than leisure participants. This section will consider both paid employees and unpaid volunteers as internal customers.

The internal customer requires services from other areas of the organization; for example, front-line staff need the support of back-of-house services to enable them to carry out their roles successfully. Depending on the organizational context, front-line staff may require the direct services of the IT, maintenance and cleaning teams to perform their roles and deliver good service, but at other times will need the services of the generic back-room functional areas, for example human resources for recruiting staff and volunteers, also finance and marketing departments. The delivery of excellent services to external customers is dependent on both front-of-house and generic back-of-house staff fulfilling their individual roles in an efficient and timely manner.

This can be illustrated utilizing the example in Table 3.2 of a school visit to a heritage attraction. The internal customer relationships can be considered as will the role of each internal customer.

To facilitate a successful school visit all the above individual functional areas need to deliver their element of the service to an appropriate level. By doing so they will fulfil the needs of the pupils, teaching staff and parents and repeat visits will most likely ensue. In some organizations, employees that do not directly interface with external customers consider they are nothing to do with the delivery of a service and forget they can be crucial in serving their internal customers in their service delivery tasks.

VOLUNTEERS AS INTERNAL CUSTOMERS

Many LETS organizations rely on volunteers to improve the range and quality of the service offered, over and above what paid staff can achieve. Volunteers are frequently used by charitable organizations not only to raise funds to secure the ongoing provision of their services but in many cases to deliver the service. It is said that 40% of UK adults are involved in some form of volunteering (Taylor, 2011), with 2 million people giving 1 hour per week in the sporting context (Sport England, 2015b). The UK public sector encourages volunteers in libraries and heritage attractions to enable them to retain service levels at a time of reduced funding for paid employees. Manchester City Council Library Service has formal volunteering opportunity descriptions not unlike paid job descriptions. These set out what is expected from the volunteer and what will be given in return, for example, the simple provision of support training and library T-shirt and goody bag together with enabling the volunteer to acquire transferable skills, such as planning, working as team, and experience of working with the general public. Manchester City Council library volunteers deliver story time, arrange events and activities and help with the First World War Archives (Manchester City Council Libraries, 2015).

As one might expect, the not-for-profit sector of the LETS industry would not function without the use of volunteers. The National Trust, whose main function is to protect unique

Table 3.2. Internal customers at a heritage attraction to facilitate a school visit.

Heritage attraction functional areas	Internal customers	Role[a]
Marketing and web design team	Education service Curatorial departments Commercial business department	To promote and inform the teaching staff in schools of the service on offer
Group bookings administration	Education service Catering facilities Coach parking facilities Cleaning	To ensure the attraction can provide the services required by the school
Education services	Curatorial departments Publications department Group bookings administration Marketing and web design team AVA technicians	To ensure that the attraction can provide all the academic services that the school requires including teaching materials prior to the visit
Customer service team	Education service Curatorial departments Commercial business department Catering facilities Coach parking facilities Cleaning Group bookings administration Marketing and web design team AVA technicians	To gather feedback from external customers and disseminate it to internal departments

[a]Note that many of these roles may be fulfilled by volunteers.

sites, requires over 60,000 volunteers to enable them to carry out conservation work in the countryside, historical properties and gardens (National Trust, 2015). Another example in an outdoor setting is that of The Canal and River Trust (formally the British Waterways Authority, a government agency), who ask for volunteers to help maintain the towpaths alongside the waterways to enable access for walking, fishing, as well as by the boaters. Volunteer lock-keepers also help boaters open and close the locks, which is invaluable at the height of summer. It is estimated that 480 volunteer lock-keepers spoke to 7000 people per week in 2014, becoming 'the face of the waterways' (Canal and River Trust, 2015).

One area where volunteers are vital is when staging mega-events where large numbers of temporary, short-term staff are required, for example The Olympic and Paralympic Games (Fig. 3.2). In the case of these one-off events Wilks (2014) suggests that the Beijing Olympics engaged over 100,000 volunteers and London 2012 recruited 70,000 Games Makers. Wilks' (2014) research showed that some volunteers interviewed at London 2012 Olympic Games did not stay for the 5 weeks requested and found they were bored and under-utilized, whilst others stated they were just too tired to continue due to starting every day very early and finishing very late. This is contradicted by Taylor (2011), who suggests that the problems of being a volunteer are more concerned with too much work, the need to undertake demanding leadership roles, and limited resources and no succession planning.

All of these volunteering scenarios require paid employees to play their part by executing their responsibilities to the internal customers no matter whether they are paid or not so that the external customers receive an exceptional experience.

Volunteer tourism

Another variation on the theme of volunteering is the advent of volunteer tourism whereby people pay to carry out voluntary work overseas. The notion of value-in-use and co-production

Fig. 3.2. An example of internal and external customers at London 2012 Olympic and Paralympic Games transport exit. Volunteers (known as 'Games Makers') in their purple and red uniforms help spectators during the Games.

can be seen in this context especially when volunteers intend to help not only themselves but other individuals and the organization plus the wider community (Stebbins, 2013). This is evident in the relatively new concept of volunteer tourism.

It is thought that some 70,545 people participate in volunteer tourism each year, generating revenue of between £832 million and £1.3 billion (TRAM, 2008 cited by Tomazos and Butler, 2012). Tomazos and Butler (2012) suggest that this is a fusion between work and leisure, but to the service provider they could be considered either as consumers of a tourism service, or a quasi-employee or both tourist (external customer) and employee (internal customer) at any one time during the vacation. If the LETS industry had to pay volunteers to fulfil these many and diverse roles, charities and mega-events would not be financially viable; therefore volunteers are central to delivering these services and to raising funds for the service to survive, working alongside paid employees.

In conclusion to this section on the differences between consumers, external and internal customers including volunteers, in practice many employers only use the terms customers, employees and volunteers (if appropriate). Even if the LETS organization considers a customer-centric approach to be paramount this encompasses external customers but not necessarily internal ones.

To continue the debate on 'who are our customers?' we may also note that consumers, internal and external customers, and volunteers are known as stakeholders. A stakeholder is anyone who has an interest in a service provider's offerings. The next section of this chapter will discuss stakeholders and the London 2012 Olympic and Paralympic Games will be used to illustrate this concept.

OTHER STAKEHOLDERS

LETS service providers are not independent organizations: they have a multitude of stakeholders. It can be a daunting task for an organization to identify and understand all of their stakeholders and therefore to try to meet their needs. Prioritizing and understanding the importance of an organization's stakeholders is necessary (Miragaia et al., 2014). Freeman's (1984 cited in Miragaia et al., 2014) definition of stakeholders suggests it is any group that can harm the organization. Whilst this is too simplistic for the LETS context as the London 2012 Olympic and Paralympic Games case study shows, it can help the organization when prioritizing their stakeholders' needs. Although Freeman's notion of 'dangerous' stakeholders such as regulatory bodies is relevant in the LETS context, for example professional sports, people can be fined, suspended and banned from their respective games for infringement of the rules on pitch and behaviour off it. Andersson and Getz (2008), whilst acknowledging the negative elements of organizational stakeholders also consider the positive ones as well, suggesting that relationships need to be developed and maintained with key stakeholders. They see relationships taking the form of cooperation, which can be informal and without risk, or joint ventures and partnerships that carry the most risk. In the example of a festival organized by a partnership, any of the associated organizations' identities can be lost as the partnership's identity dominates.

In the case of LETS events, Fairley *et al.* (2011) have suggested that the stakeholders can be managed by dividing them into groups based on the inevitable impacts of the event. The three impact classifications used are social, economic and environmental and it would seem that this was the strategy that London 2012 Olympic and Paralympic Games organizers selected.

Environmental impacts were foremost in London's bid. They used the slogan 'Towards a One Planet Olympics' stating that they would be the first sustainable Olympic and Paralympic Games (Sadd, 2012). The diversity of the environmental stakeholders can be seen from the list of 35 diverse organizations attending the 20 September 2009 meeting to address the environmental issues arising from staging the games (Commission for a Sustainable London, 2012, 2013):

- BAA now known as Heathrow Airport Holdings Limited;
- BERR;
- BioRegional Development Group;
- British Telecom;
- British Waterways;
- Campaign for Clean Air in London;
- Chartered Association of Building Engineers;
- Chartered Institute of Environmental Health;
- CIRIA;
- Department for Environment, Food & Rural Affairs;
- Earth Champions Foundation;
- East Thames;
- Energy Savings Trust;
- Entec UK;
- Environment Agency;
- Envirowise;
- Fairtrade Foundation;
- Lee Valley Regional Park Authority;
- London Borough of Newham;
- London Chamber of Commerce;
- London Community Recycling Network;
- London Food Link;
- London Sports Forum for Disabled People;
- London Sustainability Exchange;
- London Wildlife Trust;

- Metropolitan Police Force;
- National Health Service London;
- Natural England;
- Planning Aid for London;
- Royal Institute of Chartered Surveyors Foundation;
- Shelter;
- Social Enterprise London;
- Sport England;
- Strategic Forum for Construction;
- Tourism for All.

The above is a list of the attendees at the 20 September 2009 Commission for a Sustainable London 2012 meeting and is not a definitive list of all environmental stakeholders. Another Olympic and Paralympic Games stakeholder organization chaired this meeting, the Commission for a Sustainable London 2012 (Commission for a Sustainable London, 2012, 2013).

Although Fairley *et al.*'s (2011) three category stakeholder structure of social, economic and environmental organizations may not be appropriate for managing the stakeholders of smaller events, Andersson and Getz (2008: 204) suggest that stakeholders in these cases can be divided into two categories: *primary* (employees, volunteers, sponsors, spectators and participants) and *secondary* (host community, government, essential services, media, tourist organizations and businesses)(Table 3.3). They note that small events' organizers are dependent on key stakeholders for resources, finance and continuity and it means that they sometimes have to modify their goals to fulfil their stakeholders' needs. Getz *et al.* (2007) suggest that long-standing relationships with stakeholders can bring about a commitment from them to the main organization and, via negotiations, could be flexible in their requirements – making it more likely that the original goals would be accomplished. One strategy recommended by Getz *et al.* is to try to get stakeholders who are suppliers to the event to also become sponsors so that money does not only flow from the organizing committee to the suppliers but also in the other direction.

Table 3.3. Primary and secondary stakeholders (Andersson and Getz, 2008).

Primary stakeholders	Secondary stakeholders
Employees	Host community
Volunteers	Government
Sponsors	Essential services
Spectators	Media
Participants	Tourist organizations
	Businesses

In other LETS situations, such as leisure centres and tourist attractions, there is a trend to outsource a number of functional areas such as marketing, human resources and IT to reduce costs, thereby creating more stakeholders who can be influential in an organization's service offering. The notion that suppliers become 'super vendors' and therefore part of the decision-making process as 'strategic partners' is put forward by Hansen and Rasmussen (2013: 661). Building relationships with suppliers was the cornerstone of the thoughts of many of the original quality management theorists such as Deming (1986), Peters (1987), Feigenbaum (1991) and Oakland (1993).

Trust and an equal balance of power is required if the goals of both parties are to be met. If either element is missing or limited then the relationship can break down and an alternative supplier may be sought. Trust between all parties needs to be such that allowances will be made for delays if a supplier encounters extreme circumstances outside of its control, for example strikes or natural disasters (Gummesson, 1993).

In conclusion, stakeholders are important in all LETS contexts, not just mega-events. Where multiple stakeholders are involved, a complication is that they are not of equal importance to an organization, necessitating the service provider to ascertain which are the most important. In the case of London 2012 Olympic and Paralympic Games the diversity and association of the stakeholders is vast, as illustrated in Focus Box 3.1 and the list above. Therefore it would be expected that the athletes, games officials and VIPs such as Heads of State and the IOC committee's needs would receive a greater amount of attention from the organizers than other stakeholders such as spectators and sponsors.

In conclusion, consumers, customers (external) and employees (internal customers) are easier to identify than the numerous stakeholders of a mega-event such as the London 2012 Olympic and Paralympic Games. However, they all will try to influence the service offering to accommodate their own goals and needs. Therefore a strategy of having a hierarchy of stakeholders is acceptable, but robust data need to be collected to ascertain the minimum needs with which they would be satisfied (Crosby, 1984; Presenza and Iocca, 2012). Kenny (2013: 35) advocates caution when a stakeholder-centric business strategy is rigorously followed, stating that organizations can easily drift away from their own goals to fulfil the needs of others.

The next section of this chapter will return to the notion of external customers and consumers with a discussion examining buyer behaviour when customers are looking for and pre-judging a service offered by LETS providers. First consideration will be given to the benefits that the consumers and customers seek from a specific LETS service provider, building on the earlier discussion in Chapter 1. The debate continues utilizing Lovelock and Wirtz's (2011) three-stage model of service consumption, which comprises the pre-purchase phase, the service encounter and post encounter phases. Whilst the next section examines customer behaviour over these three stages, the narrative does not include an in-depth debate on how customers' expectations and perceptions are formulated. This debate is to be found in Chapter 4.

Focus Box 3.1. London 2012 Olympics and Paralympic Games Stakeholders

The focus box below illustrates a wide diversity of stakeholders, the type of organization they are and their role played in the staging of the London 2012 Olympic and Paralympic Games (this is not a definitive list).

Name of organization	Role	Type of organization
The Commission for a Sustainable London 2012	Monitors and assures the sustainability of the games	Independent body
Olympic Delivery Committee (ODA)	Building the venues and other infrastructure	Public body established by the London Olympic Games and Paralympic Games Act, 2006
London Organising Committee of the Olympic and Paralympic Games (LOCOG)	Staging both of the Games	Private company
London 2012 Ceremonies Ltd	Opening and closing ceremonies	Set up by LOCOG
Government Olympic Executive (GOE)	Overall responsibility for the games	Public body, additional Government department
The Olympic and Paralympic Security Directorate (OSD)	Responsible for developing the Olympic security strategy	Public body, part of the Office for Security and Counter-Terrorism (OSCT) within the Home Office
Olympic Park Legacy Company (OPLC)	Management and development of the Olympic Park after the Games	Public body
Greater London Authority (GLA), previously London Development Agency	Ensure London is ready for the Games and is able to keep running during them	Public body, includes Transport for London and Local Authorities

(Continued)

Focus Box 3.1. **Continued.**

Name of organization	Role	Type of organization
International Olympic Committee (IOC)	The supreme authority of the Olympic Movement acting as a catalyst for collaboration between all parties of the Olympic family	Non-profit non-governmental organization based in Switzerland
National Olympic Committees (NOCs)	Develops, promotes and protects the Olympic Movement in their respective countries	
International Federations (IFs)	Responsible for the integrity of their sport on the international level	Non-profit non-governmental organization
British Olympic Association (BOA)	Prepares and leads the nation's finest athletes at the summer, winter and youth Olympic Games	Non-profit non-governmental organization
National Governing Bodies (NGBs)	Responsibility for managing their specific sport	Non-profit non-governmental organization
UK Sport	To ensure that the resources are available to support our Olympic and Paralympic athletes	Executive non-departmental public body advising the Department of Culture, Media and Sport
Sport England	Responsible for developing and promoting sport and physical activity in England	Executive non-departmental public body
Sport Scotland	Responsible for developing and promoting sport and physical activity in Scotland	Executive non-departmental public body, responsible to the Scottish Parliament

(Continued)

Focus Box 3.1. **Continued.**

Name of organization	Role	Type of organization
Sport Wales	Responsible for developing and promoting sport and physical activity in Wales	Executive non-departmental public body responsible to the Welsh Government
Media, e.g. British Broadcasting Corporation	To televise or photograph the events	BBC public corporation Others are private companies
Partners, e.g. BMW	Provide cars for officials and VIPs	Private companies
Licensees, e.g. online shop	Provide merchandise	There were 65 licensees in total. Private companies
Sponsors, e.g. Cadbury	Provide funding to have logos at venues	There were 44 sponsoring private companies
Financial institutions, e.g. banks	Provide finance for the Games	Private companies
National Lottery	Grants for funding the Games	Public body
Contractors	Provide goods and services	Private companies
Suppliers and other creditors	Provide goods and services to Games contractors	Subcontracts private companies
Employees	Paid workforce	Working for organizations with Games contracts
Company shareholders	Private companies are accountable to their shareholders	Owners of public limited companies
Trades Unions	Support workforce	
Athletes	Without them participating there would be no Games	
VIPs	Heads of State	

(Continued)

Focus Box 3.1. **Continued.**

Name of organization	Role	Type of organization
Volunteers	Games Makers	Unpaid workforce
Spectators	Purchase tickets and provide the Games atmosphere	
Allotment holders	Rent land for vegetable growing	Land needed for Games venues
Travellers and Romani groups	Residents of caravan site	Land needed for Games venues
Local communities, especially from the five London Boroughs and Weymouth	Lived with the disruption pre-games, during and the legacy of the games	Includes local businesses, organizations and residents
The UK public	Partly funded the Games	Taxpayers

From: ODA (2007); Sadd (2012); Commission for a Sustainable London 2012 (2013); LOCOG (2013); IOC (2014); DCMS (2015); Sport England (2015a); Sport Scotland (2015); Sport Wales (2015); UK Sport (2015).

CONSUMER/BUYER BEHAVIOUR

Benefits of participating in leisure

Beard and Ragheb (1980) have identified six motivations or benefits that come from participating in leisure, which are reflected in Horner and Swarbrooke's (2014) leisure consumer typology (Table 3.4). Unfortunately, *The Volunteer* is missing from the leisure consumer nomenclature, and depending on the volunteering opportunity, any of the six benefits in Table 3.4 could be gained.

Although Table 3.4 may suggest that each type of leisure consumer only requires one benefit, this is not the case. LETS consumers will try to fulfil their own specific needs even when multiple benefits are being sought from any one experience. For example, 'The Tourist' will seek psychological benefits of enjoyment, a sense of achievement and self-esteem but may also require educational, social and relaxation benefits from their holiday experience. Kim *et al.* (2012: 15) cite the work of many academics to produce a list of 19 constructs, some or all of which would be required from a tourism experience, including novelty (feeling of newness from a new experience) and spontaneity:

- Adventure;
- Challenge;
- Escaping pressure;
- Happiness;
- Hedonism;
- Intellectual cultivation;
- Involvement;
- Knowledge;
- Meaningfulness;
- Novelty;
- Personal relevance;
- Pleasure;
- Refreshment;
- Relaxation;
- Sense of separation;
- Social interaction;
- Spontaneity;
- Stimulation;
- Timeliness.

Table 3.4. Benefits of leisure in relation to leisure consumers (Beard and Ragheb, 1980; Horner and Swarbrooke, 2014).

Benefits of leisure Beard and Ragheb (1980)	Leisure consumer Horner and Swarbrooke (2005)
Psychological: Freedom, enjoyment, involvement and intellectual challenge	The Home Lover The Spiritualist The Tourist
Educational: Intellectual stimulation	The Student
Social: Rewarding relationships with others	The Food and Drink consumer The Shopper
Relaxation: Relief from stress and stains of life	The Hedonist
Physiological: Well-being and physical fitness	The Sportsperson
Aesthetic: Interesting, pleasing, beautiful and well designed	The Artist

Sports tourists who wish to experience adventure holidays that include such activities as jet boat rides, whitewater kayaking, bungee jumping or heli-skiing are considered to be 'thrill seekers' and would be disappointed if they did not receive this level of arousal. Heritage tourists are said to wish to fulfil their need for involvement, peace of mind and educational experiences (Chen and Chen, 2010). In both cases a single hotel resort on its own will not be able to fulfil all the customers' requirements and additional services such as sightseeing trips would need to be purchased. This is unlike the food and drink consumer where a restaurant will be able to fulfil their needs.

Consumers' needs and wants are constantly changing, influenced by friends, family, advertisements and promotions, but once a customer has recognized their needs and the benefits they require they will seek a service provider; this is known as the pre-purchase phase. This is one part of Lovelock and Wirtz's (2011) three-stage model of service consumption; the others are service encounter and post encounter stage. This model will be used in the next section of the chapter to examine customer behaviour (see Fig. 3.3).

Lovelock and Wirtz's (2011) three-stage model of service consumption will be used in this section to examine customer behaviour.

Stage 1 Pre-purchase

The pre-purchase stage of the buying process is focused on the customers' desire to fulfil a need with a service or goods (need arousal), resulting in the acquisition of information as to the services offered and its provider (see Fig. 3.3). This can be achieved in any number of ways including past experience, word of mouth from others, reviews on the Internet, information (advertisements) from the providers themselves, and if appropriate the tangible elements of a service such as the actual look of the restaurant or fitness centre can be examined. It is thought that consumers are influenced less by advertising and more by social media. Therefore the significance of the social media needs to be recognized by service providers, as well as the importance of up-to-date information on well-designed websites to enable consumers to make purchase decisions quicker and more easily. In contrast it was found that potential tourists interested in holidays to destinations with which they are unfamiliar will spend more time

Fig. 3.3. The three-stage model of service consumption (Lovelock and Wirtz, 2011).

seeking out information at the pre-purchase stage than holidaymakers revisiting familiar resorts (Andereck, 2005: 66, cited in Huertas-Garcia *et al.*, 2014).

Lovelock and Wirtz (2011) suggest that potential customers throughout the pre-purchase stage will be clarifying their needs, exploring solutions and identifying a range of service providers as a way of making sure that their other elements come into the decision-making equation such as location of the service provider, their opening hours and price (which will be examined later in this chapter). One of the main purposes of the consumer carrying out all these activities is to reduce their exposure to any risk, especially of a poor experience, wasting their money and their leisure time.

Risk reduction

One of the main aims of any potential customer at the pre-purchase stage is to reduce the perceived risk of not having an inappropriate level of service, not delivered at the correct time and by unpleasant staff. They are trying to achieve what Kim *et al.* (2012: 13) describe as a 'positive memorable tourism experience'. This is difficult in the tourism or events context as Kandampully (2002 cited in Shonk and Chelladurai, 2008: 590) suggests 'tourism is consuming a combination of fundamentally independent services in a continuous chain from the time they leave home until they return.'

As customers' needs are more sophisticated and there is increased competition (Kandampully and Suhartanto, 2000), a service provider needs to be able to give their potential customers reassurance that adverse things will not happen. For example, in Marriott's Look No Further® Best Rate Guarantee programme, Marriott Hotels state that if a customer after booking a room with them finds it offered at a lower rate they will match that lower rate and add an additional 25% discount (Marriott Hotel, 2015). Whilst this type of strategy will attract the attention of a potential client, it is necessary for them to trust that an organization will keep its promises before a purchase is made (Kandampully, 1998). Particular brands can be selected to ensure that service promises will be kept.

Brands

One way that customers have used to reduce risk is to purchase from known brands such as hotel chains or service providers. Whilst older people use these risk-reducing strategies of seeking out familiar brands, young consumers are considered to be 'enthusiastic buyers … with strong curiosity … more inquisitive' (San and Yazdanifard, 2013: 153). Young people therefore were found to be prepared to take more risk and did not respond to brands to reduce a perceived risk (San and Yazdanifard, 2013). Just as brands can reduce risk, so can a great image.

Image

The image of a service provider can aid the consumer in their pre-purchase decision-making process; one such organization is the Disney Corporation because of its long-standing reputation for customer-driven service and its obsession with cleanliness and 'getting it right'. Equally, a poor image and bad reputation will discourage a customer from engaging with a service provider. The effect of a poor image on pre-purchase judgement can extend not just to one service provider but to the whole of a tourism destination as Case Study 3.1 'Blackpool Hen and Stag parties: the re-imaging of a holiday resort' shows.

To change the image of a destination is not straightforward and indeed may be complex (Croy, 2012). To overcome the negative perceptions of a tourism destination it is suggested three factors need to be changed (Gartner, 1993, cited in Croy, 2012: 49; Baloglu and McCleary, 1999, cited in Moon *et al.*, 2011: 290):

- Cognitive;
- Affective; and
- Conative.

COGNITIVE FACTOR.   These are the images gathered by the customer over time from information sources such as newspapers, radio and TV news, and documentaries giving the potential tourist knowledge of the destination. The potential customer gives a value to each attitude of the tourist destination based on their needs. To supersede all past negative images quickly is very difficult.

AFFECTIVE FACTORS.   This refers to feelings and emotions raised in a potential tourist by a destination. This emotional component is said to be strongly affected by the motivations or benefits required by the tourists from a specific tourist destination. Again these are individualist customer requirements and not any one resort would be able to facilitate all of the tourist's needs.

CONATIVE FACTORS.   Marketers should be able to go some way to predict which specific tourist would be predisposed to selecting a particular resort. The conative factors mean that the tourist has come to a decision and will take action and will book a holiday to the destination or take the opposite view and decide not to.

As well as the image of a sports facility, destination or event, price plays a part in the decision-making of a potential customer.

Price

Price is an influential element for customers at the pre-purchase review phase. Shonk and Chelladurai (2008) investigating people going to sporting events found the price of accommodation was used by them as an indicator of service quality and perceived value. Huertas-Garcia *et al.* (2014) state that tourists will make purchase decisions in relation to the price and the value which they perceive the service providers will be providing. Their research found that purchasing a holiday was seen as a risky purchase, difficult to evaluate prior to consumption and that the price was seen by them as the most important determinant of perceived quality.

Case Study 3.1. Blackpool Hen and Stag Parties: the re-imaging of a holiday resort

Graham Cain, Blackpool Borough Council Cabinet Member for Leisure and Tourism, real-izes that Blackpool's target market of low-budget stag and hen parties has created barriers to the family market and negative perceptions of the town. To overcome this problem Blackpool is instigating a policy to zone the town so clubs will be in one area where hen and stag partying can take place without upsetting the families at the attractions at the other end of the resort (Interview BBC Radio Lancashire 10 March 2015). Blackpool has also been given powers to issue Public Spaces Protection Orders under the Anti-social Behaviour, Crime and Policing Act 2014 (Home Office, 2013; see below for issuing criteria). This is to combat 'public nudity' and the wearing of inappropriate dress during the daytime by stag and hen parties (Blackpool Council Cabinet Member Gillian Campbell Interviewed by *Daily Mail* 20 October 2014; Slack, 2014).

Issuing Criteria For Public Spaces Protection Orders (Home Office, 2013)

A local authority may make a Public Spaces Protection Order if satisfied on reasonable grounds that two conditions are met.

The first condition is that:

(a) Activities carried on in a public place within the authority's area have had a detrimental effect on the quality of life of those in the locality; or

(b) It is likely that activities will be carried on in a public place within that area and that they will have such an effect.

The second condition is that the effect, or likely effect, of the activities:

(a) Is, or is likely to be, of a persistent or continuing nature;

(b) Is, or is likely to be, such as to make the activities unreasonable; and

(c) Justifies the restrictions imposed by the notice.

Visitor Numbers

Blackpool has a total of 13.5 million day visitors generating over £430m for the local economy, but when compared with the amount spent by the 3.5 million staying guests who contribute over £863m it can be understood why the Local Council wishes to reposition this resort to target this more lucrative market (Global Tourism Solutions (UK) Ltd, 2013, cited in Blackpool Borough Council, 2015).

Blackpool is also reported to be trying to attract events and conferences to the resort, as it was once a regular destination for party political conferences. Moon *et al.* (2011) suggest that staging successful events can help to reposition a resort's image and that intangible elements of that service such as efficient and confident service personnel and feelings of safety and security can influence the customers more than tangible elements.

(Continued)

Case Study 3.1. Continued.

The strategies above may go some way to achieving the feeling of being secure, but Blackpool has also undergone some refurbishment.

The excellent refurbishment of the Blackpool Tower and the Promenade by Blackpool Borough Council and Merlin Entertainments Group Ltd in 2011 cost £20m and was funded by the North West Development Agency, the European Regional Development Fund, Homes and Communities Agency and Blackpool Council (Merlin Entertainments Group Ltd, 2015). Unfortunately, Blackpool is trying to carry out this reimaging of the resort when money from both the public and private sections is in short supply (Fig. 3.4).

Fig. 3.4. Blackpool's Golden Mile during the illuminations season.

Customer reviews on TripAdvisor and other review websites frequently mention the price of a hotel room in relation to the quality of the service received. Ye *et al.*'s (2014) research suggests that LETS customers' level of consideration of the room rate is in direct relation to the star rating of a hotel. This results in either a negative or positive emotional response prior to actually purchasing the room. Whether they purchase it or not depends on the customers' perception of the quality of service they will receive in relation to the cost of it. Ye *et al.*'s (2014) research did not find this to be an attribute of business travellers.

Unfortunately for LETS service providers, inconsistencies between different groups of customers is not the only area where needs differ. Each and every potential customer as shown above can require a different LETS experience. This will be discussed in the next section of this chapter.

Inconsistencies of consumer choice

LETS service providers not only have to take into account their consumers' level of aversion to risk when devising services but also inconsistencies in customers' choice of LETS experiences. San and Yazdanifard's (2013) research found that some older customers displayed 'defensive aging' whereby they avoided offerings exclusively for the old such as senior citizen discounts.

Another example of inconsistency of service choice can be found in the trend of selecting to use a budget no-frills airline but stay in a four- or five-star hotel. Whilst this may seem a risky decision to make, to these consumers it is not. All airlines have to fulfil the same safety checks and on short haul flights there is very little difference in the core service even though budget airlines require additional payments for food and beverages and also to put baggage in the aeroplane cargo hold. If the consumer took the opposite decision and paid for a first- or business-class flight and stayed in a one- or two-star hotel the risk of an unsatisfactory experience would be far greater.

People who are now making these types of decisions are known as hybrid consumers and clothing has been printed in Germany with the slogan 'I love Aldi + Prada' to embrace this paradox in the supermarket sector (Ehrnrooth and Grönroos, 2013). Eventually the potential customer will make the decision to source a service from a specific provider and then they move into the next phase of Lovelock and Wirtz's (2011) consumer behaviour model, the service encounter.

Stage 2 The service encounter

The service encounter, the second stage in Lovelock and Wirtz's trilogy of customer behaviour, has been defined by Mascio (2010: 63) as 'the act of giving customers what they ask for efficiently and courteously'. She continues by pointing out that relationships can be formed between internal and external customers (customers and employees) especially when staff are trying to solve their service problems. Also it has been recognized that during these encounters front-of-house staff will need to meet goals and targets set by their employer not necessarily related to service delivery such as collecting information for marketing purposes or on-the-job training of new staff. The three tasks of giving excellent service, forming relationships and meeting organizational targets can be very difficult for staff to balance at the same time. One way this can be addressed is by standardization of the service encounter.

Standardization of the service encounter

To ensure that the appropriate level of service is delivered to customers some organizations have standardized the service encounters with specific delivery systems for front-of-house staff to follow (Chiang and Wu, 2014). An example is fast-food restaurants with standardized service delivery processes. This type of standardization via the introduction of technology was advocated by Levitt as early as 1972 and it allows for the *mass production* of services previously only found in the manufacturing domain.

Standardization of the service encounter is regularly met by customers when having to telephone a call centre. These are frequently used by organizations to provide an efficient way of dealing with large volumes of sales, after-sale enquires or customer complaints. Within this framework of telephone contact taking place, call centre organizations have devised standardized scripts to manage what their staff say. In the USA 3% of the workforce are employed in call centres, with some having targets to deal with two calls a minute (Lovelock and Wirtz, 2011). Consequently customer satisfaction rates have been found to be extremely low as the customer is left to judge the service quality of intangible elements of the service such as reliability and responsiveness. It has also been found that working in the call centre environment is one of the most stressful occupations (Malhotra and Mukherjee, 2004).

Standardized services at major tourist attractions and events can be problematic as both customers and staff are not homogeneous, coming from diverse cultural backgrounds, making a uniform service encounter difficult to instigate (Thwaites and Williams, 2006; Huang and Rundle-Thiele, 2014). A good example to illustrate this is to be found on cruise ships where there are high levels of personal contact between the customers and front-of-house staff, with both parties being culturally diverse.

Even so, as shown previously, individual customers have a variety of needs that they wish to fulfil through participating in a LETS activity, where a standardized service may not suffice. Also it is possible for the competitors of an organization to introduce technology or to emulate a standardized service as seen in the plethora of fast-food chains. One unique attribute an organization has to distinguish itself from its competition is their staff. Drucker (cited in Reichheld and Teal, 2001: 92) states '*People are our greatest asset*' and it is never more so than at the service encounter stage when customers and front-of-house employees are face to face.

Employees in the service encounter

The importance of employees in the service encounter has been researched by many academics. Jung and Yoon (2013) suggested that their satisfaction is key to customer satisfaction. They suggested that a friendlier service from employees with a positive approach to customers could have a major effect not only on the customers' perceptions but also in becoming loyal to a particular service provider. Regrettably in many sectors of the LETS industry, organizations have a human resource strategy of seasonal staff on low pay and given minimum training (Williams and Thwaites, 2007). Berry (1995: 159) states that high performance standards are expected of employees but organizations limit their investment in necessary equipment for them to achieve this. The above strategies have been found to make employees dissatisfied and not necessarily predisposed to delivering exceptional service to customers, which will eventually result in low retention rates as unhappy staff leave.

Unfortunately during these unsatisfactory encounters customers will be making judgements as to whether or not their expectations are being met. Schlesinger and Heskett (1991) see this as a 'cycle of failure', demonstrating a correlation between customer dissatisfaction and poor financial performance of an organization. This will be explored next.

Cycles of failure, mediocrity and success

Schlesinger and Heskett (1991) have two theories regarding the linkages between the human resource strategies, the effects on customers and the performance of an organization: the 'cycle of failure' and the 'cycle of success'. The cycle of success is of course the direct opposite of the failing scenario. Lovelock (1995) took an intermediary perspective and in his 'cycle of mediocrity' staff have job security but very little power to work on their own initiative to solve problems. The next section will examine these three theories.

Cycles of service failure and success

Both of Schlesinger and Heskett's (1991) theories have employee and customer cycles with linkages to denote correlations between various elements. For example, in the cycle of failure high employee turnover is linked to the paucity of customer relationships formed and in the cycle of success low employee turnover is linked to the ability of the employees and the organization to form relationships with customers leading to customer loyalty with the service provider.

Schlesinger and Heskett's (1991) cycle of failure is seen as a self-perpetuating cycle as lower profits mean that an organization will not have the resources to make any fundamental strategic or operational changes. Replacing staff is a drain on the organization's limited resources, as compulsory training in areas such as health and safety and food hygiene has to be given. Whilst there are staff vacancies, service quality can reduce even further (Grönroos, 2000; Heskett *et al.*, 2003). It is evident that customer dissatisfaction and lack of loyalty are inevitable in this operational environment (Heskett, 1995; Lovelock and Wirtz, 2011).

The opposite business approach, Schlesinger and Heskett's (1991) cycle of success, is where intensive recruitment and selection procedures, effective training and higher pay rates for employees are deployed. These improvements are said to deliver customer loyalty, competitive edge and improved business performance (Berry 1995; Grönroos, 2000; Maister, cited in Heskett *et al.*, 2003: 154).

Kandampully and Subartando's (2000) research into hotels found that housekeeping services were more important to the customer than the performance of the reception or food and beverage department and had more influence over the customer's judgement of whether or not to use the provider again. The customers considered a hotel to be a substitute for a temporary home and therefore the quality of the housekeeping services were paramount. Kandampully and Subartando (2000) found that the training that housekeeping employees receive is minimal compared with reception or restaurant staff and consider that this is an area that needs to be addressed. Their thinking follows Schlesinger and Heskett's (1991) theory of cycles of failure or success, whereby extensively trained staff results in higher customer satisfaction and loyalty. Organizations should be looking beyond short-term financial gains to what will be long-term 'emotional connection' between them and their customers.

The cycles of failure and success models are not without critics. In their research, Keiningham *et al.* (2005) concluded that the correlation between customer satisfaction and profitability is far more complex than the cycles of failure and success alluded to, and Edvardsson and Gustavsson (2003) questioned whether or not the two cycles are applicable to all service contexts. Silvestro (2002), despite also being a critic of the lack of linkages in the cycles, suggests that in high contact encounters employee satisfaction is related to customer satisfaction. Staff having a positive attitude to customers is now known as emotional labour (Lovelock and Wirtz, 2011), as we see in Chapter 7.

Cycle of mediocrity

Lovelock (1995) emulates Schlesinger and Heskett's (1991) employee customer linkages in the cycles of failure and success to formulate the cycle of mediocrity. Lovelock devised this set of linkages when investigating large bureaucratic organizations where innovation is not encouraged and the following of rules is paramount with employees becoming ever more dissatisfied (see Focus Box 3.2 for an example in public sector leisure services). Unlike the cycle of failure, employees have job security, wages and other benefits are reasonable, but there is very little customer focus.

Large organizations still demonstrate elements of Lovelock's cycle of mediocrity, especially when interpreting rules inappropriately. This can be seen when local authorities tried to stop people holding street parties to celebrate Prince William and Katherine Middleton's wedding by using health and safety legislation. The Health and Safety Executive was concerned that 'health and safety' was being used as an excuse not to grant permission for street parties, stating that the act was being cited to disguise the local authority's other concerns such as additional costs to them. Even the UK Prime Minister David Cameron urged local authorities not to stop people celebrating the Royal Wedding with street parties, stating that this was an act of 'petty bureaucracy' (BBC, 2011).

Unlike other sectors of the service industry such as banking, the LETS private sector is dominated by small to medium enterprises (SMEs), many being family-run businesses. Getz *et al.*'s (2005) research into this phenomenon found that the owner's main goal was to sustain the business for family reasons, such as offering accommodation to enable the family to live in a beautiful location. Family-run businesses do not seek growth or profitability, a very different business strategy from other types of LETS organizations. Family-run business would not appreciate or value the concentration of the three models above on striving to continuously improve the business, but would wish to retain the status quo.

Focus Box 3.2. **Lovelock's (1995) Cycle of Mediocrity UK Public Sector Leisure Services**

Many UK central government politicians considered that the operational environment in the UK public sector, where much of the LETS provision especially sports facilities could be found, was one of job security; wages and other benefits were reasonable but there was very little customer focus. These facilities received public money to subsidize the running costs (revenue subsidy) and capital subsidy to enable refurbishments of the infrastructure to take place. These were the ideal conditions for Lovelock's (1995) Cycle of Mediocrity to arise.

The passing of the Local Government Act of 1988 brought into legislation Compulsory Competitive Tendering (CCT), which required UK local government involved in maintaining parks and gardens, the management of sports and leisure facilities and the cleaning of all local government buildings such as theatres, libraries, museums and art galleries to allow other organizations including the private sector to bid for this work. Local government could undertake these activities if they had set up a Direct Service Organization (DSO), but this had to be removed from the day-to-day operations of the local authority and they had to win the right to do this work in fair competition with others.

The advent of this new operational régime was that even DSOs, not only when trying to win but retain these contracts, had to become innovative and customer focused, but this limited the pay levels, bonuses and benefits of staff. The main incentive for this innovative, customer-focused cultural change was that most contracts were awarded with elements of profit sharing or at least a share of any reduction in the subsidies needed to run the facility. It should be noted that many decisions such as setting admission prices were not in the gift of the managing organizations but remained with the local authorities. This operation regime, whilst it has undergone a number of changes, is still in place and is now known as Best Value (Department of Communities and Local Government, 2012).

The new legislation, the Local Government Act, 1999, was less prescriptive than CCT but it contained a statutory 'Duty of Best Value' whereby local councils have to continuously improve their services in terms of economy, efficiency and effectiveness (the 3Es). A major element of the Best Value procurement process is for local authorities to seek the maximum benefit (social value) for the community before a purchase order or contract is awarded. For local government to be knowledgeable to achieve this, consultations must take place with the local community, voluntary groups, small businesses and other stakeholders. If services are going to be de-commissioned consultations are required.

In conclusion, whilst not all employees have the ability to have face-to-face service encounters with customers, front-line staff are in a position to help them have a satisfactory experience but only if organizational culture supports them in this quest, as Chapter 7 explores in more depth. During and after the service encounter customers will reflect on the quality of the experience received and make a decision as to whether or not they were satisfied and had been given appropriate value in terms of the time and money invested. When customers make post-encounter judgements, Chen and Chen (2010) suggest that there is a direct correlation between the level of their satisfaction and their intention to make further purchases from that specific provider. The post-encounter is the third stage in Lovelock and Wirtz's (2011) consumer behaviour trilogy.

Stage 3 Post-encounter

Throughout the pre-purchase stage the customer is formulating their expectations of what they will receive from their chosen service provider and this will be used to judge the actual service in the service encounter stage. The customer will judge if their needs have been fulfilled and whether or not the organization has kept its promises (Mattila and Wirtz 2000; Huang and Dubinsky, 2014). This multi-dimensional judgement is known as 'the perceived value' of the service the customer has received and is not only concerned with price paid (Sabiote-Ortiz *et al.*, 2014).

Unfortunately, customers' needs and desired benefits from a service provider are individualistic and the same level of service can elicit a different judgement from each and every consumer. These subjective customer judgements at the post-encounter phase will influence whether or not they will purchase the experience from the same provider. Positive perceived value from a service will influence post-encounter judgements and can lead to customer loyalty (Chen and Chen, 2010).

Customer loyalty

Although many service providers concentrate on attracting new customers it is far easier and cheaper to retain existing ones and their loyalty plays a part in their decision to make a repeat purchase. Looy *et al.* (2003: 62) point out the importance of repeat purchases to the profitability of a business, stating that a loyal pizza-eating customer can have a 'lifetime value' of £5600. Loyal customers will also express their opinions of great service and its providers on the various websites, thus influencing potential customers.

Looy *et al.* (2003) suggest that there are four levels of customer loyalty that organizations need to be aware of.

1. *Truly loyal* – customers who look for a particular service provider as past experience has met their needs, for example a hotel or restaurant chain.
2. *Spuriously loyal* – customers who go to the same provider due to its convenience or habit, for example a theatre or gym.
3. *Latent loyalty* – loyal because there is no alternative, such as ski and snow boarding at the Chill Factore Manchester.
4. *No loyalty at all* – 'they shop around'. This is easy to do with airlines and hotels but not possible where unique attractions or one-off events are concerned.

A strategy used in the LETS context to create 'truly loyal' customers is to have frequent flyers programmes or fitness club memberships where free or reduced amounts of money are paid for services in relation to the points awarded to a customer for using the service in the past. Sometimes the customers do not form a bond with the organization but with specific front-of-house employees, and if the latter move to another service provider customers can go with some of them as in the case of fitness instructors or sports coaches. The reason for customers wanting to follow front-of-house staff to another employer is not only due to their professional competence but can be based on the formation of a social relationship (Kandampully, 1998).

Traditionally people used to drink alcohol in what was known as their 'local', the public house nearest their home or place of work. The retirement of a friendly pub landlord or landlady or the loss of a particular member of the bar staff was a major talking point in the community. Nowadays, many public houses cannot survive on the sale of alcohol alone as supermarkets drive down the price. The sale of food and the staging of events such as quiz nights and live music are frequently offered to compensate for the loss of custom, but despite this the Campaign for Real Ale states that almost 30 public houses a week are closing down (Gander, 2014) and the social relationship is also being lost.

Kandampully (1998) has also observed the opposite with some front-of-house staff having a greater loyalty to their customers than their employers, especially in organizations that keep trying to attract new customers. Although there seem to be disadvantages with this type of relationship there are benefits to the organization as these customers are more willing to express their dissatisfaction to staff about the service rather than say nothing and not return.

In either of the two scenarios, loyal customers with strong relationships with a service provider will try to influence the service when they perceive their needs are not being met. They would rather do this than seek out a new service supplier to purchase from. Loyal customers will also express their opinions of great service on the various social media websites, thus influencing potential customers.

We can see therefore that customers in the LETS environment have increased choice, excellent value for their money and in many instances organizations give an augmented service. This has been brought about by increased competition, with little to distinguish one provider from another. To gain and retain competitive edge from their rivals, customer loyalty is imperative to the success of LETS service organizations (Kandampully and Suhartanto, 2000).

CONCLUSIONS

This chapter is summarized in Fig. 3.5. Schlesinger and Heskett (1991) have shown that one of the main elements in delivering exceptional customer service is down to treating staff appropriately. Excellent employees can be the unique selling point of a LETS organization, not only giving competitive edge over their rival service providers, but attracting and retaining

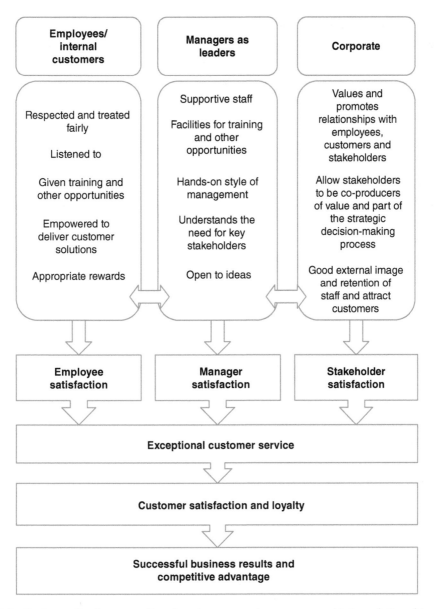

Fig. 3.5. Best practice for exceptional customer service: causes and inter-relationships (Williams and Shaw, 2006).

new customers. Examples have been given of how staff are not helped by organizations to achieve satisfactory service as they do not provide continuity of contracts, training and resources. The importance of other stakeholders to the service providers has been explored and the need to build relationships with them is also a key element of providing an excellent service. Finally, organizations need to understand the buying decision process of their target customers, especially their ever-changing needs and benefits sought from the LETS experience. Customers' satisfaction and how to measure the phenomenon will be explored in depth in Chapters 9 and 10.

QUESTIONS

1. Why is it advantageous for a service provider to distinguish between consumers and customers?

2. What are the advantages and disadvantages of delivering a customer experience using a multi-dimensional approach?

3. Utilizing a range of specific LETS experiences, explain in detail the benefits to the customer of participating in them.

4. Consider the influence of employees at each of the three stages of consumer-buyer behaviour process.

FURTHER READING

Getz, D., Andersson, T. and Larson, M. (2007) Festival stakeholders roles: concepts and case studies. *Event Management* 10, 103–122.

Heskett, J.L., Sasser, E.W. and Schlesinger, L.A. (2003) *The Value Profit Chain: Treat Employees like Customers and Customers like Employees*. Free Press, New York.

Lovelock, C. and Wirtz, J. (2011) *Services Marketing. People Technology Strategy*, 7th edn. Pearson, Harlow, UK.

Taylor, P. (2011) *Torkildsen's Sport and Leisure Management*, 6th edn. Routledge, Oxford, UK.

Wilks, L. (2014) The lived experience of London 2012 Olympic and Paralympic Games volunteers: a serious leisure perspective. *Leisure Studies* 1–16.

REFERENCES

Andersson, T.D. and Getz, D. (2008) Stakeholder management strategies of festivals. *Journal of Conventions and Event Tourism* 9(3), 199–220.

BBC (2011) Royal wedding: Cameron urges street party celebrations. BBC News UK 11 April 10.53. Available at: http://www.bbc.co.uk/news/uk-13032370 (accessed 22 March 2015).

Beard, J.G. and Ragheb, M.G. (1980) Measuring leisure satisfaction. *Leisure Research* 1, 21–33.

Berry, L.L. (1995) *On Great Service: a Framework for Action*. The Free Press, New York.

Blackpool Borough Council (2015) Resort Place-Making 2015–2017 A destination management plan for Blackpool. Blackpool Borough Council. Available at: https://www.blackpool.gov.uk/Residents/Planning-environment-and-community/Documents/Destination-Blackpool-2015---2017 (accessed 25 March 2015).

Canal and River Trust (2015) Volunteer. Available at: http://canalrivertrust.org.uk/volunteering (accessed 20 February 2015).

Chen, C.-F. and Chen, F.-S. (2010) Experience quality, perceived value, satisfaction and behavioural intentions for heritage tourists. *Tourism Management* 31, 29–35.

Chiang, C.-F. and Wu, K.-P. (2014) The influence of internal service quality and job standardization on job satisfaction with supports as mediators: flight attendants at branch workplace. *The International Journal of Human Resource Management* 25(19), 2644–2666.

Commission for a Sustainable London 2012 (2009) *Annual Review Stakeholder Engagement Programme: Annual Review Stakeholder Feedback 2008*. Commission for a Sustainable London 2012. London. Available at: http://www.cslondon.org/wp-content/uploads/downloads/2010/11/2010.10.18-CSL-2009-Annual-Review-Feedback-from-Stakeholders.doc (accessed 7 April 2015).

Commission for a Sustainable London 2012 (2013) *Thematic Review: In Sight of the Finishing Line. A Review of the Preparations to Stage A Sustainable Games February 2012*. Commission for a Sustainable London 2012. London. Available at: http://www.cslondon.org/wp-content/uploads/downloads/2012/02/In_sight_of_the_finishing_line.pdf (accessed 7 April 2015).

Crosby, P.B. (1984) *Quality without Tears*. McGraw-Hill, London.

Croy, G. (2012) Destination image. In: Robinson, P. (ed.) *Tourism: The Key Concepts*. Routledge, Oxford, UK, pp. 49–83.

DCMS (2015) Department of culture, media and sport, what we do. Available at: http://www.gov.uk/government/organisations/department-for-culture-media-sport (accessed 10 March 2015).

Deming, W.E. (1986) *Out of Crisis: Quality, Production and Competitive Position*. MIT Press, Cambridge, Massachusetts.

Department of Communities and Local Government (2012) Best value statutory guidance. Available at: http://www.gov.uk/government/uploads/system/uploads/attachment_data/file/5945/1976926.pdf (accessed 24 April 2015).

Edvardsson, B. and Gustavsson, A. (2003) Quality in the work environment: a prerequisite for success in new service development. *Managing Service Quality* 13(2), 148–163.

Ehrnrooth, H. and Grönroos, C. (2013) The hybrid consumer: exploring hybrid consumption behaviour. *Management Decision* 31(9), 1793–1820.

Fairley, S., Tyler, B.D., Kellet, P. and D'Elia, K. (2011) The Formula One Australian Grand Prix: exploring the triple bottom line. *Sports Management Review* 14, 141–152.

Feigenbaum, A.V. (1991) *Total Quality Control*, 3rd edn. McGraw-Hill, London.

Gander, K. (2014) Camra Calls for Government Help as Almost 30 Pubs Close Every Week. *The Independent* 03 March 2014. Available at: http://www.independent.co.uk/news/uk/home-news/almost-30-pubs-close-every-week-9165968.html (accessed 14 March 2015).

Getz, D., Carlsen, J. and Morrison, A. (2005) Quality issues for the family business. In: Jones, E.E. and Haven, C. (eds) *Tourism SMEs, Service Quality and Destination Competitiveness*. CAB International, Wallingford, UK, pp. 73–85.

Getz, D., Andersson, T. and Larson, M. (2007) Festival stakeholders roles: concepts and case studies. *Event Management* 10, 103–122.

Grönroos, C. (2000) *Service Management and Marketing: A Customer Approach*, 2nd edn. Wiley, Chichester, UK.

Gummesson, E. (1993) Service productivity: a blasphemous approach. *Proceedings of the Service Management and Marketing Conference,* Cardiff (July), pp. 1–15.

Hansen, Z.N.L. and Rasmussen, L.B. (2013) Outsourcing relationships: changes in power and dependency. *European Management Journal* 31, 655–667.

Heskett, J.L. (1995) Strategic services management: examining and understanding. In: Glynn, W.L. and Barnes, J.G. (eds) *Understanding Management*. Wiley, Chichester, UK, pp. 449–473.

Heskett, J.L., Sasser, E.W. and Schlesinger, L.A. (2003) *The Value Profit Chain: Treat Employees like Customers and Customers like Employees*. Free Press, New York.

Home Office (2013) Anti-social Behaviour, Crime and Policing Act 2014. The National Achieve. Available at: http://www.legislation.gov.uk/ukpga/2014/12/enacted (accessed 25 March 2015).

Horner, S. and Swarbrooke, J. (2014) *Leisure Marketing: A Global Perspective*. Routledge, Oxon, UK.

Huang, W.Y. and Dubinsky, A.J. (2014) Measuring customer pre-purchase satisfaction in a retail setting. *The Service Industries Journal* 34(3), 212–229.

Huang, Y.-T. and Rundle-Thiele, S. (2014) The moderating effect of cultural congruence on the internal marketing practice and employee satisfaction relationship: an empirical examination of Australian and Taiwanese born tourism employees. *Tourism Management* 42, 196–206.

Huertas-Garcia, R., García, M.L. and Consolación, C. (2014) Conjoint analysis of tourist choice of hotel attributes presented in travel agent brochures. *International Journal of Tourism Research* 16, 65–75.

IOC (2014) The International Olympic Committee. Available at: http://www.olympic.org/ioc (accessed 10 March 2015).

Jung, H.S. and Yoon, H.H. (2013) Do employees' satisfied customers respond with an satisfactory relationship? The effects of employees' satisfaction on customers' satisfaction and loyalty in a family restaurant. *International Journal of Hospitality Management* 34, 1–8.

Kandampully, J. (1998) Service quality to service loyalty: a relationship which goes beyond customer services. *Total Quality Management* 9(6), 431–443.

Kandampully, J. and Suhartanto, D. (2000) Customer loyalty in the hotel industry: the role of customer satisfaction and image. *International Journal of Contemporary Hospitality Management* 12(6), 346–351.

Keiningham, T.L., Perkins-Munn, T., Aksoy, L. and Estrin, D. (2005) Does customer satisfaction lead to profitability? The meditation role of share-of-wallet. *Managing Service Quality* 15(2), 172–181.

Kenny, G. (2013) The stakeholder or the firm? Balancing the strategic framework. *Journal of Business Strategy* 34(3), 33–40.

Kim, J.-K., Ritchie, J.R.B. and McCormick, B. (2012) Development of a scale to measure memorable tourism experiences. *Journal of Travel Research* 51(1), 12–25.

Levitt, T. (1972) Production-line approach to service. *Harvard Business Review* (September–October), 41–52.

LOCOG (2013) *London 2012 Olympic Games Official Report Vol*ume *3.* The London Organising Committee of the Olympic Games and Paralympic Games Limited, London. Available at: http://www.olympic.org/documents/Reports/OfficialPastGamesReports/Summer/eng/2012-ro-s-London_V3_eng.pdf (accessed 10 March 2015).

Looy, B.V., Gemmel, P. and Dierdonck, R.V. (2003) *Services Management, an Integrated Approach*, 2nd edn. Prentice Hall, Harlow, UK.

Lovelock, C.H. (1995) Managing services: the human factor. In: Glynn, W.L. and Barnes, J.G. (eds) *Understanding Services Management.* Wiley, Chichester, UK, pp. 203–243.

Lovelock, C. and Wirtz, J. (2011) *Services Marketing. People Technology Strategy*, 7th edn. Pearson, Harlow, UK.

Malhotra, N. and Mukherjee, A. (2004) The relative influence of organisational commitment and job satisfaction on service quality of customer-contact employees in banking call centres. *Journal of Services Marketing* 18(3), 162–174.

Manchester City Council Libraries (2015) Volunteer with Manchester Libraries. Available at: http://www.manchester.gov.uk/downloads/download/272/volunteer_with_manchester_libraries-role_profiles (accessed 20 February 2015).

Marriott Hotel (2015) Marriott's look no further best rate guarantee. Available at: http://www.marriott.co.uk/hotel-prices/best-rate.mi (accessed 17 February 2015).

Mascio, R.D. (2010) The service models of frontline employees. *Journal of Marketing* 74(July), 63–80.

Mattila, A. and Wirtz, J. (2000) The role of preconsumption affect in postpurchase evaluation of services. *Psychology and Marketing* 17(7), 587–605.

Merlin Entertainments Group Ltd (2015) Funding Partners Blackpool Tower. Available at: https://www.theblackpooltower.com/misc/funding-partners.aspx (accessed 25 March 2015).

Miragaia, D.A.M., Ferreira, J. and Carreira, A. (2014) Do stakeholders matter in strategic decision making of a sports organisation? *Revista de Administracae de Empresas* 54(6), 647–658.

Moon, K.S., Kim, M., Ko, Y.J., Connaughton, D.P. and Lee, J.H. (2011) The influence of consumer's event quality perception on destination image. *Managing Service Quality* 21(3), 287–303.

National Trust (2015) Get Involved, Ways to Volunteer. Available at: http://www.nationaltrust.org.uk/Volunteer (accessed 20 February 2015).

Oakland, J.S. (1993) *Total Quality Management: The Route to Improving Performance*, 2nd edn. Butterworth Heinemann, London.

ODA (2007) *The Olympic Delivery Authority Annual Report and Accounts 2006–2007*. The Stationery Office, London.

Peters, T. (1987) *Thriving on Chaos*. Pan, London.

Presenza, A. and Iocca, S. (2012) The weight of stakeholders on festival management. The case of music festivals in Italy. *Pasos Revista de Turismo y Patrimonio Cultural* 10(2), 25–35.

Reichheld, F.F. and Teal, T. (2001) *The Loyalty Effect*. Harvard Business School Press, Boston, Massachusetts.

Sabiote-Ortiz, C.M., Frías-Jamilena, D.M. and Castañeda-García, J.A. (2014) Overall perceived value of a tourism service delivered via different media: a cross-cultural perspective. *Journal of Travel Research*, doi: 10.1177/0047287514535844.

Sadd, D.E. (2012) Mega-Events, Community Stakeholders and Legacy: London 2012. PhD Thesis, Bournemouth University, Bournemouth, UK. Available at: http://eprints.bournemouth. ac.uk/20305/1/SADD,Deborah_Jane_Ph.D._2012.pdf (accessed 7 April 2002).

San, Y.W. and Yazdanifard, R. (2013) How consumer decision making process differ from youngster to older consumer generation. *Journal of Research in Marketing* 2(2), 151–156.

Schlesinger, L.A. and Heskett, J.L. (1991) Breaking the cycle of failure in services. *Sloan Management Review* (Spring), 17–28.

Shonk, D.J. and Chelladurai, P. (2008) Service quality, satisfaction, and intent to return in event sport tourism. *Journal of Sport Management* 22, 587–602.

Silvestro, R. (2002) Dispelling the modern myth: employee satisfaction and loyalty drive service profitability. *International Journal of Operations and Production Management* 22(1), 30–49.

Slack, J. (2014) Stag and hen weekends face clampdown after officials rule to ban inappropriate dress. *Daily Mail* 20 and 21 October 2014.

Sport England (2015a) About Us - What We Do. Available at: https://www.sportengland.org (accessed 10 March 2015).

Sport England (2015b) Volunteering. Available at: https://www.sportengland.org (accessed 13 April 2015).

Sport Scotland (2015) About Us. Available at: http://www.sportscotland.org.uk (accessed 10 March 2015).

Sport Wales (2015) About Us. Available at: http://www.sportwales.org.uk (accessed 10 March 2015).

Stebbins, R. (2013) Unpaid work of love: defining the work-leisure axis of volunteering. *Leisure Studies* 32(3), 339–345.

Taylor, P. (2011) *Torkildsen's Sport and Leisure Management*, 6th edn. Routledge, Oxford, UK.

Thwaites, E. and Williams, C. (2006) Service recovery: a naturalistic decision-making approach. *Managing Service Quality* 16(6), 641–653.

Tomazos, K. and Butler, R. (2012) Volunteer tourists in the field: a question of balance? *Tourism Management* 33, 177–187.

UK Sport (2015) Our Work - How We Invest in Elite Sport. Available at: http://www.uksport.gov.uk (accessed 10 March 2015).

Wilks, L. (2014) The Lived Experience of London 2012 Olympic and Paralympic games volunteers: a serious leisure perspective. *Leisure Studies*, DOI: 10.1080/02614367.2014.993334..

Williams, C. and Shaw, J. (2006) *Customer Satisfaction Through Exceptional Service Delivery: Best Practice Case-Study*. Department of Tourism and Leisure Management, University of Central Lancashire, Preston, UK.

Williams, C. and Thwaites, E. (2007) Adding value to tourism and leisure organisations through front-line staff. *Tourism Recreation Research* 32(1), 95–106.

Ye, Q., Li, H. and Wang, Z. (2014) The influence of hotel price on perceived service quality and value in e-tourism: an empirical investigation based on online traveller reviews. *Journal of Hospitality and Tourism Research* 38(1), 23–39.

chapter 4

Quality and Satisfaction Concepts

LEARNING OBJECTIVES

- To explore the challenges facing the LETS industry in providing the service quality and value that customers expect;
- To understand the importance of expectations and perceptions in managing the LETS customer experience;
- To explore the shift from measuring and managing satisfaction to engagement by customers and employees;
- To discover the best practice principles within the LETS industry.

INTRODUCTION

It is appropriate to suggest that consumers from around the globe are beginning to respect organizations that strive to be 'human' and, therefore, exceed inherent customer expectations (Parasuraman et al., 1985; Zeithaml et al., 1990). Moreover, service organizations in general, and LETS organizations in particular, have also increasingly come to recognize the growing importance of service quality management. That is, growing competition and increasingly demanding customers, as well as recessionary and globalization pressures, have emphasized the need for these businesses and sectors to focus on improving service quality in order to achieve strategic objectives and ultimately competitive advantage. At the same time, there is a new type of consumer in the industry who is more demanding, more sophisticated and more educated than before (Pirnar et al., 2010) and, thus, the implementation of quality management initiatives is fundamental to ensuring that customer and employee satisfaction and retention is maintained (Gupta and Zeithaml, 2006). Consequently, within the service sector, many providers have adopted corporate strategies that include the use of a broad range of tools, techniques and approaches that attempt to exceed customer expectations and, ultimately, to improve business performance. Within this chapter you will read about a number of current industry examples and in particular how they are measuring and managing the customer and employee experience. For example, one such approach is Human Sigma (Fleming and Asplund, 2007a), a relatively new concept developed specifically for the service sector, but, as discussed later in this chapter, one that sees a shift away from managing and measuring satisfaction. Before we discuss such approaches, we must first understand the components that contribute to customer and employee satisfaction.

CONNECTING EXPECTATIONS WITH EXPERIENCES

Not only are customer expectations and perceptions constantly shifting, customer and employee concepts of quality shift as well (Parasuraman *et al.*, 1988). 'What do customers expect?' is a challenging question and never simple to answer. Whilst there is debate and numerous responses to this important and powerful question, the original service quality research suggests that customers expect:

- To be told the truth and treated fairly;
- To be treated with respect;
- To receive careful, reliable service;
- To receive prompt solutions to problems;
- To receive accurate answers from employees;
- To receive personal attention and genuine interest;
- To wait as short a time as possible;
- To be kept informed about recovery efforts;
- To receive assistance rendered willingly; and
- To have their interests come first.

(Len Berry, cited in Ford *et al.*, 2012)

Certainly, defining the concept of quality has proven to be a difficult task. Nevertheless, the most commonly accepted definition of quality within a service context, or service quality, is that proposed and tested through research by Parasuraman *et al.* (1985, 1988) and Zeithaml *et al.* (1990). Based upon the notion that service quality can only be defined from the perspective of the customer with reference to how well the service, both delivered and perceived, matches their expectations, Parasuraman *et al.* (1985), who have played a leading role in the conceptualization of the service quality construct, state that the customer's overall perception of quality is the disconfirmation of their expectation and evaluation of services delivered, e.g. Customer Satisfaction = Perceptions − Expectations. Based around this concept, we can consider the importance of connecting expectations with experiences with a leading tourism business such as Disney.

A guestologist, a term defined and introduced by Disney, seeks to understand and plan for the expectations of an organization's customers before they enter the service, so that each 'guest' has an enjoyable and successful experience (Ford *et al.*, 2012). Table 4.1 illustrates how Disney define guestology into four workable actions: Needs, Wants, Emotions and Stereotypes.

Specifically then, guestology consists of two activities:

1. Knowing your guests – demographics.
2. Understanding your guests – psychographics.

Table 4.1 displays how Disney put both key areas of guestology into practice.

After reading the example, is this what makes Disney different? The response suggests that LETS customers do not just buy 'things'; they buy expectations about performance, service and values. Grönroos (2008) defines this as a Service-Logic and it is becoming the dominant way of thinking about how to manage organizations. For example, it is not just about the types of offering the organization or business have, e.g. the physical product or the tangible elements, it is what the offerings 'do', e.g. the emotion you may experience or personal values such as relaxation, excitement and pleasure, as we saw in Chapter 1. It is apparent from the examples used by Disney that emotions include building and achieving engagement with both customers and employees (see Table 4.1). In addition to public consumers, the LETS industry has within itself many internal customers that depend on each other and also serve each other (Ford

Table 4.1. Guestology in practice.

Demographics in practice	Psychographics in practice
Dedicated research department Face-to-face surveys via electronic pads within the park Telephone survey (at random and within 30 days of return visit) Utilization studies (e.g. rubbish bins and food items) Listening posts Focus groups Mystery shopping programmes (every other day by hospitality graduates) E-mail, comment cards and guest letters	Needs: Basic (water, food, shelter) Situational (requiring a product or service at a particular time). Disney uses service mapping to the finest of details
	Wants: Define wants in terms of exceeding customer expectations (e.g. delight or wow!)
	Stereotypes: What are the negative stereotypes? What are the positive stereotypes? (e.g. clean, friendly, fun)
	Emotions: To achieve long-term relations with employees and customers (e.g. engagement)

et al., 2012). Therefore, this concept must be extended to the level of the individual employee. Equally then, 'What do employees expect?' is a vital question.

Subsequently, it was proposed by Parasuraman and Berry (1991) that the 'zone of tolerance' model assists in managing customer perceptions during the process of service delivery. Within this context, 'moments of truth' reflect a fundamental point of service quality management (Williams and Buswell, 2003); that is, employee–customer encounters are a critical aspect of service quality management. Specifically, Parasuraman (2004) suggests that customers, rather than having a single ideal level of expectations, actually have a range of expectations – namely, a 'zone of tolerance', bounded by 'desired service' (the service level customers believe can and should be delivered) at the top and 'adequate service' (the minimum service level customers are willing to accept) at the bottom. For example, if the delivered service falls within the zone, customers will be satisfied. If the service is better than their desired service level, customers will be delighted. However, if the service falls below the zone of tolerance, customers will be 'appalled' and look elsewhere for the service. Thus, the zone of tolerance provides a range within which customers are willing to accept variations in service delivery. Interestingly, for example, Zainol *et al.* (2010), in the context of service failure, found that individuals appear to have a larger zone of tolerance when dealing with negative encounters and a narrow zone for positive encounters. As noted, the inherent nature of service makes consistent service delivery difficult across employees in the same organization and even by the same service employee from day to day. In consideration to this, the employees may also have desired and adequate service levels including a zone of tolerance during the service encounter. Understanding this process from both sides of the dyad could reveal differences in their attitudes, expectations and perceptions. This has been illustrated in Fig. 4.1.

For example, organizations not only need to manage external customer expectations and subsequent experiences, they must also meet or exceed employee expectations/experience, and often those employees within the LETS environment include volunteers.

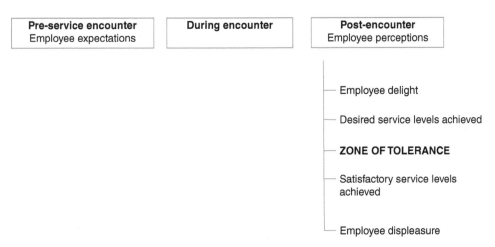

Fig. 4.1. Employee Zone of Tolerance theory.

The expectations of volunteers

A study conducted by Ralston *et al.* (2004) on expectations of volunteers prior to the XVII Commonwealth Games suggested that event volunteer satisfaction is influenced by expectations prior to the event as well as actual experiences during the event, which includes the administration and management attributes that influence how effective the event itself is organized. As noted above, failure to match the requirements and expectation of the job with those of the volunteers will make the event's management even more challenging. The researchers provide substantial evidence on the factors that typically influence volunteer satisfaction and retention levels. The volunteer satisfaction criteria include:

- Work assignment (role assigned, job fit for skills, convenience and empowerment);
- Adequate and sufficient information to enable the volunteer to do their job, clarity, recognition, feedback, face to face;
- Participation efficacy (task competency, intended result, benefits to others, importance of their role and contribution to target population);
- Organizational empathy with the volunteers and understanding the event from the volunteers' perspective;
- Recognition that volunteers have other commitments;
- Careful planning and scheduling of workloads, daily activities, tasks, and related event responsibilities;
- Orientation, philosophical underpinning and training;
- Recognition of lack of previous or similar volunteering experience;
- Quality of organizational support (training and emotional support, supportive environment, supportive supervisors, availability of help when needed);
- Communication and organizational guidance and support systems;
- Volunteer networks and informal support systems and activities;
- Group integration (contact and social aspects of relationships with other volunteers and paid staff) as correlations with volunteer satisfaction and predictors of intent to remain;
- Continuous encouragement, support and recognition;
- Specialized recognition and memorabilia;
- No distinction within groups of volunteers and with other staff;
- Relationships with supervisors, managers, other volunteers, paid staff, visitors and the wider community;
- Not being taken for granted;
- Good supervision and sorting out problems early on, good volunteer management;
- Physical facilities and event environment, food, toilets and transport; and
- Access to formal event venues and an opportunity to be involved in special and more prestigious parts of the event (e.g. ceremonies).

However, Getz (2012) points to the large, and often unique, number of stressors for event volunteers that are potential causes of burn-out, resulting in diminished volunteer involvement.

These include factors such as: intense time and energy commitment; over-demanding work-loads; insufficient numbers of volunteers; tensions between volunteers, staff and others; disempowerment; lack of effective leadership; absence of tangible rewards; insecurity over one's appointment or volunteer role; and boring or unfulfilling labour.

An example of best practice principles can be seen at the recent Olympic Games in London 2012. The London Organising Committee for the Olympic Games (LOCOG) developed a set of values, a clear statement of intent to anyone joining the organization, which also assisted in managing volunteer expectations. In concurrence with these values, all employees (Olympic Games Makers) conducted the Welcome Host customer service training and Fig. 4.2 illustrates those values.

LOCOG's values explained

1. Open: I know that my voice is heard and that my opinion is respected. We share knowledge, news good and bad and do so authentically. Every person in our team embraces challenges/disagreement as readily as praise and success.

2. Respectful: I treat everyone, whoever they are and whatever the situation, as I would like to be treated and view every interaction, no matter how minor, as an opportunity to deliver on the vision of the Games.

3. Team: I work in a team where we organize ourselves so that we succeed together and learn from our mistakes in a collaborative environment where all contributions are valued and every decision is supported as a group.

4. Deliver: I make doing my absolute best – both in what I deliver and the attitude I adopt – the minimum standard I work to for every task, no matter how routine. I take personal responsibility to deliver my promises (and those of my team), so that we fulfil the London 2012 vision.

5. Distinctive: I feel we are distinctive because we are brave and bold and genuinely seek to challenge and inspire change, and will use the opportunity handed to us to create a strong future for Olympic and Paralympic movements.

6. Inspiration: I take my inspiration, not just from our achievements but also from the effort required to deliver them, no matter how big or small the task involved. I believe in change and want to inspire this in everyone I interact with.

Critically, within the LETS environment, measuring and managing employee expectations and in particular employee engagement has been limited. Extending customer engagement to

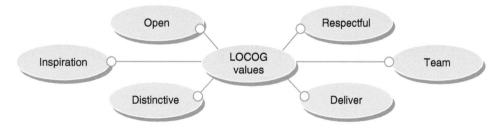

Fig. 4.2. The LOCOG value chain.

employee engagement is so important to organizational success. Specifically therefore, a new angle that moves away from managing and measuring satisfaction to managing and measuring engagement with both internal and external customers is considered next.

A NEW ANGLE: ENGAGEMENT REBRANDS SATISFACTION

Many businesses including those within the LETS sector utilize satisfaction metrics to measure employee and customer service quality to improve business performance, as we see in Chapters 9 and 10. However, the evidence suggests that managing and measuring through satisfaction, described as meeting customer expectations, is not enough to drive financial performance and service excellence (Torres and Kline, 2006; Fleming and Asplund, 2007a). Consequently, there has been a shift away from satisfaction and proposing a concept that extends well beyond traditional considerations of employee and customer satisfaction is engagement (Fleming and Asplund, 2007a).

Engagement is defined by these two key experts (Fleming and Asplund) as managing engagement as an emotional construct, and therefore the measurement and management of the employee–customer encounter must acknowledge and incorporate the critical emotional infrastructure of human behaviour or what they call 'Human Sigma'. As noted, although some businesses including those within the LETS industry succumb to employee and customer satisfaction surveys, they often measure and manage them as separate entities. For example, often these initiatives are owned by different functional areas of the business that operate in isolation, e.g. employee measurement programmes are often owned by HR and customer measurement programmes are often owned by marketing or operations (Lovelock and Wirtz, 2011). Critically then, in order to improve business performance, both customer and employee engagement must be measured and managed together.

Fleming and Asplund (2007a) describe engaged employees as loyal and psychologically committed to their job and the organization. Engaged individuals are two to three times more productive than other employees and are responsible for most of the innovations and creative ideas within an organization. Actively disengaged individuals are physically present but psychologically absent, and these individuals insist upon sharing their unhappiness with others. Organizations have an opportunity to build employee engagement, which in turn builds customer engagement within their business. Customer engagement is a measure of the extent to which customers are committed to a company, organization, a brand and/or the employees of that company (Buckingham and Coffman, 1999). Customers who are fully engaged represent an average 23% premium in terms of profitability, revenue and relationship growth as compared with the average customer (Fleming and Asplund, 2007a).

The Human Sigma rules to achieve employee and customer engagement in order to bring excellence to the way employees engage and interact with customers are the following.

Rule 1: You cannot measure and manage the employee and customer experiences as separate entities.
Rule 2: Emotion frames the employee–customer encounter.

Rule 3: You must measure and manage the employee–customer encounter at the local level (e.g. within the department or unit).

Rule 4: Quantify and summarize the effectiveness of the employee–customer encounter through the Human Sigma metric.

Rule 5: Improvement in local Human Sigma performance requires deliberate and active intervention through attention to a combination of transactional and transformational intervention activities.

It could be argued, therefore, that Human Sigma is a 'critical avenue' for business performance improvement via the employee–customer encounter (Fleming *et al.*, 2005). As noted in Chapters 1 and 2, in the service sector in general, and in the LETS sector in particular, value is created when an employee meets and interacts with a customer. Therefore, in order to achieve operational and financial improvements, the employee–customer encounter must be measured and managed (Fleming and Asplund, 2007a). Currently, in the tourism sector for example, employers are challenged to find every advantage possible to thrive, grow or simply stay in business. However, some employers have already restrained hiring and many have downsized their workforce. Certainly, a common theme is for management to value control over quality by scripting employee behaviours when they interact with customers, something that is undoubtedly apparent in the tourism industry. Often, they view employees as mistakes waiting to happen and as costs to be minimized (Lovelock and Wirtz, 2011). For example, the 'Terminator School of Management' is a metaphor for a desire to control human interaction from business (Fleming and Asplund, 2007a). Therefore, the principles of Human Sigma focus organizations on accepting human nature and capitalizing on it to manage employees, motivate them, and accelerate development to ultimately engage the emotions of the organization's customers.

Customer engagement

The first key principle surrounding the Human Sigma concept is customer engagement. Indeed, as suggested earlier, traditional measures of customer satisfaction, such as guest/attendee satisfaction surveys, have been criticized for failing to capture the depth of customer responses to service performance. For example, Bowden (2009) seeks to redirect satisfaction research toward an approach that encompasses an understanding of the role of commitment, involvement and trust in the creation of engaged and loyal customers. At the organization level, this is evidenced by the continued reliance of organizations on satisfaction metrics to assess customer feedback/responses to their products and services in the belief that high levels of satisfaction may lead to increased customer loyalty, intention to purchase, word of mouth, profit and market share (Heskett *et al.*, 1994). Satisfaction has, for some, become the ubiquitous mantra for corporate success (Chu, 2002). As noted at the start of this chapter, the most commonly used measurement approach to assessing customer satisfaction has been the confirmation–disconfirmation of expectations approach, which conceptualizes satisfaction as a post-consumption, cognitive process (Parasuraman *et al.*, 1988). However, satisfaction measurement has been criticized for failing to measure the depth of customer responses to consumption situations (Oliver *et al.*, 1997; Giese and Cote, 2000) and for providing an unreliable predictor of attitudinal loyalty. Despite these criticisms however, it seems that measures of satisfaction continue to be used as key performance and change indicators. Typically, conventional models of customer satisfaction are variations of the disconfirmation of expectation or gap models. This framework assumes that customers have specific expectations about their interactions with service organizations and personnel. Some models differentiate between perceptions of quality and customer satisfaction and others use various approaches to assess expectations. Therefore, the desired outcome of expectations is getting what one anticipates from a service encounter. However, some organizations are now realizing that engagement is also a more strategic way of looking at customer and stakeholder relationships. As noted earlier, in this emerging approach, engagement refers to the creation of a deeper, more meaningful connection between the organization and the customer (Fleming and Asplund, 2007a), and one that endures over time (Kumar *et al.*, 2010). Similar to Fleming and Asplund (2007a), Kumar *et al.* (2010) suggest that engagement is seen as a way to create customer interaction and participation. In addition, Van Doorn *et al.* (2010) consider the term 'engagement' to be behavioural in nature and they propose that customer engagement goes beyond transactions, and is specifically defined as a customer's behavioural manifestation toward a brand or firm, beyond purchase, resulting from motivational drivers. However, Kumar *et al.* (2010) argue that engagement would be incomplete without the inclusion of customer purchases from the firm.

Given that the concept of engagement is still novel and in the development phase, there are differing and conflicting opinions regarding its conceptualization. For example, Schneider and Bowen (1999) argue for a more sophisticated view of the customer experience beyond mere conformance to functional requirements and an estimate of overall satisfaction. In their research, they analysed hundreds of customer comments made about organizations that delighted or outraged them. They then classified those comments into groups with similar themes. Based on their analysis, Schneider and Bowen (1999) suggest that extreme expressions of customer delight and outrage can be characterized by whether companies meet or fail to meet a set of emotional requirements. These emotional requirements are organized in a similar manner to Maslow's Hierarchy of Needs (physiological, safety, belonging, esteem and self-actualization). At the same time, Fleming and Asplund (2007a) believe that customers have a hierarchy of needs similar in form to Maslow's. This hierarchy begins with the fulfilment of basic emotional needs and moves through the fulfilment of higher order, aspirational ones. Therefore, the underlying structure of this hierarchy is 'emotional attachment' (Fleming and Asplund, 2007a). Accordingly, Fleming and Asplund (2007a) propose four levels of customer engagement.

1. Fully engaged customers.
2. Engaged customers.
3. Not engaged customers.
4. Actively disengaged customers.

Ultimately, a customer has a strong need to enhance his/her self-esteem. Unlike Maslow's and Schneider and Bowen's hierarchies, Fleming and Asplund's research suggests that there are four key dimensions to a customer's emotional attachment to an organization.

1. Confidence.
2. Integrity.
3. Pride.
4. Passion.

Fleming and Asplund (2007a) suggest that passion is the highest level of emotional engagement. Passionate customers cannot imagine a world without the organization. They suggest that the key is to keep customers and customer engagement at the top of the mind of every employee every day. However, in a study conducted by Sutton (2015), many tourism businesses do not know exactly what a customer engagement strategy entails, primarily because they do not know how to measure and manage it. Fleming and Asplund (2007a) report that most companies do not do a good job of balancing the ways they measure, evaluate and reward their managers and employees. Most sales representatives, for example, are rewarded when they meet financial goals, not when they generate customer loyalty or high levels of engagement (Marr, 2006, 2012). Furthermore, Kumar *et al.* (2010) argue that customers can generate value to the organization through more ways than only their purchase behaviours and that a more comprehensive assessment is needed. They suggest that customers provide value to the firm through their: (i) own transactions; (ii) behaviour of referring prospects; (iii) encouragement on other customers and individuals to make/or not make initial or additional purchases; and (iv) feedback to the firm on ideas for innovation/improvement. The authors present a conceptual model of customer engagement, which is based on multiple behaviours such as word of mouth, blogging and providing customer ratings.

The concepts of engagement have also been explored in the organizational behaviour literature as a means of explaining organizational commitment and organizational citizenship behaviour, and have been utilized as a means of predicting financial performance (Saks, 2006). Within the organizational behaviour literature, engagement has been defined as 'task behaviours that promote connections to work and to others', which are expressed physically, cognitively and emotionally and which stimulate personal development and increase employee motivation (Kahn, 1990). Bowden (2009) also notes that employee engagement may act to further increase group morale, cohesion and rapport via positive psychological contagion processes. Clearly, then, engagement has an important place in contributing to an understanding of service performance and customer outcomes.

The issue of engagement and its measurement should, therefore, be considered as a fundamental concern for managers who wish to move beyond the notion of merely satisfying customers. Specifically, Bowden and Dagger (2011) consider the importance of customer satisfaction and have stated that, in order to delight customers, the LETS industry needs to move beyond merely satisfying customers. But, what is meant by the construct, 'customer delight'?

Customer delight

Plutchik (1980) originally proposed the customer delight construct in a study in which he identified eight emotions that could interact in various combinations to derive a number of second-order emotions. Customer delight was found to be the result of interaction between joy and surprise. While customer satisfaction is widely viewed as the result of meeting expectations, most existing studies indicate that customer delight requires that the customer receives a positive surprise beyond his/her expectations (Oliver *et al.*, 1997; Rust and Oliver, 2000; Arnold *et al.*, 2005). As with customer engagement, customer delight resides in Oliver's (1980) expectancy disconfirmation paradigm, as discussed earlier in the chapter, which suggests that individuals compare their actual experiences with their expectations. Therefore, disconfirmation can be associated with various levels of unexpectedness, spawning a surprise disconfirmation (Oliver *et al.*, 1997).

Schneider and Bowen (1999) suggest that a service consists of an exchange relationship, that is, a psychological construct to have needs gratified in exchange for money, time and effort. They suggest that the challenge for service firms is to gratify and perhaps delight customers, while avoiding the perception that they do not respect customer needs. Schneider and Bowen (1999) describe customer delight simply as exceeding customer expectations. That is, a customer's expectations are positively disconfirmed, which activates an aroused state. The customer experiences this pleasant state as the emotion of delight. However, achieving customer delight by exceeding customer expectations is a difficult management task. Evidence indicates that satisfying customers is not enough to retain them because even satisfied customers defect at a high rate (Fleming and Asplund, 2007a). The scales that researchers commonly use to measure satisfaction do not translate linearly into outcomes such as loyalty in terms of purchases. Like Fleming and Asplund, Schneider and Bowen (1999) suggest that focusing on customer delight and outrage – emotions more intense than satisfaction or dissatisfaction – may lead to a better understanding of the dynamics of customer emotions and their effect on customer behaviour and loyalty.

However, affective approaches, such as delight, have been criticized for increasing customer's expectations (Santos and Boote, 2003). Research has yet to determine whether delight is more effective in the initial attraction of new customers than in the retention of existing customers, due to its short-term and transient nature. Chandler (1989) describes customer delight as a reaction extended by the customer when they receive a service that not only satisfies but also provides an unexpected value or unanticipated satisfaction. It is about how a service provider handles the customer's needs of security, justice and self-esteem (Schneider and Bowen, 1999).

As noted, they propose that customer delight and outrage in service business originates with the three basic needs: security, justice and self-esteem. These coincide with the Human Sigma dimensions of engagement:

- Security: the need to feel unthreatened by physical or economic harm;
- Justice: the need to be fairly treated; and
- Self-esteem: the need to maintain and enhance one's self-image.

Certainly, the evidence suggests that a simple meeting or exceeding of customer expectations model is not sufficient for emotionally charged customers. Therefore, it may be concluded that traditional service quality and satisfaction research is outdated.

Crotts and Magnini (2011) recognize the difficulty in delighting loyal customers that engage in regular transactions with the service provider. Kumar *et al.* (2001) argue that customer delight does not require a surprise component. In their research, they adopted Plutchik's (1980) research design, providing subjects with numerous positive emotions to choose from during the experiment. At the same time, Torres and Kline (2006) in their research demonstrated how customer delight was correlated to outcomes such as positive word of mouth and repurchase intent. Crotts and Magnini (2011) also provide evidence that customer delight is a valid and measurable construct that has a strong association with guest loyalty as measured by willingness to recommend and repeat purchase. The data clearly indicated that the addition of a surprise component is more robustly correlated to loyalty. They thus pose the question: is it possible to provide an element of positive surprise each time a customer visits? They suggest that in a tourism context where encounters are typically infrequent the answer is yes, and is evidenced by the commitment made by benchmark organizations in the tourism industry to service quality (Crotts *et al.*, 2005).

Having established that Human Sigma focuses on engagement from both sides of the service encounter and goes beyond traditional considerations of employee performance and customer satisfaction, the following section now turns to the employee engagement construct.

Employee engagement

Engaged employees want their organization to succeed because they feel connected emotionally, socially and even spiritually to its mission, vision and purpose (Fleming and Asplund, 2007a: 160). Indeed, some have suggested that the principal prerequisite to achieving business success is to create a good environment, well-trained staff, with good morale and incentives to offer the best service possible (Wiley *et al.*, 2006). Traditionally, Buchanan and Gillies' (1990) basic customer loyalty model included customer satisfaction, customer loyalty, and high sales and profit margins. To this model, Schlesinger and Heskett (1991) and Lovelock (1992) added employee loyalty and developed the idea of the three cycles: Cycle of Success, Cycle of Mediocrity and Cycle of Failure. The prominent feature of the cycles became the link between the employees and the customers. Schlesinger and Heskett proposed that investing in employees gives them the ability (through training and development opportunities) and empowerment to provide superior customer service.

In contrast, Williams and Buswell (2003) noted how cultural change is one of the hardest areas for organizations to achieve. Kandampully (2003) agrees, suggesting that managers find it difficult to 'let the power out' and empower front-line staff. Williams and Buswell (2003) explain how the essence of employee engagement is the flexibility and self-judgement required of many front-line staff in tourism organizations. Nevertheless, it could be suggested here that seasonal staff working in the LETS sector find it difficult to be motivated with such concepts. Often with limited training and a minimum wage culture, front-line employees limit their levels of responsibility and engagement with the organization and the customer. Thus, Harrington and Lenehan (1998) describe internal marketing's role as the requirement to market to staff their role in providing service for the customer within a supportive organizational environment. Similarly, Grönroos (1994) argues that without active and continuous internal marketing efforts, service quality will suffer. "Internal marketing" includes both an attitude management aspect and a communications management aspect' (Grönroos, 1990). Grönroos (1994) advocates that internal marketing techniques offer an umbrella, which makes the development of personnel a strategic issue.

At the same time, according to Fisher *et al.* (2006), a number of aspects are required by organizations to be competitive, including physical resources, financial resources, marketing capability and human resources. However, the factor most likely to provide potential competitive advantage is human resources and how these resources are managed (Endres, 2008). The authors emphasize that employee engagement is a complex subject with many related issues, from employee trust to employee development, for example, therefore yielding a concept that extends well beyond traditional considerations of employee 'satisfaction' – a concept Fleming and Asplund (2007a) refer to as employee engagement. They define engagement as the individual's involvement and satisfaction with, as well as enthusiasm for work. At the same time, Fernandez (2007) states that employee satisfaction is not the same as employee engagement and, since managers cannot rely on employee satisfaction to help retain the best and brightest, employee engagement becomes a critical concept. By definition, engagement includes the involvement and enthusiasm of employees and the emotional attachment of customers (Harter *et al.*, 2004). Similarly, Harter *et al.* (2002: 269) define employee engagement as 'the individual's involvement and satisfaction with as well as enthusiasm for work'. However, a problem exists with the term employee engagement. Endres' (2008) critique of Harter *et al.*'s (2004) research on employee engagement suggests that not enough emphasis has been put on defining and validating the construct of employee engagement. Because of this lack of construct definition, subsequent users interpret the construct in different ways. For example, Lucey *et al.* (2005: 12) interpret their engagement index as measuring 'how each individual employee connects with his or her company and how each individual connects with their customers'.

Not surprisingly, therefore, Little and Little (2006) describe the following four problems with the construct of employee engagement.

1. The definitions are not clear as to whether engagement is an attitude or behaviour.
2. The definitions are not clear as to whether engagement is an individual or a group-level phenomenon.
3. The definitions do not make clear the relationship between engagement and other well-known and accepted constructs.
4. There are measurement issues that obscure the true meaning of the construct.

For organizations, the difference between an energized and disengaged workforce can mean success or failure (Fleming and Asplund, 2007a). However, like customer engagement, employee engagement has a number of challenges in its path to achieve highly engaged employees. For example, often routine and duty jobs which are typical in the LETS sector have difficulty leaving a deep impression. Therefore, in order to measure and manage predictors of employee engagement, Lockwood (2005) suggests using a combination of tools including internal surveys, focus groups and detailed gap analysis by location and department. Lockwood also suggests that there are many pathways to foster engagement, with no one kit that fits all organizations. Ultimately, the key to effective engagement will be rooted in the flexibility of approach most appropriate for each individual firm (Lockwood, 2005). Furthermore, leadership does play a very important role in employee engagement (Endres, 2008). For example, an empowering leader tends to enhance and drive the meaningfulness of the employee's job role and contributions.

Therefore, measuring engagement plays a major part in the industry as a monitor and evaluation of service delivery quality. It is apparent, that in its present format, the measurement tools and techniques do not always address the needs of the internal customer. How to maximize employee engagement and performance is an issue on the minds of many employers and managers. In our information-driven society, the planning, control and improvement of quality becomes more complex and demanding. For example, it is apparent from the research that instead of the sole emphasis being on the customer needs and expectations, all stakeholders are now concerned, including employees. Such developments, including the shift away from satisfaction, continue to challenge the industry. However, Mohr and Bitner (1995) state how the interaction between an organization's employees and its customers is key to its very survival.

Evidently then, managing and measuring the employee–customer encounter interdependently has a greater impact. With Human Sigma, critical links between employee and customer engagement have been identified, demonstrating that organizations that only drive high employee engagement can fail to engage customers. Organizations that focus only on their customers may succeed temporarily, but the results are not sustainable unless employees are also engaged. Consequently, customer engagement and employee engagement interact to promote financial performance. Therefore, front-line employees and customers together need to be the centre of management focus. Finally, this chapter concludes with Focus Box 4.1, which highlights how organizations can measure and manage employee and customer expectations and experience.

CONCLUSIONS

Thus far, then, this chapter has highlighted a number of key themes and issues in relation to the nature of the LETS industry, including the challenge of service quality management in a society that is increasingly more experienced and subsequently has increasing expectations and experiences. Recognizing that traditional satisfaction research is outdated, this chapter has revealed the shift away from measuring and managing satisfaction. At the same time,

Focus Box 4.1. **How British Airways value customer and employee expectations when designing and delivering the brand service**

BA agree that both internal and external customers are a driving force in how they design services and manage expectations. BA are constantly monitoring their feedback and identifying ways of continuous improvement to enhance both their ground and on-board experiences. For example, BA have a Research and Insights team based within a Brands department, who regularly engage with customers through customer focus groups, a customer survey titled 'customer voice' or mystery shop reports that allow them to gain both qualitative and quantitative data from customers directly. These data are then fed back through to the relevant teams who will analyse the data and then utilize this to identify focus areas. For example, the inflight service development team found recently, through mystery shop reports, that cabin crew were not completing juice rounds every 30 minutes – sometimes they weren't being done at all. Customers used the feedback methods to express how important juice rounds are to them and how they appreciate being offered a drink every half hour. Therefore, BA launched a campaign called 'Be There', which helped raise awareness of the importance of juice rounds amongst the crew community. Since the campaign was launched approximately 3 months ago, BA have seen a rise in mystery shopper scores when evaluating juice rounds, and overall customer satisfaction scores have improved on long-haul flights where juice rounds should be being completed.

Not only do BA focus on the end-users to manage expectations, they also focus on the internal employee in managing and understanding expectations. For example, BA host regular Cabin Crew Focus Groups and it was from one of these focus groups that crew reported that their customers did not like the new First Class and Club World washbags BA had recently implemented. They had changed from a unisex bag to a male and female bag, and this provided logistics issues in terms of passenger ratios. This was not only a problem logistically, the customers actually did not like the new washbag design – they deemed it cheap looking. The focus group was an excellent mechanism for quickly bringing this to the attention of BA management, and following their feedback they further identified this as an issue through their other research channels. BA were then able to revert back to a unisex more premium-feeling washbag to ensure customer satisfaction levels were increased.

it has discussed a number of approaches to aid managers in their quest for improvement. Human Sigma in particular is a new approach that measures an important service quality determinant in the LETS industry – that is, employee and customer engagement. Therefore, Chapter 5 will examine the conceptual underpinning and industry practices relevant to designing and delivering quality within a *service culture* that adopts the concept of engagement.

QUESTIONS

1. What are the main variances between satisfaction and engagement?
2. Should organizations move from satisfaction to delight in an effort to obtain loyal customers and profitable operations?
3. Guestology consists of which two activities?
4. What does the Human Sigma approach aim to achieve?

FURTHER READING

Fleming, J.H. and Asplund, J. (2007) *Human Sigma: Managing the Employee-Customer Encounter.* Gallup Press, Washington, DC.
Fleming, J.H. and Asplund, J. (2008) *Where Employee Engagement Happens.* Gallup Press, Washington, DC.
Marr, B. (2012) *Key Performance Indicators (KPI).* Financial Times/Prentice Hall, London.
Torres, E. and Kline, S. (2006) From satisfaction to delight: a model for the hotel industry. *International Journal of Contemporary Hospitality Management* 18(4), 290–301.

REFERENCES

Arnold, M.J., Reynolds, K.E., Ponder, N. and Lueg, J.E. (2005) Customer delight in a retail context: investigating delightful and terrible shopping experiences. *Journal of Business Research* 58(8), 1132–1145.
Bowden, J. (2009) The process of customer engagement: a conceptual framework. *Journal of Marketing Theory and Practice* 17(1), 63–74.
Bowden, J.L. and Dagger, T.S. (2011) To delight or not to delight? An investigation of loyalty formation in the restaurant industry. *Journal of Hospitality Marketing & Management* 20(5), 501–524.
Buchanan, R.W. and Gillies, C.S. (1990) Value managed relationships: the key to customer retention and profitability. *European Management Journal* 8(4), 523–526.
Buckingham, M. and Coffman, C. (1999) *First, Break All the Rules: What the World's Greatest Managers do Differently.* Simon & Schuster, New York.
Chandler, C.H. (1989) Quality: beyond customer satisfaction. *Quality Progress* 22(2), 30–32.
Chu, R. (2002) Stated-importance versus derived-importance customer satisfaction measurement. *Journal of Services Marketing* 16(4), 285–301.
Crotts, J. and Magnini, V. (2011) The customer delight construct: is surprise essential. *Annals of Tourism Research* 38(2), 719–722.
Crotts, J., Dickson, D. and Ford, R. (2005) Auditing organizational alignment for guest service excellence. *Academy of Management Executives* 19(3), 54–68.
Endres, G.M. (2008) The human resource craze: human performance improvement and employee engagement. *Organisation Development Journal* 26(1), 69–78.
Fernandez, C.P. (2007) Employee engagement. *Journal of Public Health Management and Practice* 13(5), 524–526.
Fisher, C.D., Schoenfeldt, L.F. and Shaw, J.B. (2006) *Advanced Human Resource Management.* Houghton Mifflin Customer Publishing, Boston, Massachusetts.
Fleming, J.H. and Asplund, J. (2007a) *Human Sigma: Managing the Employee-Customer Encounter.* Gallup Press, Washington, DC.
Fleming, J.H. and Asplund, J. (2007b) Interview with John Fleming and James Asplund. *Human Resource Management International Digest* 15(7), 39–41.

Fleming, J.H., Coffman, C. and Harter, J.K. (2005) Manage your human sigma. *Harvard Business Review*, July–August, 106–114.

Ford, C., Sturman, M. and Heaton, C. (2012) *Managing Quality Service in Hospitality*. International Edition. Cengage, London.

Getz, D. (2012) *Event Studies: Theory, Research and Policy for Planned Events*. Routledge, London.

Giese, J. and Cote, J. (2000) Defining consumer satisfaction. *Academy of Marketing Science Review*, 2000(1), 1–26.

Grönroos, C. (1990) *Service Management and Marketing*. Lexington Books, Lexington, Massachusetts.

Grönroos, C. (1994) From scientific management to service management: a management perspective for the age of service competition. *International Journal of Service Industry Management* 5(1), 5–20.

Grönroos, C. (2008) Service logic revisited: who creates value? And who co-creates? *European Business Review* 20(4), 298–314.

Gupta, S. and Zeithaml, V. (2006) Customer metrics and their impact on financial performance. *Marketing Science* 25(6), 718–739.

Harrington, D. and Lenehan, T. (1998) *Managing Quality in Tourism: Theory and Practice*. Oak Tree Press, Dublin.

Harter, J.K., Schmidt, F.L. and Hayes, T.L. (2002) Business-unit-level relationship between employee satisfaction, employee engagement, and business outcomes: a meta-analysis. *Journal of Applied Psychology* 87(2), 268–279.

Harter, J.K., Asplund, J. and Fleming, J. (2004) *Human Sigma: A Meta-Analysis*. Gallup Management Journal, Washington, DC.

Heskett, J.L., Jones, T.O., Loveman, G.W., Sasser, W.E. and Schlesinger, L.A. (1994) Putting the service profit chain to work. *Harvard Business Review* 72(2), 164–174.

Kahn, W. (1990) Psychological conditions of personal engagement and disengagement at work. *Academy of Management Journal* 33(4), 692–724.

Kandampully, J. (2003) *Services Management: The New Paradigm in Hospitality*. Prentice Hall, New Jersey.

Kumar, A., Olshavsky, R. and King, M. (2001) Exploring alternative antecedents of customer delight. *Journal of Consumer Satisfaction, Dissatisfaction and Complaining Behavior* 14, 14–26.

Kumar, V., Aksony, L., Donkers, B., Venkatesan, R., Wiesel, T. and Tillmanns, S. (2010) Undervalued or overvalued customers: capturing total customer engagement value. *Journal of Service Research* 13(3), 297–310.

Little, B. and Little, P. (2006) Employee engagement: conceptual issues. *Journal of Organisational Culture, Communication and Conflict* 10(1), 111–120.

Lockwood, N.R. (2005) Employee Engagement. Available at: https://www.shrm.org/Research/Articles/Articles/Documents/07MarResearchQuarterly.pdf (accessed on 15 April 2014).

Lovelock, C. (1992) *Managing Services: Marketing, Operations and Human Resources*. Prentice Hall, New Jersey.

Lovelock, C. and Wirtz, J. (2011) *Services Marketing: People, Technology, Strategy*. Pearson/Prentice-Hall, New Jersey.

Lucey, J., Bateman, N. and Hines, P. (2005) Why major lean transitions have not been sustained. *Management Services* 49(2), 9–14.

Marr, B. (2006) *Strategic Performance Management*. Butterworth-Heinemann, Oxford, UK.

Marr, B. (2012) *Key Performance Indicators (KPI)*. Financial Times/Prentice-Hall, London.

Mohr, L.A. and Bitner, M.J. (1995) Process factors in service delivery: what employee effort means to customers. *Advances in Service Marketing and Management* 4, 91–117.

Oliver, R.L. (1980) A cognitive model of the antecedents and consequences of satisfaction decisions. *Journal of Marketing Research* 17(11), 460–469.

Oliver, R., Rust, R. and Varki, S. (1997) Customer delight: foundations, findings, and managerial insight. *Journal of Retailing* 73(3), 311–336.

Parasuraman, A. (2004) Assessing and improving service performance for maximum impact: insights from a two-decade-long research journey. *Performance Management and Metrics* 5(2), 45–52.

Parasuraman, A. and Berry, L.L. (1991) Understanding customer expectations of service. *Sloan Management Review* 32(3), 42.

Parasuraman, A., Zeithaml, V.A. and Berry, L.L. (1985) A conceptual model of service quality and its implications for future research. *Journal of Marketing* 49(4), 41–50.

Parasuraman, A., Zeithaml, V.A. and Berry, L.L. (1988) SERVQUAL: a multi-item scale for measuring consumer perceptions of service quality. *Journal of Retailing* 64(1), 12–40.

Pirnar, I., Icoz, O. and Icoz, O. (2010) *The New Tourist: Impacts on the hospitality marketing strategies.* EuroCHRIE Amsterdam 2010, Passion for Hospitality Excellence, 25–28 October 2010.

Plutchik, R. (1980) *Emotions: A Psychoevolutionary Synthesis.* Harper and Row, New York.

Ralston, R., Downward, P. and Lumsdon, L. (2004) The expectations of volunteers prior to the XVII Commonwealth Games, 2002: a qualitative study. *Event Management* 9(1–2), 13–26.

Rust, R. and Oliver, R. (2000) Should we delight the customer? *Journal of the Academy of Marketing Science* 28(1), 86–94.

Saks, A. (2006) Antecedents and consequences of employee engagement. *Journal of Managerial Psychology* 21(7), 600–619.

Santos, J. and Boote, J. (2003) A theoretical explanation and model of consumer expectations, post-purchase affective states and affective behaviour. *Journal of Consumer Behaviour* 3(2), 142–156.

Schlesinger, L.A. and Heskett, J.L. (1991) Breaking the cycle of failure in services. *Sloan Management Review* 32(3), 17–28.

Schneider, B. and Bowen, D. (1999) Understanding customer delight and outrage. *Sloan Management Review* 41(1), 35–45.

Sutton, C. (2015) The human sigma approach to business improvement in tourism SMEs. *Journal of Small Business and Enterprise Development* 22(2), 302–319.

Torres, E. and Kline, S. (2006) From satisfaction to delight: a model for the hotel industry. *International Journal of Contemporary Hospitality Management* 18(4), 290–301.

Van Doorn, J., Lemon, K., Mittal, V., Nab, S., Pick, D., Pirner, P. and Verhoef, P. (2010) Customer engagement behaviour: theoretical foundations and research directions. *Journal of Service Research* 13(3), 253–266.

Wiley, J.W., Brooks, S.M. and Lundby, K.M. (2006) Put your employees on the other side of the microscope. *Human Resource Planning* 29(2), 15.

Williams, C. and Buswell, J. (2003) *Service Quality in Leisure and Tourism.* CAB International, Wallingford, UK.

Zainol, N.A., Lockwood, A. and Kutsch, E. (2010) Relating the zone of tolerance to service failure in the hospitality industry. *Journal of Travel & Tourism Marketing* 27(3), 324–333.

Zeithaml, V.A., Parasuraman, A. and Berry, L.L. (1990) *Delivering Quality Service: Balancing Customer Perceptions and Expectations.* Free Press, New York.

Part 2

Designing and Delivering Quality in the LETS Product

INTRODUCTION

The four chapters in Part 1 provided the conceptual and contextual underpinnings to the study of service quality in the leisure, events, tourism and sport industry. We noted the emergence of the experience economy and how, therefore, the nature of LETS products and services is an increasingly complex challenge in achieving customer satisfaction and service quality. Specific service characteristics of perishability (services cannot be stored) and inseparability (generally customers need to be present when the service is performed) and experiential properties (emotions and senses) add to the operational management difficulty. These need to be addressed at the service concept and design stage, and to acknowledge that consumer needs and wants are constantly changing and are affected by the immediacy of web-based commentary and feedback.

The next four chapters build on the knowledge and understanding of concepts and principles developed in Part 1. They examine the challenges facing organizations in designing and delivering service quality to their customers in the context of a dynamic and competitive market and an increasingly complex experience economy. Part 2 relates the emotional and behavioural responses of customers to the service logic of a systematic design process, the service culture of the organization, capacity management and the application of quality models and tools.

It builds on the analysis of the service encounter in Part 1 and emphasizes its centrality to the design and management of service quality. It suggests that this aspect is becoming increasingly influential and more difficult to manage as commentary on an organization's performance through Web 2 technology is instantaneously available, and for some customers becomes the first point of contact or encounter. Effective management of the service encounter requires a systematic approach and the deployment of a number of quality techniques and measures, some of which have implications for management of the human resource.

Part 2 also highlights the growing importance of planning and innovation in the management of the customer experience and the achievement of customer satisfaction. Chapter 5 examines the design process (now referred to as service and experience design) including the key factors to consider, the models and tools of design and the creation of opportunities for co-created value and customer involvement in the process. The relationship between capacity management and service quality is assessed in Chapter 6, including the need to plan for fluctuations in demand and especially the impact of queuing in particular settings such as visitor attractions and events.

The significance of an appropriate service culture for the delivery and management of service quality is examined in Chapter 7. The process of engagement is applied to staff and points to the need for an organizational pyramid that supports frontline staff and encourages their emotional labour in the process of interaction with customers.

Finally, Chapter 8 addresses the role and place of quality, tools, models and awards in business improvement strategies and also underlines the importance of fully understanding the customer in developing the most appropriate approaches to achieving service quality. It demonstrates how the use of such techniques does not simply improve what the organization does but is also reflective of the type of service culture highlighted in Chapter 7, and encapsulated by the Business Excellence Model reviewed in Chapter 8.

chapter 5

Service and Experience Design

LEARNING OBJECTIVES

- To examine the background to service and its evolution into experience design;
- To develop a knowledge and understanding of the principles of experience design;
- To appreciate the challenges facing experience designers and the key factors they have to take into account, particularly the management of the service encounter and the involvement of the customer;
- To develop a model of experience design which draws together the principles and factors into the four component of service concept, process, system and value;
- To explore the main tools and methods of service and experience design.

INTRODUCTION

In the first edition of the book, we suggested that service design had not been as extensively researched or written about as other aspects of the service management and service quality literature. This was despite service design and process management representing, perhaps, the first stage of service quality in LETS services, and connecting the delivery of service quality to the commitment to continuous improvement which is at the core of service quality. Indeed, we also reported that service design methodologies showed the need for customer requirements to be fully assimilated and built into the features of the product and service.

The last decade or so has seen more interest in service design, as this chapter will illustrate, but a key challenge is to extend this thinking into customer experience management and to relate it to the trends in the LETS experience economy. According to Zomerdijk and Voss

(2010), experiential services, whose focus is on the experience of customers, is an emergent scientific area, and for many service organizations designing customer emotions is a new territory. Gruber *et al.* (2015) agree with this view and suggest that in many instances the customer experience is not purposely designed, but is the consequence of design decisions about process elements such as workflows, websites, booking systems and tangibles. Heinonen *et al.* (2010: 540) suggest that 'It is assumed that the service company can more or less control the customer's experience, which thus represents both the planned process and intended outcome designed by the company.'

We saw in Chapter 1 how, historically, many 'offerings' in the LETS industry almost appear to have arisen through serendipitous circumstances and have been managed without a systematic approach to defining and understanding their relationship with the customers, and without establishing clearly the co-creation of value and the involvement of the customer as a co-producer in the service process. Where there has been a systematic approach, service design has often followed the principles of product design and has embraced the significance of service encounters, their moments of truth and the experiential properties of the LETS product and service. Therefore the term 'customer experience design' more appropriately represents such trends, although this chapter will examine the progression in thinking about the principles and methodologies of service design and its application to experience design.

BACKGROUND TO SERVICE AND EXPERIENCE DESIGN

Our examination of the nature and significance of service and experience design builds on the work of earlier chapters. Chapter 1 analysed the nature of the LETS experience economy and the increasing complexity of the LETS customer experience and the engagement of staff and customers in the process. Chapter 4 showed how the characteristics of services provide a backcloth against which to examine service design. The features of intangibility, heterogeneity, perishability and inseparability of production and consumption exemplify the distinctiveness, if not the difficulties, of managing LETS services and highlight the lack of complete control over the activity by the provider (because of the nature of LETS experiences, timing, the unpredictability of consumer behaviour or conditions such as the weather). When mistakes are made by the provider, in many instances it is impossible to rectify them because the customer consumes the product or service package as it is offered in real time. Many LETS products and services involve a process with few tangible reference points and are potentially subject to considerable variation in the way they are delivered because of this real-time delivery as well as the difficulty of standardizing approaches by staff or volunteers. In fact it is not just the variability of different staff that causes uncertainty but the variable approaches of the same staff (even the best may have an off-day).

The customer as a co-producer in many contexts also provides another element of unpredictability and the increasing significance of emotional elements in the LETS experience is a further test of the rationality and consistency of the provider's approach. Furthermore, many customers cannot always easily explain and articulate their experiences and feelings, making it very difficult for providers to satisfy every customer (Klaus and Maklan, 2013) and consequently to achieve service quality. This can be exacerbated by poor service design, which will lead to problems with service delivery (Gummesson, 1994; Bitner *et al.*, 2008). Whilst Fawcett *et al.* (2014) suggest that customer service failings often result from a lack of management commitment and poor service design, Maylor (2000) argued that a clear understanding of quality is necessary in order to design systems that deliver it; therefore, the two aspects are inextricably linked and require a systematic process, which can also account for the nature of LETS activities in a variety of settings.

Indeed, there are a number of different contexts or levels, which the design process addresses in the LETS industry, in either new service development or service enhancement, including:

- Sites such as theme parks, other visitor attractions, urban parks, country parks, retail and leisure sites, festival sites like Glastonbury, sports stadia and even town centres and their layout and management;
- Buildings such as leisure complexes, theatres, museums, heritage centres and conference and exhibition centres;
- Services such as tourism information centres, travel agencies, airlines and sports development; and
- The interface with websites, other contact points and Web 2 technology. The latter represents a major development in the last decade, as Sigala (2012: 553) suggests that 'organisations can use online social communities for actively co-operating and interacting with customers and customer communities to generate and evaluate new ideas, design and test new products'.

Whatever the context, service design can offer a systematic process that can enhance service quality. It involves the translation of ideas, solutions and intentions into a specific configuration or arrangement of equipment, space and other resources, as in a theme park with its complex circulation of people with different requirements, or a venue for special events with its equally complex movement of people and temporal concentration of resources. According to Gummesson (1994: 85):

> service design covers hands-on activities to describe and detail a service, the service system and service delivery process ... it is the process of presenting needs in some physical form, initially as a solution, and then as a specific configuration or arrangement of materials, resources, equipment and people.

More recently, Ferreira and Texeira (2013) argued that customer experience design seeks to create an emotional connection with customers through careful planning of tangible and intangible service. The skills and techniques of service and experience design have therefore become increasingly significant in recent years as they are adapted for customer experience management and the delivery of service quality. As Howitt and McManus (2014: 42) suggest, 'Service design assumes a significant importance in the pursuit of quality'. The next section examines why.

THE RELATIONSHIP BETWEEN CUSTOMER EXPERIENCE DESIGN AND SERVICE QUALITY IN LETS SERVICES

There are several reasons why customer experience design requires a knowledgeable and systematic approach in order to enhance service quality:

First, the classification of services demonstrates the nature of the service act and the importance of the service encounter in the management of the service process. The service encounter or the interaction between customers and staff and systems is important in many services but particularly in the LETS industry, where outcomes or benefits are inextricably linked to the process and the individual experience. Strategically, organizations also have to consider how the customization or standardization of a service shapes the way it is designed and delivered or, indeed, is determined itself by the design process. The simultaneity of production and consumption means that the features of the process and product, including scripting, need to be planned carefully and managed systematically to avoid mistakes and variations in service quality. Examples include the management of crowds at special events, booking systems and how entry is controlled to sites and facilities or the procedures for picking up litter.

The emphasis on the experiential properties of the LETS product and service where motivational and emotional elements are significant provides an additional challenge in the design of systems and processes as does the encouragement of co-production and co-created value in the experience. Johnston and Kong (2011) assert that managers need to consider the design of not only the service they deliver but also the experiences they provide. Indeed, in the context of events, Berridge (2012: 8) suggests that 'modern event management is largely about delivery of experiences or experience opportunities', and it could be argued that the Olympic Games are an example of this, not just as the largest event in the world, but as an experience that engages the emotions and senses (Fig. 5.1). Fawcett *et al.* (2014) suggest that there is a need to design service value systems that enhance the customer experience which is distinctive and encourage customers to return.

Second, operations are therefore now more complex in many LETS settings and have more points of contact or stages where the 'moments of truth' will be present. The notion of a multi-faceted customer experience is more widespread; it represents both the multiplicity of activities or experiences available to the consumer in the same setting and the increasingly differentiated market for the same facilities, for example the former represented by theme parks and the latter by some holiday complexes. Operations, of course, are also more challenging because consumers are more complex and sophisticated in their motives and requirements as we see in Chapter 3.

Fig. 5.1. The Olympic Games: experience design on a grand scale.

Third, many contexts are influenced by the technology available and how it is utilized, from health and fitness facilities using sophisticated equipment to visitor attractions incorporating animatronics, simulators, virtual reality and white-knuckle rides. Online booking systems, computerized access to facilities or ski lifts and improved information, signage and access all help to enhance the overall experience and the way it is managed.

Fourth, good design is also necessary for the operationalization of aims and objectives. LETS organizations represent a very wide range of contexts, purposes and functions across the public, commercial and voluntary sectors. Comparisons, through the use of some perform-ance indicators, are possible but many organizations should be judged on how effective they are in achieving the set objectives. Service design is an important element in implementing aims and objectives and identifying their implications for operations. As Kingman-Brundage (1991: 48) suggested: 'operationalising service quality dimensions is a crucial element of ser-vice design.'

Fifth, the service design process enables the necessary systematic planning to take place, par-ticularly when it uses the tools and techniques examined at the end of this chapter, and an integrated and unified approach to its operations. The challenge in all operations is to achieve a balance between maximizing customer satisfaction and the optimum use of resources, the two ostensibly conflicting objectives of service operations. Good service design ensures that resources are allocated as effectively as possible, that this occurs within a cross-functional and integrated approach, and that it follows a number of core principles.

Finally, service quality is related to innovation and the basis of this is service design (Lagrosen and Lagrosen, 2007), particularly where it is driven by the responses to the monitoring approaches examined in Chapters 9 and 10. They suggest that all services must be designed more or less consciously, and this is therefore an aspect of services management that requires more attention.

THE PRINCIPLES OF CUSTOMER EXPERIENCE DESIGN

The chapter will conclude by examining the tools of service design, but it is important at this stage to consider the recent literature that provides the underpinnings to such approaches. The process of designing services and experiences in the LETS industry is founded on a number of principles and approaches.

First there is a need to understand the customer and where there is a problem and scope for improvement. Meyer and Schwager (2007) pointed to research by Bain & Company that highlighted problems with the perceptions of many organizations about the experience they are delivering to customers and their unrealistic assessments of how well they were doing. They reported 80% of the companies surveyed believed that the experience they were providing was superior, yet only 8% of customers described this experience as 'superior'. The principles and methods of customer satisfaction measurement outlined in Chapter 11 are therefore crucial to this process.

Second, there is a need to extend this understanding to the whole customer experience, as examined in Chapter 1. We saw in Chapters 1 and 4 how Disney's approach to understanding fully their customers' requirements involved their 'guestologists' setting out to understand what customers expect, what they can do and where co-production can be encouraged and planned. Guestologists translate this understanding into two aspects of operations: experience design and staff training (Ford and Dickson, 2012). This involves the shift in emphasis from functional delivery to the emotional elements of the experience and the value of the experience to the customer, particularly when deeply valued and rich experiences are anticipated and planned for. Ferreira and Teixeira (2013) highlight the importance of engaging the customer's five senses in order to provide personal and memorable customer experiences, building on Pine and Gilmore's assertion that customers are willing to pay a premium for experiences and that service organizations should try to make them more fun. Chase and Dasu (2014), on the other hand, suggest that psychological principles can be used to deliver positive experiences for any kind of service, not just those that lend themselves to fun and the psychological aspects of service delivery and that service encounters require the same rigorous and systematic approach to design processes that deliver the technical features of the service. Berridge (2012) also identifies the need to systematically plan for such co-created experiences in the events sector, especially when the factors involved, such as the characteristics of the customer, nature of the experience and features of the setting, produce a complex relationship. Indeed, he suggests that events may be classified to reflect such factors and to elicit different experiences involving feelings, emotions and values from customers.

Third, there is a need to identify opportunities for co-creation and how they can be achieved. The growing significance of the customer as a co-producer and the more recently established concept of co-created value suggest the need to systematically plan service encounters that are flexible, situated and adapted to the setting (Grönroos, 2011). For example, Frow and Payne (2007) report on the approach adopted by Guinness to recognize the co-creation of value in the provision and consumption of a pint of Guinness beer. Case Study 5.1 explains how the customer can actively participate in achieving the perfect customer experience. Guinness found that customers needed to be taught their role, illustrating the essence of service dominant logic theory where the customer and supplier work together to co-create value. Sorensen and Jensen (2015) suggest that the challenge is to design robust and integrated service environments in which service encounters are situated and adapted to the setting and therefore planned to support the co-creation of the experience. In contexts that involve performance of physical skills and the concept of flow that we examined in Chapter 1, experience designers might consider such matters as optimizing the match between challenges and skills, minimizing distractions, and ensuring that immediate feedback occurs following participants' actions. We see in heritage settings how staff as characters from the period being depicted, and the demonstrations of skills and techniques, are designed to appeal to multiple senses and to draw the guest into the atmosphere and context of the historical setting, for example, where cotton spinning in the late 1700s is demonstrated by trained staff at Styal Mill near Manchester, or actors depict scenes from the First World War when Dunham Massey stately home near Manchester was used as a hospital for wounded soldiers. In outdoor settings, the relationship between the context and the human experience is also complex and can be dominated by instrumental goals, involving a sense of achievement as for example in climbing a mountain, to more subtle goals involving aesthetic, cultural or symbolic and expressive factors where the overriding experience is the beauty of the landscape or the meanings or memories associated with it (Backlund and Stewart, 2012).

Fourth, the shift from service design to experience design requires different interaction between employees and customers, with more customized and flexible responses. This underlines the importance of emotional engagement by staff, examined in Chapter 7, which Sorensen and Jensen (2015) refer to as 'experiential intelligence'. Indeed, they suggest that:

> This is a kind of social capability that allows tourism employees to empathise and interact with their customers and identify with their expectations and requirements, experientially and emotionally.
>
> (Sorensen and Jensen, 2015: 339)

Fifth, the principles we have explored can be thought of as part of the growing body of core knowledge and skills and tools in customer experience management contributing to what Ellis and Rosman (2008) describe as the technology of service and experience design that can be

Case Study 5.1. Guinness and the Perfect Pint of Beer

Guinness beer is brewed in over 35 countries and a global brand, but has sometimes suffered from a perception that its distinctive beer is not always consistent, especially away from its origins in Ireland. To ensure a perfect consumer experience at the point of delivery, Guinness formed a special cross-functional process improvement team charged with the job of delivering the 'Perfect Pint', which was first developed in the UK where research by Guinness (GB) revealed problems with variability. They identified four main stages to address; the first two – the quality of the raw materials supplied to Guinness and the quality within the brewing and packaging processes – are not our concern here, but the other two stages do have resonance with the issues addressed by this chapter. How the publican serves the perfect pint and how the customer is educated in how to enjoy the consumption experience offer some thoughts on aspects of service and experience design.

The famous 'two partpour' that is required to deliver a perfect glass of Guinness needs practice. Detailed instructions and training were provided by Guinness to ensure that the 'Perfect Pint' was dispensed properly and drunk correctly by consumers. Publicans needed to understand their role in delivering the perfect customer experience and the benefits to them in terms of customer loyalty. Every person involved in producing and delivering the Perfect Pint was trained to recognize their responsibility in ensuring that the customer experience is consistently excellent.

'Hold the glass at a 45 degree angle close to the spout to prevent large bubbles from forming in the head. Pull the tap fully open and fill the glass 75% full. Allow the stout to settle completely before filling the rest of the glass. The creamy head will separate from the dark body. To top off the pint push the tap forward slightly until the head rises just proud of the rim. Never allow the stout to overflow or run down the glass.'

But achieving the 'Perfect Pint' did not stop there. Research showed Guinness that consumer education was also critical if the consumption experience was going to be consistent – every time. Guinness needed to communicate to consumers their part in securing the 'Perfect Pint'. Point-of-sale laminated cards were used that explained, on one side, how to pour the 'Perfect Pint', and on the reverse side, the correct serving temperature and a ruler that allowed consumers to measure the correct thickness of the head on their pint. Consumers were also targeted with a highly successful advertising campaign that extolled the virtues of waiting for a perfect pint – as it takes between 90 and 120 seconds for a perfect pint of Guinness to settle. This activity needed to emotionally involve customers in playing their part in co-creating the perfect pint. Thirsty customers now wait patiently for their Guinness. They have become educated and involved and are now part of the process. They are now convinced that if it is worth having the perfect pint, then it is worth waiting for. This strategy, based on the cross-functional involvement of all aspects of Guinness'

(Continued)

> Case Study 5.1. **Continued.**
>
> operations, has successfully delivered the 'perfect' customer experience. It has propelled Guinness to achieve its highest ever share of the total draught beer market. Guinness recognized that the presentation of beer is critical in terms of ensuring repeat purchase – and this requires a total integration of all aspects of the supply chain – including the consumer. The Perfect Pint project, launched initially in the UK, has been so successful that the approach has been applied worldwide.

applied to many different settings. This supports Pine and Gilmore's five principles for staging encounters to enhance the customer experience and to yield maximum value for customers and providers:

- Fully theme the encounter;
- Identify an appropriate 'theatrical form' appropriate to the theme, and ensure that employees stay in character that is consistent with the theme and the theatrical form;
- Customize the encounter to the individual (rather than only to the market);
- Stimulate multiple senses during the encounter; and
- Provide ('mix in') memorabilia (Ellis and Rosman, 2008: 6).

The principles of service design illustrate the growing complexity of customer experience management in the LETS industry and the challenges facing operators.

FACTORS IN SERVICE DESIGN

There are a number of key questions for the LETS operator to answer in determining the approach to service design in any particular context:

- What are the experiential properties of the product and service?
- What are the service concept and service package?
- Who are your customers?
- At what standards do you wish to operate?
- How can the service operation be delivered to the customers?

There are also supplementary questions:

- How standardized or customized is the product and service?
- What is the level of psychological encounter?
- What emotions might these experiences evoke?
- What are the customer's expectations?
- What is the level of customer participation and how is value co-created?
- How technological is the operation?

- How complex is the process?
- What is the capacity of the operation?
- How productive is the delivery system and use of resources?

These questions underpin the entire process of planning and designing LETS services and experiences and represent a systematic approach. They also highlight a number of factors to be taken into account in designing the LETS product and service; they transcend the discreteness of the components in the model in Fig. 5.3 and indeed impact on them, but relate in particular to the service system. Bitner's early work (1992) on the servicescape identified the three key elements of ambience, layout and signs, symbols and artefacts, whilst others more recently have added to these thoughts. Edvardsson *et al.* (2010) referred to the 'experience room' in their theorizing about the wider service setting and suggested there were six factors: physical artefacts; intangible artefacts; technology; customer placement; customer involvement; and interaction with employees. Others have examined aspects such as timing and queueing (Bitran *et al.*, 2008). We shall examine tangible and operational factors, social accountability, the service encounter and customer involvement.

Tangibles

An inevitable starting point is the tangibles of a product, since they are so often associated with the core element of the product and are integral to the first impressions created and the image presented. Tangibles also comprise several important elements.

Setting

A key element in service and experience design is the context. Indeed, Ponsignon *et al.* (2012: 1278) suggest that 'design of service processes is driven by contextual factors'. Indeed, the effect of the servicescape on customer behavioural intentions in LETS settings is well documented, as we saw in Chapter 1. The setting refers to the physical and technical environments for the activity and also less tangible features such as atmosphere, image and ambience:

- *Atmosphere and ambience.* The subjectivity of consumer perceptions is even more acute in the impact of the atmosphere of a facility and is perhaps the most difficult feature of the servicescape to design into a service package. Many factors contribute to its overall impact, including lighting, temperature, music and theming. Customers will often point to the atmosphere of a restaurant or theatre, or even a leisure complex, as part of its attractiveness, but the co-creation of value is significant here because of the contribution to the atmosphere that customers can make. Fans at football stadia, racegoers at the Cheltenham Gold Cup (horse racing) Festival, visitors to the Edinburgh Fringe Festival or music fans at the Glastonbury Festival all shape the very atmosphere to which they are attracted.

- *Aesthetic appeal.* The concept of quality is a very subjective one, but the LETS provider knows that the consumer experience is often affected by reaction to the decor, furnishings, colour scheme, architecture, landscaping or design of equipment and the challenge is to identify the features with the most widespread appeal. Center Parcs, with an 'all-the-year-round' holiday concept, have a large 'tropical dome' containing pools and other water features as the centrepiece of their operations. Disney, in all its parks, has placed great importance on the quality of the environment with the visual impact of themed areas as well as making the landscaping a priority.

- *Access and location.* This ranges from the physical proximity of the facility to its market, transportation to it and parking (or provision of a train station in the case of Disneyland Paris), to provision for the disabled, and opening hours and programming policies. It can be a challenge with many events, whether the size of the Glastonbury Festival or a small local event.

- *Signage and sightlines.* Circulation of people in large sites or buildings such as theme parks and airports can be greatly affected by the clarity and positioning of signs and notices (and the number – in some instances there are too many unnecessary notices). Sightlines for viewing in special events or museums or exhibitions, or signage for cycle sportive events, are also critical in shaping consumer perceptions of the experience. Technology has helped, with sports stadia erecting large screens of the action, or providing more flexible configurations.

Operational factors

- *Health and safety and security.* Many LETS contexts contain a risk to safety, whether they are activities involving movement, or the congregation of people as spectators, or the provision of food and drink. There is the paradox in the case of, for example, theme parks or outdoor pursuits where the 'risk environment' or thrills from the activity are part of the attraction but where the consumer still likes to feel that safety measures are in place. In recent years, the design process has seen much attention to detail and procedures in white-knuckle rides, flumes and water slides, sun, outdoor pursuits and sports stadia, although, unfortunately, cannot always prevent mistakes as the Alton Towers accident in 2015 demonstrated. The need for perceived security is more subtle as we see at Disney's parks where their obsession with cleanliness and tidiness reflects their view that this enhances perceptions of security by their guests. The growing threat of terrorism is also affecting the way in which tourism operators, airports and airlines and special events venues design their procedures and control the flow of people.

- *Flexibility.* It was noted earlier how the dynamism of LETS markets means that organizations must be able to respond quickly to market changes or, indeed, the competitive edge, which requires operators to innovate and experiment. Flexibility and adaptability built into facilities and systems and processes will enable the good operator to modify their product or service. Flexible specialization, where the provider is constantly appraising the potential for adaptation of a facility or activity or the fine-tuning of a product or service, is part of the process of experience design and can also provide for elements of customization where this is appropriate and will enhance the experience. This has been seen to occur in facilities such as squash courts that have been converted into fitness suites or soft play areas or in conference and exhibition centres like the Scottish Exhibition and Conference Centre in Glasgow, which is designed for flexibility and responsiveness in how its space is used, or the Millennium Stadium in Cardiff, which can switch seamlessly from staging rugby matches to pop concerts.

- *Technology*. The impact of technology is particularly significant. It can have a bearing on the nature of a product in, for example, the rides in theme parks or the interactive activities in museums or science parks, or the equipment in a health and fitness club. Technology, in booking and membership systems and control of tickets and access as well as communications, also shapes the design of the service and the management of the service process. The hotel sector has extensively embraced the use of technology but Virgin Hotels are leading the way with their new chain of hotels in Chicago. They have set out to eliminate the elements that annoy customers such as charges for WiFi and excessive mini-bar charges and muzak in the rooms, but have designed access around technology including checking in online using the hotels' app and scanning a QR code at a kiosk for the key (although there are 'real-life' ambassadors to check the less technologically savvy guests in) and using the app on a phone or iPad to control the temperature of the room or for room service.

In other words, the very product and the way it is delivered are not simply underpinned in many contexts by technology, but manifestly based on the ability of the experience to inform, animate, excite, stimulate and entertain. The potential of such technical resources, in relation to other resources, adds to the complexity and the challenge to the design process as well as the scope for product development and for engaging with the customer.

Social accountability

The two greatest benefits of design for the service sector according to Johnston and Kong (2011) relate to 'brand image' either for the organization or for the organization's service closely followed by 'increased profits'. There is increasing pressure to take issues of sustainability, ethics and community relations into account in designing and redesigning services in the LETS sector. Examples include energy consumption, ecotourism, conflict between recreational users and landowners and localism. The Eden Project in Cornwall provides a good example of a major leisure development that had made a huge economic contribution to the region but has also set out not just to work to some principles of sustainability but also to build them into their core product and the educational messages they are promoting.

The service encounter and customer involvement

The service encounter and how it is managed by the organization is a crucial element of service and experience design, particularly when it embraces the involvement of the customer in the co-creation of value (see Fig. 5.2). The level of psychological encounter between staff and customers varies greatly across the LETS industry but its importance in achieving customer satisfaction is well documented. Cook *et al.* (2002) identified three aspects of the service encounter that raise challenges for the design and management of customer experiences, and which resonate with aspects of the experience economy highlighted in Chapter 1.

First, the various touch points or contacts make up a flow of experiences for the customer or sequencing that involve three characteristics:

1. Customers prefer sequencing of experiences that improve over time, whether it is a long temporal experience like a holiday or a much shorter one like a visit to the gym or attending a special event.
2. The flow of time as it is perceived by the customer is central to the absorption and immersion in the activity, and therefore its enjoyment, and is determined by the setting and service process and how they are managed; for example, ensuring that yoga classes take place in a quiet and relaxing area.
3. Where there is disconfirmation of expectations (whether negative or positive) customers intuitively seek explanations (especially where something goes wrong as part of a process of rationalization, which social psychologists call 'counterfactual thinking').

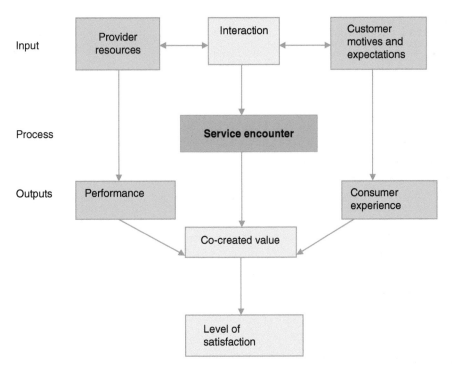

Fig. 5.2. The service encounter.

This dovetails with behavioural principles of service encounter design (Chase and Dasu, 2014; Dixon and Walsman, 2014), which state that:

- The service encounter should finish strongly;
- Any weak aspects therefore should occur early on;
- Any weak aspects should also occur together in a single stage, but the pleasurable aspects should be segmented into multiple stages to have maximum impact;
- The customer should control the process; and
- Standardized aspects should therefore be consistently delivered.

A further aspect is the temporal nature of the service encounter, which Bitran *et al.* (2008) argue requires more extensive research. They suggest that the duration of the experience and waiting times often require a compromise between additional revenue from longer waiting, as in drinks in a restaurant between placing the order and being called to the table, and the dissatisfaction that can arise if the wait is too long, an aspect of demand management we expand upon in Chapter 6. It has also been noted that dissatisfaction with queuing times can be reduced by a positive experience from the core product, although the corollary also applies.

Dixon and Verma (2013) on the other hand were more concerned with sequences of activity within time-elapsing service bundles. They felt that the service offering could be perceived as either a series of connected elements or several separate episodes, with the perceived value of the event as utility depending on the customer's evaluation of each stage in the sequence. They found that high perceived utility in the early stages had a positive effect on evaluation of later stages.

Finally, scripting and the level of standardization or customization of the service encounter are significant factors in the design process. The nature and the extent of the scripting will vary according to the bundle of attributes offered and the appropriateness of features of standardization or customization. The script will embrace the approaches to be followed by staff in ensuring consistency, but also extends to customer scripts in the ways in which they experience the service process and respond to either cues or to perceived changes or mistakes. Communications to customers about rules and procedures to follow are central to this, as we see in following signage or the usage of a swimming pool or following a nature trail. There is a need for balance in some cases where for example the explicit scripts in some events and ceremonies like weddings and sporting events highlight the importance of standardization but also enable the trend towards more customized experiences to flourish because of fewer distractions to the customer.

Some operations (e.g. TGI Fridays or Disney) build customer contact into their service concept and package, and train and prepare key personnel for engaging in conversation with guests. The use of script theory provides further evidence for the opportunity in the design process to manage and manipulate exchange and rapport between staff and customers.

DESIGNING THE SERVICE ENCOUNTER FOR CUSTOMER INVOLVEMENT

The involvement of the customer in many LETS contexts has clear implications for service and experience design. It can be argued that the customer can appear twice in the service management system, both as a consumer and as a co-producer, with the customer's own contribution perhaps enhancing the overall experience and reinforcing the view that the customer be regarded as a resource or input to be managed.

There are several ways in which the customer can participate in the service process:

1. The customer can *specify* some aspects of the service with different-priced tickets in theatres or airlines, different categories of membership in health and fitness facilities and golf clubs, or the design of a 'tailor-made' holiday.
2. The customer can be a *co-producer* in performing certain tasks, as in many facets of the voluntary sector such as sports clubs, and participate in *co-creating value*.
3. The customer can help to *maintain the ethos* of the organization in that the service encounter and the interaction can provide staff with great job satisfaction and fulfilment, particularly where there is some empowerment in place.
4. Customers can often be seen as *quality control* in that they observe and receive the work of employees and act as a check if things go wrong. The mystery guest method employed by many organizations illustrates the possibilities of this (see Chapter 9).
5. Customers are also involved in *selling and promoting* facilities and establishments through word of mouth or the use of their happy smiling faces in publicity material, as seen in holiday brochures or advertisements.

In designing the service package and service delivery system, the way in which the customer is involved raises several questions:

- *How much customer participation is required?* We have seen how some LETS contexts require, or allow, considerable participation in the service and its creation. Many instructional classes in a range of activities are highly participative; interactive experiences in museums and heritage centres, audiences in sports and entertainment venues or education as leisure all provide opportunities for active and creative participation.
- *How much interaction with staff is encouraged?* It is also necessary to consider the impact that both customer and provider have on each other and how this is particularly significant in some contexts. There is the recognition (Svensson, 2001) that the service encounter should be viewed as a dyadic or even triadic relationship in which the various actors (consumer, front-line employee and possibly manager) help to shape each other's perceptions, and the growing view that such encounters are embedded in the series of experiences customers have with organizations (Tax *et al.*, 2013). For example, the aerobics class will certainly respond positively to an enthusiastic, competent and warm instructor and,

likewise, the instructor's performance and attitude will be affected by the approach and response of the class. Thus, there is a shared experience between staff and customer and the contribution of one will impact on the levels of satisfaction of the other (see Case Study 5.2 on TGI Fridays).

- *How is the interaction between customers/participants planned for?* Not only can customers be regarded as partial employees but also their contribution to the features of the product and service can be an additional dimension, and in some cases an integral part, of the overall experience. The interaction between customers provides much satisfaction for many people and much participation in a range of activities incorporates the motive of socialization. Therefore, the very presence of other people is an important prerequisite to social events, many sporting activities, certain aspects of visitor attraction sites and other social contexts such as restaurants and bars. One of the attractions of the Cheltenham Gold Cup horse-racing festival every March, despite queues and crowded conditions, is the very atmosphere created by the 50,000 people squeezed into the racecourse. Similarly, thousands of spectators in sports such as football, rugby and ice hockey are attracted by the noise, singing and social bonding of which they are part. Furthermore, it can also be recognized that providers are also affected by the actions and behaviours of customers.

- *What are the implications for management of the customer as a productive resource?* In viewing the interaction between customers and the organization, the implications for resource efficiency must also be considered. There is a continuum from reducing the impact of customer participation to a minimum, to avoid the potential for mistakes or variation or demands on staff, to seeing the customer as a productive resource. As Bitner *et al.* (1997: 202) suggested: 'Services can be delivered most efficiently if customers truly are viewed as partial employees and their participative roles are designed to maximise their contributions to the service creation process.'

- *What are the implications for the skills of consumption?* Ford and Dickson (2012: 180) suggest that 'service experiences almost always involve co-production whereby consumers must successfully perform some task or group of tasks'. Such confidence and capability is regarded as 'self-efficacy' (Bandura, 2001), and where participation is encouraged and where service design accounts and plans for it, the skills or competences required of customers also raise important questions. How is the level of customer competence identified, to what extent is the provider involved in developing such competences, and what is its potential for enhancing the quality of the experience and overall customer satisfaction? Canziani (1997) defined customer competency in terms of the fit between customer inputs (knowledge, skills and motivation) and the task roles required of customers. Service and experience design involves a pre-experience stage in achieving customer competency; where there are queues customers can be prepared for what is to be expected of them through visual clues and specific information, as we have seen in airlines encouraging passengers to check in at airports themselves, or Disney in introducing its virtual queueing system FASTPASS, where guests are given computer-generated entry times and are encouraged and assisted in becoming more confident to use the technology by customer service representatives.

Case Study 5.2. TGI Fridays

TGI Fridays, with over 900 restaurants in 60 countries, is one of the more innovative organizations in the leisure industry and sees itself as offering more than simply food and drink. It has a distinctive approach to service and experience design. Its service concept is to create a certain atmosphere in its restaurants and, with the provision for birthdays and other party groups and its high level of engagement with customers, its core product is more part of leisure provision than most food outlets.

Today, our goal is to deliver memorable guest dining experiences, reward members for their loyalty, inspire social sharing and create brand fans (Malish). Their corporate attitude is 'In here, it's always Friday', with fun an integral part of the mix in everything they do.

Product development involves managers in the marketing department at headquarters eating out several times a week to gain ideas, with other innovations coming from the USA. Feedback is also gained from mystery customer surveys, which are carried out every month, with results received by every restaurant every 4 months based on the overall percentage. Although the organization places great emphasis on the service encounter and the training of staff, technology is an important component in the delivery system. A computer system makes ordering quicker and more accurate and is also used to track the popularity of various offerings. A recent introduction is a computer-aided control system at the door to enhance the flow and seating arrangements of customers.

Service value

TGI Fridays recognize that on the loyalty continuum, behavioural loyalty – 'I buy because I receive points' (reciprocity) – is not as strong as emotional loyalty – 'I buy because I trust Fridays' (brand trust). Customer loyalty is an important thread woven throughout the company. They manage customer loyalty to reflect the brand and reinforce this mutual exchange of value in every department. For example, IT provides real-time access to redeeming stripes in the Fridays mobile app, finance works internally on offering an equitable rewards chart, Fridays operations training integrates the Give Me More Stripes programme into new team member onboarding and marketing uses relevant and targeted communications to start the one-on-one dialogue that offers tangible demonstrations of a customer's importance to Fridays. TGI Fridays applies that thinking to its Give Me More Stripes loyalty programme, with games, playful social media campaigns, easy-to-earn rewards like desserts and appetizers and showy perks like allowing members to occasionally cut the queue in a busy restaurant.

Technology

The casual restaurant chain puts a premium on keeping technology fresh, with high-profile refinements to its Stripes website and app. It has also been piloting a six-city test where

(Continued)

Case Study 5.2. Continued.

servers use tablets for table-top ordering as well as payment and loyalty processing, and is about to roll out the tablet programme to another 80 restaurants.

Customer involvement

TGI Fridays' Give Me More Stripes was one of the first loyalty programmes in the casual-dining category, and has been a leader in recognizing and rewarding members for their engagement with the brand since 2008. The programme has been modified in recent years to focus on member flexibility, control and choice, primarily driven by guest insights; this has been achieved through social/digital sentiment, member surveys and input from their restaurant operators. Give Me More Stripes now has millions of members who enjoy first-to-know news and promotions, menu sneak previews, access to events and private invitations, and special offers via digital, mobile and social channels.

Emotional engagement through feedback and the use of social media

Everything TGI Fridays does relates very closely to the points made in this chapter and in Chapter 1 about the creation and management of a customer experience that develops over a period of time and a number of visits and is enhanced by the feedback obtained from guests and their involvement in the design of the product and service. According to Malisch:

'The trust we've built is not tied to a single visit or a specific membership perk, but has been achieved over time by a number of actions and occurrences that we measure. We monitor guest relations feedback and social sentiment by evaluating channel engagement including email open rate/click through rates (CTRs), mobile CTRs and posts to social sites like Facebook, Twitter and Tumblr. We assess event/party RSVPs, ratings and reviews and experiential reward redemptions. We periodically conduct qualitative and quantitative member research. Of course financial metrics are evaluated in terms of visits frequency and sales revenue trends.

'Social media and the Fridays' app have been integral in the growth of the Give Me More Stripes programme today and will continue to be a cornerstone moving forward. Today's customers know they are being advertised to and why they are being rewarded. We try to keep it real by engaging our guests with relevant exchanges and content – through rating their recent Fridays' visits, managing their accounts from their mobile devices and even asking members to share helpful holiday tips with each other on the Fridays Tumblr site. Our most loyal guests are very interested in tangible, immediate benefits and experiences that recognize "who they are", and let them know that we are listening to them'.

TGI Fridays topped the list in 2014 of dunnhumby's second Customer Centricity Index (CCI) on food service retailers. They were measured on how well they respond to the needs and

(Continued)

Case Study 5.2. **Continued.**

wants of their guests. Customers were surveyed on what dunnhumby calls the Seven Pillars of Customer Centricity: menu assortment, price, overall experience, feedback, promotions, loyalty and communications.

Some of the key findings from the report include the following:

- Food offerings matter. Blending staple menu items with new and exciting options is a constant struggle and it's important keep customers excited about the menu.
- Customer experience matters. Restaurant ambience and overall dining experience can affect customer loyalty.
- Fast food chains rank low in loyalty. Brands must differentiate and focus on engagement and personalization strategies.
- Fast food chains scored low in feedback and communication, presenting an opportunity to leverage mobile, social media and direct feedback to make customers' voices heard.

Source: Bell (2014) dunnhumby USA

Ford and Dickson (2012) point to the benefits of encouraging self-efficacy in customers and suggest that there are four sets of techniques and strategies for doing this.

1. *Enactive Mastery*, where repeated performance builds confidence and competency through careful task design, an understanding of what customers are capable of and the support from staff where necessary.

2. *Vicarious Experience* involving modelling by others or by technology as in white-knuckle rides where screens can show previous customers enjoying themselves, or gyms with demonstrations of how to use equipment and facilities.

3. *Verbal Persuasion*, which can be useful in contexts like bungee-jumping or interactive settings like Epcot's Living Seas Turtle Talk, which encourages engagement in questions and activities by children.

4. *Physiological Arousal* in which customers are activated by sensory stimuli like music, sound effects and smells (for example the Jorvik Museum in York).

Such techniques and strategies exemplify the recent developments in service design and customer experience management in which the customer is central to the process. The desirability of the customer to have more control and influence and the operational imperatives and technological levers of providers combine to provide an increasingly complex challenge to their service delivery and management of service quality requiring a coherent and unified approach. It can be concluded, perhaps, from the previous section that just as quality management should be an integration of services marketing, service operations and human resources management, service or experience design should be seen as a total process combining functions and adopting an integrated approach. It clearly links in with many aspects of services management including the development of a service culture, the management of service en-counters and measurement of customer satisfaction as well as the more specific components of customer co-creation, systems thinking, customer relationship management, managing service failure and recovery, building capabilities, and customer-to-customer interactions.

The model in Fig. 5.3 demonstrates the relationship between the various elements in the ser-vice design process. It does not offer a technique or a method for service design but contributes to an understanding of the complex process of designing systems and processes.

MODEL OF LETS SERVICE AND EXPERIENCE DESIGN AND DELIVERY

Service operations management and experience design require managers to balance aspirations for service quality against the limitations of budgets and resources available. This means that there are a number of elements that need to be considered in the design of customer experi-ences. Ferreira and Teixeira (2013) list the four key theatrical components of: (i) the actors (service personnel); (ii) the audience (consumers); (iii) the setting (physical evidence); and (iv) the service performance itself. As we saw a little earlier, Cook *et al.* (2002) more specifically suggested that the service encounter can be viewed as a triad between the organization which defines the service concept and the customer and staff who both influence the process and system and the experiential properties of the product. We have incorporated these factors into a model of design and delivery in Fig. 5.3 to apply to the LETS sector around the following components: the service concept; the service process; the service system; and service value.

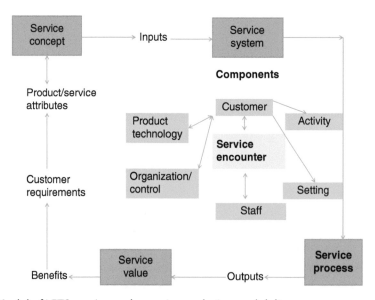

Fig. 5.3. Model of LETS service and experience design and delivery.

The LETS service concept

The first component is the LETS service concept. This represents customer needs and the features of the product or transaction, and as Dixon and Verma (2013: 138) suggest is as much pragmatic as it is aspirational: 'Effective service design and capacity scheduling involves developing a service concept that appeals to end users while considering operational constraints'.

Customer utility and benefit – both the description of the customer needs to be satisfied and how they are to be satisfied through the design of service package – are important elements in the LETS experience. The LETS service concept contains the bundle of attributes or benefits that the consumer is seeking and relates to the core product or activity and the augmented product or additional services such as hospitality, in addition to the nature of the experience sought by the customer. It also defines what business the organization is in and how it should promote and organize itself. Clearly, the approach to staging experiences and invoking emotional and sensory responses, as we saw in Chapter 1, offers a distinctive package and a means of achieving a competitive edge, although, increasingly, it also embraces digital service encounters, as exemplified by the National Trust. Their service concept is traditionally associated with heritage and the experience of visiting stately homes and other houses as well as the stretches of coastline and mountain that it owns. However, they are branching out into urban parks to help councils maintain them, which will alter the image of the trust to some extent and the nature of their service offering. Their approach to service and experience design is also concerned with the initial service encounters with many members through their digital platforms of website and mobile devices. According to Sarah Flannigan, their Chief Information Officer, they want the visitor experience to be as 'rich online as it is offline.' However, an increasing number of visitors – as many as 50%, she estimates – use mobile devices to view trust information online. 'And they wouldn't have a great experience,' says Flannigan, adding that mobile forms a key element of her transformation strategy. 'As an organization, we must adapt to the fact that a high proportion of our customers are using mobile devices.' The aim, she says, will be to use apps to increase personalization and to tailor benefits, such as an invitation for members to a particular event. This illustrates how the service concept represents the tangible and intangible elements of the service offering and needs to be aligned with the service process (Ponsignon *et al.*, 2012).

Indeed, when designing services, it is important to understand that service is a process and not a single encounter or task (Vargo and Lusch, 2008). The LETS service process is the chain of activities and stages the customer goes through; it involves much interaction between the customer and the other inputs that make up the service system. It refers to functional quality (the how) as opposed to technical quality (the what) and, in many contexts, is more important in determining the overall quality of the consumer experience. Furthermore, it is argued that customers tend to evaluate the whole process in their experience as opposed to individual encounters within the process (Bitner *et al.*, 2008), and the key to achieving service quality is the extent to which the provider understands how customers experience and evaluate the process, and incorporates this knowledge into the design of the experience. The service process involves the variables of value, job task and the job environment as created by the core logic and the three interfaces between service delivery by staff and customer perceptions of the service received. These three interfaces are described as: (i) the encounter interface, which links customer and employee logic through the values of the organization and the job environment, particularly with the significance of interpersonal relationships in high-contact services such as health and fitness and hospitality; (ii) the technical interface, which links customer and technical logic through value and work tasks and the customer's direct contact with technology and systems (important aspects are booking systems and the technology in visitor attraction sites); and (iii) the support interface, which links employee and technical logic through work tasks and the relationships between front-line and backstage staff.

The LETS service system

The production management model of adding value and converting inputs into outputs, adapted to apply to service industries, is further modified here to embrace LETS management and its service system. As Fig. 5.3 demonstrates, the LETS service system establishes what is needed in order to meet the customer requirements and the product features described by the service concept. It refers to the resources and inputs to the service process and how they are deployed, and helps to identify the service standards in all aspects of the operation. The LETS service system draws together a number of elements we have covered in this chapter: (i) the customer; (ii) the activity; (iii) the setting; (iv) product technology; (v) staff; and (vi) organization and control, as Focus Box 5.1 on the David Lloyd Group illustrates.

The customer

The relationship between the goals and motives, and increasingly the emotions, of the customer and the attributes of the product or service offering also helps to shape the outcomes of the transaction and the quality of the LETS experience. Organizations increasingly differentiate their markets based on typologies and behavioural characteristics and the use of 'big data'.

The activity

The interaction between the customer and the opportunities provided by the activity embraces the service concept and service process and naturally represents the core element of the product such as a game of badminton, a concert seat or a walk in a national park. It represents the customer's needs, motives and experiences and underpins the design, programming and delivery of all activities.

The setting

We have seen how design influences the setting and how it is used, from the infrastructure of a skiing area to the purpose-built facilities and controlled flow of people in theme parks or conference centres.

Focus Box 5.1. The David Lloyd Group

A key element of their approach to service design and service quality is their distinctive service concept allied to a clear service system. Their resources are impressive:

- 88 UK and European David Lloyd Leisure Clubs, two exclusive Harbour Clubs, one Next Generation Club and five David Lloyd Studios;
- More than 12,500 exercise machines, 150 swimming pools and over 7000 exercise classes a week. They assert that their racquets facilities are second to none with 800 tennis courts, 180 badminton courts and 140 squash courts across the UK;
- A membership of around 440,000; and
- 6000 staff, including an expert health and fitness team of over 1800 and the contracted services of over 450 tennis professionals.

Indeed, the Group believes that its core product – the activities provided by its sports and leisure facilities – is important but is underpinned by highly trained staff, high standards of cleanliness and maintenance, friendly attentive service and a pleasant and relaxing environment. It is the company's aim to exceed its members' expectations by providing an enhanced service, delighting members and increasing their perceived value of their membership. The aim is also to give all members individual attention and to try to meet every service encounter with care and compassion. The David Lloyd core values are 'caring, passion and trust' and its philosophy on service quality is to offer every member the best combination of quality product, standard of service and value for money in the leisure industry, as we see in the Group's statement about its service concept:

'WHAT WE'RE ABOUT

Our entire team are united under the principle of giving our personal best to allow others to achieve theirs. Our clubs and our highly trained team are there solely for the benefit of our members, and the better we are, the more we can help. We're passionate about offering a first-rate service, matched by a full range of high quality, innovative and family-friendly products. A vast team of highly qualified health and fitness experts and tennis and swimming professionals enables us to provide a warm, personal approach. Their knowledge and experience perfectly complements our outstanding facilities and equipment. Our members are genuinely encouraged and supported in the achievement of their goals and aspirations.'

Product technology

We have also considered how product technology is concerned with tangibles such as facilities, equipment and technology in the activity itself. It includes buildings such as cinemas and conference centres, the equipment within them and their use of technology as a feature of the product, such as screen and sound systems in cinemas or white-knuckle rides or simulators in visitor attractions.

Staff

Staff are also a key factor, because of the service encounter in many LETS contexts, and the interaction in such social settings defines the critical moments of truth. Receptionists, instructors, guides, attendants and waiters and waitresses are particular front-line staff whose role is to animate, motivate and engage with customers.

Organization and control

This is the final element and, although regarded as bureaucratic, work procedures and other documentation and communication with customers are important aspects of service quality and also help with customer flow and circulation, as well as shaping attitudes and perceptions. They can include ticket purchase, automatic entry, signage and sight lines, booking systems and the technology concerned with underpinning the delivery of the product.

Service value

The final component of the model in Fig. 5.3 returns to the needs and motives of the customer as identified or disseminated by the service concept. The model described provides a picture of the elements in the design of both the service and its system of production and delivery in LETS contexts. It demonstrates the traditional view of production in which inputs are converted through a process into outputs or outcomes but also emphasizes the link, in the loop, between the organization's service concept and, eventually, the benefits that customers take away with them and their satisfaction with how the benefits have been created. It also needs to acknowledge the process of co-creating value.

Service value does not simply relate to the concept of value for money but also accounts for other variables such as cost, time (including travelling) and the general effort required for the activity as in, for example, queuing for an attraction or event. These factors all have to be viewed within the context of increasing competing interests including not just other managed contexts for LETS activities but also the attractions of digital entertainment.

The model provides a backcloth against which the LETS experience can be analysed and broken down to enhance its understanding by staff (and customers) and the way it is designed and managed. It highlights the key factors in service and experience design that have to be considered and understood and provides the underpinning to the various tools and methods of design that can be used in the LETS industry. Its essence is the view that the customer experience has to be considered as a total experience, and the philosophy towards service and experience design therefore need a cohesive and unified approach that links the service concept with the process, system and value creation and recognizes the whole customer journey. Indeed, Rawson *et al.* (2013) found that many successful companies they studied set up a central change leadership team, with executive powers, to oversee the redesign of processes and systems to move away from isolated functions to more cross-functional processes based on journey-centric approaches. This helped to deliver not just excellent service encounters but complete journeys (i.e. the whole experience). In such cases the approaches to design will also have been enhanced by the use of particular tools and methods, and the final section in this chapter considers several tools that have application to the LETS industry.

TOOLS OF SERVICE DESIGN

The model of service delivery in Fig. 5.3 demonstrates the interaction between various components of service and experience design and the translation of the service concept into a managed process with particular outcomes. It highlights the way service delivery is designed, controlled and managed through setting out to systematically design processes and systems, and we conclude by examining the various methods or tools that can be used for service and experience design.

Customer journey mapping: a co-design method

A recently developed method in service design that addresses the process is customer journey mapping, where the customer engages with the organization through multiple channels such as website, mobile devices and tablets as well as their physical presence. It sets out to describe the process of experiencing service through different service encounters from the customer's perspective. It is really about understanding what the end-to-end experience is for a customer today, and what the ideal experience, or 'journey' will be for customers in the future. The service journey could describe how a person books tickets for a concert, travels to the venue and accesses it, is welcomed and guided through signage and personnel to their seat, how they use peripheral services providing food and refreshments and toilets. It can also be used in a wider context to identify positive and negative experiences and perceptions. For example, both the English Football Association and AFL (Australian Football League) have spent a lot of time:

- Defining who their customers are (they are clearly broad);
- Identifying their typical journey of participation/engagement in football from a youngster through to an armchair fan;
- Understanding the points at which they lose participation and interest and defining these as 'moments of truth' (e.g. both codes lose lots of fans and players at age 18 as they move from home), and understanding what 'interventions' are possible to drive a better experience – for example marketing interventions to keep engagement with relevant content, identifying new products/services for those specific moments of truth (e.g. Aus Kicks is a game the AFL designed to get young children into AFL at schools).

It is therefore a tool of design that emphasizes and defines the service process. It is a form of usability testing (Myron, 2014), which catalogues and analyses the key service encounters and moments of truth. It can extend to talking to the customer about their experiences and link in with customer satisfaction measurement; indeed, Kankainen *et al.* (2012) describe the Storytelling Group method where the provider talks to customers in order to co-design activities with an in-depth understanding of the customer and their needs and feelings. It involves focus groups of four to six people and scenario building through describing the ideal type of experience (we can see its links with the SERVQUAL model's expectations in Chapter 10). It uses a Moderator and a Creative Secretary to facilitate the discussion and to build up a timeline journey on paper. It takes into account multiple channels and harnesses users' experiences of other services to perhaps describe new touchpoints or changes to procedures and processes. It also accounts for both the transient experience as well as the value creation process.

Flowcharting and service blueprints

Flowcharting and service blueprinting are also concerned with the consumer process and the sequence of actions, stages and activities that the consumer encounters and experiences, but their essence is the graphic representation of the process and its understanding by staff. A service process flowchart follows the same principles as a manufacturing process and in engineering style will involve yes/no questions and responses. It incorporates an analysis of the duties and tasks of each front-line member of staff, but also demonstrates how they are linked. A receptionist in a leisure complex deals with bookings, ticket sales, enquiries and queries but is not necessarily aware what happens when users encounter attendants, instructors or catering staff. What the flowchart fails to reveal is the actions and operations of the organization, which take place away from the service encounters but which impact on them. It is important to note how the operations interact not only with the external customer but also with the internal customer and, particularly, how the front-line employee is supported behind the scenes. A method of demonstrating this is service blueprinting.

Service blueprinting is a more complex approach that matches the consumer process with the service system and demonstrates the interactions that take place. It shows how a *service map* (Kingman-Brundage, 1992) or *blueprint* (Shostack, 1984) depicts a consumer process and its relationship with the service process and the service system. The blueprint embraces the management function and intent at the bottom and how it relates to the requirements of customers who enter the map at the top. According to Bitner *et al.* (2008: 67):

> Service blueprints are first and foremost customer-focused, allowing firms to visualize the service processes, points of customer contact, and the physical evidence associated with their services from their customers' perspective … and also illuminate and connect the underlying support processes throughout the organisation that drive and support customer-focused service execution.

Service blueprinting therefore provides many useful insights into the technical, and particularly functional, aspects of service quality. The performance of the organization, its interactive nature and outcomes achieved make up the service process but also require a wider view than this. In addition to process, service blueprinting also considers structure and how process and structure are inextricably linked in the best organizations. Service blueprints help to illustrate the model of service delivery and the interaction between its various components and enable the design and implementation of the service package and delivery system to be much more informed and appropriate. Fache (2000) argued that blueprinting enables attention to be focused on three key factors in achieving service quality: design; the role of staff; and the interactions between staff and customers. Milton and Johnson (2012) suggested that it shows everyone how to visualize the entire service process and make explicit all points of contact.

To plot and read a service blueprint effectively requires systematic thinking, which embraces both the customer process and the service process or organizational structure. Their features include:

- *The customer's actions.* These are shown chronologically as the customer follows the service process and are the starting point for the whole blueprint, emphasizing the centrality of the customer to the method;
- *The clarification of roles of staff.* This comprises both front-line staff at the service encounters as well as the staff who are back-stage supporting or leading the contact staff;
- *Details of the service process.* This includes stages like reception or check-in counters as well as all other touch-points or service encounters;
- *Details of the service system.* These are the tangible elements, including facilities and equipment as well as access and, perhaps, parking.

To examine the customer process and the service encounter with staff involves following the map in Fig. 5.4 horizontally from left to right and along the *line of interaction*, and this highlights the potential moments of truth. Following the map from bottom to top through several lines of demarcation reveals the nature and clarity of the service logic and the structure of backstage and support functions in the organization. The *line of visibility* separates the front-line or on-stage operations from the backstage functions. On-stage duties are those that are visible to the public. Backstage duties are performed by contact staff but away from public gaze. It might be fitness instructors preparing their session, entertainers practising their routines, retail operators restocking or tour guides being trained for the substance and delivery of their material. Both on-stage and backstage operations are supported by other functions and these are separated by the *line of internal interaction* and emphasize the importance of the quality chain and the concept of the internal customer. Disney theme parks are noted for their costumed characters and the friendliness and knowledge of other on-stage staff; yet they are dependent on thousands of support staff who supply the costumes (the largest theatrical wardrobes in the world) and uniforms, train staff in the 'Disney University', service the rides or supply the shops, restaurants and bars. This line, in particular, demonstrates the importance of understanding the 'wider picture' incorporating the service concept and the service logic of the organization. Finally,

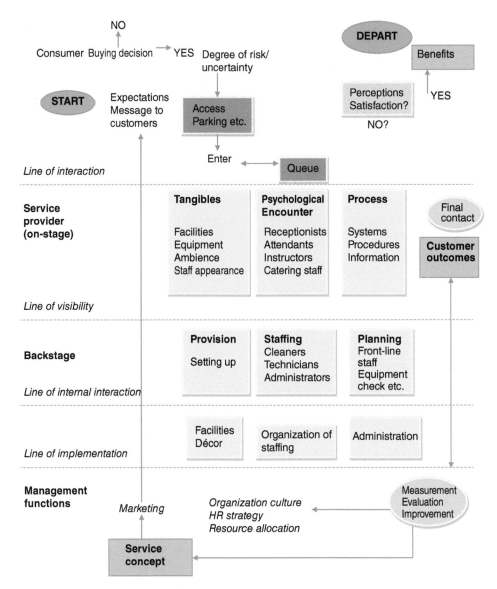

Fig. 5.4. Service blueprinting of a health club.

the *line of implementation* separates the on-stage, backstage and support functions from the planning and organizing functions of management and the policy making and decision making this requires.

We have focused on service blueprinting because it is a relatively simple approach for understanding and dealing with a complex process. Service blueprints can be used to design new services, to evaluate and modify existing ones and to control and manage service delivery. They therefore have a number of specific benefits, which Bitner *et al.* (2008) have identified from their work with companies:

- They provide a common platform for innovation and new service development. They help to communicate the values and nature of the service concept to everybody in the organization and give an overview of the service process and how it can be improved;
- They help understanding and recognition of roles and their impact on moments of truth. In doing so they also help in identifying service failure and how improvements can be made;
- They transfer and store innovation knowledge. They can be stored electronically and made available to all staff and can be used for internal discussions and blogs;
- They design moments of truth;
- They clarify competitive positioning;
- They facilitate understanding of the ideal service experience;
- They can also offer insights into enhancing customer to customer interactions – a particular feature of many LETS experiences.

They connect employees with each other as well as with the external customer; they help different departments or functions to understand the notion of the internal customer. They represent, in particular, the unified or integrated approach so critical to the achievement of service quality and enhance the provision and management of service encounters and are an important stage in the process of operationalizing dimensions of quality in specific contexts. However, their ability to determine the dimensions or attributes of quality is less secure and, increasingly, organizations must formalize the way they identify customer requirements and incorporate them into the planning process.

Quality function deployment

Third, a tool for planning and designing LETS services and experiences that addresses customer requirements, is based on a method called quality function deployment (QFD). QFD has been regarded as a useful method to understand customer requirements and to develop comprehensive products or service specifications (Stuart and Tax, 1996; Lin and Pekkarinen, 2011). QFD has been applied successfully to the manufacturing industry, particularly by the Japanese (it started in the Mitsubishi organization at the Kobe shipyards in 1972), but although its potential for services has been acknowledged in recent years (Ghobadian and Terry, 1995; Stuart and Tax, 1996; Chin *et al.*, 2001) little application, including in the LETS sector, has occurred to date. QFD has been variously described as a system, method, process or philosophy, but its distinctiveness is the systematic way in which customer requirements are translated into the technical requirements of the product or service. Han *et al.* (2001: 797) defined QFD as:

> a structured approach to seek out customers and understand their needs. It begins by matching customer requirements with the necessary corresponding design requirements, which in turn match with the necessary corresponding production requirements, and so on, to ensure that the needs of the customer are met.

QFD also emphasizes customer requirements, continuous improvement and an integrated or holistic approach across the organization. It also embraces the constant need to listen to the

Focus Box 5.2. **Alitalia's Use of QFD**

Ghobadian and Terry (1995) explained the use of a form of QFD by the airline Alitalia, for designing a new Intercontinental Business Class service. They went through six phases in the process:

Phase 1: Identification of Customer Requirements. Alitalia, interestingly, used a team of managers to identify customer requirements in three categories: quality of flight attendants; quality of in-flight products; and quality of cabin environment. Ideally, customers would be involved, and the various techniques for measuring customers' views highlighted in Chapters 9 and 10 would be used.

Phase 2: Obtaining Customer Importance Ratings. This phase also takes us back to customer satisfaction measurement and the benefits of establishing the importance that customers attach to different attributes of the service. Alitalia asked 3000 customers to rate the importance of service features and to compare Alitalia's performance with the 'ideal airline'. Cross-functional team meetings then determined the target quality level for each attribute as they were ranked by customers.

Phase 3: Identification of Quality Elements. This phase is related to functional quality and the team identified the measurable design features of the service together with the methods and processes necessary for the service delivery.

Phase 4: Construction of Correlation Mix. This phase is important in order to achieve quality. Phases 1 and 3 enhanced understanding, but there is a need to demonstrate how the quality elements would meet customer requirements. Alitalia used a matrix with 47 customer requirements and 87 quality elements to establish the strength of the correlation between them (1 weak, 3 average and 9 strong).

Phase 5: Feasibility Study. Pragmatism determines that the improvement to quality elements has to be planned over a number of cycles because of the technical, cost and reliability constraints. Alitalia attempted to quantify these by calculating the difficulty involved on a scale of 1 to 10 (10 being the most difficult) for each quality element and placing them in a matrix, which also presented the significance of each element by multiplying the correlations in Phase 4 by the absolute weights of the customer requirements and adding them together.

Phase 6: Quality Planning and Implementation. This is what makes all the work in the first five phases worthwhile. The first four phases were concerned with identifying customer requirements, setting targets and determining how the service package could meet those requirements. Phase 5 acknowledged the constraints, which meant that the inevitable trade-offs would have to be managed by prioritizing planned improvements. Phase 6 represents the planning and implementation of the improvements. Alitalia achieved this by setting up four cross-functional teams, with each addressing a different facet. As a result a new business class service was introduced and improvements were made to seat pitch, seat comfort, seat design, interior design, food and duty-free range.

customer, the VOC (voice of the customer), and all the methods considered in Chapter 10 for identifying customer requirements and measuring customer satisfaction levels, as we see in the example of its use in Focus Box 5.2.

We can see from the example in Focus Box 5.2 that the features and assumptions of QFD are extremely relevant to services and can effectively meet the needs of service design. Indeed, Stuart and Tax (1996) highlighted several principles in presenting their case for QFD:

1. *QFD provides a common focus for the marketing, human resource management, service operations and ICT functions* in the organization and encourages the unified approach that is so important in service design and delivery. A clearer understanding of the service logic in the organization is likely, with everybody more conscious of the impact of their decisions and actions on attributes of the service.

2. In particular, *QFD encourages a team work approach* since it is best approached through the use of multidisciplinary teams from across all functions (Ozgener, 2003).

3. *QFD recognizes that service design and process management must be customer led* and that the attributes of the service align with customer needs and wants. The causes of Gap 1 in the SERVQUAL model in Chapter 10 would be addressed by the QFD process and the service concept would be sensitive to market factors.

4. QFD, therefore, highlights the importance of the service encounter and moments of truth *and the need to analyse each interaction in the service process.*

5. *The overview provided by QFD enables the 'trade-offs' between features to be weighed up and evaluated;* for example, improving access to a site and enhancing its amenities but attracting visitors who may then impact on its perceptual capacity and quality; or adding to the features of an airline service (as does Virgin Airlines) with the risk of making more mistakes or standardizing or speeding up the delivery of a service but with the danger of making it less personal (some budget airlines).

QFD in services is based on a three-part process that represents service planning (design requirements), element planning (service process elements and service delivery development)

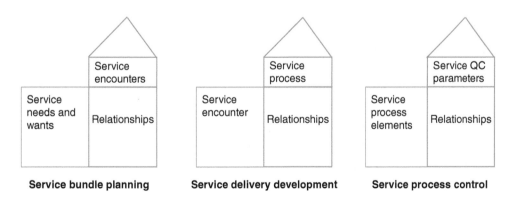

Service bundle planning **Service delivery development** **Service process control**

Fig. 5.5. The houses of quality.

Case Study 5.3. Application of QFD to the Olympic Museum, Lausanne

A modern visitor attraction can be used to illustrate the application of QFD to the analysis of the service's attributes and the needs of its customers. The process is progressive and begins with the identification of the attributes of the product or service, which, of course, draw on the service concept. The service concept of the Olympic Museum in Lausanne might be an up-to-date, technologically sophisticated, informative and exciting presentation in delightful surroundings overlooking Lake Geneva. The technique translates the service concept into service bundle attributes and their relationship with service encounters in House 1 (Fig. 5.6).

Key		Service encounters		
□ Strong positive relationship		Reception	Displays	Restaurant
□ Weak positive relationship				
Ease of access	Speed of entry	□	□	□
	Clarity of information	□	□	□
Use of technology	Sophisticated	□	□	□
	Reliable	□	□	□
Staff attitude	Speed of response	□	□	□
	Helpfulness	□	□	□
	Friendliness	□	□	□

Fig. 5.6. House 1: service bundle planning, Olympic Museum, Lausanne.

The attributes might be an extremely pleasant location, interesting/educational display, consumer participation and demeanour of staff, which might be broken down further into more specific attributes. Service encounters, representing moments of truth (positive or negative), would occur at entry (reception), each major display, points of information and the restaurant.

House 2 (Fig. 5.7) then takes each service encounter and identifies the elements of the service process that represent customer needs. The encounters with the different displays or aspects of the museum would be concerned with the visual impact of the displays, their

(Continued)

Case Study 5.3. Continued.

interest and excitement, their educational value, ease of circulation and the nature of the technology and overall environment. We shall address the service encounter at reception. The staff at the ticket desk have an important role in not simply admitting customers but also providing information about customer flow, timing, the technology (including tokens for viewing videos) and retail and catering opportunities – all done with a smile. The key characteristics are therefore the attentiveness, friendliness and helpfulness of staff, the speed of response, and the accuracy and clarity of information provided. It is necessary to bear in mind here the importance of service attributes and how they can be classified, and explained, as satisfiers, dissatisfiers and delighters. Satisfiers tend to be associated with the core product (such as the film at a cinema or the game of squash at a leisure complex) and are constantly assessed by the customer – and have the potential to delight. Dissatisfiers tend not to be noticed until they go wrong because they are not the main attraction but enable the core product to be consumed – examples are parking or toilets or reception. The right-hand side of the house therefore denotes the relative importance of the customer attributes.

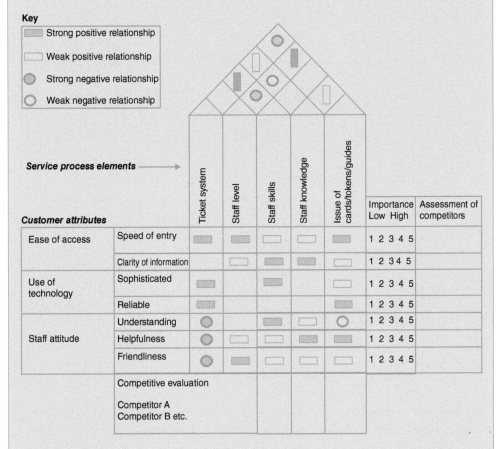

Fig. 5.7. House 2: service delivery development in the reception service encounter.

(Continued)

Case Study 5.3. Continued.

The next step is the development of counterpart characteristics. They represent the means of the organization to meet the attributes and requirements of the customer for each service encounter. For example, the scope for some involvement or participation is facilitated by the museum's use of state-of-the-art technology. However, the museum's use of technology also means that much of the usage or access to areas of provision is automatic, resulting in lack of contact with staff; this mitigates against the customer attribute of attentiveness and friendliness of staff and illustrates the benefits of QFD in identifying the trade-offs involved in planning and designing services. There will be positive and negative relationships between attributes and different counterpart characteristics. The house helps the organization to establish these relationships much more quickly and accurately. It is important to note that if a row in the house remains empty then the organization has failed to identify an element of provision to meet the specific customer requirement, requiring one of them to be reassessed.

The next stage in the house examines the interrelationships between counterpart characteristics and is shown in the roof of the house. It represents an effective way of making strategic decisions in the allocation of resources and the design of the delivery system and the consideration of further trade-offs. For example, the customer attributes of speed of response/access (no queues) is difficult to square with the desired attentiveness and helpfulness of staff who may have a number of questions to answer. The museum has to decide whether to provide more staff at reception, which may reduce its ability to direct resources into updating displays, or to have more staff around the different displays to provide the attentive and responsive service desired by customers.

The aspect to this stage provides the opportunity to measure the importance of each customer attribute and to gauge them against those of close competitors, thereby further refining QFD's ability to address the two objectives of maximizing customer satisfaction and optimizing the use of resources. A high importance rating for an attribute together with low rating for a competitor signifies considerable competitive advantage. A low rating for an attribute and a high rating for a competitor suggests a low priority for action. The museum, perhaps, can give slightly less attention to the range and attractiveness of its food and drink items because of the beautiful views over Lake Geneva from its rooftop terrace. A health club may find that its customers tend to regard the competence and attitude of staff more highly than the nature and extent of equipment – the feature of a rival facility.

House 3 finally links the service process elements with key aspects of operations that control the process and its outputs to ensure customer satisfaction for each service encounter and builds on the format of House 1. At reception, for example, staff's speed at admitting people could be enhanced by training in the use of technology and their knowledge of

(Continued)

Case Study 5.3. **Continued.**

the whole process in order to answer any specific questions. Their attitude will be affected by their dress, what they say to customers (script theory) and their manner (courtesy, friendliness and helpfulness). An additional advantage of QFD is its ability to identify the existence, and strength, of any relationships between different elements.

QFD, therefore, is a reasonably complex and quantitative approach to planning and designing services that encapsulates many of the facets of service quality that this book has examined. However, Shahin and Chan (2006) have highlighted the limitations of QFD in some instances in dealing with a diverse market, and argue for segmentation around service encounters to identify more specific characteristics, the term customer requirement segmentation (CSR) as a prerequisite for QFD. In their case study of a 4-star hotel they showed how cultural differences or characteristics like age and gender can prove challenging for standardized practices. They suggest that CSR can offer a compromise though mass customization with differently designed service encounters such as front desk. For it to work fully, however, the meaning of the total experience and customer journey needs to be examined.

Fig. 5.8. **The Olympic Museum, Lausanne.**

and operations planning (process control) as we see in Fig. 5.5. QFD, therefore, has three principal objectives: (i) to identify the customer; (ii) to identify what the customer needs or wants; and (iii) how to meet the customer's requirements. We apply these objectives and principles to a specific context in Case Study 5.3 on the Olympic Museum in Lausanne.

Customer experience analysis and evaluation

Finally, there are a number of approaches, recently developed or modified, that are more concerned with an in-depth understanding of the customer experience in order to effect changes to service process and systems. They also overlap with approaches to measuring customer satisfaction covered in Chapter 10, but their starting point is the meaning that customers attach to their experiences and the service encounters, or touchpoints that comprise and impact on the overall experience. Johnston (1999) called this transaction analysis, later to become customer experience analysis and it is also referred to as customer-firm touchpoint analysis (Frow and Payne, 2007; Zomerdijk and Voss, 2010) and customer experience modelling (Teixeira *et al.*, 2012). Berridge (2012) also highlights symbolic interaction (SI) analysis in the context of events in particular in which SI analysis helps the designers understand more about the experiences they have created, but also to provide an analytical framework for deriving the real meaning from the experience for the customer (and possibly the designer). He points out how the social world of individuals is not simply made up of physical objects and emotions but the actions that individuals take towards them and to staff and co-participants. Any method for exploring the meanings attached to such actions and responses can underpin more direct methods of planning service processes, encounters and experiences. It can also address the need to review and understand sequencing of events and encounters in the service journey that we highlighted earlier and to fully embrace the customer's emotions and motivations perhaps not fully addressed by service blueprinting or QFD. If skilfully undertaken, it adopts the theatre and storytelling approaches to designing and delivering memorable experiences we referred to in Chapter 1 as well as possibly acknowledging and catering for 'flow' in the process.

CONCLUSIONS

This chapter has examined the principles and methods involved in designing quality into the LETS product or service and the way it is experienced by the consumer. In highlighting the factors that are significant in designing service systems and processes, it has examined the elements and components of service and experience design and presented an integrated approach to their management to meet customer requirements as fully as possible. Methods and tools such as blueprinting and quality function deployment help to achieve integration as well as reflecting customer-driven approaches, although, perhaps, they need to be underpinned by other approaches that fully explore the meaning and impact of the various encounters and touchpoints within the total customer journey and experience. Such approaches also highlight the need to achieve productive potential, as well as to maximize customer satisfaction, and the next chapter considers the management of capacity across LETS operations and its relationship with the achievement of service quality.

QUESTIONS

1. How is the service concept translated into a service offering?
2. What does an integrated approach to service delivery mean?
3. How are customers involved in service delivery as co-producers?
4. Why is it important to plan and design the management of service encounters?

FURTHER READING

Bitner, M.J., Ostrom, A.L. and Morgan, F.N. (2008) Service blueprinting: a practical technique for service innovation. *California Management Review* 50, 66–95.
Zomerdijk, L. and Voss, C. (2009) Service design for experience-centric services. *Journal of Service Research* 13, 67–82.

REFERENCES

Backlund, E.A. and Stewart, W.P. (2012) Effects of setting-based management on visitor experience outcomes: differences across a management continuum. *Journal of Leisure Research* 44(3), 392–415.
Bandura, A. (2001) Social cognitive theory: an agentic perspective. *Annual Review of Psychology* 52, 1–26.
Bell, K. (2014) News Report on TGI Fridays. Available at: https://www.colloquy.com/latest-news/report-in-n-out-burger-t-g-i-fridays-top-list-of-customer-focused-restaurants (accessed March 2015).
Berridge, G. (2012) Event experience: a case study of differences in the way in which organisers plan an event experience and the way in which guests receive the experience. *Journal of Park and Recreation Administration* 30(3), 7–23.
Bitner, M.J. (1992) Servicescapes: the impact of physical surroundings on customers and employees. *Journal of Marketing* 56(2), 57–71.
Bitner, M.J., Faranda, W.T., Hubbert, A.R. and Zeithaml, V.A. (1997) Customer contributions and roles in service delivery. *International Journal of Service Industry Management* 3, 193–205.
Bitner, M.J., Ostrom, A.L. and Morgan, F.N. (2008) Service blueprinting: a practical technique for service innovation. *California Management Review* 50, 66–95.
Bitran, G.R., Ferrer, J.-C. and Oliveira, P.R. (2008) Managing customer experiences: perspectives on the temporal aspects of service encounters. *Manufacturing and Service Operations* 10(1), 61–83.
Canziani, B.F. (1997) Leveraging customer competency in service firms. *International Journal of Service Industry Management* 1, 5–25.
Chase, R.B. and Dasu, S. (2014) Experience psychology – a proposed new subfield of service management. *Journal of Service Management* 25(5), 574–577.
Chin, K.S., Pun, K.-F., Leung, W.M. and Lau, H. (2001) A quality function deployment approach for improving technical library and information services: a case study. *Library Management* 22(4/5), 195–204.
Cook, L.S., Bowen, D.E., Chase, R.B., Dasu, S., Stewart, D.M. and Tansik, D.A. (2002) Human issues in service design. *Journal of Operations Management* 20, 159–174.
Dixon, M. and Verma, R. (2013) Sequence effects in service bundles: implications for service design and scheduling. *Journal of Operations Management* 31, 138–152.

Dixon, M.J. and Walsman, M.C. (2014) Using behavioral research to design better customer experiences. *Cornell Hospitality Quarterly* 55(3), 221–227.

Edvardsson, B., Enquist, B. and Johnston, R. (2010) Design dimensions of experience rooms for service test drives: case studies in several service contexts. *Managing Service Quality* 20(4), 312–327.

Ellis, G.D. and Rosman, J.R. (2008) Creating value for participants through experience staging: parks, recreation and tourism in the experience industry. *Journal of Park and Recreation Administration Winter 2008* 26(4), 1–20.

Fache, W. (2000) Methodologies for innovation and improvement of service in tourism. *Managing Service Quality* 10, 356–366.

Fawcett, A.M., Fawcett, E., Cooper, M.B. and Daynes, K.S. (2014) Moments of angst: a critical incident approach to designing customer-experience value systems. *Benchmarking: An International Journal* 21(3), 450–480.

Ferreira, H. and Teixeira, A.C. (2013) 'Welcome to the experience economy': assessing the role of customer experience literature through bibliometric analysis. *FEP Working Paper 481*, University of Porto, Portugal.

Ford, R.C. and Dickson, D.R. (2012) Enhancing customer self-efficacy in co-producing service experiences. *Business Horizons* 55, 179–188.

Frow, P. and Payne, A. (2007) Towards the 'perfect' customer experience. *Journal of Brand Management* 15, 89–101.

Ghobadian, A. and Terry, A.J. (1995) How Alitalia improves service quality through quality function deployment. *Managing Service Quality* 5, 1–8.

Grönroos, C. (2011) A service perspective on business relationships: the value creation, interaction and marketing interface. *Industrial Marketing Management* 40, 240–247.

Gruber, M., de Leon, N., George, G. and Thompson, P. (2015) Managing by design. *Academy of Management Journal* 58(1), 1–7.

Gummesson, E. (1994) Service management: an evaluation and the future. *International Journal of Service Industry Management* 5, 77–96.

Han, S.B., Chen, S.K., Ebrahimpou, M. and Manbir, S. (2001) A conceptual QFD planning model. *International Journal of Quality and Reliability* 18(8), 796–812.

Heinonen, K., Strandvik, T., Mickelsson, K., Edvardsson, B. and Sundström, E. (2010) A customer-dominant logic of service. *Journal of Service Management* 21(4), 531–548.

Howitt, M. and McManus, J. (2014) Creating the service design interface. *Management Services* 2014(Winter), 38–45.

Johnston, R. (1999) Service operations management: return to roots. *International Journal of Operations and Production Management* 2, 104–124.

Johnston, R. and Kong, X. (2011) The customer experience: a road-map for improvement. *Managing Service Quality* 21(1), 5–24.

Kankainen, A., Vaajakalli, K., Kantola, V. and Mattelma, T. (2012) Storytelling group – a co-design method for service design. *Behaviour & Information Technology* 31(3), 221–230.

Kingman-Brundage, J. (1991) Technology, design and service quality. *International Journal of Service Industry Management* 3, 47–59.

Kingman-Brundage, J. (1992) The ABCs of service system blueprinting. In: Lovelock, C.H. (ed.) *Managing Services: Marketing, Operations and Human Resources*, 2nd edn. Prentice-Hall, Hemel Hempstead, UK, pp. 96–102.

Klaus, P. and Maklan, S. (2013) Towards a better measure of customer experience. *International Journal of Market Research* 55(2), 227–246.

Lagrosen, L. and Lagrosen, Y. (2007) Exploring service quality in the health and fitness industry. *Managing Service Quality* 17(1), 41–53.

Lin, Y. and Pekkarinen, S. (2011) QFD-based modular logistics service design. *Journal of Business & Industrial Marketing* 26(5), 344–356.

Maylor, H. (2000) Strategic quality management. In: Moutinho, L. (ed.) *Strategic Management in Tourism*. CAB International, Wallingford, UK, pp. 239–256.

Meyer, C. and Schwager, A. (2007) Understanding customer experience. *Harvard Business Review* 85(2), 117–126.

Milton, S.K. and Johnson, L.W. (2012) Service blueprinting and BPMN: a comparison. *Managing Service Quality* 22(6), 606–621.

Myron, D. (2014) Why you should consider customer journey mapping. *Customer Relationship Management* (December), 2 pp.

Ozgener, S. (2003) Quality function deployment: a teamwork approach. *TQM and Business Excellence* 14(9), 969–979.

Ponsignon, F., Smart, P.A. and Maull, R.S. (2012) Process design principles in service firms: universal or context dependent? A literature review and new research directions. *Total Quality Management* 23(11), 1273–1296.

Rawson, A., Duncan, E. and Jones, C. (2013) The truth about customer experience. *Harvard Business Review* 91(9), 90–98.

Shahin, A. and Chan, J.F.L. (2006) Customer requirements segmentation (CRS): a prerequisite for quality function deployment (QFD). *Total Quality Management* 17(5), 567–587.

Shostack, L. (1984) Designing services that deliver. *Harvard Business Review* 62, 133–139.

Sigala, M. (2012) Exploiting web 2.0 for new service development: findings and implications from the Greek Tourism Industry. *International Journal of Tourism Research* 14, 551–566.

Sorensen, F. and Jensen, F.J. (2015) Value creation and knowledge development in tourism experience encounters. *Tourism Management* 46, 336–346.

Stuart, I.F. and Tax, S.S. (1996) Planning for service quality: an integrative approach. *International Journal of Service Industry Management* 4, 8–77.

Svensson, G. (2001) The quality of bi-directional service quality in dyadic service encounters. *Journal of Services Marketing* 15, 357–378.

Tax, S.S., McCutcheon, D. and Wilkinson, I.F. (2013) The service delivery network (SDN): a customer-centric perspective of the customer journey. *Journal of Service Research* 16(4), 454–470.

Teixeira, J., Patrício, L., Nunes, N.J., Nobrega, L. and Fisk, R.P. (2012) Customer experience modeling: from customer experience to service design. *Journal of Service Management* 23(3), 362–376.

Vargo, S.L. and Lusch, R.F. (2008) Service dominant logic: continuing the evolution. *Journal of the Academy of Marketing Science* 36(1), 1–10.

Zomerdijk, G.L. and Voss, A.C. (2010) Service design for experience-centric services. *Journal of Service Research* 13(1), 67–82.

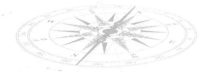

chapter 6

Capacity Management

LEARNING OBJECTIVES

- To understand the relationship between capacity management and service quality;
- To apply the knowledge and skills of controlling supply and manipulating demand;
- To understand the process and psychology of queuing and the means for reducing customer dissatisfaction with waiting;
- To appreciate the principles of yield management and their implications for the management of capacity.

INTRODUCTION

This chapter addresses a number of operational issues that are particularly significant in the management of service quality in leisure, events, tourism and sport. They link with other aspects of the book and especially the principles of service design in Chapter 5. The management of capacity draws on the core elements of service operations management, and in particular, the aim of reconciling the tensions between maximizing customer satisfaction, optimizing the use of resources and managing resource budgets. In the context of visitor attractions there is now a national code of practice to encourage high standards of customer care, maintenance and safety, and, of course, similar codes of practice in adventure leisure and tourism.

The purpose of this chapter is to examine the nature of leisure and tourism services and products, highlighting the challenges of managing service supply for variable demand and their implications for the delivery of service quality.

SERVICE QUALITY AND OPERATIONS MANAGEMENT

There is a key relationship between the management of resources and the management of service quality. Johnston *et al.* (2012) suggested that service operations are the configuration of resources and processes to create and deliver the service offering to customers. Many of the facets of capacity management are linked with the control and regulation of demand. They can be viewed as problems or as natural elements of the consumption experience and even, perhaps, an opportunity to be exploited to improve service quality. Good capacity management means that the organization can cope with any level of demand without adversely affecting levels of customer satisfaction; it can meet its targets and its customers' requirements whilst its systems, procedures and resources are stretched. Most contexts in the LETS context experience pressures of this nature.

Visitor attractions, especially theme parks, are affected by seasonality and can experience long queues, in particular on popular rides. For example, one of the authors visited a French theme park with his young family during peak season and the queues were such that they experienced just four of the main rides in one day. Tickets could be purchased to be 'fast tracked' to the front of the queues, but these were a very expensive, additional cost for the experience. Airlines have queues at their check-in desks and often have to manage the problem of delays or overbooking, through, for example, online or self-service check-in machines for those with only carry-on luggage. National parks are a popular form of 'public good' (Tribe, 2005) that can experience real problems with human overcrowding and use various methods to control this. There can be problems of erosion, limited car parking and dissatisfaction with the visitor experience for those seeking a more solitary, heterogeneous space in the outdoors, rather than an enclavic space (Beedie and Hudson, 2003) of people in groups. For example, the Peak District National Park is the most visited in the UK and the managing authority has tried to actively de-market it, to reduce visitor numbers at peak times and smooth that visitor demand.

Capacity management is concerned with achieving a balance between extreme positions and clearly reflects the objectives of service operations management, which are to reconcile the maximization of customer satisfaction with the optimum usage of resources. The problems of overloading, especially at peak times when there are queues or perceived overcrowding, can affect customer satisfaction and service quality and, indeed, lose custom through people going elsewhere either at the time or subsequently after a poor experience. Pressure on resources, especially staff, can lead to mistakes or rushed impersonal service, leading to customer dissatisfaction and a drop in service standards.

However, problems of unfilled overcapacity, or underwhelmed customers, can also affect the quality of the consumption experience. For example, a ticket for a music gig is perishable – if it is not sold it generates no revenue for the artist – and low crowd numbers can have a negative effect on the atmosphere, a key element of the servicescape expectations that attracts people in the first instance. This may also present images of failure or unpopularity in the minds of suspicious customers. For example, when on holiday, one of the authors always searches for restaurants that are busy with local people, rather than empty with unoccupied staff, as a tacit recommendation of good service quality by other customers. Staff in empty LETS environments rarely enjoy the lack of involvement and atmosphere and can begin to build up a negative image of their organization.

CAPACITY MANAGEMENT AND 'REAL TIME' SERVICE DELIVERY

Capacity, therefore, is not necessarily a straightforward concept to examine. It can certainly be viewed in terms of its resources and their impact on numbers of customers at any given time, as with a cinema, fitness club, airport or theme park. Yet time is also a key variable and much depends on the speed with which customers are processed, whether there is a fixed time (as with some sports, a special event or a guided tour) or the duration of the visit or experience is highly variable (as with tourists on a beach, or visitors to a museum or art gallery). In catering, the service concept incorporates this approach as in 'fast-food' outlets encouraging a rapid throughput and turnover (even through the use of bright colours in their décor and playing quick-tempo music – which stimulates people to eat more quickly) or the 'fine dining' restaurant, which offers the table for the entire evening and time is not pressured. The Jorvik Centre in York, in contrast, received complaints when it attempted to speed up its ride to reduce the length of queues.

The concept of capacity is also complicated by the characteristics of service delivery considered in Chapter 2. The issue of intangibility means that output cannot be stored and unfilled capacity in the guise of theatre seats, cruise ship cabins or cyclists at a sportive event, cannot be recovered. The corollary means that uneven demand cannot be smoothed out since consumption takes place as the service is produced (inseparability). Furthermore, the uncertainty of demand and delivery in many contexts is compounded by the uncertainty over the time it takes to process some customers as highlighted in the previous paragraph – a 'stochastic' pattern, which results in queuing and is one of the main features and problems of capacity management in LETS operations. It is easier to predict demand and patterns of usage where there is a single product, such as a cinema film or a gym, but where the product is mixed and complex, as in multi-activity sports and leisure facilities or theme parks, the notion of heterogeneous consumption means that it is very difficult to predict with any accuracy the decision making of consumers as they move around the service environment.

The real-time nature of LETS services means that the likelihood of consistently matching actual output to potential output is very uncertain and is dependent on three main factors: (i) the management of demand through the range of services, pricing policies and marketing; (ii) the management of usage through programming, scheduling, queuing theory and coping strategies; and (iii) the extent of capacity leakages when staff are late or absent or when facilities or equipment are out of commission. Output, sales and usage in LETS operations are determined by productive capacity, which also affects customers' perceptions and their overall satisfaction with the experience. Perceptual capacity is a difficult facet of provision for organizations to plan for because of variations in consumer behaviour and helps to explain the fine line that LETS providers have to tread between customer satisfaction and maximizing participation (which is considered a little later in this chapter). Whatever the nature of perceptual capacity and the context being managed, organizations need to plan their operations strategically.

OPERATIONAL STRATEGIES

There are two broad strategies that organizations adopt to manage their capacity and their productive potential: (i) control of the supply, which can be fixed or variable; and (ii) management of demand.

Control of supply

Fixed supply

The first challenge is to manage capacity or supply, but there are limited opportunities for this in LETS services, where there are fixed capacities or limits that cannot be exceeded once they have been planned. Some operations require a fairly elastic capacity (e.g. special events with pressures on their catering facilities and toilets) but many contexts have a relatively inelastic or fixed capacity as determined by factors such as the car parking spaces or rules (e.g. fire regulations or the number involved in particular sports). There may be upper limits but there are also fixed resources to be used, which means that the operational goal is to maintain demand as far as possible.

Service quality can suffer with this approach. Airlines, for example, regularly overbook scheduled flights in order to (ultimately) match their fixed capacity and, hence, maximize the revenue per available seat mile. The limit of overbooking is determined by a mathematical algorithm in the airline's revenue management system. According to Belobab *et al.* (2009), airlines have an average operating profit margin of 5%, but at peak holiday times the volume of no-show passengers can be as high as 20%, so the revenue 'spoilage', or loss, is 15% on that flight. Overbooking is thus a capacity control response to the variability of passenger behaviour. However, when all passengers do show up, it means that the airline has to refuse seats at check-in or to ask for volunteers to receive compensation and accept the next available flight (be 'bumped off'). Wangenheim and Bayón (2007) found that in this scenario, although customers feel that overbooking is unfair, airlines always provide a solution with an alternative flight and often compensation; therefore they perceive that this service recovery redresses the balance of fairness. These authors' research found that in reality, this deliberate 'denied boarding' and recovery strategy provokes less dissatisfaction than providing a lesser service or even a downgrade for premium-paying passengers. Interestingly, the 'bumping off' situation can lead to a scenario of dissatisfied passengers who do not wish to be moved from their flight, but also very satisfied customers who have the flexibility to do this. Going a step further, there are some websites that give passengers advice on how to actively seek out and profit from such overbooking activity!

Some reservations systems, for example sports arenas and theatres, can match supply with demand directly. In other cases, the resulting problem for service quality is the queue. Disneyland Resort Paris provides such an example. In its first few years it experienced a number of problems with capacity because of both demand and supply factors. Income was affected by inevitably poor take-up in winter months and also the lower-than-expected secondary spend in shops and restaurants (compared with the American parks). There were also problems with queues at the busiest times in the summer because of limited provision of rides: 29 rides in total, with a capacity of 50,000 people per day (1724 per ride), compared with Disney World's 72 rides with a capacity of 90,000 guests (1250 per ride). At the time of writing this chapter, Disneyland Resort Paris has 58 rides (attractions) and Thunder Mountain – a train with five trucks – has a capacity of 2400 per day. With a fixed maximum capacity, management can vary the number of trucks used through the day with respect to customer demand. Focus Box 6.1 gives an example of using information to help consumers themselves to take a significant role in queue reduction.

Variable supply

In some LETS contexts there is a need for as much flexibility as possible, with the attempt to match supply to demand referred to as the 'chase' strategy (Sasser, 1976). This requires either more resources being made available (such as staff or equipment) or a quicker response time (in a busy travel agency shop). Flexible staffing levels and skills are the most important factor in the chase strategy but, in some operations, facilities can be closed off or opened, depending on demand, as in catering outlets at sports stadia or in special events. There is the need for flexible staff; for example, leisure centres often employ leisure attendants or assistants who can also coach sports. Special events in leisure and conference facilities are often staffed by a high proportion of casual employees, who therefore represent a variable cost. There is also the need

---

Focus Box 6.1. Rugby World Cup 2015: Birmingham (UK)

On one weekend in September 2015, Birmingham hosted two Rugby World Cup matches, two soccer Premiership matches and seven other major cultural events, including the new Grand Central Shopping Centre opening and the UK Cycle Show. There was huge potential for gridlock around the city but this never materialized, due to web information being posted and updated for people to be able to plan their journeys and choose quieter times. For example, the organizers of the Rugby World Cup 2015 established a web resource in advance called 'Gameplan'. This provided information on likely visitor volumes, routes and locations, likely people and traffic flows at different times during the weekend, and information about the other events taking place at the same time. Gameplan was used in a similar way for other major city venues and encouraged event participants to adjust their travel behaviour to help reduce queuing. One of the authors attended one of these Birmingham events that weekend and in adjusting his travel times each way found only a small increase in traffic volumes.

for elasticity in other areas; for example, there is no use increasing capacity of a facility if its car parking or access is limited or it does not have the catering facilities to cope.

There are, therefore, circumstances where insufficient capacity to cope with demand means the provider can only adopt a 'coping' strategy and effectively maintain a 'level capacity' (Sasser, 1976), in which demand is constant or customers are forced to wait. In these cases, there are implications for service standards; there may be no control of any elements of the service offering, or there is an attempt to maintain standards in the core product and some aspects of the augmented product will suffer.

An example of the former used to occur around the Channel Tunnel between England and France. When opened it was advertised extensively that motorists could just turn up and go straight on to the train; they were met with many hours of queues and extremely disgruntled holidaymakers. Although this is still possible, over time customers have learned to book their crossings in advance and reduce the chances of long queues. Examples of the latter are stately homes unable to offer guided tours at their busiest times or health and fitness facilities offering more personal guidance and help at slacker times.

There are, therefore, a number of options in day-to-day capacity management for adjusting capacity to meet variable demand and they can be viewed as long-term or short-term options (Table 6.1). Although this table is from the 1990s, the principles still prevail and many of the options in Table 6.1 are used right across the LETS industry – an industry known for its use of part-time and casual staff and its scheduling of customers. The Cheltenham Racing Festival again provides many examples. Hundreds of casual staff are employed over a 4-day period and additional viewing and catering space is created through renting marquees and temporary stands; it requires a 'superhuman' effort from the staff employed. They use a number of the options listed, as do most organizations, and it is important to note that rarely are they independent of each other. For example, cross-training of staff to increased flexibility probably means fewer staff employed. Several of the options, such as changing location and hours or providing automated entry, overlap with the control of demand.

Management of demand

The other strategy is to manage the pattern of customer demand and much of this is achieved through encouraging customers to change their behaviour in relation to timing and frequency. This is where service quality has close links with services marketing and consumer behaviour, and an understanding of the market and its segments is particularly important. There are predictable patterns of demand associated with work and other commitments, the weather and seasonality, which affect all aspects of provision, and the challenge is to move some peak-time demand to off-peak times. An example of this is the use of price reductions to encourage participants in health and fitness facilities to attend at off-peak times, such as early morning sessions before work. The willingness of tourists to travel more cheaply out of season is another example. The scheduling of major events and festivals (such as the Munich Beer Festival) requires an

Table 6.1. Capacity management options (CMOs; Klaasen and Rohleder, 2000).

	Longer-term CMOs	Shorter-term CMOs
Base CMOs (must do)	Hiring full-time employees	Hourly/daily scheduling
	Lay off full-time employees Yearly scheduling (e.g. annual leave)	Weekly shift scheduling
Optional CMOs	Part-time employees	Temporary employees
	Rent capacity	Overtime
	Share capacity	Idle time
	Cross-train	Schedule extra staff
	Provide more information to servers	Periods of super-human effort
	Simplify the service process	Customers wait
	Reorganize servers to specialize	Non-urgent work falls behind
	Redesign service	Do non-urgent work when quiet
	Build excess capacity	Turn away custom
	Change hours of operation	Allow customers to reserve/ book
	Change location	Subcontract out
	Automation (e.g. entry) Change level of customer participation	Change allocation of resources

understanding of the motives and requirements of various target groups and the resources and processes needed to meet them. All large visitor attractions undertake a considerable amount of systematic research and planning in order to adapt their operations through knowledge of demand and customer requirements. Time-series data on usage are used to establish demand patterns and hence inform different temporal capacity requirements.

The approaches to manipulating demand include the following.

Price incentives

Pricing strategies can be used as both an incentive and disincentive to smooth demand and usage, aiming to increase demand at less popular times and reduce demand at the most popular times. The rationale for this is also based on the concept of marginal costing, in which the price is linked to just the direct costs of the additional usage, and the public sector traditionally has been slow to use this practice. It is limited by the speed of local government decision making and less dynamic practices. Examples from the commercial sector include nightclubs that are cheaper during the week, pubs that offer 'happy hours' during early evening and golf clubs that offer reduced rates for play at certain times.

Non-financial incentives

Similar to price, if a customer knows they could face greater costs in time or effort at certain times, they may be encouraged to avoid those times.

Promotional activities

In some cases aggressive marketing and advertising, linked to pricing policies, is sufficient to adjust consumers' purchase behaviour. In other cases, programming and scheduling methods and skills can pay off in promoting demand and take-up at less popular times. Leisure centres use their programming policies to schedule more popular activities such as five-a-side at less popular times to increase usage (if they can get away with it). Ski resorts have promoted their facilities, including lifts, for year-round 'mountain activity' usage such as mountain biking. Theme parks have targeted schools through their educational features in order to fill off-peak times.

Product development

Another approach is to alter the product, especially in order to fill unused times or capacity. The development of racket ball as an alternative to squash was seen a number of years ago, as was the conversion of squash courts to soft play areas when the demand for squash began to decline. A further example is at a public swimming pool where family fun sessions with large floating play objects are promoted, to increase demand on typically quieter Sunday afternoons.

Booking systems

Where organizations can 'reserve' capacity there are fewer problems managing demand, as exemplified by airlines, restaurants, hotels and some sporting events. Booking systems are in place in facilities such as golf clubs, leisure centres and health and fitness clubs to help to even out demand and prevent queues from a customer perspective, and under-utilization from the organization's perspective. Other contexts such as bars, cinemas and travel agencies cannot always accurately predict demand and require contingency plans to manage the extra numbers and the problem of the queue.

Yield management/revenue management

Yield management (now more commonly called revenue management) was developed in the 1980s to help an ailing global airline industry maximize revenues, whilst constrained by fixed, perishable capacity. The aim is to find the most profitable combination of different customer segments through differential pricing to those segments, based on their demand characteristics, and influence their purchase behaviour. Scheduled airlines offer seats with different in-flight service levels (for example, first class, business class, economy class) and charge different prices for those. In addition, many airlines encourage early advance purchase with lower fares that increase closer to departure. As each seat is purchased and as the date of departure moves closer, an algorithm in the reservation system recalculates the optimum price at which to sell each remaining seat, based on time-series data of previous seat sales. Constantanidis and Diercjx (2014) described this as pricing dynamically with respect to different customer profiles, further arguing that such prices do not increase linearly over time. They posited that any Internet cookies could be used as indirect data to create more highly refined profiles – not just direct cookies from airlines – but their research findings were inconclusive.

These may seem like over-sophisticated attempts to develop capacity management techniques, but in 2015 the International Air Transport Association (IATA) reported that the average profit/passenger across all airlines in the world was $8.27 (http://www.IATA.com/). With such a low profit margin, managing capacity and demand effectively is imperative for all airlines to achieve long-term profitability.

Revenue management techniques in consumer markets are now being adopted by other LETS organizations, for example, large visitor attractions and the Channel Tunnel (mentioned above). However, the techniques are also relevant to industrial markets, for example, seaports, which are income-generating public resources with a fixed overall capacity. Different vessels have different requirements when carrying passengers or cargo and some ships even need dedicated facilities, which further limit a seaport's carrying capacity. One delayed vessel can have a further delaying effect on other vessels; therefore to manage service quality for all users, revenue management is effective in that context, with differential pricing being a key tool to minimize over-use (Hong *et al.*, 2015).

The study of the manipulation of demand to manage capacity also contains some variables that affect overall approaches. Whether the demand for a particular product or activity is independent or is dependent on other products and services is a key factor. The number of participants or customers at many facilities or events will be directly related to the demand for food and beverage operations, although, interestingly, Disneyland Resort Paris in its early years overestimated the secondary spend by visitors in the restaurants and shops.

Queuing or waiting

Despite the application of these demand and supply management methods, a significant feature of many LETS contexts (though not always a source of dissatisfaction) is the queue; as Lovelock and Wirtz (2011: 260) observe: 'Waiting is a universal phenomenon'. However, in many cases there are constraints on the extent to which supply or demand can be manipulated and some problems of under-capacity, from the customer perspective, will always be apparent, as in the queues that feature in particular establishments. This is the problem of fluctuating service demand, which managers in some contexts regard as the most difficult aspect of demand and capacity management. Queuing is a major problem in certain situations but an established feature in others. Theme parks expect queues with their more popular rides, especially their recently introduced ones, and even argue that, in some cases, their customers perceive an attraction or ride to be less appealing if it does not have a regular queue. They are often managed to enhance the overall experience by adding information or displays to entertain, to allow views of happy/excited riders at key points, or are controlled and communicated with signage to pleasantly surprise customers eventually (a good technique is slightly to overestimate the time it takes from a certain point so that expectations are exceeded). Communications are especially important when delays are not expected or are not part of the experience (as with airlines and train companies) and, when sensitively and promptly effected, can greatly dissipate feelings of unrest.

Queuing is particularly acute in visitor attractions such as theme parks and museums and with airlines, but can also be present in operations such as travel agencies, ski lifts, special events and sports stadia. Many LETS operations face waits or delays in the receiving or processing of customers as well as the actual activity or experience. In this examination of service quality, customer satisfaction and the management of operations, the queue can be the one factor that impairs the overall experience for the consumer, especially since the wait often occurs at the first service encounter and also provides ample opportunity for the individual to dwell on the experience. The contexts and consumer motives or requirements may be different but there are some aspects of commonality. The delivery system and its design, particularly where it relates to the temporal nature of the service encounter (examined in Chapter 5), interact or engage with customers and the customer process at the point of queues.

There are several consumer characteristics that can have an influence on the consumer's perception, and tolerance, of the wait: (i) the (perceived) pressures of time on the individual (e.g. holiday-makers might be more tolerant of a wait); (ii) where there are children (especially young ones), the wait can be a test of the most patient; (iii) where the waiting environment is uncomfortable; (v) prior experience and therefore expectations; (vi) the mood of the consumer on joining the queue; and (vii) individual customers perceiving the fairness of their position and movement in the line relative to others. Illustrating this last point of equity, one of the authors experienced a ski lift queue in the Pyrenees where a large male adult skier tried to push past a small child. The child's indignant parent reached across with his ski pole and unclipped the protagonist from one of his skis and the people immediately adjacent applauded this action. However, Gillam *et al.* (2014) argued that in Middle Eastern countries it is entirely acceptable to walk to the front of a queue and be served; therefore queuing requires sensitive management in international service environments.

Maister (1985) proposed eight customer perceptions of queuing, and if these are well-managed in a LETS service environment, their adverse effect on service quality perceptions should be reduced:

- Occupied time feels shorter than unoccupied time;
- People want to get started (with the experience);

- Anxiety makes waits seem longer (related to this: the other line always moves faster!);
- Uncertain waits are longer than known, finite waits;
- Unexplained waits are longer than explained waits;
- Unfair waits are longer than equitable waits;
- The more valuable the service, the longer the customer will wait; and
- Solo waits feel longer than group waits.

The conclusions of the research on the psychology of waiting times demonstrate that it tends to have an overall negative effect on customer perceptions of satisfaction. Also, according to Kokkinou and Cranage (2013), the dissatisfaction caused by waiting in line is not linear over time; there is a timescale of satisfied tolerance, beyond which dissatisfaction increases exponentially. Clearly this differs for every customer and every queuing context, providing the LETS manager with a significant challenge to anticipate. For example, skiers and snowboarders often look for shorter queues on the mountain – even planning routes to avoid them from vantage points on ski lifts – in order to maximize their activity time and minimize queuing. On the other hand, theme park managers argue that customers do expect to queue for certain rides and place an additional value on the ride if there are long queues. Extending this point culturally, Gillam *et al.* (2014) argued that Japanese consumers often prefer to join longer queues as an indicator of high potential quality.

When faced with a choice of different queues many people become anxious that their chosen queue is moving more slowly than others they could have chosen, for example at a supermarket checkout. Or, within that checkout queue, anxiety can grow if there is a delay, due to technology breakdown, or possibly perceived as even worse, due to the person at the front of the queue. Janakirman *et al.* (2011: 981) acknowledged that people in queues 'can experience an emotional rollercoaster whilst waiting' and that this can lead to a customer deciding to abandon the line, as Focus Box 6.2 illustrates. These authors continue to explain that people in queues are in a constant psychological tension between 'waiting disutility' (queue abandonment) and completion commitment (staying put).

There are several methods that LETS providers can use to improve customer satisfaction with waiting and its impact on the overall experience.

1. *Provide details of the time it takes from certain points in the queue.* This is a popular technique and widely used in visitor attractions, such that this information is now expected by customers. It also helps if managers overestimate the time left, to under-promise and over-deliver on customer perceptions.
2. *At the initial point of service entry, provide customer information on peak and off-peak times so that they have an opportunity to enter the service at a less busy time.* An example of this was a sign promoting self-service breakfast times at a popular hotel chain. Using a traffic light system to show how relatively busy different time slots are, it enabled guests with more flexibility to avoid the busy 'red' times and either chance the 'amber' times, or target the quiet 'green' times.
3. *Keep people occupied as they queue (which has the effect of reducing the perceived time).* Some visitor attractions employ performers to entertain people queueing; others provide promotional videos; and Disney designs features, related to the themed area, into their queuing space to

> **Focus Box 6.2. The importance of queue design**
>
> At a newly opened motorway services restaurant in the UK, one of the authors encountered a single queue of around 30 people waiting at the beginning of a long food counter, where customers had to walk past each server before the next one was prepared to serve them. People at the front of the line were mainly stopping for food at the first or second server, leaving the others unoccupied, and the queue was barely moving. The author only wanted coffee and went directly to that end station – six servers along the counter – only to be asked to re-join the line and wait, yet the person ostensibly serving the coffee had no customers to serve. The author chose to abandon the queue and continue his journey, very dissatisfied. This decision may have been made by judging the disutility of a lengthy wait against the benefits of the coffee, or it may have been a subjective, irrational response to the situation (you decide!). Either way, this shows that LETS managers must understand the nature of queues in their context in order to manage customer satisfaction effectively.

relieve the boredom or uses sound as a means of distracting or stimulating. A hotel with queues at certain times for its lifts installed mirrors by each one and this immediately reduced the number of complaints.

4. *Consider alternative queuing layouts.* For example, physically organize the queue so that parts of it are out of sight for a time and the wait appears shorter. Or be creative, as ski park operators in the USA have been: people tend to ski and snowboard in small groups, so at all chair-lifts there is a queue just for singletons to join groups on lifts with empty seats, to try to maximize the up-lift capacity usage. This principle is understood by all users and no-one objects to the singletons effectively jumping the main queue.

5. *Convince customers that the wait was worth it, even for a 45-second white-knuckle ride.* In other words, promote the perception (hopefully the reality!) that the quality of the activity or experience is high enough to justify the wait and word of mouth will help to establish the expectations of others.

6. *Use technology to reduce the waiting experience.* Wittmer (2011) found that airlines' self-service e-check-in systems (web- or mobile-based) reduced passenger waiting times and thus increased their satisfaction with the check-in process. Kalakou *et al.* (2015) then noted that around 70% of airline passengers checked in this way and such a dramatic speeding up of the process has led to an unanticipated capacity gain in airports' physical building space, where traditional check-in counter areas are now under-utilized.

7. *Use a virtual queuing system.* Some theme parks use both a physical and virtual queuing system. For example, Legoland uses the virtual system 'Q-Bot' (Focus Box 6.3), where customers pay a premium to rent a hand-held device that lists availability for a range of rides and enables the user to book a place in the queue for a specified time. The cheaper rental price promises to reduce queueing time by half, whereas the more expensive price promises near-instant access to the ride.

8. *Understand how customer behaviour in the customer–technology interface may affect waiting time and mitigate against that.* As biometric passports have been introduced at airport self-service

---

Focus Box 6.3. **Virtual queuing technology at Legoland**

The following is quoted directly from the Legoland website (http://www.legoland.co.uk/Plan/qbot/):

Q-Bot is a ride reservation device and it allows you to reserve your place in the queue line for your favourite rides without having to actually stand in line!

Rent your Q-Bot from either of the Q-Bot pick-up-points in The Beginning or Adventure Land and then simply follow the steps below:

- Select one ride from your choice of over 20 attractions using the Q-Bot buttons*.
- Receive your ride time on the Q-Bot screen.
- Explore the park, visit our shops and restaurants or, maybe even ride a different ride!
- Go to your chosen ride on or after your allocated time.
- Enter via the Q-Bot entrance.
- Enjoy the ride!
- Repeat this simple process for your next ride.

---

security checks, one of the authors travelling frequently has observed that at peak times, queues for these can move more slowly than the queues for real security staff; thus he chooses the latter facility in those scenarios. Passengers are required to present themselves to the biometric scanner in a specified way, but many do not do this and delay themselves and others in the line, requiring frequent security staff intervention to make the process work. Liu (2012) found that customers should not be forced to use self-service technology and must be given other options, especially if they do not fully trust that the technology will work.

Beyond queuing

There are several other factors that shape the approach to capacity management in the LETS industry.

First, there is the problem of *perishability*, which was elaborated on in Chapter 2. The 'real-time' delivery of the LETS experience means that capacity cannot be stored and sold at a later time. Unused sports facilities or vacant seats in a cinema or theatre cannot be sold again for that particular session and represent lost income.

Second, the problem can be alleviated and exacerbated by the features of *seasonality and peak usage times*. For example, most theme parks receive the majority of their customers in 4 months or so, with weekends especially busy. Many facilities, such as leisure centres, tend to be underused during the day and parts of the weekend but often with over-demand in the early evening and weekend mornings. Connell *et al.* (2015) researched visitor attractions in Scotland and found that as a key aspect of their business strategy, 39% of them put on special events in the low season to address seasonal dips in demand. The local community was the main market and the events were linked to cultural-historical reference points, such as the Burns' Night celebration.

Third, the challenges of capacity management also highlight the *need for balance* in emphasizing organizational performance and customer satisfaction in the optimal use of capacity, so as not to diminish the service experience. On the one hand, capacity management is concerned with maximizing productivity through revenue/yield management and embraces the use of performance indicators in aspects such as sales, throughput and usage, especially in relation to space and resources. Yet, an over-emphasis on achieving greater throughput or usage can run the risk of affecting customer perceptions and satisfaction. To illustrate this, Wang's (2012) research explored the tensions between revenue management (RM) and customer relationship management (CRM), which found that in hotels the former is more prevalent, with a sales focus on maximizing shorter run revenues by managing the perishable inventory through price and customer segmentation; this can improve annual profit by up to 8%. On the other hand, CRM focuses on longer run customer satisfaction, to retain the most profitable customers and increase the patronage and profitability of other customers. Many hotels try to do both and these differing priorities in the same organization can potentially work against each other.

Fourth, allowing for appropriate service capacity should be a key aspect of service design. Capacity management techniques such as those discussed here should be considered at the design stage, not simply retro-fitted in the short term to solve a longer term capacity problem (see again, Chapter 5). In cases of rapidly growing demand it may be advisable for a LETS organization to review its service design and invest in alternative capacity. For example, Branch and Robarts (2014) found that the use of floating ferry terminals and vehicle parks can extend tourist (dis)embarkation capacity in crowded cities and ports (e.g. Gothenburg, Sweden), and large ferries can berth where they could not otherwise be able to. Clearly, such an approach does not then rely on the physical constraints of the littoral land resource and both the location and customer/vehicle movement process can be designed as required.

CONCLUSIONS

Managers in the LETS industry must understand that effective service capacity management has a significant impact upon customer satisfaction and use appropriate operational techniques to assure this. These techniques involve controlling supply and/or manipulating demand skilfully, so that service capacity is not over-reached. This requires achieving a balance between meeting customer needs and using resources as cost-effectively as possible, which may be challenging. A deliberate and systematic capacity management strategy should be part of the initial design of a service and LETS managers should not underestimate the need to review and revise their service design if longer term capacity issues arise.

QUESTIONS

1. What are the different ways in which a LETS organization can manage its capacity with respect to variable demand?

2. What are the key customer perceptions of queuing that LETS managers should understand and influence to minimize dissatisfaction with the waiting experience?

3. How could these principles be applied to the sustainable carrying capacity of the tourist destination?

FURTHER READING

Chen, C.-M., Chiu, H.-H., Chi, Y.-P. and Wu, S.-C. (2015) Does uncertain demand affect service quality? *International Journal of Hospitality Management* 46(April), 6–78.

Connell, J., Page, S.J. and Meyer, D. (2015) Visitor attractions and events: responding to seasonality. *Tourism Management* 46, 283–298.

Lovelock, C. and Wirtz, J. (2011) *Services Marketing: People, Technology, Strategy*, Global edn. Pearson, Boston, Massachusetts, pp. 250–271.

Madangolu, M. and Ozdemir, O. (2016) Is more better? The relationship between meeting space capacity and hotel operating performance. *Tourism Management* 52(February), 74–81.

Ponting, J. and O'Brien, D. (2015) Regulating 'Nirvana': sustainable surf tourism in a climate of increasing regulation. *Sport Management Review* 18, 99–110.

REFERENCES

Beedie, P. and Hudson, S. (2003) Emergence of mountain-based adventure tourism. *Annals of Tourism Research* 30(3), 625–643.

Belobab, P., Odoni, A. and Barnhart, C. (eds) (2009) *The Global Airline Industry*. Wiley, Chichester, UK.

Branch, A.E. and Robarts, M. (2014) *Branch's Elements of Shipping*. Routledge, London.

Connell, J., Page, S. and Meyer, D. (2015) Visitor attractions and events: responding to seasonality. *Tourism Management* 46, 283–298.

Constantanidis, E. and Diercjx, R.H.J. (2014) Airline price discrimination: a practice of yield management or customer profiling. *EMAC Conference Paper*, Valencia (June), Spain.

Gillam, G., Simmons, K., Stevenson, D. and Weiss, E. (2014) Line, line, everywhere a line: cultural considerations for waiting line managers. *Business Horizons* 57, 533–539.

Hong, L.J., Xu, X. and Zhang, S.H. (2015) Capacity reservation for time-sensitive service providers: an application in seaport management. *European Journal of Operational Research* 245, 470–479.

Janakirman, N., Meyer, R.J. and Hoch, S.J. (2011) The psychology of decisions to abandon waits for service. *Journal of Marketing Research* XLVIII(December), 970–984.

Johnston, R., Clark, G. and Shulver, M. (2012) *Service Operations Management: Improving Service Delivery*, 4th edn. Pearson, Harlow, UK.

Kalakou, S., Psaraki-Kalouptsidi, V. and Moura, F. (2015) Future airport terminals: new technologies promise capacity gains. *Journal of Air Transport Management* 42, 203–212.

Klassen, J.K. and Rohleder, T.R. (2000) Combining operations and marketing to manage capacity and demand in service. *Service Industries Journal* 2, 1–30.

Kokkinou, A. and Cranage, D.A. (2013) Using self-service technology to reduce customer waiting times. *International Journal of Hospitality Management* 33, 435–445.

Liu, S. (2012) The impact of forced use on customer adoption of self-service technologies. *Computers in Human Behaviour* 28, 1194–1201.

Lovelock, C. and Wirtz, J. (2011) *Services Marketing: People, Technology, Strategy*, Global edn. Pearson, Boston, Massachusetts.

Maister, D.H. (1985) The psychology of waiting lines. In: Czepiel, J.A., Solomon, M.R. and Suprenant, C. (eds) *The Service Encounter*. Lexington Books, Lexington, Massachusetts, 113–123.

Sasser, W.E. (1976) Match supply and demand in service industries. *Harvard Business Review* 54(6), 133–140.

Tribe, J. (2005) *The Economics of Leisure and Tourism*, 3rd edn. Butterworth-Heinemann, Oxford, UK.

Wang, L. (2012) Relationship or revenue: potential management conflicts between customer relationship management and hotel revenue management. *International Journal of Hospitality Management* 31, 864–874.

Wangenheim, F.v. and Bayón, T. (2007) Behavioral consequences of overbooking service capacity. *Journal of Marketing* 71(October), 36–47.

Wittmer, A. (2011) Acceptance of self-service check-in at Zurich airport. *Research in Transportation Business & Management* 1, 136–143.

chapter 7

Service Culture

LEARNING OBJECTIVES

- To define service culture;
- To appreciate the importance of linking culture to employee and customer engagement;
- To adopt an engaging service culture for competitive advantage;
- To understand the sources of service culture conflict;
- To appreciate why an event organization's culture is vital to service excellence, productivity and competitive advantage.

INTRODUCTION

The strong link between an organization's culture and its performance has been widely recognized by both practitioners and academics. For continuing relationships and engaged customers and employees it is vital for organizations to be equipped with an effective employee–customer focused culture. Put simply, without such a culture, organizations should not expect survival, let alone success, in the long-term. So, what are its key components and characteristics?

An organization's service culture in any sector is difficult to define and can be divided into many different types. Examples include those emphasizing employee engagement, power and results, constant organizational change and those that under-invest in their workforce. Furthermore, many organizations in the LETS industry embed a range of strategies that aim to improve their service culture in a systematic and strategic way. This chapter will identify a number of these strategies, including corporate social responsibility and sustainability. Many organizations and in particular those within the LETS industry define their service culture as 'a way of behaving, thinking and acting that is learned and shared by the organizations' members' (Ford *et al.*, 2012: 119). In fact, the Ritz-Carlton defines their service culture as simply as: 'It's the way we do things around here'. In more detail, Lovelock *et al.* (2009: 296) define service culture as:

- Shared ideas of what is important in an organization; and
- Shared values and beliefs of why those *things* are important.

For example, over the last 7 years, Hilton Worldwide has focused on aligning their widespread organization and culture around a shared vision, mission, values and set of key strategic priorities. These foundational elements have enabled their success and ensure that they have a common sense of who they are, where they are going and what they stand for as a company. Travel with Purpose, their corporate responsibility strategy, is embedded in the culture and throughout their business. It allows them to take advantage of their global footprint and scale while also realizing the need for local solutions (Nasetta, 2015).

In terms of sharing these values and beliefs, some organizations within the LETS industry such as the Ritz-Carlton, Marriott, JetBlue Airlines and the London Olympic Games, teach employees core values instead of implementing a rule-book culture. It was evident in Chapter 4 how the Olympic Games Committee used their values to recruit the right volunteers or Olympic Games Makers. Also, adopting this style of service culture often empowers and engages employees into making their own decisions. Certainly within the LETS service environment where the majority of service encounters are face to face and create moments of truth, strong cultural values are vital in ensuring their employees do the right things the right way for their customers.

For example, the Ritz-Carlton translates its service culture into the New Gold Standards and includes five leadership principles for creating a 'legendary customer experience' (Michelli, 2008). These principles include:

Principle 1 Define and refine (Communicating core identity and culture).
Principle 2 Empower through trust (Select – Do not Hire, Trust).
Principle 3 It's not about you (Build a business focused on others, support front-line empathy).
Principle 4 Deliver Wow! (The ultimate guest experience, turn WOW into action).
Principle 5 Leave a lasting footprint (Aspire, Achieve, Teach, Sustainability and Stewardship).

Michelli (2008) suggests that success of the Ritz-Carlton's service culture is largely dependent on a highly engaged workforce, creating a highly engaged customer base. The Ritz-Carlton's leadership objectively examines and improves engagement in both these sectors of the business by utilizing the Human Sigma approach as described in Chapter 7. To assess the engagement of staff, Ritz-Carlton administers the Q^{12} tool (Employee Engagement Metric). The data led to a renewed effort to increase the engagement of professionals and staff. Examples of engagement at the Ritz-Carlton include: 'By asking our Ladies and Gentlemen (employees and customers) how they perceive our efforts to create an environment where they can grow and make a purposeful difference, we can make adjustments in the work environment that help our people drive our key business objectives' (Michelli, 2008).

Ritz-Carlton leaders have executed action plans that have been developed at the department (local) level for each of the company's properties (including making employee engagement part of management performance rewards and prioritizing staff engagement as a key business factor). Accordingly, in Ritz-Carlton properties where employee engagement improves, the hotel's revPAR (revenue per available room) increases at a rate higher than in hotels that did not show Q[12] improvement (Michelli, 2008).

Consistent with their quest for excellence, Ritz-Carlton listened to the purported advantages of measuring customer engagement (a metric of the emotional connection and perceived fit held by a customer toward a business, and overall customer loyalty). Ritz-Carlton further adopted the CE[11] customer engagement metric – the measurement for customer engagement intuitively fits a business that is committed to offering the guest an emotional experience and long-term loyalty (Fleming and Asplund, 2007). In 2003, Ritz-Carlton agreed to conduct a pilot test and the results identified that the organization has further increased revenues through attention to customer engagement, a stronger metric than customer satisfaction.

At the Ritz-Carlton, CE[11] is well understood and valued by management; however, time has been taken to help front-line staff understand what customer engagement means, how it is measured, and the relationship between the results of CE metrics and the overall viability of the business (Michelli, 2008). Specifically, Human Sigma identifies the importance of measuring and managing locally, whereas the Ritz-Carlton localizes to ensure that information is readily available to all employees. Therefore Ritz-Carlton adopts an engaging service culture where ideas of what is important within the organization are shared and valued.

As suggested by Michelli (2008) and agreed by Marr (2012), customer engagement measurement has to go beyond an infrequent exercise of data collection. To truly build life-long customers, receive recognition for service and quality, enhance customer spending patterns and produce customer evangelism, businesses must place the information they receive from customers directly in the view of leadership and the front line. The open-communication policies and involvement of the employees in the planning of their work and decision making drive employee engagement and reflect sound business sense. It's about creating an engaging service culture with both customers and employees. Mitchelli suggests 'an engaged workforce personally invests in success and business growth, while creating an engaged clientele' (Michelli, 2008: 44).

Creating an engaging service culture can also involve embedding corporate social responsibility (CSR) into corporate culture. CSR is a term associated with the activities that an organization is performing for the benefit of the community it serves. Certainly, LETS organizations have been involved in CSR for many years, but it is clear that many services such as events, tour operators and airlines are becoming more and more socially conscious. For example, many LETS services recruit CSR ambassadors to support the statement that 'care for the environment and community is important in our organization's culture'. For example, British Airways are really passionate about corporate social responsibility – 'we even have a community learning centre, where local schools can visit for the day and learn all about BA' (Fig. 7.1). Within the community,

Fig. 7.1. BA Community Learning Centre, London.

BA employees are encouraged in their teams to support local initiatives – 'last year our team went to a local dementia day care centre in uniform and helped serve the lunches and organize social activities' (BA Employee, 2015). Additionally, on a larger scale, BA have a charity partnership with Comic Relief called 'Flying Start'. This project runs collections on-board and raises money at a number of corporate events. BA raised £2 million on-board alone last year!

Moreover, allowing employees time to volunteer or recruiting volunteers is widely acknowledged as an integral component of a LETS company's CSR activity. However, as noted in Chapter 4, managing volunteers and understanding their expectations is vital to its success. It must also be acknowledged that small to medium sized businesses (SMEs) may find allowing employees time to volunteer difficult due to the lack of resources.

Many LETS services set strategies that consider the local community and the impact of the activities on the environment. For example, Hilton Worldwide's sustainability practices are embedded within the business' culture where hotel teams drive local solutions that result in new opportunities for youth, the development of responsible supply chains, conservation of scarce natural resources, as well as greater cultural understanding and encouragement of human rights. Each of these examples demonstrates shared value, not only for the business but also for society. Some examples include:

- Reducing energy use and carbon output by 20.2%, waste output by 26.8% and water use by 13.1% since 2009;
- Announcing our global 'Open Doors' commitment that aims to impact at least 1 million young people by 2019 by helping them to reach their full potential;
- Achieving ISO 50001 certification for energy management across our entire portfolio of hotels;
- Hiring over 2000 veterans since launching Operation: Opportunity in 2013;
- Hosting over 600 career awareness events as part of Careers@HiltonLive, impacting more than 73,000 young people;
- Training nearly 2000 general managers and department heads on child trafficking awareness and reaching more than 45,000 Team Members through our Code of Conduct training;
- Activating nearly 2400 global projects during our second annual Global Week of Service and achieving nearly 200,000 volunteer hours across our global footprint;
- Participating for the first time in the Carbon Disclosure project;
- Supporting more than 700 hotels with our Living Sustainably environmental awareness campaign.

(Hilton Worldwide, Travel with Purpose Agenda, 2015)

In many situations including those mentioned and within community leisure and event services, the main strategic objectives are to provide high quality community engagement. Not only can engagement with the external community be a strategic objective but research by Swanson (2014) reveals that embedding CSR into corporate culture strengthens employee engagement. Therefore both business and society benefit. There is significant evidence to support the engaged employee argument (Gallup, 2006; MacLeod and Clarke, 2009) including reduced staff turnover, higher levels of productivity and profitability, fewer sick days, increased levels of innovation and improved morale. However, these employees within the LETS industry work in some of the most demanding roles. Considering this, we will next discuss the sources of service culture conflict.

SOURCES OF SERVICE CULTURE CONFLICT

Not only is service culture difficult to define, cultural change is one of the hardest areas for organizations to achieve (Williams and Buswell, 2003). For instance, one of the most common organizational change initiatives as mentioned in the first edition (Williams and Buswell, 2003) is Total Quality Management (TQM). However, since then, many firms have labelled TQM a failure and started to cut back their quality budgets. In many cases, the failure of TQM was due to the culture remaining the same. The initiative was often treated as a technique or programme of change, not as a fundamental shift in the organization's direction, values and culture. In other words, when TQM initiatives were implemented independent of a culture change, they were unsuccessful. For this to be successful, Senge (2014) argues that organizations need to discover how to tap in to people's commitment and capacity to learn at all levels. Senge labels these types of organizations as 'learning organizations' where 'people continually expand their capacity to create the results they truly desire, where new and expansive patterns of thinking are nurtured, where collective aspiration is set free, and where people are continually learning to see the whole together'.

Also in the first edition, Williams and Buswell (2003) explain how the essence of attaining service culture is through employee empowerment and empowerment is the flexibility and self-judgement required of many front-line staff. In a later publication (Williams and Thwaites, 2006), 'naturalistic decision making' is identified as an important approach linking to empowerment and as a means for improving service quality. Certainly however, it could be argued that seasonal staff or volunteers working in the LETS industry find it difficult to be motivated with such concepts. Often with limited training and a minimum wage culture, front-line employees limit their levels of responsibility and engagement with the organization and the customer. Furthermore, organizations, including management or leaders, can also limit levels of front-line empowerment. Often they see the front line as 'mistakes waiting to happen' and therefore do not let the power out! Subsequently, front-line staff cannot respond with the flexibility to customer needs, non-routine encounters and service failures.

Certainly, a strong service culture as noted is where the organization focuses on employee and customer engagement. A good way to illustrate this is through the inverted pyramid (Fig. 7.2) devised by Lovelock *et al.* (2009), which highlights the importance of the front line in achieving a strong and valued culture.

Therefore, as a requirement, ensuring staff understand their role in the service encounter must be within a supportive organizational culture. Despite this, many service organizations still continue to script and standardize service encounters, some of the most 'shocking'

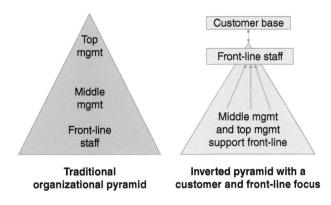

Legend: ‡ = Service encounters, or 'Moments of Truth.'

Fig. 7.2. The inverted organizational pyramid (Lovelock *et al.*, 2009).

examples of repetitive service scripts being found within the banking and retail sectors. In many cases, the importance of the service encounter is not a shared cultural value but instead perceived as an opportunity to maximize sales. Not surprisingly, therefore, Lovelock and Wirtz (2011) suggest that too much rigidity causes role stress and the causes of role stress can include:

- *Person versus Role:* Conflicts between what jobs require and the employee's own personality and beliefs; and
- *Organization versus Customer:* Dilemma whether to follow company rules or to satisfy customer demands.

At the same time, in continuous occupations that have no single end product as described by Riley *et al.* (2002), service workers often create the satisfied customer as an object (end product). Therefore, new approaches to service quality should include the notion that role interpretation can take place during a service encounter (Riley, 2007). Riley argues that an employee's interpretation of their role is not a constant but is a device that can be manipulated both in a self-seeking manner and as a defence mechanism that can be applied where coping with stress is required. One of the strongest explanatory theories of how people conduct themselves and cope in encounters is that of emotional labour (Riley, 2007). Riley suggests that if coping is part of the encounter process, then it will inevitably influence the outcome of that process: the quality of service.

Emotional labour (emotions management)

Emotional labour research has been conducted in a broad range of contexts and more recently in tourism (Kinman, 2009; Van Dijk *et al.*, 2009). Emotional labour, as described by Morris and Feldman (1996), is the effort, planning and control required to display organizationally desired emotions during interpersonal transactions. However, Hochschild (1983), who first introduced the concept, specifies that expectations exist regarding the appropriate or inappropriate emotional display of employees whose jobs involve a considerable degree of contact with the public. However, more recently, it has been recognized that emotional labour should be conceptualized as a subjective phenomenon encompassing different dimensions (Mann, 1999). Therefore, emotional labour is described by Mann (1999) as the effort required to fake or suppress an emotional display because of the demands of the work role. The Emotional Labour Inventory developed by Mann (1999) assesses three components of emotional labour.

1. Expectations/rules for emotional display – rules or scripts.
2. Emotional suppression – suppress to hide negative emotions.
3. Emotional faking – fake 'not being me'.

Similarly, Van Dijk *et al.* (2009) describe it as the management of emotional display by staff to satisfy organizational expectations during voice-to-voice or face-to-face interpersonal interactions. Furthermore, emotional labour is considered by Kinman (2009) to include both an external component (employees' perceptions of organizational emotional display rules and the demands made upon them to comply with these rules) and an internal component (the effort involved in regulating emotions in order to display emotions that are required by the job role but not genuinely felt, or to suppress inappropriate emotions that are felt). For example, when performing emotional labour, a tour guide can choose to either display false emotion (surface acting) or try and manage experienced emotion (deep acting). Any attempt by an employee to surface act and fake emotion may lead to 'leakage' in that true emotions are detected by service receivers resulting in poorer customer service performance than if a genuine display of emotion is employed (Grandey *et al.*, 2005). Deep acting is a more motivated display of managed felt emotion for the purpose of customer service interactions and, as such, is suggested to have provided benefits beyond that of surface acting (Grandey *et al.*, 2005). Both Ashforth and Humphey (1993) and Morris and Feldman (1997) recognize that workers may genuinely feel the emotions displayed. In turn, Lam and Chen (2012) developed and tested a model of emotional labour in the hotel industry using affective event theory. The results showed that negative emotions relate positively to surface acting and negatively to deep acting. Furthermore, surface acting leads to lower job satisfaction, whereas deep acting leads to higher job satisfaction, service quality and lower turnover.

As suggested earlier, Hochschild (1983) theorized the consequences of emotional labour based on the service provider's capacity to strike a balance between the requirements of the self and the demands of the work role. Consequently, display rules are learned norms regarding when and how emotion should be experienced in public (Ekman, 1972). For example, LETS organizations implement display rules to regulate behaviour and service providers are expected to act friendly and disguise anger (Augustine and Joseph, 2008). This is apparent in Disney parks where cast members are 'on show' and with display rules being to interact with guests, smiling and having fun and providing that all important magical service. In particular, emotional display rules may be communicated through mission statements, staff handbooks, training and appraisals. Rules and scripts are often enforced through customer and mystery shopping feedback (Erstad, 1998). Furthermore, it has been observed that customer service providers are typically subordinate to their consumers, and that their interactions with members of the public tend to be more routine and often scripted, thus constraining opportunities for personal expression (Grandey and Fisk, 2006). The quality of employee–customer interaction, and how to enhance this, is therefore a considerable concern for management.

LETS-based service provision therefore requires emotion management in the service provider and the service receiver in order to meet service quality expectations (Lashley *et al.*, 2005). Van Dijk *et al.* (2009) suggest the need to engage in emotion management through the use of emotional labour for tourism-based employees is going to increase. As consumer demands and expectations for quality service rise, so too does the demand from employers or organizational representatives to satisfy these expectations.

It could be argued, therefore, that emotional labour is one of the main factors that determine the perception of service quality, and the interaction between the service provider and customer is the core of service experiences that influences customer's perceptions of service quality. However, no universal conclusion exists about the consequences of emotional labour, a major reason for the confusion in results being the lack of clear definitions of what actually constitutes emotional labour. Researchers have recognized the importance of individual characteristics in determining the consequences of emotional labour (Wharton, 1999), and Chu and Murrmann (2006) created the Hospitality Emotional Labour Scale (HELS) as an instrument to better measure the emotions of front-line employees (see Table 7.1).

Furthermore, Sarbin and Allen (1968) identify eight levels of role involvement along a continuum of self-role differentiation. They describe role theory as the enactment of roles in various social settings.

Role theory

Role theory is based on a dramaturgical metaphor (Solomon *et al.*, 1985). The study of a role, described by Solomon *et al.* (1985) as the cluster of social cues that guide and direct an individual's behaviour in a given setting, is the study of the conduct associated with certain socially defined positions rather than of the particular individuals who occupy these positions. Constructs adapted from role theory have been used to explain consumer behaviour, especially with regards to expectation formation (Sheth, 1967). A role theoretic approach (Solomon *et al.*, 1985) emphasizes the nature of people as social actors who learn behaviour appropriate to the positions they occupy in society and each role that a person plays is learned. Furthermore, one's confidence that one is 'doing the right thing' leads to satisfaction with a performance (termed role validation) and can be linked to the employee zone of tolerance theory (as noted in Chapter 4) and subsequent success in interacting with others who are playing their respective roles. At the same time, within LETS organizations, the desire to perform a service role well should also be a function of a group- or team-based performance (Solomon *et al.*, 1985; Fleming and Asplund, 2007), as service personnel are typically members of an organization/department or team. However, recruiting volunteers for sporting events such as the Glasgow 2014 Commonwealth Games, can often result in insecurity over one's appointment

Table 7.1. Emotional labour scale (Chu and Murrmann, 2006: 1184).

1	I fake a good mood when interacting with customers.
2	I fake the emotions I show when dealing with customers.
3	I put on a mask in order to express the right emotions for my job.
4	The emotions I show to customers match what I truly feel.
5	I behave in a way that differs from how I really feel.
6	I put on an act in order to deal with customers in an appropriate way.
7	My interactions with customers are very robotic.

or volunteer role (Getz, 2012). For this reason, the issue of accountability can be viewed as a question of commitment to a role identity.

Certainly, the evidence suggests that viewing service encounters from a role theory perspective has a number of advantages. As noted above, role theory compels us to adopt an interactive approach, since roles are defined in a social context. The concept of role expectation is, therefore, an especially powerful one in determining the quality of the service experience. However, issues may occur because the participants do not share common role definitions (Solomon *et al.*, 1985). Nevertheless, role theory and the related concepts make it possible to consider both customer and employee interactions and connections. Heskett *et al.* (1997) labelled this connection between employee and customer experiences the 'satisfaction mirror', which vividly conveys the notion that business success results from employee satisfaction being 'reflected' in terms of customer satisfaction. Therefore the emphasis is on the joint behaviours of the 'actors' and since control of the LETS service experience is a crucial area of managerial concern and a difficult task to accomplish, further analysis of these theories is important.

Social identity

Of particular relevance to the concepts of role theory and the emphasis on joint behaviours is social identification, which reflects the extent to which an individual senses a oneness or sameness with others in a social group (Tajfel and Turner, 1986). For example, this could be related to LETS employees working within a team or the customer's interaction with those employees. It is most commonly manifested as references to the social group 'we'. Moreover, research by Solnet (2006) displays factors that increase a sense of social identity making people: more willing to communicate; more open to others' communications; and more likely to interpret communicative actions in similar ways (Haslam *et al.*, 2003). At the same time, inter-role congruence is a term described by Solomon *et al.* (1985) as the degree of agreement between both parties involved in the service transaction regarding the appropriate roles to be played. For example, many interactions within the LETS industry such as hotel check-in are learned norms, meaning service employees and customers understand the service system and roles are quickly made and acted upon. However, a lack of congruence in roles towards communication can lead to decreased efficacy of dyadic communication performance. It seems then likely that the accurate mutual comprehension of role expectations is a prerequisite for a quality service experience (Bitner *et al.*, 1990). Furthermore, it could be argued that problems arise when there is a discrepancy somewhere in the system or a role discrepancy. Examples include, inconsistencies with expectations such as the employee's perception of the job duties differing from the customer's expectations or the customer's conception of the customer's role varying from the employee's notion of that role (Solomon *et al.*, 1985).

Power imbalance

Not only are there inconsistencies with expectations during the service encounter, but also in many dyads of social interaction; one person is more powerful than the other (Lee, 2010).

Power is not necessarily owned by an individual. For example, in the tourism industry a service employee's expertise, knowledge and judgement would place the service employee in a position of power over the customer. Such differences in power may place less powerful service customers in an uncomfortable position. However, when customers are not dependent upon the service provider, competitor alternatives are often sourced or the use of self-service technologies utilized.

Typically, research on power imbalance often focuses on the customer. However, perceived power imbalance is apparent in service employees. In short, when an employee is 'serving' a customer who is perceived to have greater social power, such as first class passengers, the employee's cognition, emotion, communication pattern and behaviours are adjusted to the situation. According to the theory of 'personal control', individuals in this situation of limited control in an environment tend to perceive emotional stress, anxiety and frustration more easily than those in the situation of higher control (Averill, 1973). The theory of 'self-induced' dependence explains that the perception of lower status makes one feel less competent in performing the necessary tasks for goal attainment (Lockwood, 1958; Lewis and Blanchard, 1971). However, both employees and customers are often responsible for performing specific actions that negatively influence the quality of the service experience. However, the desire for affiliation stems from the need for human interaction and friendly relationships along with the necessity to be accepted and liked by others (McClelland, 1961). Furthermore, the need for power stems directly from the desire to direct and make a difference (McClelland, 1961). This type of need, as observed by Jelencic (2011), usually exhibits itself in one or two ways: the first is viewed as undesirable by others in that they often desire and want power over others; the second and more desirable need for power relates to institutional power where individuals wish to control and support the work of others in order to progress the aims and ambitions of the organization.

Social psychology

Given that mutual understanding is a desirable goal for service encounters, how do we go about achieving it? A review of the social psychology literature reveals two concepts that help explain mutual understanding: customer–employee identification and employee–customer identification. These are two distinct concepts, which are, however, strongly interrelated and will be discussed below. First, however, at a social psychological level, each act is a purposive transaction whose outcome is dependent upon coordinated actions of both participants (Solomon *et al.*, 1985). As noted, much of social behaviour consists of joint activity and a major task for the interacting person is the mutual coordination of appropriate behaviour with the other person (Thibaut and Kelley, 1959). Social psychology implies that interpersonal behaviour is people taking up roles as discussed earlier (Broderick, 1998; Parker and Ward, 2000). However, Jones and Lockwood (2004) describe the perspective of social psychology as not the differences between individuals but the nature of the interaction itself, between people and their environments, and the sharing of this behaviour and experience. More recently, Riley (2007) suggests that, in terms of customer–employee service encounters, three specific themes emerge.

1. Successful encounters are something to do with job satisfaction.
2. Encounters are potentially stressful to the employee.
3. As a consequence coping strategies are required by employees.

Critically, however, emotion work as described by Bolton (2004) is a risky business that requires adaptability rather than rigidity and routinization. Furthermore, when socio-psychological boundaries are dissolved through employee–customer identification, the collectivistic aspects of the identity become more salient. This collectivistic orientation tends to foster relational exchanges, in contrast to individualistic identity orientations, which maintain a norm of transactional exchange (Flynn, 2005). Relational forms of exchange are analogous to customer orientation as outlined by Saxe and Weitz (1982), because each interaction is embedded in the context of a long-term commitment to exchanging value. This reasoning leads the researcher to construe that the more perceived boundaries between employees and customers are dissolved, and an identity emerges (employee↔customer identification), the more front-line employees will seek to exceed customer's expectations.

Customer–employee identification

As noted therefore, customer–employee identification is a type or classification of social identification and the rationale behind this comes from the social psychology literature. During the service encounter, the service employee image interacts with the customer's self-concept generating a subjective experience. It is argued that people try to protect and enhance their self-concept by affiliating with people whom they perceive to be the same as them (Turner, 1985). From a social psychological perspective, individuals attempt to make sense of one another in order to guide their own actions, as well as the social interaction process with others (Fiske, 1993). During the consumption process, a particular product/service user-image interacts with the consumer's self-concept, generating a subjective experience referred to as self-image congruence (Sirgy *et al.*, 1997). During the service encounter, customers may use some congruent traits that are associated with the human personality and structures that can be used to make sense of other people (Leyens and Fiske, 1994), and many form these impressions in even the briefest social interactions (Ambady and Rosenthal, 1992). McGinnies and Ward (1980) argue that perceived similarity between customers and employees facilitates communications concerning specific service attributes. Furthermore, Coulter and Coulter (2002) believe that perceived similarity helps individuals to reduce interpersonal barriers, allows them to identify with others on a personal basis and generates a level of trust and assessment of others according to perceived similarity with themselves. Later, Jamal and Adelowore (2008) extended the concepts of self-congruence to the context of customer–employee interactions in the retail banking sector. They argue that, during the service interaction, the service employee image interacts with the customer's self-concept to generate a subjective experience called 'self-employee congruence'. The findings of their empirical research revealed that self–employee congruence has a significant impact on customer interactions, relationships, satisfaction and loyalty. In a similar approach, Stinglhamber *et al.* (2002) identified the importance of affective commitment in the service encounter. They developed a three-component model to examine the extent to which the employee felt 'a connection with customers', agreed that they 'were on the same team', used 'we' rather than 'they' to describe customers, and identified strongly with customers. Such findings reflect the theory of homophily (Lazarsfeld and Merton, 1964), which argues that individuals enjoy the comfort of interacting with others who are similar to themselves.

Employee–customer identification

As suggested earlier, employee–customer identification is simply the type or classification of social identification. Therefore, an employee's identification with the customer is how much the employee senses a oneness or sameness with them. Other drivers of employee–customer identification are how front-line employees construe the distinctiveness, similarity and prestige of the customer's identity (Ashforth and Mael, 1989). For example, many roles in the LETS sector, such as those of front-line employees, inherently contain a substantial relational component (Sluss and Ashforth, 2007), where employees work at the boundary between the company and the customer. In these cases, conditions are ripe for employees to assess their place in a complex social landscape (Lockwood, 1958). Certainly, the evidence suggests that employee–customer identification enhances the quality of the service encounter.

Fundamentally, however, for front-line employees who span the boundary between the company and its customers, the complexity of the 'social landscape' may result in an assessment of the self-concept in relation to the organization and its customers. It was noted in Chapter 4 how the Human Sigma scale measures organization identification and the organization can be a powerful emblem of group identity for employees. Nevertheless, recent advances in social identity theory and management suggest that employees can identify with more than the organizational identity (Ashforth *et al.*, 2008). It has been argued that relational identities, those which relate to a work relationship with another individual or group (Sluss and Ashforth, 2007), can also be a powerful source of self-definition. Consequently, it is suggested that employees identify with customers (employee–customer identification). By identifying with customers, employees perceive themselves to be relatively interchangeable exemplars within the social category, where the employee–customer relationship is a basis for self-definition (Sluss and Ashforth, 2007). For example, employee–customer identification functions independently from identification with the company. However, the two can coexist, converging or competing with one another (Sluss and Ashforth, 2008).

In summary, employee–customer identification is a new concept, but the notion that employees can construe the disposition or values of those on the other side of the corporate boundary is already present in the literature. As such, customer–employee identification is thought of as a mirror image of employee–customer identification where customers also identify with the employees.

Organization identification

Given that the two can coexist, organization identification is a form of social identification in which an employee or customer experiences a sense of oneness or sameness with the organization. Ashforth and Mael (1989) first introduced organizational identification to the field of management and later validated a scale to measure it. It built on Ouchi's suggestion (1981) that goal or value congruence between employees and the organization may motivate employees to behave in ways that are consistent with the organization's objectives. According to Dutton and Dukerich (1994), organizational identification aligns individual's interests and behaviours with interests and behaviours that benefit the organization. Therefore, employees who strongly identify with the organization are likely to focus on tasks that benefit the whole organization rather than purely self-interest objectives (Bell and Menguc, 2002).

Indeed, it has been observed by Anderson and Onyemah (2006) that employees can struggle, and sometimes receive conflicting signals from management, as to whether the customer or company is 'king'. Critically, therefore, LETS organizations need to show that the two identities are positively related. Exploring further, organizational identification has successfully predicted behaviour among art museum members (Bhattacharya *et al.*, 1995), employees (Wieseke *et al.*, 2007) and customers (Ahearne *et al.*, 2005). It has also been implicated as a mediating process for corporate social responsibility (Sen and Bhattacharya, 2001), leadership (Wieseke *et al.*, 2007) and the service profit chain (Homburg *et al.*, 2009).

Before we conclude this chapter, a case study will be shared in order to represent some of the theories and principles discussed.

SERVICE CULTURE INDUSTRY INSIGHTS

Case study 7.1 highlights the vital components as discussed in this chapter for adopting an engaging service culture.

CONCLUSIONS

To conclude, this chapter has analysed the underpinning theories and concepts that contribute to managing service culture. Whilst evaluating service culture concepts, determinants and causes of conflict, it is apparent that it is increasingly being viewed as a highly complex and multidimensional process of interaction between the customers, employees and the organization. Furthermore, issues related to social identity, role discrepancies and power imbalance can all contribute and affect the organizational culture. The examples such as Ritz-Carlton, TGI Fridays in Chapter 5 and the case study highlighted in this chapter, all support the view that employee engagement is a vital component of service culture and in turn customer engagement. Understandably, other examples also emphasize the importance of organizational

Case Study 7.1. Establishing an engaging service culture in an event organization is vital to service excellence, productivity and competitive advantage

Service Culture Definition: As 'a shared purpose where everyone is focused on creating value for others inside and outside the organization'.

Event: University Experience Days (UEDs).

Event Duration: These events are 4-hour taster experiences.

Attendees: Target 16–17-year-old college students based in the UK.

Event Opportunities: Provide an exciting experience, so that they should consider us as an appealing study destination if they progress their education after college.

Event Challenges: In particular, the raising of UK student tuition fees from £3375 to £9000 per annum in 2012 was a critical event. This affected higher education significantly; it resulted in high increases in consumer expectations. This was not just confined to current students paying the new higher rates, but also prospective students who attended recruitment events as they researched their options.

Service Culture: We appreciate that people are crucial to the success of our UEDs. This applies to both our front-line staff and visiting college students and staff. As change is so common, we have a strong emphasis on gaining both qualitative and quantitative feedback from all those involved in our events. To elaborate, we have strong interests in the level of service that our frontline staff produce and many of our frontline employees are aged between 18 and 20 with limited work experience. During each event, we employ buddy/mentoring 1-2-1 relationships. Participants are paired in twos where new staff are partnered with more accomplished colleagues. This allows us to build friendships and mutual learning/development relationships amongst those involved. We empower them to make decisions by themselves as well. Where problems might arise, if they feel capable of repairing issues by themselves without the help of their supervisors, we allow them the powers to do that.

In our UEDs, our employees' quality of networking and communication with guests is important to the overall success of our events. Our frontline staff are predominantly current students; this is significant because research tells us college learners value their experiences and opinions as much as that of academic university staff. An important responsibility which our frontline staff host are our university campus tours. They are approximately 75 minutes long and have group sizes averaging at 15 persons. While working, they are also tasked with being our eyes and ears by listening in to and observing visitor interactions and conversations amongst each other. As tours conclude, they feed back their information in quality circles. These are team meetings where all frontline employees collectively

(Continued)

Case Study 7.1. **Continued.**

Fig. 7.3. **University Experience Days.**

meet with their supervisor. This allows everyone an opportunity to feed back and share information with all colleagues. These are forms of self and group reflection that help to ensure everyone feels valued. Not only do we receive feedback about the event in question, but we also gain information about how we work as a team. For instance, recently our staff said they did not like the new orange T-shirts they had to wear. Others took exception to how some academic staff looked down on them during our UEDs. Afterwards, we are able to respond to such feedback and make sure that it is visible to staff so they see we do respect and value their opinions. We celebrate outstanding service by rewarding the individuals or teams concerned and then naming them amongst the wider team.

culture, and the contribution of quality tools, systems and approaches should not be forgotten. Therefore, the following chapter addresses these aspects.

QUESTIONS

1. How do organizations create emotional connections between employees and customers? In your experience, what organizations are able to do this?

2. What is emotional labour? Explain the ways in which it may cause stress for employees in specific jobs. Give suitable examples.

3. Do all service organizations need to create strong human connections?

4. Will a service-oriented culture lead to customer loyalty?

FURTHER READING

Lam, W. and Chen, Z. (2012) When I put on my service mask: determinants and outcomes of emotional labour among hotel service providers according to affective event theory. *International Journal of Hospitality Management* 31(1), 3–11.

Michelli, J.A. (2008) *The New Gold Standard*. McGrawHill, New York.

Solnet, D. (2006) Introducing employee social identification to customer satisfaction research: a hotel industry study. *Managing Service Quality* 16(6), 575–594.

Swanson, D. (2014) *Embedding CSR into Corporate Culture: Challenging the Executive*. Palgrave Macmillan, UK.

REFERENCES

Ahearne, M., Bhattacharya, C.B. and Gruen, T. (2005) Antecedents and consequences of customer-company identification: expanding the role of relationship marketing. *Journal of Applied Psychology* 90(3), 574.

Ambady, N. and Rosenthal, R. (1992) Thin slices of expressive behavior as predictors of interpersonal consequences: a meta-analysis. *Psychological Bulletin* 111(2), 256–274.

Anderson, E. and Onyemah, V. (2006) How right should the customer be? *Harvard Business Review* 84(7/8), 59–67.

Ashforth, B.E. and Humphery, R.H. (1993) Emotional labour in service roles: the influence of identity. *The Academy of Management Review* 18(1), 88–115.

Ashforth, B.E. and Mael, F.A. (1989) Social identity and the organization. *Academy of Management Review* 14(1), 20–39.

Ashforth, B.E., Harrison, S.H. and Corley, K.G. (2008) Identification in organizations: an examination of four fundamental questions. *Journal of Management* 34(3), 325–374.

Augustine, S.K. and Joseph, B. (2008) Emotional labour among the frontline employees of the hotel industry in India. In: Jauhari, V. (ed.) *Global Cases on Hospitality Industry*. The Howarth Press, New York.

Averill, J. (1973) Personal control over aversive stimuli and its relationship to stress. *Psychological Bulletin* 80(4), 286–303.

Bell, S.J. and Menguc, B. (2002) The employee-organization relationship, organizational citizenship behaviors, and superior service quality. *Journal of Retailing* 78(2), 131–146.

Bhattacharya, C.B., Rao, H. and Glynn, M.A. (1995) Understanding the bond of identification: an investigation of its correlates among art museum members. *Journal of Marketing* 59(4), 46–57.

Bitner, M.J., Booms, B.H. and Tetreault, M.S. (1990) The service encounter: diagnosing favourable and unfavourable incidents. *The Service Encounter* 54(1), 71–84.

Bolton, S. (2004) Conceptual confusions: emotion work as skilled work. In: Warhurst, C., Keep, E. and Grugulis, I. (eds) *Skills That Matter*. Palgrave/Macmillan, Basingstoke, UK, pp. 19–37.

Broderick, A. (1998) Role theory, role management and service performance. *Journal of Services Marketing* 12(5), 348–361.

Chu, K.H.L. and Murrmann, S.K. (2006) Development and validation of the hospitality emotional labor scale. *Tourism Management* 27(6), 1181–1191.

Coulter, K.S. and Coulter, R.A. (2002) Determinants of trust in a service provider: the moderating role of length of relationship. *Journal of Services Marketing* 16(1), 35–50.

Dutton, J.E. and Dukerich, C.V. (1994) Organizational images and member identification. *Administrative Science Quarterly* 39 (June), 239–263.

Ekman, P. (1972) Universal and cultural differences in facial expressions of emotion. In: Cole, J.R. (ed.) *Nebraska Symposium on Motivation.* University of Nebraska Press, Lincoln, Nebraska, pp. 207–283.

Erstad, M. (1998) Mystery shopping programmes and human resource management. *International Journal of Contemporary Hospitality Management* 10(1), 34–38.

Fiske, S. (1993) Social cognition and social perception. *Annual Review of Psychology* 44(2), 155–194.

Fleming, J.H. and Asplund, J. (2007) *Human Sigma: Managing the Employee-Customer Encounter.* Gallup Press, Washington, DC.

Flynn, F.J. (2005) Identity orientations and forms of social exchange in organizations. *Academy of Management Review* 30(4), 737–750.

Ford, C., Sturman, M. and Heaton, C. (2012) *Managing Quality Service in Hospitality*, International edn. Cengage, London.

Gallup (2006) Gallup Study: At Work, Feeling Good Matters. Available at: http://www.gallup.com/businessjournal/20311/work-feeling-good-matters.aspx (accessed 1 April 2015).

Getz, D. (2012) *Event Studies: Theory, Research and Policy for Planned Events.* Routledge, London.

Grandey, A. and Fisk, G. (2006) Display rules and strain in service jobs: what's fairness got to do with it? In: Perrewe, P. and Ganster, D. (eds) *Research in Occupational Stress and Wellbeing*, Vol. 3. Elsevier, Oxford, UK.

Grandey, A., Fisk, G., Mattila, A., Jensen, K. and Sideman, L.A. (2005) Is service with a smile enough? Authenticity of positive displays during service encounters. *Organisational Behaviour and Human Decision Processes* 91(1), 38–55.

Haslam, S.A., Postmes, T. and Ellemers, N. (2003) More than a metaphor: organizational identity makes organizational life possible. *British Journal of Management* 14(4), 357–369.

Heskett, J.L., Sasser, W.E. and Schlesinger, L.A. (1997) *The Service Profit Chain: How Leading Companies Link Profit and Growth to Loyalty, Satisfaction and Value.* Free Press, New York.

Hochschild, A. (1983) *The Managed Heart: Commercialisation of Human Feeling.* University of California Press, Berkeley, California.

Homburg, C., Wieseke, J. and Hoyer, W.D. (2009) Social identity and the service-profit chain. *Journal of Marketing* 73(2), 38–54.

Jamal, A. and Adelowore, A. (2008) Customer-employee relationship: the role of self-employee congruence. *European Journal of Marketing* 42(11/12), 1316–1345.

Jelencic, M. (2011) Motivation Theories: An Overview. Seminar Paper. Druck and Bindang, Norderstedt, Germany.

Jones, P.C. and Lockwood, A. (2004) *The Management of Hotel Operations.* Thomson, London.

Kinman, G. (2009) Emotional labour and strain in 'Front-Line' service employees: does mode of delivery matter? *Journal of Managerial Psychology* 24(2), 118–135.

Lam, W. and Chen, Z. (2012) When I put on my service mask: determinants and outcomes of emotional labor among hotel service providers according to affective event theory. *International Journal of Hospitality Management* 31(1), 3–11.

Lashley, C., Morrison, A. and Randall, S. (2005) More than a service encounter? Insights into the emotions of hospitality through special meal occasions. *Journal of Hospitality and Tourism Management* 12(1), 80–92.

Lazarsfeld, P. and Merton, R. (1964) Friendship as social process: a substantive and methodological analysis. In: Berger, M. (ed.) *Freedom and Control in Modern Society.* Octagon, New York.

Lee, J. (2010) Perceived power imbalance and customer dissatisfaction. *The Service Industries Journal* 30(7), 1113–1137.

Lewis, P. and Blanchard, E. (1971) Perception of choice and locus of control. *Psychological Reports* 28(1), 67–70.

Leyens, J.-P. and Fiske, S.T. (1994) Impression formation: from recitals to symphonie fantastique. In: Devine, P.G., Hamilton, D.L. and Ostrom, T.M. (eds) *Social Cognition: Impact on Social Psychology.* Academic Press, San Diego, California, pp. 39–75.

Lockwood, D. (1958) *The Blackcoated Worker: a study in class consciousness*. Clarendon Press, Oxford, UK.

Lovelock, C. and Wirtz, J. (2011) *Services Marketing: People, Technology, Strategy*. Pearson/Prentice-Hall, New Jersey.

Lovelock, C., Wirtz, J. and Chew, P. (2009) *Essentials of Services Marketing*. Pearson Education, South Asia.

MacLeod, D. and Clarke, N. (2009) *Engaging for Success: Enhancing Performance Through Employee Engagement*. Available at: http://www.acas.org.uk/media/pdf/7/6/08140-MacLeod-Clarkes-Concept-of-Employee-Engagement.pdf (accessed 28 March 2015).

Mann, S. (1999) Emotion at work: to what extent are we expressing, suppressing, or faking it? *European Journal of Work and Organizational Psychology* 8(3), 347–369.

Marr, B. (2012) *Key Performance Indicators (KPI)*. Financial Times/Prentice Hall, London.

McClelland, D. (1961) *The Achieving Society*. The Free Press, New York.

McGinnies, E. and Ward, C. (1980) Better liked than right: trustworthiness and expertise in credibility. *Personality and Social Psychological Bulletin* 6(September), 467–472.

Michelli, J.A. (2008) *The New Gold Standard*. McGraw Hill, New York.

Morris, J.A. and Feldman, D.C. (1996) The dimensions, antecedents, and consequences of emotional labour. *Academy of Management Review* 21(4), 986–1010.

Morris, J.A. and Feldman, D.C. (1997) Managing emotions in the workplace. *Journal of Management Issues* 9(3), 257–274.

Nasetta, C. (2015) President & CEO, Hilton Worldwide. Available at: http://cr.hiltonworldwide.com/approach/ceoMessage.php (accessed 24 March 2015).

Ouchi, W.G. (1981) *Theory Z: How American Businesses Can Meet the Japanese Challenge*. Avon, New York.

Parker, C. and Ward, P. (2000) An analysis of role adoptions and scripts during customer-to-customer encounters. *European Journal of Marketing* 43(34), 341–358.

Riley, M. (2007) Role interpretation during service encounters: a critical review of modern approaches to service quality management. *International Journal of Hospitality Management* 26(2), 409–420.

Riley, M., Ladkin, A. and Szivas, E. (2002) *Tourism Employment: Analysis and Planning*. Channel View, Clevedon, UK.

Sarbin, T.R. and Allen, V.L. (1968) Role Theory. In: Lindzey, G. and Aronson, E. (eds) *The Handbook of Social Psychology*. Addison-Wesley, Reading, Massachusetts.

Saxe, R. and Weitz, B.A. (1982) The SOCO scale: a measure of the customer orientation of salespeople. *Journal of Marketing Research* 19(3), 343–351.

Sen, S. and Bhattacharya, C.B. (2001) Does doing good always lead to doing better? Consumer reactions to corporate social responsibility. *Journal of Marketing Research* 38, 225–243.

Senge, P. (2014) *The Dance of Change: The Challenges to Sustaining Momentum in a Learning Organization*. Crown Business, UK.

Sheth, J.N. (1967) A review of buyer behaviour. *Management Science* 13(12), 8718–8756.

Sirgy, M., Grewal, D., Mangleburg, T., Park, J., Chon, K., Claiborne, C., Johar, J. and Berkman, H. (1997) Assessing the predictive validity of two methods of measuring self-image congruence. *Journal of the Academy of Marketing Science* 25(3), 229–241.

Sluss, D.M. and Ashforth, B.E. (2007) Relational identity and identification: defining ourselves through work relationships. *Academy of Management Review* 32(1), 9–32.

Sluss, D.M. and Ashforth, B.E. (2008) How relational and organizational identification converge: processes and conditions. *Organization Science* 19(6), 807–823.

Solnet, D. (2006) Introducing employee social identification to customer satisfaction research: a hotel industry study. *Managing Service Quality* 16(6), 575–594.

Solomon, M.R., Surprenant, C.F., Czepiel, J.A. and Gutman, E.G. (1985) A role theory perspective on dyadic interactions. *Journal of Marketing* 49(1), 99–111.

Stinglhamber, F., Bentein, K. and Vandenberghe, C. (2002) Extension of the three-component model of commitment to five foci: development of measures and a substantive test. *European Journal of Psychological Assessment* 18(2), 123–138.

Swanson, D. (2014) *Embedding CSR into Corporate Culture: Challenging the Executive.* Palgrave Macmillan, Basingstoke, UK.

Tajfel, H. and Turner, J.C. (1986) The social identity theory of inter-group behavior. In: Worchel, S. and Austin, L.W. (eds) *Psychology of Intergroup Relations.* Nelson-Hall, Chicago, Illinois.

Thibaut, J.W. and Kelley, H.H. (1959) *The Social Psychology of Groups.* Wiley, New York.

Turner, J. (1985) Social categorization and the self-concept: a social cognitive theory of group behavior. In: Lawler E. (ed.) *Advances in Group Processes: Theory and Research.* JAI Press, Greenwich, Connecticut, pp. 77–121.

Van Dijk, P.A., Smith, L. and Cooper, B. (2009) Are you for real? An evaluation of the relationship between emotional labour and visitor outcomes. *Tourism Management* 32(1), 39–45.

Wharton, A. (1999) The psychosocial consequences of emotional labour. *The Annals of the American Academy of Political and Social Science* 561(1), 158–176.

Wieseke, J., Ullrich, J., Christ, O. and Van Dick, R. (2007) Organizational identification as a determinant of customer orientation in service organizations. *Marketing Letters* 18(4), 265–278.

Williams, C. and Buswell, J. (2003) *Service Quality in Leisure and Tourism.* CAB International, Wallingford, UK.

Williams, C. and Thwaites, E. (2006) Service recovery: a naturalistic decision–making approach. *Managing Service Quality: An International Journal* 16(6), 641–653.

chapter 8

Business Improvement Through the Use of Quality Systems and Models

LEARNING OBJECTIVES

- To explore how LETS organizations can improve through the implementation of business improvement strategies;
- To examine whether or not accredited or non-accredited business improvement strategies should be implemented by LETS organizations;
- To present an overview of both integrated management and quality assurance systems;
- To gain an insight into a number of specific business improvement strategies utilized within the LETS operational environment.

INTRODUCTION

Business improvement strategies can be used to manage every aspect of an organization by taking a holistic approach such as the EFQM business excellence model or by just focusing on one element of the organization's processes (such as inspection of goods or services) (Dale *et al.*, 2007). Examples of inspection techniques can be found in many sectors of the LETS operational environment such as a checklist for hotel supervisors to inspect the preparation of guest bedrooms.

An organizational culture that continuously seeks business improvements is hard to achieve without a clear vision embedded within a strategic framework. The International Standards

Organization (ISO, 2005) calls this framework a quality management system (QMS) and defines it as a way 'to direct and control an organization' when considering quality matters. A QMS encompasses the organization's quality policy ('overall intentions and directions') and quality objectives ('something sought or aimed for') (ISO, 2005). Organizations can select from a vast array of business improvement strategies from sophisticated integrated management system (IMS) such as EFQM to a simplistic customer online feedback questionnaire, implementing as few or as many as they consider to be appropriate in their situation. The selection and introduction of business improvement strategies in the LETS environment will be discussed in Chapter 11. This current chapter will give an overview of the main integrated management systems to facilitate business improvement strategies, especially those implemented by LETS organizations.

EVOLUTION FROM INSPECTION TO INTEGRATED MANAGEMENT SYSTEMS

Although this section is entitled an evolution it should be noted that all of the four types of business improvement strategies are still in use today.

Inspection

The quality evolution started as early as the 1930s in the manufacturing sector when inspection methods were devised by Shewhart. These were developed further in the 1950s by Juran and Deming (Williams and Buswell, 2003; Dale *et al.*, 2007). Their main concern was to reduce the number of items leaving factories with faults (non-conformities) and suggested that this could be achieved by the inspection of goods using specific objective values known as statistical process control (SPC) (Williams and Buswell, 2003; Dale *et al.*, 2007). As the example of a hotel guest bedroom checklist shows, inspection techniques are internal measures with no ability to monitor customers' needs. Although LETS organizations do not implement SPC to the same extent as manufacturing, fast-food outlets, hotel receptions and housekeeping as well as EPOS systems in retailing utilize elements of inspection techniques.

Quality control

Quality control tools and techniques were initially used in the manufacturing sector. Whilst still looking inward and advocating testing and inspection, Juran in his 'Fitness in Use' theory moved to a proactive approach and suggested that quality needed to be planned for (Juran and Godfrey, 1999 cited in Williams and Buswell, 2003). Juran and Godfrey were in favour of setting what are now known as key performance indicators (KPIs) to aid the control of quality and therefore written procedures and quality manuals were produced. Quantitative KPIs are still the cornerstone of many business improvement strategies used by LETS organizations. Ryanair needs their planes to turn around from touch-down to lift-off in 25 minutes for their operations to be cost effective (CAPA, 2013; Ryanair, 2014). Dale *et al.* (2007: 25) state that quality control is still a detection-based concept 'getting rid of bad things after it has taken place' similar to inspection. The American Society of Quality (ASQ) suggests that quality control and assurance (the next stage in the evolution of quality) are used incorrectly to mean the same thing and this is explored below.

Quality assurance systems

The ASQ's (2015) definition of quality assurance system is:

> The planned and systematic activities implemented in a quality system so that quality requirements for a product or service will be fulfilled.

Dale *et al.* (2007) see this as a move towards prevention rather than the detection-based strategy that was previously implemented. It is suggested by ASQ that organizations have more confidence in the goods or service provided by having a quality assurance system (QAS) framework in place. This is due to the implementation of advanced quality planning such as examining what Evans *et al.* (2014) call the softer quality issues such as training needs of employees and gathering feedback from customers. Both Juran in his Managing for Quality Trilogy and Deming's continuous improvement cycle advocate a prevention-based strategy, which is fundamental to a QAS framework (see Table 8.1).

Before the introduction of a QAS a change of organizational culture is necessary, whereby the finding of non-conformances does not automatically lead to blame being allocated to an employee. The finding of mistakes is used to improve performance and the prevention of re-occurrence errors.

A QAS provides the framework by which monitoring and measuring, utilizing a variety of quality tools, can be controlled, replicating Deming's continuous improvement cycle (see Table 8.1). Although a QAS can be devised by an organization (see Focus Box 8.5 Marriott Hotels) there are a number of accredited generic ones such as BS EN ISO 9001:2015 (CQI,

Table 8.1. Illustrating the stages in Juran's Managing for Quality Trilogy and Deming's Continuous Improvement Cycle (Williams and Buswell, 2003).

Juran's Managing for Quality Trilogy	Deming's Continuous Improvement Cycle
Quality planning (including customers' needs)	Plan
Quality control	Do
Quality improvement	Check
	Act

2015a) as well as those for specific sectors such as Quest, the UK Quality Scheme for Sport and Leisure. Quest has two QAS frameworks, one for facilities management and the second for sports development (Right Directions/Leisure-Net Solutions Ltd, 2014a).

Many LETS organizations implement QMS so that improvements are not only made in the operational environment but also maintained, which can lead ultimately to total quality management (TQM) (Dale *et al.*, 2007).

Integrated management systems

Total Quality Management is seen as the ultimate level for organizations to achieve requiring a cultural change, but it is not a prescriptive system (Dale *et al.*, 2007) as we saw in Chapter 7. Therefore a number of IMS frameworks have been devised to enable a holistic approach to business improvement to be taken. Therefore the whole of the organization including branches can be managed, even when there is a high degree of complexity, and e-services can also be included. It is said (Dale *et al.*, 2007) that an integrated system is more efficient and effective in reducing conflict and duplication.

Many IMS frameworks have been based on the excellence award model (EFQM, 2013a) that allows for integration of other monitoring and inspection techniques, quality control tools and quality assurance systems (see Fig. 8.1). Dale *et al.* (2007) state that an organization can easily monitor its performance and progress using the self-assessment features of these frameworks. Another advantage of IMS frameworks is that they can accommodate other areas of the organization that require monitoring either for statutory generic compliance, such as the Health and Safety at Work Act, or sector specific compliance, for example alcohol licensing (see Fig. 8.1).

The evolution of business improvement strategies has not yet reached maturity. Technology brings the service and manufacturing sectors ever closer together, giving consumers a wider choice of experiences and a greater number of potential providers. Therefore, the implementation of existing business improvement strategies is necessary as well as devising new ones to retain the organization's competitive edge.

It should be noted that as small- to medium-sized businesses (SMEs) are predominant in the LETS industry a philosophical approach to business improvement strategies can be taken as most owner-managers are constantly on the front line of their provision and can gain informal feedback from customers and staff. Although SMEs will have to implement less complex monitoring tools for statutory compliance, it is difficult for them to implement QMS and IMS frameworks. This is partly due to the costs involved, but also the low number of employees, which means it is difficult to find time to allow staff to be absent to attend training sessions and to carry out the additional duties of managing a business improvement strategy. The selection and implementation of business improvement systems, techniques and tools will be considered in Chapter 11.

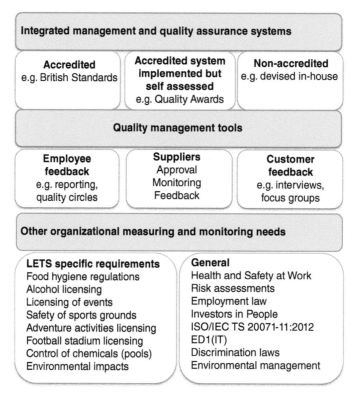

Fig. 8.1. Overview of business improvement strategies.

Although there is a vast array of continuous improvement methods they can be divided into two distinct types: accredited and self-assessed non-accredited methods. The next section explores the differences, advantages and disadvantages of each; as Fig. 8.1 shows the LETS organizations use both.

SELF-ASSESSED NON-ACCREDITED AND ACCREDITED BUSINESS IMPROVEMENT STRATEGIES

Self-assessed non-accredited systems and tools

Self-assessed non-accredited systems and tools are those devised in-house by the organization such as those implemented by Disney and Marriott Hotels (see Focus Box 8.5). Most of the quality tools used to gather feedback from customers and staff are self-assessed such as quality circles, questionnaires, and focus groups (see Chapter 10 for details of these quality tools). The widely used SERVQUAL (Zeithaml *et al.*, 1990) and its derivatives that measure and analyse five operational gaps using a 22-item instrument do not have the infrastructure in place to be assessed externally. Managers can purchase an easy-to-use book for £12.99 (2016 price) and carry out an internal audit of the organization; a diagnostic checklist based on gap scores suggests improvements (see Chapter 10 more information).

Advantages of self-assessed non-accredited systems and tools include:

- Can be bespoke to a specific type of organization's needs;
- Costs can be lower but training of staff still required; and
- Can be frequently carried out.

Disadvantages of self-assessed non-accredited systems and tools include:

- Not recognized unless devised by a global brand;
- Existing custom and practice can proliferate;
- Existing organizational culture retained; and
- Internal monitoring and measurement not always impartial, nor robust and infrequently carried out, plus data collected are not always analysed.

Accredited systems and tools

Accredited systems and tools, such as the excellence model (EFQM, 2013a) and Investors in People (2015), are ones that are monitored by an outside organization known as a third-party assessment. The organization will be assessed using a set of specific criteria to indicate how successful they have been and where improvements have to or can be made.

Advantages of accredited systems and tools include:

- Externally recognized within the sector (QUEST);
- Some recognized by customers (hotel star ratings);
- Introduction can act as an agent for change within an organization;
- Continuous improvement possible as frequent re-assessments required; and
- Impartial external assessors.

Disadvantages of accredited systems and tools include:

- Some criteria not relevant when generic systems and tools imposed, for example on SMEs;
- Additional cost of staff training, cost of preparing for first and subsequent assessment visits, and fees for assessments. The British Quality Foundation (BQF) UK Excellence Award charges a fee of £4137+VAT for establishments with fewer than 50 employees (BQF, 2015a); and
- Another additional cost can be the engagement of consultants to train and prepare the organization for the initial assessment.

Accredited systems and tools not externally assessed

There is another context in which accredited systems and tools are implemented by an organization but without engaging with the third-party assessment. An organization has many of the advantages of accreditation and self-assessment without some of the disadvantages. For instance, costs are reduced and criteria that are felt not to be appropriate can be ignored. If internal assessors are externally trained, the issues of robustness and impartiality can to some extent be eliminated.

Each year only a few organizations are selected as winners of a quality award. An organization could be a few points below the winners and be seen as having 'failed'. For example, Marriott Hotels were a finalist in the UK Excellence Award 2000 but not 'winners' (BQF, 2015b). Therefore some organizations choose to use the quality award scoring criteria for internal assessment but without submitting the results. EFQM (2013c) recognizes this and has a set of basic assessment guidelines for self-assessment purposes available free of charge on their website. The next section will examine a number of widely used quality systems. This includes Quality Awards, Six Sigma and Human Sigma, Balanced Scorecard and BS EN ISO 9001:2015.

BUSINESS IMPROVEMENT STRATEGIES FOR THE LETS INDUSTRY

Robinson (2003, cited in Ramchandani and Taylor, 2011), when interviewing leisure centre managers, found that the frequently stated reason for adopting a quality management programme was to improve both the service and organizational efficiency.

QUALITY AWARDS BASED ON THE EXCELLENCE MODEL

The Excellence Model was devised by the European Foundation for Quality (now known as EFQM) and is said to be suitable for any organization, regardless of location, size or sector (BQF, 2015c). The generic model allows for a holistic approach to be taken when managing the whole of an organization, known as an integrated management system (see Fig. 8.2).

The model has eight fundamental concepts, which underpin what an excellent organization should be (adapted from EFQM, 2013b):

1. The need to add value for customers.
2. Creating a sustainable future by simultaneously improving the organization's performance as well as the economy, environment and local social conditions.
3. Manage change within the organization to enhance its capabilities.
4. Continuously improve and innovate by harnessing all stakeholders' creativity, thus generating increases in value and level of performance.
5. Leaders of the organization must have values and ethics and act as role models.

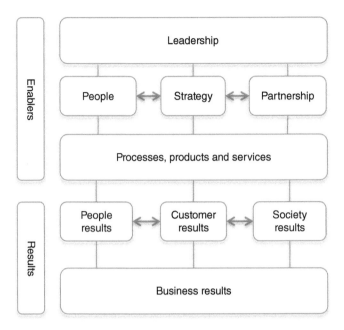

Fig. 8.2. The EFQM Excellence model criteria (EFQM, 2012).

6. Organizations must be known for their capability to recognize opportunities and threats and therefore achieve an effective and efficient response.

7. An organizational culture of not only valuing people but also empowering them needs to be created and therefore achieve organizational and personal goals.

8. Within the context of the operating sector an organization must be able to sustain outstanding results in both the short and long term, meeting the needs of all stakeholders.

The eight fundamental concepts drive the assessment criteria for each of the model's five 'enablers' (*which strategies need to be developed and how they are going to implement them*) and the four 'results' (*these are the results an organization achieves in comparison to their strategic goals*).

The model's criteria are shown in Fig. 8.2 divided into enablers and results. One of the enablers is 'people' and one of the results is 'people results'. These two elements of the model's criteria will be explored in Focus Box 8.1.

Although EFQM presents the European Excellence Awards there are many others that utilize this model. For example, the excellence awards in the UK are generally based on geographical location of the organization. Table 8.2 gives example of other awards and LETS award winners.

Wongrassamee *et al.* (2003) and Dror (2008) state that the Excellence Model is based on the concepts of TQM but suggest that long-term strategies are not accommodated by it. The fact that there is a quality award associated with this model is viewed favourably as organizations can be benchmarked against each other (Wongrassamee *et al.*, 2003; Dror, 2008). Calvo-Mora *et al.* (2015: 3) support benchmarking via this model as a 'continuous process of learning, innovation and improvement.' Heras-Saizarbitoria *et al.* (2011), when evaluating the main benefits of implementing the model, noted an improvement to the organization's external image followed closely by improvements to the goods and services produced, thus impacting on profitability as the example in Focus Box 8.2 illustrates.

Focus Box 8.1. Integrated Management System Properties of the Excellence Model – People Enabler and Results

One of the easiest ways for an organization to meet the requirements of an excellence model enabler is to consider using an existing quality tool. Investors in People (IiP) is a generic and frequently used quality tool to ensure that human resource management utilizes best practices, such as empowerment, and leadership. The IiP assessment requires feedback from all staff enabling the organization to understand their strengths and focus on areas of weakness (Investors in People, 2015). Accreditation to IiP would go some way towards fulfilling the People enabler criteria (see below).

EFQM basic assessment criteria for People (EFQM, 2013c):

1. Our strategy includes a plan on the people we need for the future.
2. We develop our people's knowledge and skills.
3. Our people understand the mission, vision, values and strategy and their evaluation is based on those.
4. We have created a culture that develops and rewards people's dedication, skills, talents and creativity.
5. Our internal communication is efficient and works in all directions: top-down, bottom-up and lateral.
6. We ensure that all necessary data and information are appropriately shared and understood.
7. We take care of the health and safety of our people and we provide good working conditions.
8. We have a system of rewards and recognition to honour and motivate our people.

For the People Results evidence must be provided of implementing the human resource strategies and the fact that an organization was accredited to IiP would be one way. This can be enhanced by data from implementing other quality tools such as minutes of staff quality circles, staff development records, thus integrating existing business improvement strategies.

EFQM basic assessment criteria are scored using:
No evidence / don't know
We have a plan
On our way
Close to good
Fully done

Using the above results organizations are then asked to reflect on both their areas of strength and instead of using the words 'failure' or 'weaknesses' EFQM ask that areas of opportunity be considered.

Table 8.2. **Example of quality awards based on the Excellence model.**

Excellence award	Awarding body	LETS recipient
European Excellence Award (see Focus Box 8.2 for best practice example)	EFQM	Alpenresort Schwarz Winner 2013 Pirktl Alpen Resort Austria Finalist 2008 Edinburgh International Conference Centre Scotland Winner 2003 (Fig. 8.3), Finalist 2001, 2000 Landhotel Schindlerhof Germany Winner 1998
UK Excellence Award	BQF (formally British Quality Foundation)	First Trans Pennine Express 2014 Winner, Finalist 2012 Northern Rail Finalist 2012, 2011 Seaview Hotel Isle of Wight Winner 1998
The WOW! Award	Scotland Quality	Inverclyde Leisure 2015
Excellence Award – The Customer Satisfaction Prize	Wales Quality Centre	Cardiff Marriott Hotel 1999
Excellence Award – The Service Sector Prize	Wales Quality Centre	Swansea Marriott Hotel 2000
Excellence Award – The Tourism Prize	Wales Quality Centre	Furcroft Hotel 2001 Broneiron Limited Conference Centre 2002
Excellence Award – The Small Business Prize	Wales Quality Centre	Broneirion Limited 2003
Excellence Award – The Prize for the Most Improved Organization	Wales Quality Centre	Broneirion Limited 2004
Ireland Excellence Award	Centre for Competitiveness (Northern Ireland and Ireland)	
North of England Business Excellence	North of England Excellence	First Trans Pennine Express Winner 2010, Special Award 2014–2012 Northern Rail Special Award Merseyrail Ltd Winner 2014, 2011 Manchester Airport Winner 2010 The Mersey Forest 2007

Fig. 8.3. Edinburgh International Conference Centre Scotland – Winner of the EFQM Business Excellence Award 2003.

Dror (2008) states that this model's criteria are broader than most other improvement strategies and that cultural changes are expected within the leadership enabler.

Calvo-Mora *et al.* (2015) consider the leadership enabler as a means of knowledge creation with the process enabler as the application of knowledge. Their view is that the model enables stakeholders including suppliers and customers to be part of the knowledge creation and application. A criticism of the model by Calvo-Mora *et al.* (2015) is that when a self-assessment or external assessment has generated a number of areas for improvement it is difficult to know which ones will have the greatest positive impact on the organization. Heras-Saizarbitoria *et al.*'s (2011) research showed that quality of external assessment and the need for physical and financial resources were two main concerns when implementing EFQM. They also encountered a degree of difficulty from organizations not understanding the principles and assessment criteria when they were trying to implement it.

To conclude, notwithstanding the criticism above, the Excellence Model has the ability to be an integrated management framework over the five 'enablers'. Organizational strategies can be accommodated and the evidence of carrying them out is contained within the four 'results' section. The Excellence Model, whilst having specific assessment criteria within the five enablers, does not specify a series of KPIs that must be met and therefore has the ability to be applicable to all sectors.

Focus Box 8.2. **Excellence Model Good Practice – Alpenresort Schwarz, Austria**

The EFQM Model in Action Good Practice demonstrates how Alpenresort Schwarz, Austria became one of the EFQM award winners in 2013 (EFQM, 2014).

It was stated that Alpenresort Schwarz, Austria showed:

Development and Learning from Employees – Succeeding Through Talented People

'There is a well-developed recruitment process and a thorough induction programme, aimed at ensuring that new employees are developed to fit with the resort ethos.'

Ability to Change via Employee Involvement – Managing With Agility

One way of implementing improvements is via four project teams (Guest, Health, Schwarz Inside and Green Schwarz flower).

Living The Values – Leading with Vision, Inspiration and Integrity

'The Pirktl family has developed the resort Mission, Vision and Values with involvement from all Alpenresort Schwarz department and unit leaders, deputies and the project team leaders. The Pirktl family and all leaders with more than two employees undertake annual leadership feedback reviews.'

Strategic Partner Programme – Developing Organizational Capacity

'Schwarz has achieved long term beneficial relationship with (strategic) partners and suppliers based on mutual trust, respect and openness. This has been achieved through the use of an internal supplier rating system that is shared with the partners.'

Think Guest and Show Heartiness – Adding Value For Customers

'The Guest is at the centre of all that Alpenresort Schwarz represents. The facilities, the range of offers to the Guest profile and, in particular, the focus on the Guest is exemplary – they are invited to become a part of the 'family' operational ethos; employees continuously "Think Guest" and show Heartiness.'

QUALITY AWARDS *NOT* BASED ON THE EXCELLENCE MODEL

A vast and seemingly growing number of international, national, local and internal business quality awards exist that are not based on the Excellence Model. The popularity of trying to gain these awards has grown rapidly over recent years as more businesses compete within the marketplace, especially in the LETS industry. Many of these quality awards are also the basis of an assessment of the applicant's performance against a set of criteria and often within certain categories (CQI, 2015a). For example, Visit Lancashire (2015) in partnership with Visit England awards for excellence has 20 award categories including: Best Visitor Experience, Outstanding

Customer Service, Best Sustainable Tourism Practices and the Best Tourism Event Award. Another award that is promoted by the UK Government and is widely sought within the public-sector LETS provision is Customer Service Excellence.

Customer Service Excellence

Although Customer Service Excellence is the title of this award, this standard is not based on the Excellence Model but could be used to partly fulfil the criteria in the customer enabler and results sections. The UK government requires services financed by the public sector to be managed in efficient, effective, excellent, equitable and empowering ways with the citizen at the heart of service provision (CSE, 2015a). The underpinning ethos is that a service should be customer-focused and assessment (either externally or self-assessed) is against five criteria (CSE, 2015a):

1. Customer insight.
2. The culture of the organization.
3. Information and access.
4. Delivery.
5. Timeliness and quality of service.

The benefits to Merseytravel of accreditation to this quality award are illustrated in Focus Box 8.3.

Although this award is open to other organizations such as university services and housing associations, only the current LETS holders are shown in Table 8.3.

In conclusion, Customer Service Excellence can be externally assessed or self-assessed and can monitor all elements of the customer and employee interface. It also has the ability to be part of an IMS such as the EFQM excellence model. A similar customer-focused quality award has been specifically devised for the hospitality industry.

Focus Box 8.3. Customer Service Excellence – Merseytravel

Merseytravel is responsible for the integrated passenger network for the whole of Merseyside. In 2008 Merseytravel accomplished the customer service excellence award for their bus gateway, reaching the appropriate level of performance in all 57 elements over the five criteria of the standard and with no development needs identified.

They concluded that the benefits of this accreditation were:

- Recognition that best practice through accreditation has enhanced staff morale as well as supporting customer relations;
- Managing change effectively;
- Effective team working and project management.

(Centre for Assessment Ltd, 2015)

Table 8.3. Customer Service Excellence accredited LETS providers (CSE, 2015b).

LETS provider	Service provision	LETS provider	Service provision
Birmingham City Council	Events, Libraries, Sport & Leisure and Parks & Nature Conservation	Lisburn City Council	Arts Services Sport Services
Medway Council	Leisure, Sport & Tourism Services	North Yorkshire	National Park Authority
Northamptonshire County Council	Library and Information Services	Oxford City Council	Parks and Communities
Royal Borough of Kensington and Chelsea	Leisure and Park Services	Salford City Council	Grounds Maintenance, Environment & Community Safety
Snowdonia	National Park Authority	Yorkshire Dales	National Park Authority

Hospitality Assured

The Hospitality Assured award is said to encourage organizations to appraise their operational processes for the customer's perspective and to see if there is any way that improvements can be made. One of the benefits stated by Hospitality Assured of gaining this award is that it leads to a reduction in staff turnover, a major factor and cost in the hospitality industry (Hospitality Assured, 2011). The 2015 Hospitality Assured Award Winner was Edinburgh International Conference Centre (Hospitality Assured, 2015). Again, this award can partly fulfil the needs of the customer and customer results section of the Excellence Model. The growth in sport and leisure facilities has led to a specific quality award being devised for this sector, known as Quest, the UK Quality Scheme for Sport and Leisure.

UK Quality Scheme for Sport and Leisure (Quest)

Quest has two frameworks: one is for managing sport and leisure facilities and the other for sports development. It is said that Quest defines industry standards and good practice and it enables managers of sports facilities and sport development to compare their performance with equivalent facilities across the UK. This is known as benchmarking and requires a third-party external assessment, but both frameworks have the ability to be used as a self-assessment improvement strategy (Right Directions/Leisure-Net Solutions

Ltd, 2014a). Quest training and assessment is currently contracted to Right Directions in partnership with Leisure-Net Solutions Ltd by Sport England, Sport Scotland, Sport Wales and Sport Northern Ireland.

The Quest assessment criteria are arranged into categories with multiple modules, with a number of modules applicable to both frameworks (see Table 8.4).

As well as the core modules, Quest has a range of 19 'generic plus' modules, such as Young People Participation 5-19 Years and Quality/Integrated Management Systems (see Focus Box 8.4), and 27 'specific plus' modules, including Event Management, Pool Water Management and Entrepreneurship (Right Directions/Leisure-Net Solutions Ltd, 2014b). Whilst a specific number of modules from each category is required, the selection from a large number of modules allows for a bespoke, flexible business improvement strategy to be implemented. The 'generic plus' module Quality/Integrated Management Systems will be examined to illustrate the criteria and guidance given to participating leisure facilities and sports development programmes (see Focus Box 8.4).

Deming's Plan, Do, Check and Act theory (cited in Williams and Buswell, 2003) underpins the continuous improvement philosophy of Quest and this is actioned as a template for each module's assessment criteria as Plan, Do, Measure, Review and Impact.

Although Quest's two frameworks would not fulfil all the criteria of the Excellence Model due to the optionality of the modules, it would fulfil some. Other LETS awards devised by trade

Table 8.4. Quest core assessment modules.

Core assessment category	Examples of modules
Operations (not sports development)	Cleaning & Housekeeping Maintenance & Equipment Environmental Health & Safety Declaration
People	Customer Experience & Insight (not sports development) Team & Skills Development Leadership
Purpose	Financial & Budget Management Outcomes & Impact Measurement Community Outcomes (not sports development) Planning to Improve Marketing, Research & Communications
Delivery	Partnerships Policies, Procedure & Standards

Focus Box 8.4. **Quest Assessment Criteria and Guidance – Generic Plus Module Quality/Integrated Management Systems**

PLAN

How do you plan to develop your integrated management system (IMS) or quality management system (QMS)?

DO

How do you ensure that staff are involved with the development process and have access to the system?

What best practice, legislation and statutory requirements have you considered?

What training is in place to ensure staff are updated with the procedural content of both new and revised documentation?

What resources are allocated to achieve both the development and delivery of the system?

MEASURE

How do you measure?

REVIEW

How do you review what you have measured?

IMPACT

Has what you have done made a difference?

Each criterion question is followed by examples of best practice thereby expanding on *'How do you measure?'*

Examples of Best Practice for this specific criterion include:

- Audits, internal and external;
- Training; and
- Staff feedback
  Additional Guidance for this question includes:
- Are internal audits undertaken in a timely manner?
- Are external audits used to measure the success and implementation of the system?
- Is training undertaken and measured for its effectiveness and knowledge of the staff?
- Is training undertaken and measured for its effectiveness and knowledge of the staff?
- Does the organization seek to achieve nationally recognized accreditation for the practice; safeguarding; customer service or equalities work for example? (*Customer service excellence could fulfil this.*)

(Right Directions/Leisure-Net Solutions Ltd, 2014c)

bodies would not achieve this due to their simplistic nature. For example, the UK Event Award requires an organization to submit a 1250 word report (UK Events, 2015).

In-house quality awards

Similar to the trade body awards, any organization can devise their own awards and use them to self-assess their organization. A variety of awards has been devised by Marriott Hotel Group, examples of which are shown in Focus Box 8.5 (there is further information relating to Marriott Hotel Group's best practice in Chapter 11).

In conclusion, most quality awards require a considerable amount of effort, time and resources. Can the benefits surpass any potential limitations? Table 8.5 below considers the potential advantages and limitations of entering and winning a quality award.

Moving on from LETS specific business improvement strategies, the next section of the chapter will examine a number of generic ones such as Six Sigma, Human Sigma, Balanced Scorecard and BS EN ISO 9001:2015.

SIX SIGMA IN SERVICE ORGANIZATIONS

Six Sigma is both a philosophy and a goal of performance (Process Management International, 2006). The objective of a Six Sigma strategy is to understand how defects occur and then to devise process improvements. A defect in the context of Six Sigma is defined as 'anything that does not meet the customer requirement' (Adams, 2003: 19). Antony (2004) suggests that Six Sigma has a strong statistical foundation but that customer requirements need to be determined (Harry and Schroeder, 2000). As the service sector

---

Focus Box 8.5. Internal Self-Assessment Quality Awards

Marriott Hospitality Awards and Recognition

Listed below are examples of the internal awards set and managed within the Marriott Hotel Group. Some awards are used to benchmark against other Marriott hotels, others are used for internal purposes only:

- Marriott Partnership Circle Award;
- Marriott Overall Satisfaction Award;
- Marriott Service Excellence Award;
- Marriott Food & Beverage Award;
- Marriott eCommerce Achievement Award;
- Marriott International Franchise Award.

(Marriott, 2015)

Table 8.5. The advantages and limitations of quality awards.

Advantages	Limitations
Popularity	Effort
Marketing/PR exposure	Timeliness and time consuming
Increase market share	Expense
Change market positioning	Resources
Employee engagement	Political infighting
Increase morale	Detailed application process and preparation of documents
Employee reward and recognition	Scoring methods
International, national, local and company recognition	Not winning!
Improved quality and productivity	
Become a role model	
Attend an awards event	

tends to implement less quantitatively oriented quality improvement programmes it is suggested (Hensley and Dobie, 2005; Antony *et al.*, 2007) that they do not need many of the quantitative tools and techniques of the Six Sigma toolbox such as cause and effect diagrams and flowcharts.

It is stated that services adopting a Six Sigma business strategy will have the following benefits (Antony, 2005a, b):

1. Improved cross-functional teamwork throughout the entire organization.
2. Transformation of the organizational culture from fire-fighting mode to fire-prevention mode.
3. Increased employee morale.
4. Reduced number of non-value added steps in critical business processes through systematic elimination, leading to faster delivery of service.
5. Reduced cost of poor quality.
6. Increased awareness of various problem-solving tools and techniques, leading to greater job satisfaction for employees.
7. Improved consistency level of service through systematic reduction of variability in processes.
8. Effective management decisions due to reliance on data and facts rather than assumptions and gut-feelings.

Six Sigma is most successful when it is adopted as a management philosophy (Hensley and Dobie, 2005). Research by Hensley and Dobie (2005) identified four potential complications encountered when implementing Six Sigma in a service environment.

1. It is generally considered to be more difficult to gather data in service settings than in manufacturing.
2. Measurements of customer satisfaction may be more difficult in services because the interactions between customer and service provider can create complications.
3. The measure and control phases of Six Sigma may be more difficult to control in services because service sub-processes are harder to quantify and the measurement data are harder to gather.
4. Much of the data in services are collected manually in face-to-face interactions.

It is said that Six Sigma cannot be effectively implemented within SMEs (Antony, 2008) as there are difficulties in dedicating full-time staff known as Six Sigma 'black belts' to executing projects. Employees in SMEs often perform many different functions unlike those in larger organizations and SMEs can lack financial resources and technical structure (Wessel and Burcher, 2004). Research suggests that the successful implementation of Six Sigma in services depends on the organization's ability to apply the underlying concepts (Bane, 2002). Therefore, Fleming and Asplund (2007), as noted in Chapter 7, developed Human Sigma to address the ineffectiveness of the Six Sigma methodology in areas of human resources.

Human Sigma for the LETS industry

Human Sigma is a way to measure and manage the human systems of business. Both employee and customer engagement levels are assessed as these scores are leading indicators of the financial performance that a business hopes to achieve (Fleming and Asplund, 2007). Gallup identified 12 key questions (the Q survey) that serve as indicators of:

- The degree of employee engagement: engaged, non-engaged or actively disengaged categories;
- The level of emotional connection between an employee and employer;
- Whether employees have the materials they need to do their job;
- Whether expectations placed on employees are clear;
- Whether a supervisor takes an interest in employees;
- Whether employees' opinions matter; and
- Whether they are afforded opportunities to learn and grow (Michelli, 2008).

Gallup also identified 11 key questions (the CE11) that serve as an indicator of an organization's degree of customer engagement. Taken together, the Q12 and the CE11 questions form the basis for Human Sigma.

Extensive research conducted by the Gallup organization has established a link between the engagement levels of employees and those of customers. Fleming and Asplund's (2007) meta-analysis studied 1926 business units in ten different companies, including Ritz-Carlton, and demonstrated that organizations that adopted Human Sigma management systems have outperformed their rivals by 26% in gross margin and 85% in sales growth over a 1-year period. Therefore, LETS organizations have an opportunity to build employee engagement, which in turn builds customer engagement within their business.

Though the Human Sigma management model may be implemented in various ways, the underlying philosophy is based on the five rules that suggest a new approach for the employee–customer encounter (see Chapter 4). This model is designed to be applied to almost any organization, but is particulary applicable to organizations with a high degree of direct customer contact as in the LETS industry.

Consequently, Six Sigma is a method to improve quality and reduce errors in business processes. Human Sigma, in contrast, reduces variance in key employee and customer outcomes by improving an organization's human performance and moving it towards excellence. Its goal is to reduce the number of disengaged employees and customers and move them towards engagement with the organization. Six Sigma focuses on materials, methods and measurements to drive business improvements. Human Sigma focuses on people to optimize business performance. Overall, the conclusion is that the Human Sigma approach to business improvement is potentially more beneficial to the LETS industry.

Whilst Ritz-Carlton has adopted Human Sigma, the Hilton Hotels and Resorts have taken another generic business improvement strategy and have implemented the Balanced Scorecard.

BALANCED SCORECARD

Devised by Kaplan and Norton in 1992, the Balanced Scorecard is a generic *performance measurement framework* that enables strategic planning and management control of an organization (Kaplan and Norton, 1992; Balanced Scorecard Institute, 2015). By 2001 it had been adopted by 44% of worldwide organizations (Neely, 2008), the Hilton Hotels and Resorts being one (see Focus Box 8.6). Strategic planning is said by Anthony (1965: 16, cited in Kaplan, 2010) to be dependent 'on an estimate of a cause and effect relationship between a course of action and a desired outcome.' Managers are able to devise measures to enable the organizational vision and goals to be achieved. This is translated into four separate but interlinking perspectives so that a balanced view of the organization can be obtained.

1. Financial.
2. Customers.
3. Internal business processes (includes communities).
4. Innovation, learning and growth (includes stakeholders) (Kaplan and Norton 1992; Kaplan, 2010).

Focus Box 8.6. Hilton Hotels and Resorts Balanced Scorecard Measurements	
Total Revpar[a]	Concentrates the team on ensuring every penny sold counts
Market Share	Comparison with competitors' benchmark of how business is doing in varied markets
No Show Revenue	Ensures that the team are managing quality of reservations and of course the revenue
BDRC[b] Venue Verdict	Conference organizers feed back, aim to see where business processes need improvement and capex[c] requirements

[a]Total Revpar is the abbreviation for total revenue per available room.
[b]Most of the world's leading hotel companies use the BDRC's Hotel Guest Survey.
[c]Capex is the abbreviation for capital expenditure.

Each one of the four perspectives of the Balanced Scorecard requires:

- *Objectives* – e.g. specific delivery times (linking to measures and targets);
- *Measures* – how is the objective to be measured? For example specific KPIs;
- *Targets* – the level of performance required; and
- *Initiatives* – are there any specific programmes needed, for example staff training, to enable them to meet the objectives?

Examples of Hilton Hotel and Resorts measurements can be seen in Focus Box 8.6.

It has been suggested by Dror (2008) that this structure enables long-term strategies to be supported, but points out that whilst an organization has the flexibility to devise any KPI or targets, none are recommended. Wongrassamee *et al.* (2003) on the other hand, do not see this as a problem, stating that KPIs can easily be changed.

Kaplan (2010) expresses the opinion that front-line staff should be exposed to financial as well as non-financial data. Research into tourism SMEs adopting the balanced scorecard showed that there was an over-reliance on 'hard' financial data such as sales, rather than including 'soft' data such as staff satisfaction and empowerment, thereby not achieving a holistic view of the organization (Phillips and Louvieris, 2010). Kaplan (2010) goes so far as to say that the 'Learning and Growth perspective' was a 'black hole' to some organizations, but goes on to point out that Heskett *et al.*'s (1997) Service Profit Chain (see Chapter 7) also has linkages between human resources and financial outcomes.

The model can accommodate other stakeholders such as suppliers, but Kaplan (2010) suggests that a strategy should be devised by the organization first before exposing it to the opinions of others. Although the original four perspectives of the Balanced Scorecard remain, due to empirical research findings an interactive six-stage closed loop management system for strategy execution has been added (Kaplan and Norton, 1992; Kaplan, 2010). This third generation of the Balanced Scorecard enables causality between objectives and performance to be identified.

The Six Stage Closed-loop Management System

1. Develop the strategy.
2. Translate the strategy.
3. Align the organization.
4. Plan operations.
5. Monitor and learn.
6. Test and adapt the strategy.

Kaplin (2007), in a presentation on the closed loop management system, said that it enabled organizations to link strategic planning with the operational environment. He suggests that this is achieved by devising a strategic map to create a solution strategy and through the appropriate balanced scorecard perspectives an action plan will be produced. The subsequent business processes can be readily actioned and monitored throughout the relevant areas of the organization via the objectives, measures, targets and initiatives of each balanced scorecard perspective.

Benefits of the Balanced Scorecard

It is suggested that the benefits of the balanced scorecard are:

- It focuses managers on the critical measures;
- It enables the impact of the implementation of an objective on other areas of the organization to be measured;
- Is customer oriented; and
- It allows for all critical information to be contained within one reporting medium.

In conclusion the balanced scorecard is useful even if it is only used in a specific functional area, e.g. human resources or marketing, but it has the advantage of being able to translate corporate objectives into operational procedures across the whole organization (Looy *et al.*, 2003).

THE BRITISH STANDARDS INSTITUTE

The British Standards Institute (BSI), in partnership with other similar organizations such as the International Standards Organization, devises standards and assesses organizations against them. This enables organizations certified to a BSI standard to 'embed excellence' 'making it a habit' (BSI, 2015a). BSI administers an array of standards, both generic and sector specific, as Table 8.6 illustrates.

Table 8.6. British Standards Institute generic and specific standards appropriate to the LETS industry (BSI, 2015b).

	Appropriate to LETS organizations
Generic Standards	
BS EN ISO 9001:2015	Quality Management Systems
BS EN ISO 9004:2000	QMS Guidelines for performance improvements
PAS99	Integrated Management System
BS ISO 13053-1:2011	Quantitative methods in process improvement. Six Sigma. DMAIC methodology
BS ISO 13053-2:2011	Quantitative methods in process improvement. Six Sigma. Tools and techniques
ISO 14001:2015	Environmental Management
BS ISO 31000	Risk Management
BS 13500:2013	Organizational Governance
BS 11000:2011	Collaborative Relationships
BS ISO 10002:2014	Complaints Management
CCA Global Standard	Contact Centre Management
BS ISO 50001:2014	Energy Management System
ISO/IEC 27001:2013	Information Security
BS ISO/IEC 20000-1:2011	Information technology. Service management. Service management system requirements
BS OHSAS 18001:2007	Occupational health and safety management systems. Requirements
Specific Standards	
BS OHSAS 18001	Food Safety
BS7960:1999	BS Code of Practice for Door Supervisors
ISO 201201	Sustainable Events Management
PAS 51:2004	Guide to Industry Best Practice for Organizing Outdoor Events

Amongst the generic BSI standards listed in Table 8.6 there are a number to safeguard the environment such as ISO 14001:2015 and BS ISO 50001:2014. Focus Box 8.7 illustrates a European Union initiative, the Eco-Management and Audit Scheme (EMAS), that advocates that more than these minimum standards need to be achieved.

From the lists in Table 8.6 it can easily be seen that there is a diverse range of standards and guidance that can be applied to the LETS environment, including statutory obligations such as food safety and health and safety. This can be disconcerting for all but the largest LETS organizations, but BSI have introduced PAS99 Integrated Management Systems and BS EN ISO 9001:2015 to enable organizations to coordinate the management and continuous improvement of their organizations.

PAS99 Integrated Management Systems

The PAS99 framework was devised to integrate the management of a multitude of standards. It is said to have the benefit of:

- Meeting all standard requirements with one set of policies and procedures;
- Auditing more than one system at a time to save money and resources;
- Improving overall efficiency by removing the need to duplicate tasks;
- Clearly defining roles and responsibilities and highlighting common objectives; and
- Making it easier to continually improve all management systems (BSI, 2015c).

It is suggested that SMEs (prevalent in the LETS industry) will save time and money by utilizing PAS99, compared with other IMS and QMS. PAS99 is currently under review as the revisions to BS EN ISO 9001:2015 and other management standards may have negated the need for it.

Focus Box 8.7. The Eco-Management and Audit Scheme

The need to protect the environment is not only promoted by laws and standards; there is a European Union initiative EMAS designed to improve companies' environmental performance and that recognizes organizations that exceed the minimum legal requirements.

EMAS is a voluntary scheme that promotes continuous improvement of environmental performance in organizations, which it also verifies. Good environmental management can have the benefit of cost savings by reducing the amount of waste and energy consumption. This in turn helps the sustainability of the environment as well as that of the organization. IEMA (2015) recognizes the different needs of small- and medium-sized businesses (SMEs) by producing an EMAS toolkit for small organizations.

(IEMA, 2015)

BS EN ISO 9001:2015 Quality Management System

BS EN ISO 9001:2015 is an accredited QMS that is audited by third-party organizations. Although the information below concerns the recently released 2015 version of the standard, this has not been implemented as yet as there is a 3-year transition period for organizations already certified to the 2008 version. There is also going to be a change from third-party auditing of an organization to assessing by means of subjective and objective evaluations of the data. Green (2015) suggests that generalist and specialist assessors will be required, especially when the organization is utilizing high levels of technology.

A number of writers, including Seddon (1997, cited in Williams and Buswell, 2003), have criticized previous versions of ISO 9001 stating that the prescriptive nature of the standard did not address customers' needs; it was a means of inspection not quality assurance and levels of improvement did not reach beyond what was required in the standard. Pekovic (2010), when writing about the limitations of the 2008 edition of the standard, suggested that it was not relevant in the service context as it did not recognize that it was difficult to control service outputs before delivery and also it took time to improve service quality. He also pointed out the advantage that larger organizations have over SMEs when trying to absorb costs of certification and training, but suggested that they can be recouped by the reduction in mistakes (non-conformance).

Psomas *et al.* (2013) investigated the effectiveness in service SMEs, including e-services and tourism, of ISO 9001:2008 after 3 years of implementation. Whilst they recognized an improvement in operation performance and service quality when ISO 9001:2008 was adopted, they did not find the two were necessarily linked. Their results also questioned the direct impact of ISO 9001 on financial performance. Although Heras-Saizarbitoria *et al.* (2011) consider that there are a number of motivators for instigating ISO 9001, such as demand from clients, pressure from competitors, image and the need to improve efficiency, they were similar to the EFQM findings in the same study. BQF found that many organizations were demanding that their suppliers certify to ISO 9001 and the suppliers were doing so to gain or retain contracts rather than as a business improvement strategy (BQF, 2015d).

The revised standard BS EN ISO 9001:2015 goes some way to addressing these issues as there is an emphasis on encompassing customer needs and organizational leadership. This is accommodated by a number of new clauses, 'Context of the Organisation' (stakeholder requirements) and 'Leadership' (see standard structure in Focus Box 8.8). The standard also requires risk to be considered, not only the negative effects of uncertainty but the positive ones as well (opportunities).

An integrated approach has been taken in the review so that BS EN ISO 9001:2015 is fully integrated with other management standards, such as ISO 14001:2015 environmental management. ISO are utilizing a template known as Annex SL and the 2015 revision of BS EN ISO 9001 is based on this, and it ensures that all management system standards have an integrated approach in areas such as evidence and documentation. BS EN ISO 9001:2015 is

---

Focus Box 8.8. BS EN ISO 9001:2015 Structure Clauses

1. **Scope**.
2. **Normative references**.
3. **Terms and definitions**.
4. **Context of the organization** – understand the needs of interested parties (stakeholders).
5. **Leadership** – top management need to demonstrate they are engaged in the activities. Must be customer focused and their satisfaction must be maintained.
6. **Planning**, including actions necessary to address risks and opportunities (see Risk-based thinking in the text).
7. **Support resources**, including people, plus monitoring and measuring resources traceability. Communications including documentation and documentation control indicated.
8. **Operation–customer requirements**. This encompasses review, design and development of products and services; supply chain communications and controls. Customers and external suppliers' property should also be cared for.
9. **Performance evaluation** including customer satisfaction measures. Internal audits and management reviews are necessary.
10. **Improvement**.

(BSI 2015e; CQI, 2015b)

---

able to fulfil many but not all of the criteria within the Excellence Model 'enablers and results criteria' (BQF, 2015e).

BS EN ISO 9001:2015 is said to be applicable to any organization to ensure that they focus on customer requirements and continuously improve all systems and processes that impact upon them. This standard utilizes Deming's (1986, cited in Williams and Buswell, 2003) Plan, Do, Check and Act theory to inform its seven principles.

1. Customer focus.
2. Leadership.
3. Engagement of people.
4. Process approach.
5. Improvement.
6. Evidence-based decision making.
7. Relationship management (BSI, 2015e).

The process approach and risk-based thinking

The definition from ISO (2015a) is that the process approach is the systematic management of processes and their interactions to achieve intended results. The interlinkage comes about because the outputs from one process can be the inputs of another. It is said to create value for the customer and other stakeholders (BSI, 2015g) and is again based on Deming's Plan, Do, Check and Act theory (BSI, 2015e) (see Fig. 8.4).

The process approach allows for 'risk-based thinking' to ensue, whereby risk, both negative and positive (opportunities), is considered throughout the production of products or services (CQI, 2015b). The standard requires that possible changes are identified and examined for high levels of risk, which will impact on an organization's ability to meet customer requirements and take a preventative approach (ISO, 2015b; BSI, 2015f). The risk-based thinking requirements enable organizations to comply with statutory and regulatory laws. The process approach is not only recognized as important by the British Standards Institute but it is central to the EFQM Excellence and reducing waste in Six Sigma initiatives.

Benefits

The benefits of implementing BS EN ISO 9001:2015 to an organization are said to be:

- The revised standard's emphasis on leadership, whereby top management are actively involved in all aspects of the organization rather than overseeing the implementation of the QMS. It is said that greater involvement by the leadership team will ensure the whole organization will be motivated towards the organization's goals and objectives;
- It is said to ensure that quality management is now completely integrated and aligned with the business strategies of an organization, thereby increasing the probability of reaching organizational goals and objectives;

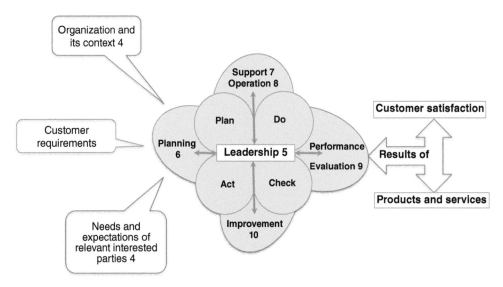

Fig. 8.4. Illustration of ISO9001:2015 Clauses 4–10 in relation to Deming's Plan, Do, Check, Act Cycle (Adapted from BSI, 2015e).

- There is a focus on risk and opportunity management;
- It is said to bring continuous improvement. Therefore, more efficient internal processes motivate and engage staff, leading to a reduction in errors and to increased profits;
- It will enable customer needs to be met, therefore leading to improved customer satisfaction and confidence in the organization; and
- Implementation of the revised standard is thought to lead to more efficiency, saving time, money and resources than with the previous version. There are fewer prescriptive requirements and evidence or documented information can be produced in any media. *No need for a quality manual or written procedures and records* (Various sources: BSI, 2015d, f; Green, 2015).

Heras-Saizarbitoria *et al.* (2011) saw the spread of ISO 9001 in its previous version as a global phenomenon. Many organizations such as the Chartered Quality Institute, International Organization for Standardization and British Standards Institute to name a few, support this growth through publications, training and podcasts etc. Although the service sector is only represented by 23.5% of the certifications compared with manufacturing at 51.6%, it is expected that further growth will come from there.

CONCLUSIONS

Ramchandani and Taylor's (2011) research demonstrated that leisure centres in their sample that had achieved a quality award had a higher performance in a variety of indicators such as utilization and satisfaction but it was not statistically significant. Many organizations enter for a number of different quality awards, but the same study found that there was a weak correlation between the number of awards a centre had and its performance in the same areas. Quest attainment was shown to strongly affect finance, and utilization performances plus customer satisfaction, but the introduction of ISO 9001 resulted in customer satisfaction being significantly higher than that of any other award. Chapter 11 will explore selection and implementation of business improvement initiatives.

QUESTIONS

1. What are the benefits and disadvantages of accredited and non-accredited business improvement strategies?

2. Why is the introduction and maintenance of business improvement strategies difficult for SMEs?

3. Why is Deming's Plan, Do, Check and Act theory so influential when business improvement strategies are devised?

4. Is a customer and employee focus paramount when implementing business improvement strategies?

FURTHER READING

Juran, J.M. and Defeo, J.A. (2010) *Juran's Quality Handbook: The Complete Guide to Performance Excellence*, 6th edn. McGraw-Hill, New York.

Kaplan, R.S. and Norton, D.P. (2006) *Alignment: Using the Balanced Scorecard to Create Corporate Synergies*. Harvard Business Review Press, Boston, Massachusetts.

Oakland, J.S. (2014) *Total Quality Management and Operational Excellence: Text with Cases*, 4th edn. Routledge, London.

REFERENCES

Adams, C.W. (2003) *Six Sigma Deployment*. Elsevier Science, Amsterdam, the Netherlands.

Antony, J. (2004) Six Sigma in the UK service organisations: results from a pilot survey. *Managerial Auditing Journal* 19(8), 1006–1013.

Antony, J. (2005a) Assessing the status of Six Sigma in the UK service organisation. *Proceedings of the Second National Conference on Six Sigma,* Wroclaw, 1–12.

Antony, J. (2005b) Six Sigma for service processes. *Business Process Management Journal* 12(2), 234–248.

Antony, J. (2008) Can Six Sigma be effectively deployed in SMEs? *International Journal of Productivity and Performance Management* 57(5), 420–423.

Antony, J., Antony, F.J. and Kumar, M. (2007) Six Sigma in service organisations. *International Journal of Quality and Reliability Management* 24(3), 294–311.

ASQ (2015) Quality Assurance vs. Quality Control. Available at: http://asq.org/learn-about-quality/quality-assurance-quality-control/overview/overview.html (accessed 24 July 2015).

Balanced Scorecard Institute (2015) About The Balanced Scorecard. Available at: http://balanced-scorecard.org/Resources/About-the-Balanced-Scorecard (accessed 13 August 2015).

Bane, R. (2002) Leading edge quality approaches in non-manufacturing organisations. *Annual Quality Congress Proceedings*, May (20–22), 245.

BQF (2015a) About the UK Excellence Award. Available at: https://www.bqf.org.uk/awards/uk-excellence-award (accessed 25 July 2015, now offline).

BQF (2015b) All UK Excellence Award Winners. Available at: https://www.bqf.org.uk/awards/uk-excellence-award/previous-winners-and-finalists (accessed 25 July 2015, now offline).

BQF (2015c) Levels of Excellence. Available at: https://www.bqf.org.uk/what-we-do/efqm-levels-of-excellence (accessed 30 May 2016).

BQF (2015d) ISO 9001. Available at: https://services.bqf.org.uk/performance-improvement/model-and-standards/iso9001 (accessed 30 May 2016).

BQF (2015e) ISO 9001 and the Excellence Model. Available at: http://www.bqf.org.uk/performance-improvement/model-and-standards/9001 (accessed 30 May 2016).

BSI (2015a) About BSI. Available at: http://www.bsigroup.com/en-GB/about-bsi (accessed 3 August 2015).

BSI (2015b) Standards. Available at: http://www.bsigroup.com/en-GB/standards (accessed 3 August 2015).

BSI (2015c) PAS 99 Integrated Management System. Available at: http://www.bsigroup.com/en-GB/pas-99-integrated-management/PAS-99-for-SMEs (accessed 3 August 2015).

BSI (2015d) ISO 9001 – Quality Management System Best Practice for Small Businesses White Paper. Available at: http://www.bsigroup.com/Documents/iso-9001/resources/BSI-ISO-9001-Management-system-White-paper-UK-EN.pdf (accessed 3 August 2015).

BSI (2015e) BS EN ISO 9001:2015 Implementation Guide. Available at: http://www.bsigroup.com/Documents/iso-9001/resources/ISO9001-IMPLEMENTATION-GUIDE-FINAL-APRIL2016.pdf (accessed 30 May 2016).

BSI (2015f) ISO 9001:2015 Revision. Available at: http://www.bsigroup.com/en-GB/iso-9001-quality-management/ISO-9001-revision-2015 (accessed 4 August 2015).

BSI (2015g) What is the difference between a process and a procedures approach? White Paper. Available at: http://www.bsigroup.com/Global/revisions/-Difference-between-process-and-procedures-approach-FINAL-June2015.pdf (accessed 28 September 2015).

Calvo-Mora, A., Navarro-Garcia, A. and Periañez-Cristobal, R. (2015) Project to improve knowledge management and key business results through the EFQM excellence model. *International Journal of Project Management* Jan, 1–14.

CAPA (2013) Ryanair SWOT Analysis. Available at: http://www.centreforaviation.com (accessed 24 July 2015).

Centre for Assessment Ltd (CFA Ltd) (2015) Best Practice Mersey Rail Ltd. Available at: http://www.customerserviceexcellence.uk.com/UserFiles/File/Case%20Study%20-%20Merseytravel.pdf (accessed 27 July 2015).

CQI (2015a) Excellence models and awards – development and evolution. Available at: http://www.thecqi.org/Knowledge-Hub/Knowledge-portal/Compliance-and-organisations/Excellence-models-and-awards (accessed 26 July 2015).

CQI (2015b) ISO 9001:2015 Understanding the International Standard White Paper. Available at: http://www.thecqi.org/Knowledge-Hub/Management-system-standards/CQI-Resources/ISO-White-Papers/ISO-90012015-and-140012015 (accessed 28 September 2015).

CSE (2015a) About the Standard. Available at: http://www.customerserviceexcellence.uk.com/aboutTheStandardCSE.html (accessed 27 July 2015).

CSE (2015b) Current Holders. Available at: http://www.customerserviceexcellence.uk.com/currentHoldersCSE.asp (accessed 27 July 2015).

Dale, B.G., Van Der Wiele, T. and Van Iwaarden, J. (2007) *Managing Quality*, 5th edn. Blackwell, Oxford, UK.

Dror, S. (2008) The balanced scorecard versus quality award models as strategic framework. *Total Quality Management and Business Excellence* 19, 583–593.

EFQM (2012) EFQM Model Criteria. Available at: http://www.efqm.org/efqm-model/model-criteria (accessed 24 July 2015).

EFQM (2013a) The EFQM Excellence model. Available at: http://www.efqm.org/the-efqm-excellence-model (accessed 24 July 2015).

EFQM (2013b) EFQM Model Fundamental Concepts. Available at: http://www.efqm.org/efqm-model/fundamental-concepts (accessed 26 July 2015).

EFQM (2013c) The EFQM Model in Action: People-Basic Assessment. Available at: http://www.efqm.org/sites/default/files/peopleassess.pdf (accessed 1 August 2015).

EFQM (2014) EFQM Model in Action Good Practice. Available at: http://www.efqm.org/efqm-model/efqm-model-in-action/leadership (accessed 1 August 2015).

Evans, J.R., Foster, S.T. Jr and Linderman, K. (2014) A content analysis of research in quality management and a proposed agenda for future research. *The Quality Management Journal* 21, 17–44.

Fleming, J.H. and Asplund, J. (2007) *Human Sigma: Managing the Employee-Customer Encounter*. Gallup Press, Washington, DC.

Green, R. (2015) ISO 9001:2015. Available at: http://quality.eqms.co.uk/iso-9001-2015-webinar-richard-green (accessed 28 September 2015).

Harry, M. and Schroeder, R. (2000) *Six Sigma: The Breakthrough Management Strategy Revolutionising the World's Top Corporations*. Doubleday Currency, New York.

Hensley, R.L. and Dobie, K. (2005) Assessing the readiness for Six Sigma in a service setting. *Managing Service Quality* 15(1), 82–101.

Heras-Saizarbitoria, I., Casadesus, M. and Marimón, F. (2011) The impact of ISO 9001 standard and the EFQM model: the view of the assessors. *Total Quality Management and Business Excellence* 20, 187–218.

Heskett, J.L., Sasser, W.E. Jr and Schlesinger, L.A. (1997) *The Service Profit Chain*. The Free Press, New York.

Hospitality Assured (2011) The standard for service and business excellence. Available at: https://www.instituteofhospitality.org/hospitality-assured/about_ha/ha (accessed 27 July 2015).

Hospitality Assured (2015) Hospitality Awards 2015. Available at: http://www.aahospitalityawards.com/awards/hospitality-awards (accessed 27 July 2015).

IEMA (2015) Introducing EMAS: The Eco-Management and Audit Scheme. Available at: http://ems.iema.net/emas (accessed 30 May 2016).

Investors in People (2015) Introduction to Investors in People. Available at: https://www.investors-inpeople.com/resources/achieving-investors-people/introduction-sixth-generation-standard (accessed 30 May 2016).

ISO (2005) ISO 9000:2005, Quality management systems – fundamentals and vocabulary. Available at: http://www.iso.org/iso/home/store/catalogue_tc/catalogue_detail.htm?csnumber=42180 (accessed 3 August 2015).

ISO (2015a) ISO 9001:2015 The Process Approach Presentation Notes. Available at: http://www.iso.org/tc176/sc02/public (accessed 28 September 2015).

ISO (2015b) Risk-Based Thinking in ISO 9001:2015. Available at: http://isotc.iso.org/livelink/live-link?slice=15867076&searchbarwidgetmode=fulltext&where1=risk+based+thinking+&-ScopeSelection=15867076%7C8835883%7CWithin+01.+Public+information&lookfor1=all-words&modifier1=relatedto&boolean2=And&lookfor2=complexquery&typeDropDownId=1&-boolean3=And&lookfor3=complexquery&dateDropDownId=1&func=search&objType=258&-SearchBarSearch=TRUE&location_id1=8835883&facets=true&fulltextMode=allwords (accessed 28 September 2015).

Kaplan, R.S. (2007) The closed loop management system for executing strategy with strategy maps and scorecards … and many other management tools, Harvard Business School presentation. Available at: http://www2.capacent.is/lisalib/getfile.aspx?itemid=22307 (accessed 1 November 2015).

Kaplan, R.S. (2010) *Conceptual Foundations of the Balanced Scorecard Working Paper 10-074*. Harvard Business School, Cambridge, Massachusetts.

Kaplan, R.S. and Norton, D.P. (1992) The balanced scorecard – measures that drive performance. *Harvard Business Review* Jan–Feb.

Looy, B.V., Gemmel, P. and Van Dierdonck, R. (2003) *Services Management, an Integrated Approach,* 2nd edn. Prentice Hall, Harlow, UK.

Marriott (2015) Awards and Recognition: Core Values and Heritage, Marriott International Corporate Values. Available at: http://www.marriott.com/culture-and-values/core-values.mi (accessed 9 October 2015).

Michelli, J.A. (2008) *The New Gold Standard*. McGraw Hill, New York.

Neely, A. (2008) Does the balanced scorecard work: an empirical investigation. Research Paper RP 1/08 School of Management, Cranfield University, UK. Available at: https://www.som.cranfield.ac.uk/som/dinamic-content/research/documents/070701-electricalstudy1.pdf (accessed 13 August 2015).

Pekovic, S. (2010) The determinants of ISO 9000 certification: a comparison of the manufacturing and service sectors. *Journal of Economic Issues* XLIV, 895–914.

Phillips, P. and Louvieris, P. (2010) Performance measurement systems in tourism, hospitality, and leis-ure small-medium-sized enterprises: a balanced scorecard perspective. *Journal of Travel Research* 44, 201–211.

Process Management International Ltd (2002–06) *Business Improvement*. Revision 1.0.1, 1–50.

Psomas, E.L., Pantouvakis, A. and Kafetzopoulos, D.P. (2013) The impact of ISO 9001 effectiveness on the performance of service companies. *Managing Service Quality* 23, 149–164.

Ramchandani, G. and Taylor, P. (2011) Quality management awards and sports facilities' performance. *Local Government Studies* 37, 121–143.

Right Directions/Leisure-Net Solutions Ltd (2014a) Quest Quality Scheme. Available at: http://quest-nbs.org (accessed 24 July 2015).

Right Directions/Leisure-Net Solutions Ltd (2014b) Guidance Notes and Assessment Preparation Forms. Available at: http://questnbs.org/quest/assessments-guidance/guidance-notes-and-preparation-forms (accessed 2 August 2015).

Right Directions/Leisure-Net Solutions Ltd (2014c) Gplus 12 Quality and Integrated Management System Guidance Notes August 2014a Issue 3. Available at: http://questnbs.org/images/PDFs/GuidanceNotes/gplus%2012%20quality%20management%20integrated%20management%20system%20guid-ance%20notes%20issue%203%20august%202014%202.pdf (accessed 2 August 2015).

Ryanair (2014) Ryanair Annual Report 2014. Ryanair (STRATEGY – Ryanair July 25 2014). Available at: http://investor.ryanair.com/wp-content/uploads/2015/04/2014-Annual-Reports-Annual-Report.pdf (accessed 30 May 2016).

UK Events (2015) The UK Events Award 2015. Available at: http://www.ukeventawards.com (accessed 2 August 2015).

Visit Lancashire (2015) Lancashire award winners. Available at: http://www.visitlancashire.com/inspire-me/lancashire-award-winners (accessed 5 October 2015).

Wessel, G. and Burcher, P. (2004) Six Sigma for small and medium-sized enterprises. *The TQM Magazine* 16(4), 264–272.

Williams, C. and Buswell, J. (2003) *Service Quality in Leisure and Tourism*. CAB International, Wallingford, UK.

Wongrassamee, S., Gardiner, P.D. and Simmons, J.E.L. (2003) Performance measuring tools: balanced scorecard and the EFQM excellence model. *Measuring Business Excellence* 7, 14–29.

Zeithaml, V.A., Parasuraman, A. and Berry, L.L. (1990) *Delivering Quality Service: Balancing Customer Perceptions and Expectations*. Free Press, New York.

Part 3

Monitoring and Enhancing Quality in the LETS Product

INTRODUCTION

Parts 1 and 2 have been more concerned with the concepts and processes of service quality in leisure, events, tourism and sport and the tools and techniques for designing and achieving service quality. The business of designing the service package, identifying the service standards and implementing a quality approach through certain methods and techniques is important and the earlier chapters highlighted these aspects. They also suggested that the nature of the service encounter and the interaction between staff and customers were key determinants in the achievement of quality service. Effective management of the service encounter requires a systematic approach and the deployment of a number of quality techniques and measures as we saw in the final chapter of Part 2. The design process and the essence of quality models and awards, including those based on the Business Excellence Model, indicated that feedback, and acting on it, is a crucial aspect of service quality as the customer evaluates the performance of the organization as well as the nature of their consumption experience.

In the service quality management literature, the meeting of customer needs and expectations is central to recognizing whether or not the appropriate quality has been delivered or achieved. We saw in the first edition that there are two moments when customers judge whether or not they are satisfied: during the service production process and again at the end (the outcome). Organizations need to be able to monitor to see whether they have been successful at both junctures and whether the customer is satisfied that value has been achieved. LETS activities have benefits linked to the customer experience, so that the features highlighted by SERVQUAL and other measurement tools in Chapters 9 and 10, like reliability, responsiveness, empathy, cleanliness and assurance, impact on the emotional and motivational dimensions of the experience. This has implications for the measuring and monitoring of customer satisfaction and service quality.

Part 3 builds on the use of an array of quality systems, tools and techniques, examined in Part 2, and highlights and evaluates ways of measuring and monitoring customer needs and satisfaction. It embraces the impact of technology and social media on such processes and considers the development of both quantitative and qualitative methods of measurement and monitoring. We know that many organizations and managers are more comfortable with numbers, but the argument for understanding behaviour and consumer experiences through qualitative measures is also persuasive.

The final chapter helps to conclude the book and highlights the strategic issue facing all LETS organizations, which is the competitive edge and the need to develop consumer-led strategies. It offers some thoughts on the options and choices available to organizations in implementing strategies for business improvement and uses a case study on the Intercontinental Hotel Group to illustrate and support many of the points in the chapter.

chapter 9

Principles of Monitoring Service Quality

LEARNING OBJECTIVES

- To understand the importance of monitoring service quality for improving the customer experience;
- To understand the principles of, and key approaches to, monitoring service quality;
- To recognize the range of stakeholders who may provide insights for improving service delivery.

INTRODUCTION

This chapter explains why it is important for LETS organizations to monitor service quality and the key approaches used to generate feedback from their consumers. No matter what quality management system, and the associated quality tools and techniques embedded within it, is implemented by an organization, there comes a point when the service delivered needs to be monitored and customers' opinions sought. A variety of qualitative and quantitative approaches can be used to carry out these two tasks.

LETS organizations need to be able to access a range of people's opinions including not only internal and external customers but also other stakeholders of the organization (shareholders, council tax payers, grant-aid bodies, etc.). The same information-gathering approach will not necessarily be used with each and every segment, partly because the type of data to be collected changes from group to group and also from context to context. For example, existing customers can be asked questions in investigating at least four different scenarios: (i) the service they have just received; (ii) the service they expected to receive; (iii) the services they would like to have in the future; and (iv) the service they receive from the organization's competitors.

The data can be gathered in three distinct ways: (i) unsolicited (e.g. written messages of thanks or complaint, informal comments to staff); (ii) passively solicited (e.g. comment cards left in every hotel bedroom); or (iii) actively solicited (e.g. asking people to fill in questionnaires, attend a focus group or give an interview). Both solicited approaches of gaining feedback require thought as to what are the objectives of the survey, which research approaches are best to achieve them, and in what format the data should be.

QUALITATIVE AND QUANTITATIVE RESEARCH APPROACHES

Johnston *et al.* (2012: 102) stated that 'a variety of means' should be used to understand customers' satisfaction with a service. The main difference between qualitative and quantitative approaches is the type of data collected that can then be processed into useful information. This initially depends on how the questions are designed and formatted, but some data-gathering methodologies can produce both qualitative and quantitative data.

Qualitative research approaches are those that result in the collection of data that are non-numerical (e.g. interviews). The purpose of generating qualitative data is to develop a deep, rich understanding of a phenomenon, rather than simply generate numerical patterns to describe it. This tends to take longer to collect and analyse, though there are a few computer software packages that can analyse qualitative data (e.g. NVIVO). It is more difficult to display the research findings visually as they do not readily fit into graphs etc., and they cannot be analysed statistically. However, that is not why qualitative data are generated; therefore, when gathering any data, their purpose should be decided upon *before* their type and approach.

This is unlike quantitative research approaches, which generate numerical data to be able to describe and test a phenomenon using statistical techniques. A variety of computer packages (e.g. SPSS, EXCEL) can be used to analyse these data quickly and display the results visually in graphical form. Depending how the questions are formatted, some surveys (e.g. electronic mail, customer surveys) can seek either qualitative or quantitative data. It is also not unusual to have a mix of qualitative and quantitative questions in the same questionnaire.

The list in Table 9.1 is divided between approaches that produce qualitative and quantitative data, or potentially both.

It is also not unusual, and is actively encouraged, to use a variety of research approaches to gain as full an evaluation of a service as possible from different perspectives. In this way the

Table 9.1. Service quality research approaches.

Type of survey approach	Qualitative approaches	Quantitative approaches	Qualitative or quantitative
Customers	Customer interviews Focus groups Customer advisory panels Complaints monitoring Critical incident technique Ombudsmen	SERVQUAL and its derivatives	Transactional surveys Customer surveys Total market surveys Internet and e-mail surveys
External organizations	Inspectors		Mystery shoppers
Internal to the organization	Suggestion schemes Employee reporting Staff surveys Quality improvement teams	SERVQUAL and its derivatives Human Sigma	

limitations of each individual research approach and its data can be reduced. Monitoring needs to be carried out on a regular basis as customer needs and expectations are constantly changing. Berry (1995) called this *systematic listening*. This chapter deals with approaches to monitoring (understanding) service quality and although these have some overlap with the content of Chapter 10, service quality *measurement* will only be covered in the next chapter.

QUALITATIVE APPROACHES

Qualitative approaches tend to be used less often than quantitative approaches when investigating service quality in the LETS product, because there is a managerial tendency to want to measure and report quickly and easily, rather than fully understand, monitor and improve, quality issues (note that quantitative measurement of service quality will be covered in Chapter 10). However, Martínez and Martínez (2010) strongly recommend the use of qualitative and quantitative techniques to understand what service quality means to customers and thus how it can be improved. To use a farming analogy, if we regularly weigh an animal we can only know how much it weighs. However, if we take time to understand its dietary needs we can nourish it and then monitor the success of that nourishment.

In-depth customer interviews

Although a very valuable way to solicit detailed customer views, interviews are used infrequently, but sometimes gain information about the organization that was not anticipated, usually in semi-structured or unstructured interviews. It is very time consuming and thus expensive, and so only a limited number can be carried out. Whilst some of the problems of administering a questionnaire are removed (e.g. misinterpreting the questions), the preparation of the data collected for analysis is also very time consuming. It takes approximately 3 hours to transcribe a tape recording of a 1-hour interview. Berry (1995) advocated structured interviews with predetermined questions as an approach for extensive service reviews. The set questions enabled comparisons to be made from one interviewee to another and from one review to another. However, this quasi-quantitative approach does not typically generate new insights. The majority of interview-based research in the LETS context utilizes semi-structured interviews, as respondents can expand upon their answers and generate richer, thicker accounts. Customers participating in LETS experiences are usually very reluctant to give up their free time to answer questions, unless waiting time is a part of that experience; for example, in an airport departure lounge or a theme park ride queue; therefore designing the location and timing of such data gathering must be given careful consideration.

Focus groups

A particular theme or topic is discussed by a small group of people with a moderator selected for the purpose. Various writers have suggested what the role of the moderator should be. Veal and Burton (2014) thought that they should direct the proceedings and make sure all items are covered, whereas others see the role as only a note taker. Williams and Parang (1997) considered whether or not there would be any advantage in using a trained moderator external to the organization. An external person would not be a stakeholder in the organization but would not be able to ask supplementary questions or extend areas of debate, due to their lack of knowledge regarding the organization. Either way, Halpern and Graham (2013) support the notion that the moderator/facilitator should be trained. According to Ghauri and Grønhaug (2010), the reason that focus groups are often used in research is that they can be a quick and relatively inexpensive way of garnering views from a range of people, and from people who may not be literate, or from groups who may be difficult to research, for example children. Unfortunately focus groups can be ineffectual if the aims and objectives are not considered and the composition is not appropriate; these are key elements of focus group design.

Researchers typically agree that using between six and twelve people for a focus group is most appropriate, although Gratton and Jones (2010) cautioned against using more than eight, to encourage the full contribution of everyone in the group. Sharpley and Jepson (2011) sought homogeneity as far as possible in their focus group memberships; however, in large and complex research this can often mean establishing multiple focus groups with different member profiles. However, Walliman (2006) suggested that member selection depends on the purpose required of their presence: a cross-section of a population; proportionate representation of elements of a population; or just a group of people who are interested in the topic. In addition, as Veal and Burton (2014) note, they are of particular value when views of a specific group of people are required, often when that group is too small to be fully represented in a larger sample.

Even when they are functioning well, focus groups necessarily cannot represent the full customer base. Also, trying to find a convenient time to convene a focus group with a representative sample is very difficult, prompting Smith and Caddick (2012) to suggest over-recruiting to ensure that a sufficient number of people arrive on the day. The corollary to this is that if there are too many people, the focus group convener must make a decision on whether or how to manage such a number.

The advantage of focus groups is that they can usually be arranged in a short period of time and so new ideas and understanding, or changes to service delivery etc., can be discussed and feedback disseminated quickly. The LETS industry frequently uses this approach, as many of its customers (e.g. school teachers, social and sports club secretaries) are not the consumers of the service (e.g. pupils, social and sports club members). In addition, some organizations use employee focus groups for improvement; for example British Airways engages flight crews in this process and these staff also undertake mystery shopping duties (see below) on-board flights.

Customer advisory panels

While customer advisory panels seem to duplicate the focus group methodology, the difference is that, whereas a focus group generally only meets once, panel members serve for a period of time and a relationship builds up. An example of this can be seen in connection with the management of Lake Windermere in the Lake District National Park. The Windermere Users Committee meets with South Lakeland District Council and the Lake District National Park Authority representatives to discuss issues to do with the management of the lake. The committee's membership includes representatives from the commercial users of Lake Windermere and the various clubs (sailing, water-skiing, motor boats, etc.). A further example is that one of the authors is a member of a readers' advisory group for a sporting magazine, to provide comments on its future focus and content.

Complaints monitoring

Organizations can view customer complaints in a number of ways. The two extremes are 'the customer is always right' and the organization uses any complaints as a learning exercise (this will be discussed later), or 'the customer is out to "get" the organization' and therefore their word cannot be trusted. The intermediate stage between these two strategies is that an organization sees customer complaints as a way of disciplining employees. Management spends time (and money) investigating and searching out the offenders rather than using the event as a learning or training opportunity and seeing that processes are reviewed, if appropriate. A culture of blame is in operation and no one takes responsibility for even minor mistakes, as the consequences are too great. Customer complaints are kept away from managers as much as possible and clients can become frustrated, as staff at low levels are not empowered to give compensation or redress in any form. This again leads to even lower perceptions of the organization.

The first strategy for dealing with customer complaints is one in which the organization thinks that 'the customer is king (or queen)'. The organization is prepared to listen to every comment or complaint from a customer and use it in a constructive way. Whilst evaluation and review of complaints is part of the process, this is an open-minded activity looking at all aspects, not just which employee to blame. These types of organization have come to be known as 'learning organizations'.

One of the main difficulties is in getting customers to comment or complain in the first place and one strategy that has been used is service guarantees. These notify the customer in advance what will happen if something goes wrong and generates feedback even if it is mostly negative in nature. Guarantees also reduce customers' perceived risk, especially if they are purchasing an expensive service (e.g. a holiday, membership of a private health club). These service guarantees are in excess of a customer's legal rights. For example, if a pizza is not delivered within 15 minutes then the customer does not have to pay for it. Or the Marriott hotel chain empowers front-desk staff with a budget they can use at their discretion, to offer a guest more benefits to recover an unsatisfactory experience (for example a free room upgrade). Some hotels in the USA will not charge a customer if there is something not to their satisfaction about their stay. This is an automatic refund with no questions asked or investigation carried out in the presence of the customer. In the latter case some customers may well take advantage of the guarantee, but the organizations considered the information they received from genuine complainants to be of great value in the longer term – more than the costs of a night's stay. On the other hand some organizations do not simply accept a customer's complaint at face value, as the following example (the 'Customer is out to "get" the organization') illustrates.

One leisure organization took this view and instigated methods to 'catch the customers out'. When receiving a complaint, employees had to call a supervisor, who then walked the complainant to a very unwelcoming room at the back of beyond. The room was spartan, poorly decorated and partly used for storage. The supervisor took a 'statement' and passed it on to a manager. The manager then investigated the complaint with the customer and any associated employees. The customer was expected to wait throughout the process and some customers left before any conclusion was delivered. Some managers were quite elated when they found in favour of the organization and not the customer. Whilst the authors are sure that some customers will make unfounded complaints, the genuine complainant is not being treated fairly and their perceptions of the organization will be even lower than before.

Lewis (2007) explained that analysing customer complaints is an important aspect of monitoring service success. Further, Au et al. (2009) noted that complaints usually emanate from service failure and if not managed properly, customers will not re-purchase from that organization and will try to denigrate its reputation through word-of-mouth. Given that we each have electronic access to a potentially global audience, Grainer *et al.* (2014) suggests that dissatisfied socially networked customers tell, on average, 280 friends about their experience. Earlier, Tripp and Grégoire (2011) found that customers experiencing severe service failure can initiate communications that go viral on the Internet, reaching millions of people immediately.

Monitoring complaints is therefore important in the LETS product and is becoming easier to achieve in real-time with the global reach of the Internet. Many LETS goods and services are purchased online and a live customer performance rating (typically 1–5 stars), supported by qualitative review comments, can be maintained, to indicate the overall quality of customers' experiences. Customer complaints in these ratings can then be investigated and responded to immediately. It is not uncommon where a complaint has been resolved for the selling organization to ask the customer to update their review subsequent to service recovery, to remove the low score.

Complaints tracking systems

This can be as simplistic as keeping a record of the number of complaints and categorizing them into specific areas of service delivery, or as sophisticated as reviewing how each individual complaint was dealt with. Organizations should be aware of the limitations of this approach, as Griffin (2002) commented that only 5–10% of customers complain and, exploring this further, Gruber *et al.* (2009) found that most dissatisfied customers do not bother to complain at all.

Horovitz and Cudennec-Poon (1990) identified five factors to account for this reluctance to complain.

1. Fear of 'hassle' or too much trouble to complain.
2. No one available to complain to.
3. Customers feel that it will do no good.
4. They do not know where to complain.
5. They attribute the problem or part of it to themselves, as they participate in the service creation and delivery process.

In addition, Bamford and Xystouri (2005) summarized earlier research and identified four further linked factors.

1. Customers think that the organization will do nothing about it.
2. Customers do not want personal confrontation with an individual.
3. Customers do not understand their rights and responsibilities.
4. Customers perceive that complaining takes a lot of time and effort.

Bodey and Grace (2006) suggested further that often people's personality traits can influence their propensity to complain about a service, and that they perceive that a complaint may harm their self-image or their image in the eyes of the person they are complaining to. These researchers concluded that organizations should try to make the complaining process more comfortable for customers, so that service failures can be monitored and understood fully. Clearly then, analysis of data needs to be fed back to appropriate areas of the organization to be used as a learning opportunity.

Whilst this seems to be an internal, informal monitoring system, a number of accredited quality systems (e.g. ISO 9001:2015, as explained in Chapter 8) require a formalized complaints monitoring system before certification can be given. They require all complaints to be logged and investigated, service recovery actions monitored and, most importantly, information provided so that managers can re-evaluate the service.

A further development has been the publication of BS ISO 10002:2014 Customer Satisfaction Complaints Handling. This gives prominence to the complaints management process, rather than integrating it into a wider quality system. The principles of the Standard (BSI, 2015) are:

- Enhancing customer satisfaction by creating a customer-focused environment that is open to feedback (including complaints), resolving any complaints received, and enhancing the organization's ability to improve its product and customer service;
- Top management involvement and commitment through adequate acquisition and deployment of resources, including personnel training;
- Recognizing and addressing the needs and expectations of complainants;
- Providing complainants with an open, effective, and easy-to-use complaints process;
- Analysing and evaluating complaints in order to improve the product and customer service quality;
- Auditing of the complaints-handling process; and
- Reviewing the effectiveness and efficiency of the complaints-handling process.

Most LETS organizations actively solicit comments from their external customers, some by placing comment cards in rooms or on tables, others by e-mailing the customer after their service experience, or even providing touchscreen technology for feedback immediately a customer leaves the service (e.g. at some Merlin Entertainment attractions). An example of the latter is the Intercontinental Hotel Group (IHG), which follows up a guest's stay with an e-mailed questionnaire seeking feedback about their experience, in addition to using guest comment cards.

The advantage of instigating a formal complaints tracking system is the potential for learning. According to Larivet and Brouard (2010), important strategic intelligence can be acquired on the customer, the complaint and how effectively it has been managed, and used with other data sources to understand its significance and not react to isolated incidents. For example, in the hospitality industry, Harris and Reynolds (2004) identified the phenomenon of '*Jaycustomers*', people who seek personal gains from deliberately complaining. Tracking and understanding complaints is, therefore, an activity in which organizations should be actively engaged.

Taking this monitoring further, Hilton uses service recovery documentation that an employee must complete when they resolve a service breakdown/complaint. This information is then fed back from their supervisors through to senior management, to be able to monitor any trends and also learn from the way in which the service has been recovered, to disseminate more widely in the organization.

Graham (1990, cited in Sampson, 1996) found that there can be a disadvantage in formally monitoring complaints, as it can make customers think negatively about the organization. However, more recently, McQuilken and Robertson (2011) identified that encouraging customers to complain about service failure can increase that customer feedback, without initiating any related word-of-mouth communications or causing the customers to leave the service. Also, with the opportunity for posting both positive and negative comments online, Grainer *et al.* (2014) found that 54% of customers will cite positive experiences, unsolicited by the service organization.

Online reviews

Since the first edition of this book, use of the online medium for consumers to comment about their LETS experiences has become normalized, post-purchase behaviour, rather than an exception. Online reviews and commentaries in social media have become so ubiquitous that the UK Competition and Markets Authority (2015) reported that 54% of adults use online reviews and 6% use blogs and vlogs to inform their purchase decisions, which are worth £23bn each year.

Online reviews are now critical to the reputation of LETS organizations, with Torres *et al.* (2015) finding that online consumer ratings have a direct impact on an organization's profitability. This virtual public arena allows consumers to report on their experiences immediately and to a global public, a phenomenon now known as ewom (electronic word of mouth) communications. Tsao *et al.* (2015) investigated the impacts of ewom in hotel reviews and established – perhaps not surprisingly – that both the total volume and proportion of positive reviews have the most impact on consumers' buying intentions, and that positive reviews were more influential than negative reviews. However, ewom also has managerial utility, beyond just informing potential consumers about the product/service they are researching to purchase. Duff's (2015) research found in the tourism context that the volume and content of reviews were important to the LETS organization to identify the homophily of consumers – hotel guests in this case – to understand typologically their wants and needs of the LETS experience.

A further development of the online review is that other people can rate the reviews themselves, creating a meta-review. Fang *et al.*'s (2016) research into online tourism reviews identified this activity as a helpful additional layer of assurance for consumers.

Because there is a huge array of online review, social media and chat forum websites giving unlimited opportunities for people to comment on a LETS product or service, Nguyen and Coudounaris (2015) recommend that organizations need an online review management (ORM) strategy to manage their online reputation. Many hotel chains already do this, but for the small to medium LETS enterprises, keeping track of this information can be almost impossible. This has led to a growth in companies that provide specialist services to collate and filter every comment placed online that relates to an organization and its products and services.

The importance of creating and developing a good online reputation has inevitably led to abuse of this public platform, through fake reviews. Mathews Hunt (2015) explained how these have increased significantly and Anderson and Simester (2014) previously discovered that 5% of reviews on a retailer's website were from non-purchasers of the retailer's products, with some reviewers even posting reviews for their own personal reasons, not influenced by the retailer! Luca and Zervas (2015) investigated fake reviews posted on Yelp about restaurants and concluded that systematic fraud exists in such reviews in the USA. More specifically they found that incidences of fraud increased where an organization had a weak reputation, very few or bad reviews, and where competition was high between similar organizations. They also found that fake reviews occurred far less in larger restaurant chains. Some of the data used in the research were from Yelp itself, who had instigated a 'sting' to identify fake reviewers. A further high profile example comes from the UK, where Mathews Hunt (2015) reported that the Advertising Standards Agency (ASA) found against TripAdvisor for not maintaining informational accuracy of reviews on its website. Subsequently, TripAdvisor has put software in place to check for anomalous or suspicious review behaviour.

As the growth in fake and paid online reviews has become increasingly understood, Filieri *et al.* (2015) noted that this has had some negative impact on consumers' trust in reviews when seeking purchase advice. Clearly, this may lead to cynicism over the value of online reviews, but the plethora of review platforms does allow consumers to search multiple sources and, in effect, conduct their own mini-literature review to evaluate the veracity of these reviews. This fake and paid reviewing activity has been called 'astroturfing' by various researchers, including Malbon (2013), who argued that it has the potential to undermine the market forces that influence sellers to behave with integrity towards their consumers, and that policy makers and regulators should respond accordingly, as the UK ASA did in the example above.

Critical incident technique

As early as 1954, Flanagan wrote that this technique comprises 'a set of procedures for collecting direct observations of human behavior in such a way as to facilitate their potential usefulness in solving practical problems'. Interestingly, Flanagan reported that one of the first studies to use this technique was by Gallon in the 1880s, observing recreational activities, but its application to an industrial setting did not occur until the late 1940s. An example of critical incident technique in practice can be seen in the following study of the effect of other customers on service delivery (Grove and Fisk, 1997) using tourists in Florida for critical incident research. The study set out to find out if, and how, critical incidents occurred and whether they were a collective (all customers) or an individual phenomenon. Whilst the majority of the literature on critical incidents concentrates on negative effects, this study also classified positive ones. Indeed, monitoring of critical success factors is seen as equally important to an organization (Wise, 1995). A series of 486 interviews was conducted, using open and closed questions. Of the 330 critical incidents recorded, 161 were positive (e.g. sociability of other customers; nobody trying to jump the queue). The negative ones included people using bad language, smoking and too many older people.

Edvardsson (1998a) first saw critical incidents in a simplistic way, citing the monitoring of customer complaints and the ability to identify when a customer is not satisfied with the service received as examples. He suggested that putting service recovery techniques in place is the solution to these incidents. In his later study of public transport, an area of major importance to the LETS industry, Edvardsson (1998b) stated that customer dissatisfaction is caused by an event and suggested that the study of these occurrences will aid continuous improvement. Not all events were classified in his study as critical incidents, only those that recur. Acknowledging this, Edvarsson and Roos (2001) later emphasized the importance of understanding the 'criticality' of a critical incident from the customer's perspective.

By identifying and concentrating on managing critical incidents, organizations can begin the process of achieving continuous improvement. These solutions may involve additional staff training, redesign of the service delivery or generating a customer profile, which can then be managed. Flanagan (1954) and Grove and Fisk (1997) described this technique as applied to the industrial setting in great detail, and the following is a summary.

1. Data collection can be carried out in a number of ways:
   i. Focus groups;
   ii. Interviews;
   iii. Questionnaires with open and closed questions.
2. Classification of data:
   i. One of the most difficult and time-consuming tasks is to devise the incident classifications into which the data can be placed. Grove and Fisk (1997) classified the data by repeating the task three times, each time using a different person. This increases the validity of the methodology;
   ii. Large categories can be divided into subgroups. A simple example is the category 'Sociability', which is divided by Grove and Fisk into 'friendly' and 'unfriendly' incidents.

In a study of adventure leisure and tourism, Donne (2009) addressed the challenge of classifying incidents by using the source of the incident within the servicescape as a category range, to help participants to identify 'critical moments of truth'.

1. Service employees.
2. Customer's own actions/performance.
3. Customer's changing disposition during the experience.
4. Tangibles.
5. Controllable servicescape.
6. Non-controllable servicescape.
7. Other users in the servicescape.
8. Service organization/management.
9. Influences of the marketing environment.

Participants were observed during their experience and field notes made of incidents within these categories. The participants were then interviewed shortly after their experience and prompted to reflect on what effect, if any, did these specific incidents have on their experience and 'other users' had a significant impact. This framework enabled structured and detailed field notes to be produced to prompt participants to reflect effectively on their experiences in a subsequent interview.

Lovelock and Wirtz (2011) suggested that managing the customer portfolio is important in the reduction of negative effects. An example they give of this being done badly is where a hotel booked two main groups of guests for the same weekend: one group attending an academic conference and the other group supporting their soccer team. These authors emphasize that other participants in the service should improve the experience, not detract from it.

In the research in Florida in the earlier example by Grove and Fisk (1997), many negative incidents were attributed to the length of time customers had to wait in theme park queues. A redesign of the service was required and they suggested that entertaining the people while they waited would reduce these encounters. Organizations such as Disney engage in this 'queuetainment' of customers (guests) at LETS visitor attractions, which, as Gnoth *et al.* (2006) found, has a positive influence on customers' emotional state of arousal and hence, their satisfaction with the experience. This management of the queueing experience is not necessary for all queues since, as Chuo and Heywood (2014) identified, there is an optimum queuing time that customers will tolerate before feelings of dissatisfaction begin. The challenge for the LETS manager then is to understand this optimum time and manage resources appropriately, to engage customers and maintain their interest. This could be by using employees in a direct 'queuetainment' role or, as with many theme parks, designing a queueing system that ensures customers will see some of the attraction as they wait, to arouse emotions and heighten the anticipation of the experience.

Limitations of the critical incident technique

When applying the critical incident technique to six different industries, Wels-Lips *et al.* (1998) found three main limitations.

1. *Customers need to rely on their memory.* As any police investigation illustrates, people interpret the same event in different ways.
2. *Multinational organizations and overseas visitors.* Wels-Lips *et al.* found that the 'determinants of critical incidents are also at least partly cultural or country specific'. The tourism industry comprises not only multinational organizations (e.g. hotel chains) but also major tourist attractions and events (e.g. Buckingham Palace, London; Beatles Experience, Liverpool) that welcome visitors from all over the world. Organizations cannot use one set of data to identify critical incidents and apply them to every country or culture.
3. *Implementation.* As with other qualitative approaches, it is very time consuming and therefore expensive. Wels-Lips *et al.*'s interviews (80 people at each of six sites) took 'several weeks'. Meyer and Westerbarkey (1996) suggested that a way to overcome this is by comment cards,

with two columns (one for positive statements and the other for negative ones), but as with all passive unsolicited approaches the reply rates will be low.

Advantages of the critical incident technique

Critical incident technique can be applied to the total customer experience, including external factors (e.g. transportation to the facility, or accommodation available in the immediate area of the site) or internal (e.g. to ascertain what the customers' positive and negative experiences have been). Internal monitoring need not be confined to customer/staff interactions but can include fellow customers, as the Florida example illustrates. Critical incident technique is a very versatile research approach and can be used both to monitor service quality and inform rewards for well-performing staff, as in the following example of a US hotel rewarding staff through critical incident. A hotel in New Hampshire, USA, made use of comment cards to solicit evidence from guests of critical incidents where employees provided especially good service. By collecting and reviewing these comment cards, management periodically rewarded employees who had the most nominations – typically every month – in order to develop a culture of employees taking the initiative to delight guests.

Inspectors

All of the externally accredited quality management systems (e.g. ISO 9001:2015) require that an 'inspection' is carried out for the initial certification and then further inspections on a cyclical basis. Most quality awards require one inspection to see if the organization can 'win' the award, usually preceded by an 'advisory visit' and many with scope for a re-inspection on a list of specified improvements. For example, the Adventure Activities Licence is a legally required safety and quality award for providing commercial adventurous activities for under 18-year olds in the UK. The licence is held for 1, 2 or 3 years, depending on the inspector's judgement.

Examples of inspection regularly encountered in the LETS industry are given below.

Restaurants

A number of organizations send out inspectors to ascertain whether the service is up to their very specific standards. Two of the most famous are Michelin and Egon Ronay, which allocate various levels of awards to restaurants. The best restaurants in the world are said to be those with the Michelin award but, apart from the inspectors, it is not known by what criteria they are judged. Whilst in both instances the inspectors act as paying customers and are not known to the establishment, the views of other customers are not included in the appraisal.

Tourist accommodation

For many years there was a number of different organizations that accredited UK hotels and guesthouses in a fragmented way, using slightly different criteria and awarding different types of 'badge'; for example, 3 stars, or 4 crowns. There were also differences between the different national schemes, and that managed by the Automobile Association (AA). Standards from the National Tourism Boards of England, Scotland, Wales and Northern Ireland have now been aligned, together with the cooperation of the AA, for a single, harmonized approach to this accreditation: the National Quality Assessment Scheme. This scheme is managed by a regulatory body called 'Quality in Tourism', which is the assessment service for VisitEngland, and its purpose is to provide information for consumers on accommodation standards in the UK. All types of accommodation are in scope for this scheme, including less obvious provision such as holiday villages, university/campuses, individual caravans and hotel boat facilities.

In making an assessment of such accommodation six overarching criteria are applied, whilst considering the nature and style of the property:

- Condition and appearance;
- Physical and personal comfort of guests;
- Service and hospitality for guests;
- Attention to detail;
- Guest choice and ease of use; and
- Cleanliness.

Within these overall criteria each specific accommodation type has its own specific standards specified (Quality in Tourism, 2015).

Sport and leisure

Quest (http://www.questnbs.org/) is the UK quality scheme for managing leisure facilities and development and sport development, endorsed by the national governing bodies: Sport England; Sport Scotland; Sport Wales; and Sport Northern Ireland as we saw in Chapter 8. It is intended to be used as a tool for continuous improvement of service quality in that sector. By defining industry standards and good practice, it aims to provide a management framework for ongoing service delivery and development. The facility management 'modules' covered by the Quest assessment are too extensive to summarize here, but there are different levels of performance and assessment that can be targeted by an organization as it grows within the framework.

Community sports clubs

Community sports clubs and their volunteer organizers are the backbone of UK sporting participation. Clubmark (http://www.clubmark.org.uk/) is a single, national, Sport England standard, to improve the country's sports club infrastructure through ensuring an appropriate environment of welfare, equity coaching and management for club members. It encourages clubs to be active and accessible in their community by focusing on four main inspection categories with their more detailed criteria:

- Activity/playing programmes;
- Duty of care and welfare;
- Knowing your club and its community; and
- Club management.

'Trade' inspectors have a valuable role to play in making sure that industry standards are adhered to or, in the case of Michelin, exceeded, but inspections have their limitations. By their very nature they are perpetuating industry customs and practices. Existing customers do not have a voice within the restaurant and hotel inspectorates.

Organizations need to embrace quality improvement strategies and gain feedback from as many sources as possible. Inspection, whether sought or not, is just another element that aids their ability to improve their service continuously. Similarly, national, independent awards such as the AA Hospitality Awards provide both public kudos and feedback on performance to an organization (see Focus Box 9.1 Thistle Hotels).

Focus Box 9.1. **Thistle Hotels**

Press Release Date: 27 September 2011

Thistle Hotels scooped the prestigious 'Hotel Group of the Year Award' last night at the AA Hospitality Awards 2011-2012. Hosted by popular BBC newsreader Sophie Raworth, at the London Hilton on Park Lane, the ceremony rewarded the best performers in the UK's hospitality industry, and was well attended by world-renowned chefs, prominent hoteliers, restaurateurs, hospitality gurus and key media.

On selecting Thistle for the award, the judging panel were particularly impressed with how the hotel group have successfully kept their focus on the guest experience and developed teams in a way that delivered this commitment – genuinely and passionately.

AA Hotel Services manager, Simon Numphud, said: 'Thistle Hotels has significantly improved their overall product and service offering over the last 18 months. This includes achievements such as full Hospitality Assured accreditation, Tourism for All audits, increasing standards particularly in hospitality and service combined by ongoing significant refurbishment. All these things combined made them a deserving choice as winner of this award.'

On receipt of the award, Heiko Figge, Managing Director of Guoman & Thistle Hotels, commented: 'We are extremely honoured to accept this award, and I'd like to thank each and every one of our Thistle colleagues for their contribution and dedication. To be named "Hotel Group of the Year" is recognition of the sheer commitment and passion our people have shown in developing and enhancing the Thistle experience. We're all very proud to be acknowledged with such a high profile industry award.'

Mystery shoppers

This is a participant observation approach used by many LETS organizations, where people pose as customers so that they can experience the service delivered by an organization. Indeed, the Quest accreditation scheme mentioned above incorporates mystery shopper visits, based on the inspection criteria. After experiencing the LETS facility, the mystery shopper uses a ratings form to ensure their evaluation is systematically structured and covers all relevant aspects of the service (Berry, 1995). Liu *et al.* (2014) extend this point in their research methodology by noting that 20 standard questions were developed to cover all aspects of customers' dining experience, but most importantly, the mystery shoppers underwent extensive training to ensure they took a consistent approach to 'shopping'.

Some breweries use mystery shoppers to ascertain whether the approaches taught on their training schemes are being put into practice; this includes greeting the customer within a specific time and serving the drinks correctly. Supporting this, Wieseke *et al.* (2011) report from their study of travel agencies that mystery shopping evaluates the service process rather than just the outcomes, and can provide valuable insights to link customer satisfaction with business performance. Further, Minghetti and Celotto (2014) deliberately link the mystery shopping process with principles of customer satisfaction in their research methodology, to investigate the performance of Tourist Information Offices in Italy and Austria.

As well as identifying poor service, mystery shopping should be used to reward good service. Berry (1995) suggested that it is necessary to instruct employees as to why this type of exercise is being used, and subsequently rewarding good service removes some of the feeling of being 'spied' upon. Of course, unsatisfactory service encounters generally result in further staff training for performance management. Latham *et al.* (2012) recommend using the feedback from a neutral mystery shopper to inform further coaching of such staff, to develop and motivate them to improve their performance. However, more fundamental service design issues can also be highlighted, which could prompt a redesign of that service. Further, Atef (2012) suggests that mystery shopper feedback could be used to inform continuous improvement.

To increase the reliability of this approach, organizations should set performance standards by which staff can be judged. The utilization of as many objective measures as possible is preferred (e.g. did the member of staff have the correct uniform on?) rather than subjective ones (e.g. was the member of staff helpful?). Whilst the use of subjective questions cannot be avoided due to the intangibility of services, the use of rating scales tries to minimize this problem, for example:

> Mystery shopper at a reception desk in a hotel.
> Were you acknowledged within 30 seconds of arriving at the check-in desk?
> Yes No   Length of time:... minutes... seconds
> Were you spoken to in a courteous manner at all times?
> Yes No
> Did you receive all the information you needed?

Yes No
Were you shown the way to the lift or stairs?
Yes No

The most successful mystery shopper exercises are those that use trained people external to the organization. Wilson (1998) stated that in 1996 over £20 million was spent on this technique and the Mystery Shopping Providers Association (http://www.mspa-eu.org/en/ 2015) asserts that this spend is now US$1.5bn worldwide, with 50,000 trips/month carried out in the UK alone. With the major growth of events management in the LETS sector, specialist companies are also now offering dedicated events mystery shopper services. However, it is not unknown for the families of head office staff to carry out this task, because using external organizations can be very costly. Apart from the fact that these people tend not to be specifically trained to be mystery shoppers, they soon start to become recognized.

External mystery shopping

By completing a series of mystery shopper observations in a number of competitor facilities as well as the organization's own outlets, a benchmarking exercise can be carried out. This enables direct comparisons to be made. Seay *et al.* (1996) considered that the data collected by using mystery shoppers in either situation had a major limitation brought on by its 'keyhole or snapshot approach'. They did not like the fact that organizational decisions are being made from a one-off observation of the service. This gives validity to the authors' original statement that a variety of survey approaches need to be used to gain an in-depth evaluation of the service provided. Wieseke *et al.* (2011) later supported this by recommending that mystery shopping should be combined with other techniques and Rood and Dziadkowiec (2013) used mystery shopping and the SERVQUAL instrument in combination to research restaurant dining experiences. However, Benjes-Small and Koceva-Wellington (2011) used the summative 'snapshot' nature of mystery shopping to recommend regular and iterative mystery shopper activity, which encourages cyclical improvement to a service.

Employee research

Whilst all the above techniques deal with soliciting customer feedback, internal customers should not be forgotten. It must be remembered that they are the only ones who can appraise internal procedures and internal service delivery, which will eventually impinge on the external customers. Berry (1995) suggested that employees, unlike external customers, will not only point out problems but can also come up with solutions to rectify them.

Many organizations have instigated suggestion schemes that reward employees if an idea is implemented. Very few of these schemes are still running after a few years, generally because there were no properly constituted systems to appraise the suggestions. Employees became disillusioned and stopped participating. Another reason for lack of participation was the lack of an appropriate reward. If employees see the organization benefiting from their ideas, especially in the area of cost saving, and they were given a 'paltry' sum as a reward, this results in them being dissatisfied.

Employee reporting

Carlzon (1987) referred to the event of front-line staff delivering services to customers as *Moments of Truth*. At this point the operations staff are privy to a whole range of comments from their customers and systems need to be in place to enable formal feedback of this information vertically and horizontally throughout the organization. Some organizations require that their senior management act as front-line staff from time to time, especially if their own position keeps them away from external customers. This also gives them insight into what it is like to work in front-line positions as well as having the opportunity to have contact with the customers. Donne's (2009) research into a LETS case organization found that senior management actively scheduled themselves as front-line staff so that they could both lead their employees by example in a subliminal staff development exercise and elicit live customer comments about their service experience. Grönroos (2007) calls these front-line encounters with customers *Moments of Opportunity* due to the potential value of the information gained from this source. Customers will be unaware that these data are being passively collected from them. As Sampson (1998) pointed out, there is no control over the sample size etc., because the respondents select themselves. However, in Donne's (2009) example, the senior management elicited qualitative comments, derived using a qualitative participant observation technique, thus sample size was unimportant and real insights were generated.

Quality circles

An extension of 'employee reporting' is the notion of quality circles, which was devised and developed by Kauru Ishikawa in the early 1960s and is arguably the most significant factor in the success of many Japanese organizations since then. Quality circles are concerned with problem solving by the employees closest to where the problems occur and, if not allowing full empowerment, can be construed as encouraging employee involvement and the process of continuous improvement. Dale and Boaden's (1994) definition of a quality circle is 'a voluntary group of between six and eight employees from the same work area'. The function of a quality circle is to allow employees to meet, in the organization's time, to solve problems for functional areas for which they are responsible. They should be trained to identify, analyse and solve some of the problems in their work, presenting solutions to management and, where possible, implementing the solutions themselves. Whilst they seem to operate in isolation, quality circles should be networked via a coordinator so that information can be passed throughout the organization.

This is an internal system with no external customer involvement and, depending on how the quality circle is constituted, can allow vertical and horizontal communications throughout the organization. The authors would disagree with Dale and Boaden that staff should always come from the same area, as this would facilitate only vertical communications. Although vertical communications are important, allowing front-line staff to disseminate customers' comments to others in different areas of the organization may be of equal importance. Quality circles comprising staff from across the organization comply with Deming's (1986) idea that institutional barriers need to be broken down for a holistic quality culture to develop. For example, at Wodin Watersports (anonymized) outdoor adventure centre, every department holds a short review meeting at the end of each day, where staff are encouraged to reflect on what can be learned for all from the day's activities in a mutually supportive environment. This is to identify areas for improvement and share examples of good practice. Then, at the end of each week there is a full staff meeting convened by the general manager, where key points are drawn out from the daily review meetings and guest feedback comments are discussed, to identify actions for improvement or good practice exemplars to share.

Service recovery may not be as immediate with quality circles as with examples of employee empowerment illustrated earlier but there are some similar principles. They encourage employees to become more active and engaged in improving the service they are delivering. They may not devolve authority quite to the extent that full empowerment does, but on occasions the solution or improvement is introduced by members of the team and the sense of ownership of the service delivery can be strong.

In order for a quality circle to be an effective tool in improving service quality and leading the way towards total quality, it must be introduced with care and sensitivity. In his early work, Mullins (1996: 543) suggested a number of criteria for successful implementation: (i) commitment and support of top management; (ii) full consultation with staff; (iii) a participative approach by management and an appropriate style of managerial behaviour; (iv) delegation of decision making; (v) trust and goodwill on both sides; (vi) an effective support structure of consultation and negotiation; (vii) support of trades unions and/or staff representatives; and (viii) continuous monitoring and review of results.

The success of quality circles depends on members being assured that they do belong to them and that they have a genuine contribution to make to enhancing service quality. There are several problems associated with quality circles. They can be dismissed as another management gimmick, especially at a time of rapid culture change. If they are used too early in the process they can be seen as management abdicating responsibility. If they are enforced they immediately lose much of their value based on the intrinsic motivation of members. The third reason for failure stems from the lack of proper training and preparation of members. The high staff turnover in some LETS organizations exacerbates this problem.

However, quality circles can offer a number of benefits for both the organization and its staff. They can offer solutions to problems that may not even have been identified in the first place. There is staff development in that group members receive additional training in communications and problem-solving skills; indeed, the literal translation of the Japanese term for quality circles is 'the gathering of the wisdom'. There may be other spin-offs in terms of increased staff morale, better teamwork and improved communication throughout the organization, as well as the main outcome in greater customer satisfaction.

CONCLUSIONS

The monitoring of service delivery and collection of feedback on customer and other stakeholders' satisfaction is important and needs to be understood by the LETS organization, to maintain and enhance service quality. This should be done deliberately and systematically, with web-based technology being a very effective mechanism. However, customer and wider stakeholder feedback should be elicited by the LETS organization using multiple media channels. Employees also provide important insights, especially those at the customer interface, as they observe at first hand the customers' experiences.

QUESTIONS

1. Why is it important for LETS organizations to monitor service quality?
2. What are the main methods of generating feedback to monitor service quality?
3. Which key stakeholders can provide the best insights into the quality of the service experience?

FURTHER READING

Bronner, F. and de Hoog, R. (2014) Social media and consumer choice. *International Journal of Marketing Research* 56(1), 51–71.
Grady, J. and James, J.D. (2013) Understanding the needs of spectators with disabilities attending sports venues. *Journal of Venue and Event Management* 4(2), 48–64.
Minghetti, V. and Celotto, E. (2014) Measuring quality of information services: combining mystery shopping and customer satisfaction research to assess the performance of tourist offices. *Journal of Travel Research* 53(5), 565–580.
Torres, E., Adler, H. and Behnke, C. (2014) Stars, diamonds and other shiny things: the use of expert and consumer feedback in the hotel industry. *Journal of Hospitality & Tourism Management* 21(December), 34–43.

REFERENCES

Anderson, E.T. and Simester, D.I. (2014) Reviews without a purchase: low ratings, loyal customers, and deception. *Journal of Marketing Research* 51(3), 249–269.
Atef, T.M. (2012) The mystery demystified: a mystery shopper's experience with hotel services and products. *Tourismos: An International Multidisciplinary Journal of Tourism* 7(1, Spring–Summer), 289–308.
Au, N., Buhalis, D. and Law, R. (2009) Complaints on the online environment – the case of Hong Kong hotels. In: *Information and Communication Technologies in Tourism. Proceedings of the International Conference in Amsterdam, The Netherlands, 2009*. Springer, Vienna, pp. 73–85.

Bamford, D. and Xystouri, T. (2005) A case study of service failure and recovery within an international airline. *Managing Service Quality: An International Journal* 15(3), 306–322.

Benjes-Small, C. and Koceva-Wellington, E. (2011) Secrets to successful mystery shopping: a case study. *College and Research Libraries News* 7(5), 274–287.

Berry, L.L. (1995) *On Great Service: A Framework for Action*. Free Press, New York.

Bodey, K. and Grace, D. (2006) Segmenting service 'complainers' and 'non-complainers' on the basis of consumer characteristics. *Journal of Services Marketing* 20(3), 178–187.

British Standards Institute (2015) *BS ISO 10002 Customer Satisfaction Complaints Handling*. British Standards Institution, London.

Carlzon, J. (1987) *Moments of Truth*. Ballinger Publications, Cambridge, Massachusetts.

Chuo, H.-J. and Heywood, J.L. (2014) An optimal queueing wait for visitors' most favourite ride at theme parks. In: Chen, J. (ed.) *Advances in Hospitality and Leisure*, Vol. 10. Emerald Group Publishing Ltd, Bingley, UK, pp. 57–73.

Competition and Markets Authority (2015) *On-line Reviews and Endorsements. Report on the CMA's Call for Information*. Crown Copyright, London.

Dale, B.G. and Boaden, R.J. (1994) The use of teams in quality management. In: Dale, B.G. (ed.) *Managing Quality*, 2nd edn. Prentice-Hall, Hemel Hempstead, UK, pp. 514–529.

Deming, W.E. (1986) *Out of the Crisis: Quality, Productivity and Competitive Position*. MIT Press, Cambridge, Massachusetts.

Donne, K.E. (2009) ADVENTUREQUAL: an extension of the SERVQUAL conceptual gap model in young people's outdoor adventure. *International Journal of Sport Management and Marketing* 6(3), 253–276.

Duff, A. (2015) Friends and fellow travellers: comparative influence of review sites and friends on hotel choice. *Journal of Hospitality & Tourism Technology* 6(2), 127–144.

Edvardsson, B. (1998a) Service quality improvement. *Managing Service Quality* 2, 142–149.

Edvardsson, B. (1998b) Causes of customer dissatisfaction – studies of public transport by critical-incident method. *Managing Service Quality* 3, 189–197.

Edvarsson, B. and Roos, I. (2001) Critical incident techniques: towards a framework for analysing the criticality of critical incidents. *International Journal of Service Industry Management* 12(3), 251–268.

Fang, B., Ye, Q., Kucukusta, D. and Law, R. (2016) Analysis of the perceived value of on-line tourism reviews: influence of readability and reviewer characteristics. *Tourism Management* 52(February), 498–506.

Filieri, R., Alguezaui, S. and McLeay, F. (2015) Why do travelers trust TripAdvisor? Antecedents of trust towards consumer-generated media and its influence on recommended adoption and word of mouth. *Tourism Management* 51 (December), 174–185.

Flanagan, J.C. (1954) The critical incident technique. *Psychological Bulletin* 51, 327–358.

Ghauri, P. and Grønhaug, K. (2010) *Research Methods in Business Studies*, 4th edn. Prentice-Hall, London.

Gnoth, J., Bigné, J.E. and Andreu, L. (2006) Waiting time effects on the leisure experience and visitor emotions. In: Kodak, M. and Andreu, L. (eds) *Progress in Tourism Marketing*. Elsevier, Oxford, UK.

Grainer, M., Noble, C.H., Bitner, M.-J. and Broetzman, S.M. (2014) What unhappy customers want. *MIT Sloan Management Review* 55(3), 31–35.

Gratton, C. and Jones, I. (2010) *Research Methods for Sports Studies*, 2nd edn. Routledge, London.

Griffin, J. (2002) *Customer Loyalty: How to Earn It, How to Keep It*. Jossey-Bass, San Francisco, California.

Grönroos, C. (2007) *Service Management and Marketing: Customer Management in Service*, 3rd edn. Wiley, Chichester, UK.

Grove, S.J. and Fisk, R.P. (1997) The impact of other customers on service experience: a critical incident examination of 'getting along'. *Journal of Retailing* 73, 63–85.

Gruber, T., Szmigin, I. and Voss, R. (2009) Handling customer complaints effectively: a comparison of the value maps of female and male complainants. *Managing Service Quality: An International Journal* 19(6), 636–656.

Halpern, N. and Graham, A. (2013) *Airport Marketing*. Routledge, London.

Harris, L.C. and Reynolds, K.L. (2004) Jaycustomer behavior: an exploration of types and motives in the hospitality industry. *Journal of Services Marketing* 18, 339–357.

Horovitz, J. and Cudennec-Poon, C. (1990) Putting service quality into gear. *Service Industries Journal* 10, 249–265.

Johnston, R., Clark, G. and Shulver, M. (2012) *Service Operations Management Improving Service Delivery*, 4th edn. Pearson, Harlow, UK.

Larivet, S. and Brouard, F. (2010) Complaints are a firm's best friend. *Journal of Strategic Marketing* 18(7), 537–551.

Latham, G.P., Ford, R.C. and Tzabbar, D. (2012) Enhancing employee and organizational performance through coaching based on mystery shopper feedback; a quasi-experimental study. *Human Resource Management* 51(2), 213–229.

Lewis, B.R. (2007) Managing service quality. In: Dale, B.G., van de Wiele, T. and van Iwaarden, J. (eds) *Managing Quality*, 5th edn. Blackwell Publishing, Malden, Massachusetts, pp. 234–257.

Liu, C.-H.S., Su, C.-S., Gan, B. and Chou, S.-F. (2014) Effective restaurant rating scale development and a mystery shopper evaluation approach. *International Journal of Hospitality Management* 43, 53–64.

Lovelock, C. and Wirtz, J. (2011) *Services Marketing: People, Technology, Strategy*. Pearson Education, Harlow, UK.

Luca, M. and Zervas, G. (2015) Fake it till you make it: reputation, competition and YELP review fraud. *Harvard Business School NOM Unit Working Paper No. 14-006*, revised edn. Harvard Business School, Boston, Massachusetts.

Malbon, J. (2013) Taking fake on-line consumer reviews seriously. *Journal of Consumer Policy* 36(2), 139–157.

Martínez, J.A. and Martínez, L. (2010) Some insights on conceptualizing and measuring service quality. *Journal of Retailing and Consumer Services* 17(1), 29–42.

Mathews Hunt, K. (2015) Gaming the system: fake online reviews vs consumer law. *Computer Law and Security Review* 31(1), 3–25.

McQuilken, L. and Robertson, N. (2011) The influence of guarantees, active requests to voice and failure severity on customer complaint behavior. *International Journal of Hospitality Management* 30(4), 953–962.

Meyer, A. and Westerbarkey, P. (1996) Measuring and managing hotel guest satisfaction. In: Olsen, M.D., Teare, R. and Gummesson, E. (eds) *Service Quality in Hospitality Organisations*. Cassell, London, pp. 185–203.

Minghetti, V. and Celotto, E. (2014) Measuring service quality of information services: combing mystery shopping and customer satisfaction research to assess the performance of Tourist Offices. *Journal of Travel Research* 53(September), 565–580.

Mullins, L.J. (1996) *Management and Organizational Behaviour*, 4th edn. Pitman, London.

Nguyen, R.A. and Coudounaris, D.N. (2015) The mechanism of online review management: A qualitative study. *Tourism Management Perspectives* 16 (October), 163–175.

Quality in Tourism (2015) The assessment service for VisitEngland. Available at: http://www.qualityintourism.com/about-quality-assessment (accessed 12 November 2015).

Rood, A.S. and Dziadkowiec, J. (2013) Cross cultural service gap analysis: comparing SERVQUAL customers and IPA mystery shoppers. *Journal of Foodservice Business Research* 16(4), 359–377.

Sampson, S.E. (1996) Ramifications of monitoring service quality through passively solicited customer feedback. *Decision Sciences* 27, 601–622.

Sampson, S.E. (1998) Gathering customer feedback via the internet: instruments and prospects. *Industrial Management & Data Systems* 9, 71–82.

Seay, T., Seaman, S. and Cohen, D. (1996) Measuring and improving the quality of public services: a hybrid approach. *Library Trends* 44, 464–490.

Sharpley, R. and Jepson, D. (2011) Rural tourism: A spiritual experience? *Annals of Tourism Research* 38(1), 52–71.

Smith, B. and Caddick, N. (2012) Qualitative methods in sport: a concise overview for guiding social scientific sport research. *Asia Pacific Journal of Sport and Social Science* 1(1), 60–73.

Torres, E.N., Singh, D. and Roberstons-Ring, A. (2015) Consumer reviews and the creation of booking transaction value: lessons from the hotel industry. *International Journal of Hospitality Management* 50(September), 77–83.

Tripp, T. and Grégoire, Y. (2011) When unhappy customers strike back on the internet. *MIT Sloan Management Review Magazine*, Spring Research Feature.

Tsao, W.-C., Hsieh, M.-T., Shih, L.-W. and Lin, T.M.Y. (2015) Compliance with eWOM: the influence of hotel reviews on booking intention from the perspective of consumer conformity. *International Journal of Hospitality Management* 46(April), 99–111.

Veal, A.J. and Burton, C. (2014) *Research Methods for Arts and Events Management*. Pearson, Harlow, UK.

Walliman, N. (2006) *Social Research Methods*. Sage, London.

Wels-Lips, I., Van der Ven, M. and Pieters, R. (1998) Critical services dimensions: an empirical investigation across six industries. *International Journal of Service Industry Management* 9, 286–309.

Wieseke, J., Malhotra, N. and Schmidt, K. (2011) Service quality: exploring the usefulness of mystery shopping for services. *AMA Summer Educators' Conference Proceedings* 22, 454–455.

Williams, S. and Parang, E. (1997) Using focus groups to match user expectations with library constraints. *Serial Librarian* 31, 335–339.

Wilson, A.M. (1998) The role of mystery shopping in the measurement of service performance. *Managing Service Quality* 8, 414–420.

Wise, D. (1995) *Performance Measurement for Charities*. ICSA Publishing, Hemel Hempstead, New York.

chapter 10

Measuring Service Quality and Satisfaction

LEARNING OBJECTIVES

- To understand the principles of measuring service quality in the LETS industry;
- To identify different techniques that are used to measure service quality;
- To understand the uses and limitations of using the SERVQUAL approach to measuring service quality.

INTRODUCTION

This chapter will explain the principles and main techniques of measuring service quality used in the LETS industry. It will concentrate on methods applied specifically to service quality and not repeat more generic research methods material that is readily available in other texts. Further, the chapter will explore the SERVQUAL approach to measuring service quality, as its variants are the most prevalent techniques applied in such research.

QUANTITATIVE METHODS OF MEASURING SERVICE QUALITY

Ferreira and Teixeira (2013) suggest that measuring the service experience is difficult, given the subjective nature of each experience and the range of possible dimensions that could apply to different services, given their different characteristics. Many different approaches have been used and are still being developed, but the main techniques applied to the LETS industry are discussed here.

Transactional or exit surveys

These are carried out immediately after the customer has received the service. An example of how this used to be done is package holiday companies giving out paper questionnaires on the flight home. As digital technology has developed, electronic mail surveys have become the norm and for many LETS services we are asked to provide some form of immediate, online feedback. For example, after visiting the Warner Bros Studio Tour London – The Making of Harry Potter, customers receive an e-mail soliciting survey feedback, incentivizing this with a draw to win gift vouchers. Most surveys of this nature are devised in-house, with the majority of the questions soliciting numerical (quantitative) data so that large survey numbers can be accommodated, but qualitative data can also be generated by this method if open-ended questions are asked. The problem with in-house surveys such as these is that they can be poorly designed and include potential – inadvertent – bias in the way questions are framed or scored. For example, one of the authors visited a French museum where the customer survey questions used a four-point Likert scale response, with three positive options and only one negative option.

Customer or user surveys

These are considered to be the easiest questionnaires to distribute, cheapest to administer and allow for a large sample to be accessed. Either qualitative or quantitative data can be generated but usually they are a mix of both. As stated earlier, this is not an exhaustive review of research methods that have their own body of knowledge, but key issues will now be identified.

Gratton and Jones (2010) noted that the advantages of surveys include ensuring a wide geographical coverage and producing highly structured data to help analysis. Extending this latter point, Veal and Burton (2014) explained that surveys allow large volumes of complex data to be interpreted succinctly and that longitudinal studies can be conducted over time using a consistent methodology.

These and other authors identified potential problems when using surveys and an example from Kim *et al.*'s (2013) research into motivations to attend an ethnic minority festival show how the impact of these can be minimized. This study focused on a food and wine festival in Australia and the statements in the questionnaire were designed to be worded and presented consistently, to avoid ambiguity and enable respondents to understand them clearly. Also, the questionnaire was administered by a team of researchers located in different areas of the festival, continuously throughout the day of the event, to ensure appropriate timing of the survey. They identified a random sample of every tenth person who passed their position, which gave control over who would be a respondent. The survey was interviewer-completed, to ensure honest and sincere answers and to maximize the response rate.

Clearly this survey could not reach non-attendees and explore their lack of motivations, but that was not the study's purpose. However, in wider services research, reaching non-users of a service is very difficult to achieve. A further limitation was identified in fieldwork by

Williams (1997) at six leisure-related organizations, which demonstrated that people do not like giving up their 'valuable' free time to be involved in a customer survey. However, given the relaxed nature of an all-day festival this may not be an issue and some LETS contexts – typically temporally extended service encounters – may be more conducive to such research than others.

General implementation of surveys

Varva (1998) advocated that four different customer groups should be surveyed.

1. *Current customers:* Ongoing monitoring of their needs and expectations as well as their perceptions of the existing service. Berry (1995) segmented current customers into two distinct categories, new and declining:

    i. *New customers:* The reasons for their attraction to the services provided by the organization are worth knowing, as are the reasons for leaving their previous service provider. Attracting new customers can be a very expensive undertaking, especially if the marketplace is saturated already (e.g. health and fitness clubs); and

    ii. *Declining customers:* Berry (1995) suggested that surveying these customers can give an indication as to the level of loyalty that customers have towards the organization as well as the reasons why they are not using the services to the same extent.

2. *Past customers:* To gain information as to the reasons they have stopped using the service and which organization they are using instead.

3. *Potential customers:* One of the most difficult groups to access but potentially worthwhile if developing new services for a different customer base. Amending existing services to fit the needs of these potential customers has a high level of risk, as it could alienate existing ones.

4. *Competitors' customers:* It is always useful to access information regarding major competitors, but this should be done in an ethical way.

Most theorists recommend that customer surveys should be carried out on a regular basis and Varva (1998) pointed out that to increase response rates, a pre-recruitment strategy should be implemented before administering the questionnaires (e.g. an e-mail or a telephone call). A popular alternative is to offer an incentive for participating (e.g. names going into a prize draw or money-off vouchers). However, this would increase the cost of the research, which is often ill-afforded in the voluntary and public sectors of the LETS industry. However, as more organizations seek feedback using incentives, this may set customers' expectations and they may not respond without one. Follow-up activities should include acknowledgement of customer participation, either individually (if not anonymous) or collectively via reports, by giving feedback on how customers' ideas or suggestions have been incorporated into the organization.

Extending Varva's work, and with reference to Chapter 9, employees are also a valuable survey population where the sample size allows. For example, at Ritz-Carlton a Human Sigma approach (see Chapter 7) was adopted, whereby employees were surveyed to establish the extent of their engagement and satisfaction with their service environment. Where the findings were acted upon hotel performance improved (Sutton, 2014).

Online surveys

Online surveys are ubiquitous, with LETS organizations seeking intelligence on how they can improve their offering and academic researchers seeking to develop bodies of knowledge. Both require efficient access to widely spread populations at a low cost, which Gratton and Jones (2010) explained are the key reasons for using the online medium. In their review of online research in hospitality and tourism, Hung and Laws (2011) found similarly that the main advantage of this medium is low cost, but also that it elicits a fast response from those respondents who do reply. Their findings supported Gratton and Jones' (2010) observation that sample representativeness/bias is a limitation, and most response rates were below 30%, which is comparable to typical postal survey response rates of around 25%.

The key disadvantage of the online medium is that only customers with access to the Internet can respond, although 75% of households in developed countries now have this. The difficulty is then researching specific populations such as the elderly and those with limited incomes (Veal and Burton, 2014). Also, because there is no public listing of e-mail addresses, and the churn rate of individual e-mail addresses is high, sampling opportunities may be limited to convenience samples with particular online communities.

If online survey research is undertaken, Costa e Silva and Duarte (2014) argued that although survey software is available, there can be compatibility issues with an organization's own system; therefore they recommend the use of online survey systems such as Survey Monkey and Zoo-merang. These are quick and easy to use and although they may have some limitations in terms of the number, type and degree of customization of questions available, they are still very effective. Overall though, the key message from these and other authors is that researchers should choose the most appropriate medium for the context of their research project, with Hung and Laws (2011) suggesting that a paper-based approach is still needed for some research populations.

An example of an online survey from Les Arcs mountain resort can be seen in Fig. 10.1. The photograph shows three different ways of gaining access to this survey: searching for the website; scanning a QR code directly; or using an SMS number. In this way customers are able to choose their access method, using the technology they prefer or have available.

These details of how to access the survey were published on the resort piste map and promoted at locations around the resort, such as the funicular termini, the Tourist Office and Ski School, and other prominently visible points around the resort. To encourage survey completion there was an incentive of a ski pass refund; thus it was necessary to specify the dates of staying at the resort. This would then provide the resort's management with very useful time-bound data about customers' experiences in specific periods, potentially identifying patterns to inform future quality enhancements.

Fig. 10.1. Les Arcs ski resort.

Net promoter score

A simpler method of obtaining feedback is the Net Promoter Score, which has gained a big following recently amongst larger organizations as a way of measuring loyalty between a customer and a business – a kind of customer satisfaction. Businesses seem to like it as it is one question, is easy to administer and can be measured at each customer touchpoint (at the end of customer service calls or visits, by incentivizing quick online forms and after complaint resolutions). It is proposed by Reichfield (2003) as the key quality measure that helps to improve business success. It identifies customer loyalty through a key survey question around how likely the customer is to recommend the company/product to a friend. On a scale of 0–10, Reichfield proposed that a rating of 0–6 is scored by 'Detractors' who would not make that recommendation, 7–8 is scored by 'Passives' who are neutral and 9–10 is given by 'Promoters' who would make that recommendation. The Net Promoter Score (NPS) is then calculated as follows:

NPS% = Promoters% – Detractors%

The imperative is thus to increase the number of Promoters and reduce the number of Detractors. Zikakis (2013) suggests that the NPS leader in an industry will outgrow its competitors by more than two and a half times and it has become a commonly used indicator in many industries. However, there is a strong debate over the effectiveness of this metric being a single solution for all organizations to achieve success. For example, Kristensen and Eskildsen's (2011) survey of 3400 Danish insurance customers concludes that the approach is methodologically flawed, especially with respect to the scaling, and that it is an 'inefficient and unreliable measure' (Kristensen and Eskildsen, 2011: 970). Williamson and Tharrett (2013) note that in the health and fitness club industry NPS can be a useful preliminary benchmark, but should not be used to compare across contexts (e.g. budget versus luxury clubs), because member expectations and business value propositions are typically different, and the score is an outcome that gives no insights into the process through which it has been achieved. These practitioners assert that NPS is not a single panacea and should be used in conjunction with other metrics.

In addition, Weill and Woerner (2015) argue that although NPS is used by major 'omni-channel' firms – especially in retail – it should be one element of a more strategic approach towards understanding 'customers' goals and life events' (Weill and Woerner, 2015: 32). They conclude that NPS should be integrated with all customer data to develop insights that are then acted upon to enhance the service encounter.

THE SERVQUAL GAP ANALYSIS MODEL

This measurement tool is based on the underpinning theory that customers judge service delivery via the formula that customer perceptions should equal or exceed customer expectations for them to be satisfied with the service provided. Customer perceptions are based on the actual service delivered, whilst customer expectations are based on past experiences, word of mouth, personal needs and the LETS organization's external communications. Urban (2013) suggested that the SERVQUAL quality attributes are prevalent in the services literature and the SERVQUAL measurement technique is used extensively by both academics and practitioners, across a wide range of sectors.

Zeithaml *et al.* (1990) devised the SERVQUAL model in the mid-1980s to measure gaps in service delivery numerically. It was originally used in the US financial sector (Parasuraman *et al.*, 1985) and subsequently made available to the remainder of the service sector. In the LETS sector, SERVQUAL or an adapted version of the instrument has been used as a measuring tool by many academic writers, either as SERVQUAL or with a new name that reflects the contextual change (Table 10.1), as this is the key factor influencing the adaptations.

Whilst the model has been applied extensively in the commercial sector of the tourism and leisure industry, not-for-profit examples are in the minority. Williams' (1997) UK research sites included two local government sports facilities (a golf course and a leisure centre), two sites funded by central government (a museum and an art gallery) and a theatre run by a charitable trust.

Implementation of the SERVQUAL instrument

Measuring the service gaps 1 to 5 (Fig. 10.2) is by three questionnaires, each one to survey a different response group: customers; managers; and operations staff.

Table 10.1. Selected adaptations of SERVQUAL.

Alternative name	Reference	Application
CASERV	Markovič and Krnetic (2014)	Casinos
DINESERV	O'Neill (2001)	Restaurants
ECOSERV	Khan (2003) Wong and Fong (2012)	Ecotourism
EVENTQUAL	Calabuig Moreno and Crespo Hervás (2009)	Sporting events
HISTOQUAL	Frochot (1996)	Heritage sites
HOLSAT	Tribe and Snaith (1998)	Holiday resort, Cuba
HOLSERV	Mei *et al.* (1999)	Hotels
LODGSERV	Knutson *et al.* (1990)	Hotels
SERVGYM	Bandyopadhyay (2013)	Gymnasia
THEMQUAL	Tsang *et al.* (2012)	Theme parks

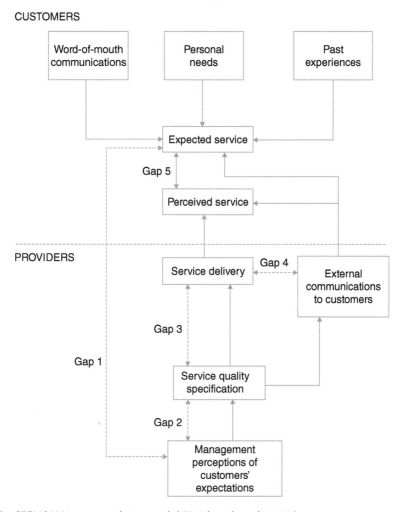

Fig. 10.2. SERVQUAL gap analysis model (Zeithaml *et al.*, 1990).

Gap 5: customer expectations versus customer perceptions

The service quality gaps can be generated both internally and externally to the organization. Gap 5 is external: customer expectations of the service judged against perceptions of the service received. Expectations of a service are affected by word-of-mouth opinions, customers' personal needs and their past experiences of their current and previous service providers (Zeithaml *et al.*, 1990).

The SERVQUAL customer questionnaire to measure Gap 5 comprises two sets of 22 statements on a seven-point Likert scale (see examples in Fig. 10.3) and has the ability to give gap scores in the range –6 to +6.

The 22 statements are categorized into five dimensions of service: tangibles, reliability, responsiveness, assurance and empathy (see Table 10.2). By analysing the scores for individual dimensions, specific elements of the customer service experience can be monitored.

Perception statements

	Strongly disagree					Strongly agree

At (X organization)
6. When a customer has a problem, excellent (X organization) will show a sincere interest in solving it.   1 2 3 4 5 6 7

11. Employees in excellent (X organization) will give prompt service to customers.   1 2 3 4 5 6 7

19. Excellent (X organization) will have operating hours convenient to all their customers.   1 2 3 4 5 6 7

Expectation statements

	Strongly disagree					Strongly agree

At (X organization)
6. When a customer has a problem, (X organization) will show a sincere interest in solving it.   1 2 3 4 5 6 7

11. Employees in (X organization) give prompt service to customers.   1 2 3 4 5 6 7

19. (X organization) has operating hours convenient to all their customers.   1 2 3 4 5 6 7

Fig. 10.3. Examples of SERVQUAL customer questions (Zeithaml *et al.*, 1990).

Table 10.2. SERVQUAL dimensions (Adapted from Ladhari, 2009).

Dimension	Definition	Questionnaire statements
Tangibles	Appearance of physical facilities, equipment, personnel and communications materials	1 to 4
Reliability	Ability to perform the promised service dependably and accurately	5 to 9
Responsiveness	Willingness to help customers and to provide prompt service	10 to 13
Assurance	Knowledge and courtesy of employees and their ability to convey trust and confidence	14 to 17
Empathy	Provision of caring individualized attention to customers	18 to 22

SERVQUAL's gap analysis theory is that the closure of Gaps 1 to 4 can rectify any discrepancies at Gap 5.

GAP 1 and 2 score generation

Gap 1 occurs when managers do not know or understand their customers' needs and expectations. The managers cannot design or specify the service that is required, creating Gap 2. The first section of the questionnaire has been designed so that a direct comparison can be made between customers' Gap 5 score and the managers' score for Gap 1. The second part enables managers' opinions to be sought on service operations.

GAP 3 and 4 score generation

The managers' questionnaire continues by measuring Gaps 3 and 4. Gap 3 is when the service specification has been designed incorrectly, thus causing the operational staff to deliver an inappropriate service. Gap 4 is when inaccurate or incomplete information is given to customers and expectations are too high. The third and final questionnaire is distributed to operational staff. This only generates scores for Gaps 3 and 4.

Constructs

Zeithaml *et al.* (1990) considered that the causes of each of these four gaps are distinct and produced by internal influences, referred to as 'constructs'. Once gaps have been detected, the checklist of 'constructs' (see Focus Box 10.1) enables organizations to make specific changes to their internal procedures and therefore reduce the gaps.

Data processing

The vehicle of three questionnaires generates a large amount of numerical data but the SERVQUAL scores can be easily calculated if a statistical software package (i.e. SPSS) or a spreadsheet (i.e. EXCEL) is used.

Criticisms of the SERVQUAL model

Although academics and practitioners have used the SERVQUAL model extensively in the service sector since its inception in the mid-1980s, both in the USA and elsewhere, it is not without its critics. However, criticism is largely concerned with the conceptualization, design and reliability of the instrument rather than its implementation.

The application of the model in different countries or cultures is very rarely commented upon. However, in more general terms Martínez and Martínez (2010) recommended developing service quality measures that are specific to a country or culture, an argument supported by Boon-itt and Rompho (2012) in their study of hotel service quality in Thailand. These authors further recommended that tourism seasons should be considered as a variable, suggesting

Focus Box 10.1. Constructs hypothesized to influence service quality gaps within the providers' organizations (Zeithaml *et al.*, 1990)

Constructs Influencing Gap 1

Market Research Orientation (MRO) Extent to which managers make an effort to understand customers' needs and expectations through formal and informal information-gathering activities.

Upward Communication (UC) Extent to which top management seeks, stimulates and facilitates the flow of information from employees at lower levels.

Level of Management (LOM) Number of managerial levels between the top-most and bottom-most levels.

Constructs Influencing Gap 2

Management Commitment to Service Quality (MCSQ) Extent to which management views service quality as a key strategic goal and allocates adequate resources to it.

Goal-Setting (GS) Existence of a formal process for setting quality of service goals.

Task Standardization (TS) Extent to which technology and training programmes are used to standardize service tasks.

Perception of Feasibility (POF) Extent to which managers believe that customers' expectations can be met.

Constructs Influencing Gap 3

Teamwork (TEAM) Extent to which all employees pull together for a common goal.

Employee-Job Fit (IT IT) Match between the skills of employees and their job.

Technology-Job Fit (TEIT) The appropriateness of the tools and technology that employees use to perform their jobs.

Perceived Control (PC) Extent to which employees perceive that they are in control of their jobs and that they can act flexibly.

Supervisory Control System (SCS) The extent to which employees are evaluated/compensated on what they do (behaviour) rather than solely on output quality.

Role Conflict (RC) Extent to which employees perceive that they cannot satisfy all the demands of all the individuals (internal and external customers) they must serve.

Role Ambiguity (RA) Extent to which employees are uncertain about what managers and supervisors expect from them and how to satisfy those expectations.

Constructs Influencing Gap 4

Horizontal Communication (HC) Extent to which communication and coordination occurs between different departments that have contact with and/or serve customers.

Propensity to Overpromise (PTO) Extent to which the firm feels pressure to promise more to customers than can be achieved.

that hotel customers may have different expectations in high and low season. However, the SERVQUAL questionnaire requires respondents to state an absolute score of excellence expectations, without reference to other variables, so this argument may not be valid.

How customers judge service

The underpinning theory of SERVQUAL (i.e. that customers are satisfied when they judge that the service they receive meets or exceeds their expectations) was questioned by Cronin and Taylor (1992, 1994), Buttle (1996) and many subsequent authors. Cronin and Taylor suggested that service customers engage in an alternative perspective of 'performance-only' evaluation and developed their 'SERVPERF' approach. The key assumption is that customers only judge the quality of their experience and do not compare their expectations and experience perceptions in making that evaluation. In the LETS industry some examples of the use of SERVPERF include: Tawse and Keogh's (1998) study of three UK leisure centres; O'Neill *et al.*'s (2000) DIVEPERF study of scuba divers to examine the five SERVQUAL attributes; Graefe and Hong's (2004) study of a Korean flower blossom festival; Tkaczynski and Stokes' (2005) study of jazz festivals and subsequent development of FESTPERF; and Lee *et al.*'s (2011) study of comparative gender perceptions of service quality in golf.

The academic debate over disconfirmation versus performance-only measurement continues, with no conclusion and strong arguments on both sides, but SERVQUAL and its variants remain more prevalent in service quality research.

Customer expectations and excellence

Zeithaml *et al.* (1990) considered the factors that influence the formulation of the customers' expectation judgement to be: word of mouth; personal needs; external communications; and past experience. The wording of the customer expectation questionnaire asks them to judge the service provided by an *excellent* facility of the same generic type, but the organization has no way of knowing what their concept of excellence is. Also, Donne (2009) found that customers often do not have 'expectations', especially if they have not experienced a service before. Instead they have 'hopes', or in some more extreme experiential contexts 'fears', for their service encounter.

Subjective judgements by staff

The SERVQUAL model is based on subjective judgements. According to Williams (1997), staff judge the services provided quite severely; they can be more critical than their customers. Two examples of this can be seen at a museum and a leisure centre. At the museum, staff commented on artefacts being out on loan, but as this site had a high number of first-time visitors, customers had no knowledge of a 'worsening or reduced' service. The consequence was that staff were inaccurate in judging their customers' expectations.

At the leisure centre, all the staff surveyed mentioned the problems of the centre's location within the boundary of a secondary school (e.g. bad behaviour of the pupils). Only one customer commented on the location as being a negative factor and the pupils' behaviour was not referred to at all.

In these instances, if the customers' gap scores do not take priority over those of the managers and operational staff, facilities may incur additional running costs by providing a level of service in excess of customer needs. Whilst this is a strategy sometimes implemented in the commercial sector of the industry, the public sector would find it difficult to sustain, necessitating reduction or even cuts in some other services.

Questionnaire design

To facilitate customer judgement via expectations and perceptions, the customer questionnaire asks two sets of similar questions. Williams (1997) observed that customers not only find this tedious but the respondents also get embarrassed at frequently choosing the number 7 when judging an excellent facility. Earlier research by Brown *et al.* (1993) confirmed this, but when Parasuraman *et al.* (1993) were responding to this criticism from others, they defended the two-part instrument as giving more accurate diagnostic information. They went on to suggest that rating expectations and perceptions on scales in adjacent columns could reduce the length of the questionnaire.

The customer questionnaire also takes a considerable time to fill in. When Williams (1997) used it as an exit survey at tourism and leisure facilities, respondents became anxious about keeping the rest of their party waiting and 'wasting' their leisure time. Putting the expectation and perception scores on adjacent columns may reduce the time but the proposed expansion of the instrument to three columns to allow transaction-specific data to be collected will exacerbate this problem (Parasuraman, 1995).

Scoring

An irregularity commented upon by both Teas (1993) and Brown *et al.* (1993) concerns the meaning of the gaps, as different numerical scores can give the same gap scores (e.g. 3 – 7 = –4; 2 – 6 = –4). Buttle (1996) questioned whether or not identical scores calculated from different values indicate the same perceived quality. Saleh and Ryan (1992), Taylor *et al.* (1993) and Mels *et al.* (1997) advanced the need for 'care' to be taken when using the numerical data, suggesting that follow-up research should be of a qualitative nature. In addition, Lee *et al.* (2011) used an alternative ratio scoring approach because they argued that SERVQUAL scoring is not sensitive enough to measure expectations versus perceptions accurately, and Humnekar and Phadtare (2011) concluded that this 'discrete' scale was not reliable for their study of hotels in India.

Dimensions

The 22 statements are grouped into Zeithaml *et al.*'s (1990) five service dimensions: tangibles, reliability, responsiveness, assurance and empathy. Babakus and Boller (1992), Cronin and Taylor (1992) and Taylor *et al.* (1993) have questioned the number and stability of them. Overlapping dimensions was experienced when SERVQUAL was implemented at an amusement park

(Williams, 1997). Customer comments indicated that the scores for the 'tangible' and 'reliability' service dimensions were both being affected by the physical environment of the site, especially the condition of the toilets. However, to the managers, the 'reliability' dimension was purely to do with the safety of the rides.

Scott and Shieff (1993) maintained that the five dimensions are only applicable to homogeneous services, which is rare to find in the LETS industry, and Calabrese and Scoglio (2012) argue that the SERVQUAL dimensions still lack variance across contexts and this is reflected by the many variations of the instrument, adapted to be industry-specific. In a specific LETS context, Guiry *et al.* (2013) concluded that other important factors should be investigated in future research into medical tourism.

Klaus and Maklan (2013) suggested that the SERVQUAL dimensions are limited and should be extended to include emotions and peer influences, which supports earlier LETS research by Donne (2009), who found that key dimensions should include what he called 'the socialscape', the customer's mood on entry into the service and their changing disposition through the service experience, especially in extended service encounters. Klaus and Maklan (2013) further proposed that they had validated a scale of customer experience quality (EXQ) with 19 determinants in four categories. This scale draws on the extant research into service attributes and determinants with a more detailed prescription of many of these, for four services' contexts. However, the authors suggest that EXQ should be tested in the context of hedonic services, proposing entertainment and tourism from the LETS industry.

In summary, and acknowledging the need to specify quality attributes for each service type, Urban (2013: 201) states: 'there is no chance of finding one universal set of quality attributes.' This is reflected by his own study linking perceived customer quality with process quality, which he tested across five different industry sectors for contextual coverage and noted that further clarification is needed for other service types.

Industry-specific adaptations

When Carman (1990), Babakus and Boller (1992) and Brown *et al.* (1993) could not replicate Zeithaml *et al.*'s research findings, Parasuraman *et al.* (1991) blamed this on the changes they made to the instrument. These authors later contradicted themselves by reasserting this issue, saying that the SERVQUAL instrument was 'the basic skeleton ... that can be supplemented with context-specific items when necessary' (Parasuraman *et al.*, 1993).

As a consequence of this potential discriminant validity limitation, many authors have produced industry-specific adaptations of the model (see Table 10.1), with the more recent versions including: EVENTQUAL (Calabuig Moreno and Crespo Hervás, 2009); THEMEQUAL (Tsang *et al.*, 2012); SERVGYM (Bandyopadhyay, 2013); and CASERV (Markovič and Krnetic, 2014). In addition, site-specific variations have been developed, such as Frochot's (1996) HISTOQUAL.

Finally, taking a more philosophical approach, Kelkar (2010) suggested SERVDIV, from the notion of Service Divinity, where in the Vedic (Hindu) tradition it is considered that 'the guest is divine' (*atithi devo bhava*). Kelkar (2010) applied this to hotels and restaurants, where the term 'guest' is commonly used, and criticized the 22-item SERVQUAL questionnaire as being 'too whiny' in its negativity, proposing instead a 16-item questionnaire in three categories. However, the questionnaire requires no customer (guest) input and is completed by the organization's employees, thus lacking a key perspective.

Despite all of these variations, the reliability of the SERVQUAL instrument may be brought into question if LETS practitioners deviate too much from the original approach, as they may not have the statistical expertise. An alternative could be to employ consultants to carry out this task (see Chapter 11).

Implementation in the LETS industry

Williams' (1997) application of the model to a number of LETS attractions highlighted a number of implementation problems, as follows.

Sampling frame

The original research of Zeithaml *et al.* (1990) was carried out in financial institutions that have a large number of managers and operational staff. This is not the case in most LETS facilities.

Non-participation in the service

Williams found that comments from most visitors were very complimentary when responding to open-ended questions about a museum, but that negative SERVQUAL gap scores had been achieved for the service dimensions of 'reliability' and 'responsiveness'. The negative gap was even more pronounced if first-time visitor scores were calculated separately.

A further analysis of the quantitative data showed that negative scores could be generated when excellent service was delivered. This is due to the customers not testing the organization's service recovery systems. As previously commented upon, tourists who are first-time visitors to a facility may not be aware of changes to service delivery that regular users may perceive as problems. These customers would therefore mark '7' against customer expectations questions and '4' on the perceptions, as instructed, if they did not know or did not have an opinion. The '4' does not act as a neutral point but influences the gap scores: 4 − 7 = −3. This again highlights how the scoring can lack stability across all responses.

Parasuraman *et al.* (1988) stated that participation in the service is a requirement for the SERVQUAL model, but in this case it would seem the visitors have in effect become partial non-participants. To try to overcome the effect of partial non-participation, Williams (1997) filtered out cases in which the respondents had chosen the number '4' for either the 'reliability' or the 'responsiveness' dimension, and positive scores were obtained but the sample size was very much reduced.

One way to overcome this is to sample only customers who have had a problem (McDougall and Levesque, 1992), but an excellent service delivery organization may have very few respondents. These organizations need to be aware of partial non-participation, as inappropriate changes to operational procedures could be undertaken. Whilst some debates arising out of these criticisms are purely in the academic domain, they have consequences for the validity of the model to practitioners.

Developments of the conceptual gap model

In addition to the contextual design and application of the SERVQUAL measurement instrument, the five-gap conceptual gap model itself has been subject to scrutiny by researchers, in terms of both the determinants of expectations and the number of potential gaps. For example, Mackay and Crompton (1988) noted 'the concept of equity' and Hanna and Wozniak (2001) suggested 'mood on entry' into the service, both of which can be determinants of expectations. Also, Luk and Layton (2002) proposed a gap between employees' and management expectations and Donne (2009) drew this research together to propose ADVENTUREQUAL, an 11-gap perceptual model with five determinants of expectations (see Fig. 10.4).

Little of this later work has been integrated into adapted versions of the SERVQUAL measurement instrument – especially the additional gaps – possibly because this would require a fundamental redesign of the 22-item questionnaire and perhaps make it too unwieldy to administer efficiently. However, if perceptual gaps and determinants are being missed by researchers ignoring these developments, there is scope to develop the measurement aspect of such extended gap models with further research.

CONCLUSIONS

Managers in the LETS industry need to understand the importance of measuring service quality, whilst seeking also to understand the qualitative factors that constitute a good service experience for customers. In this way service quality can be improved. Different measurement techniques can be used with respect to different LETS contexts, but most are either a variation of expectations–perceptions disconfirmation (e.g. SERVQUAL) or performance-only (e.g. SERVPERF) assumptions. The choice of measurement technique should be informed by its appropriateness for both the purpose and the service context.

QUESTIONS

1. How do the different possible gaps in the SERVQUAL model combine to identify areas for service improvement?
2. How can different variations of the SERVQUAL approach be adapted to suit different industry contexts?

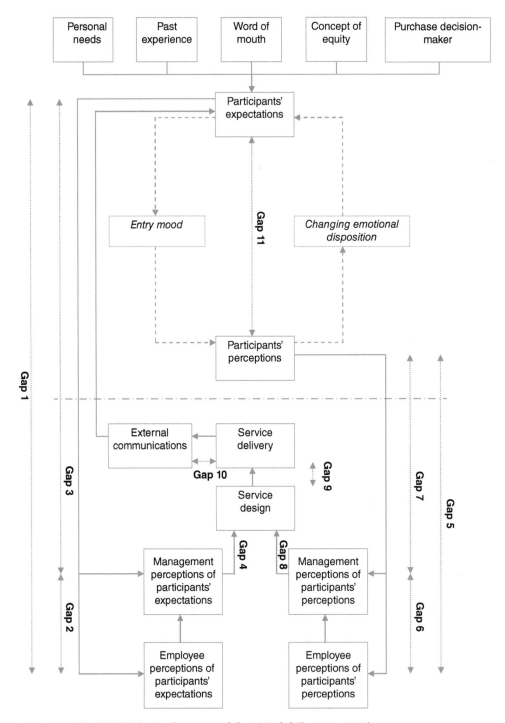

Fig. 10.4. ADVENTUREQUAL Conceptual Gap Model (Donne, 2009).

3. Which key dimensions of service quality should be measured to identify possible quality gaps?

4. Which LETS contexts may be better suited to an online survey and which may be better suited to a face-to-face questionnaire survey?

FURTHER READING

Johnston, R. (1995) The determinants of service quality: satisfiers and dissatisfiers. *International Journal of Service Industry Management* 6(5), 53–71.

Keith, N.K. and Simmers, C.S. (2013) Measuring hotel quality satisfaction: the disparity between comment cards and LODGSERV. *Academy of Marketing Studies Journal* 17(2), 119–131.

Shonk, D.J. and Chelladurai, P. (2008) Service quality, satisfaction and intent to return in event sport tourism. *Journal of Sport Management* 22, 587–602.

Williams, P. and Soutar, G.M. (2009) Value, satisfaction and behavioural intentions in an adventure tourism context. *Annals of Tourism Research* 36(3), 413–438.

REFERENCES

Babakus, E. and Boller, G.W. (1992) An empirical assessment of the Servqual scale. *Journal of Business Research* 24, 253–268.

Bandyopadhyay, N. (2013) *Service Quality, Satisfaction and Loyalty in Gymnasiums: A Study from India.* Goa Institute of Management (October 3, 2013), India.

Berry, L.L. (1995) *On Great Service: A Framework for Action.* Free Press, New York.

Boon-itt, S. and Rompho, N. (2012) Measuring service quality dimensions: an empirical analysis of Thai hotel industry. *International Journal of Business Administration* 3(5), 52–64.

Brown, T.J., Churchill, G.A. Jr and Peter, J.P. (1993) Research note: improving the measurement of service quality. *Journal of Retailing* 1, 127–139.

Buttle, F. (1996) SERVQUAL: review, critique, research agenda. *European Journal of Marketing* 30, 8–32.

Calabrese, A. and Scoglio, F. (2012) Reframing the past: A new approach to service quality assessment. *Total Quality Management and Business Excellence* 23(11/12), 1329–1343.

Calabuig Moreno, F. and Crespo Hervás, J. (2009) Using Delphi method to develop a measure of perceived quality of sport event spectators. *RETOS – Nuevas Tendencias en Educacion Fisica, Deporte y Recreacion* 15, 21–25.

Carman, J.M. (1990) Consumer perceptions of service quality: an assessment of the SERVQUAL dimensions. *Journal of Retailing* 1, 33–55.

Costa e Silva, S. and Duarte, P. (2014) Suggestions for international research using electronic surveys. *The Marketing Review* 14(3), 297–309.

Cronin, J.J. Jr and Taylor, S.A. (1992) Measuring service quality: a re-examination and extension. *Journal of Marketing* 56(July), 55–68.

Cronin, J.J. Jr and Taylor, S.A. (1994) SERVPERF versus SERVQUAL: reconciling performance-based and perceptions-minus-expectations measurement of service quality. *Journal of Marketing* (January), 125–131.

Donne, K.E. (2009) ADVENTUREQUAL: an extension of the SERVQUAL conceptual gap model in young people's outdoor adventure. *International Journal of Sport Management and Marketing* 6(3), 253–276.

Ferreira, H. and Teixeira, A.A.C. (2013) Welcome to the experience economy: assessing the influence of customer experience literature through bibliometric analysis. *FEP Working papers* 1–26.

Frochot, I. (1996) Histoqual: the evaluation of service quality in historic properties. In: Robinson, M., Evans, N. and Callaghan, P. (eds) *Proceedings of Managing Cultural Resources for the Tourist, Tourism and Culture: Towards the 21st Century Conference.* University of Nottingham Centre for Tourism and Travel/Business Education Ltd, Sunderland, UK, pp. 48–59.

Graefe, A.R. and Hong, K.-W. (2004) Predicting event satisfaction by using SERVPERF and the CIRCUMPLEX model of affect. *Journal of Tourism and Leisure Research* 16(4), 7–25.

Gratton, C. and Jones, I. (2010) *Research Methods for Sports Studies*, 2nd edn. Routledge, London.

Guiry, M., Scott, J. and Vequist, D.G. (2013) Experienced and potential medical tourists' service quality expectations. *International Journal of Health Care Quality Assurance* 26(5), 433–446.

Hanna, N. and Wozniak, R. (2001) *Consumer Behavior: An Applied Approach.* Prentice-Hall, Upper Saddle River, New Jersey.

Humnekar, T.D. and Phadtare, M. (2011) ASCI Reliability of SERVQUAL in the hotel sector of Pune City: an empirical investigation. *Journal of Management* 40(2), 60–72.

Hung, K. and Laws, R. (2011) An overview of internet-based surveys in hospitality and tourism journals. *Tourism Management* 32, 717–724.

Kelkar, M. (2010) SERVDIV: A Vedic approach to measurement of service quality. *Services Marketing Quarterly* 31(4), 420–433.

Khan, M. (2003) ECOSERV: ecotourists' quality expectations. *Annals of Tourism Research* 30(1), 109–124.

Kim, S., Savinovic, A. and Brown, S. (2013) Visitors' motivations in attending an ethnic minority cultural festival: a case study of the Fêsta Croatian Food and Wine Festival, South Australia. *Event Management* 17, 349–359.

Klaus, P. and Maklan, S. (2013) Towards a better measure of customer experience. *International Journal of Market Research* 55(2), 227–246.

Knutson, B., Stevens, P., Wullaert, C., Patton, M. and Yokoyama, F. (1990) LODGSERV: a service quality index for the lodging industry. *Hospitality Research Journal* 2, 277–284.

Kristensen, K. and Eskildsen, J. (2011) The accuracy of the net promoter under different distributional assumptions. In: *Quality, Reliability, Risk, Maintenance and Safety Engineering* (ICQR2MSE), *International Conference.* IEE, pp. 964–969.

Ladhari, R. (2009) A review of twenty years of SERVQUAL. *International Journal of Quality and Services Sciences* 1(2), 172–198.

Lee, J.-H., Kim, H.-D., Ko, Y.-J. and Sagas, M. (2011) The influence of service quality on satisfaction and intention: a gender segmentation study. *Sport Management Review* 14(1), 54–63.

Luk, S.T. and Layton, R. (2002) Perception gaps in customer expectations: managers versus service providers and customers. *Service Industries Journal* 22(2), 109–128.

Mackay, K.J. and Crompton, J.L. (1988) A conceptual model of consumer evaluation of recreation service quality. *Leisure Studies* 7, 41–49.

Markovič, M. and Krnetic, M. (2014) CASERV on casinos. *Tourism in Southern and Eastern Europe* 3, 364–379.

Martínez, J.A. and Martínez, L. (2010) Some insights on conceptualizing and measuring service quality. *Journal of Retailing and Consumer Services* 17(1), 29–42.

McDougall, G. and Levesque, T. (1992) The measurement of service quality: some methodology issues in marketing, operations and human resources insights into services. In: *2nd International Research Seminar in Service Management,* 9–12 June 1992, France, pp. 750–766.

Mei, A.W.O., Dean, A.M. and White, C.J. (1999) Analyzing service quality in the hospitality industry. *Managing Service Quality* 9(2), 136–143.

Mels, G., Boshof, C. and Nel, D. (1997) The dimensions of service quality: the original European perspective revisited. *Service Industries Journal* 17, 173–189.

O'Neill, M. (2001) Measuring service quality and customer satisfaction. In: Kandampully, J., Mok, C. and Sparks, B. (eds) *Service Quality Management in Hospitality, Tourism, and Leisure.* Haworth, New York, pp. 15–50.

O'Neill, M.A., Williams, P., MacCarthy, M. and Groves, R. (2000) Diving into service quality – the dive tour operator's perspective. *Managing Service Quality* 10(3), 131–140.

Parasuraman, A. (1995) Measuring and monitoring service quality. In: Glynn, W.J. and Barnes, J.G. (eds) *Understanding Services Management*. Wiley, Chichester, UK, pp. 143–177.

Parasuraman, A., Zeithaml, V.A. and Berry, L.L. (1985) A concept model of service quality and its implications for future research. *Journal of Marketing* 49, 41–50.

Parasuraman, A., Zeithaml, V.A. and Berry, L.L. (1988) SERVQUAL: a multiple-item scale for measuring consumer perceptions of service quality. *Journal of Retailing* 64, 12–37.

Parasuraman, A., Zeithaml, V.A. and Berry, L.L. (1991) Refinement and reassessment of the SERVQUAL scale. *Journal of Retailing* 69, 420–451.

Parasuraman, A., Zeithaml, V.A. and Berry, L.L. (1993) Research notes: more on improving service quality measurement. *Journal of Retailing* 69, 140–147.

Reichfield, F. (2003) The one number you need to grow. *Harvard Business Review* 81(12), 46–54.

Saleh, F. and Ryan, C. (1992) Analysing service quality in the hospitality industry using the Servqual model. *Service Industries Journal* 11, 324–343.

Scott, D. and Shieff, D. (1993) Service quality components and group criteria in local government. *International Journal of Service Industry Management* 4, 42–53.

Sutton, C. (2014) The applicability of the human sigma model to service quality management in the UK tourism industry: an operational analysis. PhD Thesis, University of Central Lancashire, Preston, UK.

Tawse, E.L. and Keogh, W. (1998) Quality in the leisure industry. *Total Quality Management* 9(July), 219–222.

Taylor, S.A., Sharland, A., Cronin, J.J. Jr and Bullard, W. (1993) Recreational service quality in the international setting. *International Journal of Service Industry Management* 4, 68–86.

Teas, R.K. (1993) Expectations, performance, evaluation and consumers' perceptions of quality. *Journal of Marketing* 57, 18–34.

Tkaczynski, A. and Stokes, R. (2005) All that jazz! Festival-specific predictors of service quality, satisfaction and repurchase intentions. *ANZMAC: Broadening the Boundaries* 05–07 Dec, Fremantle, Western Australia.

Tribe, J. and Snaith, T. (1998) From Servqual to Holsat: holiday satisfaction in Varadero, Cuba. *Tourism Management* 19, 25–34.

Tsang, N.K.F., Lee, L.Y.S., Wong, A. and Chong, R. (2012) THEMQUAL – adapting the SERVQUAL scale to theme park services: a case of Hong Kong Disneyland. *Journal of Travel and Tourism Marketing* 29(6), 416–429.

Urban, W. (2013) Perceived quality versus quality of process: a meta concept of service quality measurement. *The Service Industries Journal* 33(2), 200–217.

Varva, T.G. (1998) Is your satisfaction survey creating dissatisfied customers? *Quality Progress* 30(12), 51–57.

Veal, A.J. and Burton, C. (2014) *Research Methods for Arts and Events Management*. Pearson, Harlow, UK.

Weill, P. and Woerner, S.L. (2015) Thriving in an increasingly digital ecosystem MIT. *Sloan Management Review* 56(4, Summer), 27–35.

Williams, C. (1997) Is the SERVQUAL model an appropriate management tool for measuring service delivery quality in the UK leisure industry? *Managing Leisure: An International Journal* 3, 98–110.

Williamson, M. and Tharrett, S. (2013) Look Beyond Your Net Promoter Score to Drive Member Loyalty. *Club Industry* 29(11), 40.

Wong, I.A. and Fong, V.H.I. (2012) Development and validation of the casino service quality scale: CASERV. *International Journal of Hospitality Management* 31(1), 209–217.

Zeithaml, V.A., Parasuraman, A. and Berry, L.L. (1990) *Delivering Quality Service, Balancing Customer Perceptions and Expectations*. Free Press, New York.

Zikakis, B. (2013) Why you need to know about Net Promoter Scores. *Corporate Meetings & Incentives* 32(8), 11.

chapter 11

Business Improvement Strategy: A Navigation Plan for LETS Professionals

LEARNING OBJECTIVES

- To understand the need to evaluate an organization's progress in meeting its goals and achieving its visions;
- To identify solutions and opportunities needed to achieve the organization's objectives;
- To appreciate the need to prioritize the organization's plans for business improvements in line with the organization's objectives and its resource base;
- To appreciate that organizations take many business improvement routes when trying to achieve their objectives;
- To understand the effects of introducing and implementing business improvement strategies in a multi-stakeholder operational environment;
- To appreciate that monitoring and appraisal of the operational environment is potentially a never ending process.

INTRODUCTION

This final chapter is designed to help you navigate through some of the theories and instruments examined in previous chapters in order to give you an enhanced understanding of the service quality imperatives facing organizations in their strategic planning. The right set of tools, techniques or approaches provide insights to current performance and highlight areas that need attention.

To facilitate the planning of this, they have been grouped into the following key LETS *strategic* perspectives:

- Leaders' perspective;
- Multidimensional stakeholders' perspective *including customers and employees*;
- Operational perspective; and
- Research perspective.

PREPARATION

Before embarking on a new and possibly costly business improvement strategy it is necessary to ask the questions outlined below. It is quite possible that some organizations will already be able to answer many of these questions satisfactorily but it may be that they need to implement the monitoring and measuring strategies outlined in Chapters 9 and 10 before they can address the 'Where is the organization currently?' questions. This always raises the matter of cause and effect, but time spent addressing these questions and honestly appraising an organization is well worth it. This is a time for open and frank discussions through means such as focus groups or quality circles/improvement teams, chaired by people with no vested interest in the outcome and with a guarantee of no repercussion to any whistle blowers. We have included a case study (11.1) on the Intercontinental Hotel Group (IHG), which provides a good example of an organization that appears to have addressed many of the questions we pose and to have adopted a clear business strategy for improvement.

Questions to be answered include:

A. Where is the organization currently?
1. What are the organization's objectives and strategic goals?
2. What is being done successfully by the organization?
3. What is being successfully achieved in a particular section/branch/unit of the organization?
4. Are the needs of the consumers and customers being met?
5. What can be done better?

The next question 'What is the organization trying to achieve?' will be partly answered when addressing the previous question. It will be interesting to see if all areas of an organization are trying to achieve the same thing or have totally different ideas of what is expected.

Questions to be answered are:

B. What is the organization trying to achieve?
1. Where are there areas for improvement to meet the organization's objectives?
2. Are there any new goals or visions the organization needs to meet?
3. Are there any future changes, both positive and negative, which may need addressing?

The next question 'How do you get the organization to where it needs/wants to be?' may seem to be a question for managers or board members. However, following the reasoning behind employee and customer engagement examined in Chapter 7 this is undoubtedly a question that all employees address together and contribute an answer to, even though decision-making, especially when there are resource implications, will of course be left to managers. An example of this was shown in Chapter 7 where Ritz-Carlton leaders executed plans that had been developed at the department (local) level.

Questions to be answered are:

C. How do you get the organization to where it needs/wants to be?
1. Prioritize the goals, vision or changes needed.
2. Consider which business improvement strategies will enable the organization to reach its objectives.
3. Consider the resource implications of implementing a business improvement strategy.

Continue to ask the questions AGAIN and AGAIN and, more importantly, listen to the answers.

If at least the questions in A and B above have been answered, an organization is ready to consider some of the strategic objectives listed next. The first is the leaders' perspective.

LEADERS' PERSPECTIVE

Core values

Organizations are often in constant change and senior executives need to be able to cope with this whilst nurturing the company's purpose, values and goals. They need to have commitment to service quality excellence, be responsive to market pressures and refuse to countenance mediocre service with the associated low customer satisfaction levels. Even when the operational environment is difficult, leaders should not throw away the core values of their organization. Berry's (1999) evidence shows that by not changing the organization's core values, sustained success can be achieved through the strategy of constantly seeking business improvements. Core values should be limited in number (typically between five and seven) so they are memorable and deliverable. This applies to any enterprise within the LETS sector, including commercial and not-for-profit organizations.

For example, Michelli (2008) proposed the core values leaders at any company can use to provide a unique customer experience:

- *Define and refine:* Understand the ever-evolving needs of customers;
- *Empower through trust:* Empower employees by treating them with the utmost respect;
- *It's not about you:* Anticipate customers' unexpressed needs and concerns;

- *Deliver WOW!:* Enable guests to design their own experience;
- *Leave a lasting footprint: Develop and conduct an unsurpassed training regime.*

It is also important to adopt core values that can differentiate an organization from its competitors as well as providing confidence and reassurance in its approach to service quality. We have seen how the increased emphasis on the customer experience has provided opportunities to design more emotional engagement by customers into the service offer right across the LETS industry. Indeed, we see trends in developing 'immersive' experiences that reflect the values of the organization and its core product. Examples include:

- *Chester Zoo's* £40 million Islands project in 2015 aiming to 'turn guests into explorers';
- *The Guinness Storehouse* in Dublin setting out to 'emotionalize the visitor journey with a story-driven sensory experience augmented by multi-media technology';
- *Nike:* to experience the emotion of competition, winning and crushing competitors;
- *House Hotel Collections* who suggest that 'it's about a sense of place rather than simply an anonymous room'; and of course
- *Walt Disney:* 'To make people happy';
- The Intercontinental Hotel Group's 'Brand-hearted' approach (see Case Study 11.1).

We should also reiterate the view that successful and responsible organizations cannot ignore the increasingly significant issue of sustainability in their strategic planning. Core values would therefore acknowledge the role that corporate social responsibility (CSR) plays in shaping the way an organization engages with the community, as well as its contribution to a more sustainable world. The London 2012 Olympic Games for example aimed to make sustainable development part of the way it worked and a key element of its planned legacy. Core values linking to CSR can help an organization understand the many iterative ways that their business activities engage with society and the environment.

Shared values

Although it is necessary for senior managers to take responsibility to instigate and promote changes in the organization, they need to do this by inspiring and encouraging personnel throughout the organization. It is incumbent on leaders, when considering business improvements, to not exclude employees and volunteers from any area of the organization in discussions, and to nurture 'quality zealots' to embed changes throughout the organization and help overcome the difficulty of challenging the status quo.

Chapter 7 defines the importance of an engaged service culture or *'a shared purpose where everyone is focused on creating value for others inside and outside the organization'*. It examined the growing importance of 'emotional labour' as well as the emotional engagement of customers and how this links to the co-creation of value as discussed in Chapters 1 and 2. This also connects

Case Study 11.1. Intercontinental Hotel Group (IHG)

Introduction

IHG became a standalone company in 2003 and is now one of the largest hotel companies in the world, with nine brands comprising about 4000 hotels and 345,000 staff across almost 100 countries. However, it is significant to note that IHG owns very few of those hotels, although its own history goes back over 60 years and some of the brands also have a rich heritage. In fact IHG began in the 1950s with the founding of the Holiday Inn brand, which is still one of the core brands in the IHG group. IHG, instead of owning hotels, is an overall brand name, a franchise with the benefits of central marketing, operational and booking systems, but also with the challenge of ensuring and assuring quality across the brands and the individual hotels. We have focused on IHG because it ties in with many of the messages and key points highlighted in Chapter 11 and throughout the book.

Indeed, the introduction to the chapter points to the need for clear goals and objectives and an equally clear and strong vision to engage guests, staff and other stakeholders. In identifying their priorities in the last 3 years, IHG have focused on *'those things that matter the most … they are aligned with brands, people, delivery and responsible business'*. This seems to fit quite comfortably with the perspectives outlined in Chapter 11, particularly the first three – the Leaders', Stakeholders' and Operational Perspectives – and also has a resonance with our fourth perspective, Research, because of their understanding of the external environment, their analysis of the market and their use of informed consultants. In focusing on the three themes, they have identified a series of programmes for achieving the associated goals and targets, and this case study will highlight a number of these as we match the themes with the perspectives of Chapter 11.

Brands

IHG's approach links closely with the points made in Chapter 11 about core and shared values as the underpinning to the Leaders' Perspective. The IHG philosophy was manifested in 2012 by the creation of its 'BrandHearted' approach in which the brands were paramount and a number of programmes and priorities were identified to underpin this approach. This dovetails with the first perspective in Chapter 11, the Leaders' Perspective, in which the need for clear core values is emphasized. According to Richard Solomon, Chief Executive in 2014, 'We know that well-managed brand standards are at the heart of how to create preferred brands. They drive quality and consistency across our brands, giving guests the same great experience wherever and whenever they stay with us'. In recent years IHG has won over 400 awards, including: the JD Power and Associates 'Highest in Guest Satisfaction' for the Holiday Inn brand; the 'Best Business

(Continued)

Case Study 11.1. **Continued.**

Hotel Chain Worldwide' at the Business Traveller Awards; the 'Best Boutique Hotel (Hotel Indigo, Shanghai) at the TTG China Travel Awards; and the 'World's Leading Luxury Resort', The Danang Sun Peninsular (Fig. 11.1), at the World Travel Awards. Their priorities included:

- The Freshen Up phase focused on fixing the basics and raising brand quality and consistency, which included a new identity and global service training programme;
- Celebration of 60 years for Holiday Inn, building on the momentum this created and delivering a new approach to managing their brands that would give the Holiday Inn family greater distinction;
- Consolidating two new brands EVEN Hotels and HUALUXE Hotels & Resorts;
- Developing their approach to brand standards so they can consistently deliver great brand experiences;
- Continuing to develop their consumer insights in order to understand better their guests' needs;
- Introducing a General Manager training programme;
- Their Celebrate Service Week;
- Receiving high levels of responses to their Engagement Survey.

Fig. 11.1. The Danang Sun Peninsular Resort, Vietnam.

(Continued)

Case Study 11.1. Continued.

IHG identified four programme areas to help promote the brands and the core and shared values of the company.

1. Improve brand preference across the IHG family.

IHG were aware that the expectations and needs of their guests are constantly changing, and are committed to understanding the needs of their guests each time they stay; this has included using the results from a comprehensive survey of 20,000 guests to 'redefine how we think about what guests are looking for based on their needs and occasions. With this insight we can inform our portfolio strategy, identifying gaps and opportunities to grow the IHG brand family and talk about our brands in a language that makes sense to consumers'. To facilitate this, IHG:

- Have developed clear brand visions and frameworks to guide the consistent delivery of their brands around the world, from design and communications to standards and service behaviours;
- Have introduced improvements to the guest experience for the Holiday Inn® brand family as they try to differentiate each brand's position in the market better to meet guest needs; and
- Are repositioning the Crowne Plaza brand.

2. Improved quality and consistency across the brands.

This has involved developing the approach to standards, making them easier to use, to measure and maintain, including standardizing the layout and language, making them available online and providing a consistent way of managing new standards and changing existing ones. The process also embraced the 'IHG General Manager Program', a brand-specific approach to developing high-performing general managers who lead their teams to deliver the brand experience, and to build continuous development. IHG also saw the need to resolve quickly any guest issues when problems occur and launched a project to improve service recovery while guests are still in hotels – a significant aspect of service quality we have addressed throughout the book. They have also introduced a guest Internet standard that addresses price and quality across the brands to address a common source of customer dissatisfaction in hotels.

3. Use the IHG brand more effectively to strengthen guest loyalty.

IHG have identified that guests who stay in two or more brands are consistently more valuable than those who have loyalty to just one, and the IHG Rewards Club is a successful scheme to encourage lasting member loyalty through enhanced benefits.

4. Build their reputation for leadership in innovation.

This also fits closely with the developments in service and experience design we examined in Chapter 5. To achieve this, they were creating a brand innovation strategy to help the

(Continued)

Case Study 11.1. Continued.

development of the hotel of the future by testing innovations with their guests before standardization throughout the brands. For example, one of the newest brands HUALUXE Hotels & Resorts were setting out to combine tranquillity and luxurious amenities through a modern interpretation of a Chinese tea house and resort-style bathrooms, and a lobby lounge with connected gardens. IHG was also listed as one of the 'Top 10 Most Innovative Companies in Fitness' in *Fast Company*'s 2016 Most Innovative Companies issue in February 2016, for the creation of their EVEN™ Hotels brand.

Finally, we emphasized the increasing significance of sustainability and corporate social responsibility to service quality in Chapters 5 and 11, and IHG have identified three developments to support this approach:

- *IHG Academy Programmes* are partnerships between their hotels/offices and local education institutions to provide skills development and employment opportunities. Started in 2006, the programme has gained global recognition for providing quality training to over 10,000 participants in more than 150 IHG Academy Programmes;
- *The IHG Shelter Fund* raises funds to respond quickly when disaster strikes. Indeed, in 2014 IHG Shelter in a Storm Programme responded to 15 disasters, donating more than $400,000 to help those impacted;
- **Green Engage** is their award-winning environmental management system to help hotels reduce their environmental impact and operating costs (with over 50% of hotels signed up).

People

This aspect illustrates the points we have made in Chapter 11 about the Multidimensional Stakeholders' Perspective and how any approach to quality requires both customer and employee engagement and an appropriate service culture. IHG set out to 'equip our people with what they need to build a 'BrandHearted' culture in our hotels'. They worked with their hotel owners to develop a new General Manager Training Scheme and to offer new leadership competencies and an approach to project management (the IHG Way of Project Delivery), which helped their leaders gain a clearer understanding of what is expected from them in operational contexts. Chapter 7 emphasized the importance of employee engagement and the emotional labour of staff, and IHG appears to recognize this through their engagement surveys of staff (94% response in 2013) and their Celebrate Service Week Scheme, and they receive external accreditation on a number of 'Best Companies to Work For' lists. The priorities within their strategic approach focused on the following:

(Continued)

Case Study 11.1. Continued

1. Building a more effective organization.

They were concerned with how to support their teams in being even more effective and efficient through having the right structures, accountability, capabilities and ways of working, critical for delivering high performance as we have seen in the Stakeholders' Perspective in Chapter 11 and other chapters (notably 3, 7 and 8).

2. Creating a high performance culture.

They have set out to achieve this through a better linking of performance management and reward, and aligning it to company targets.

Delivery

This aspect fits closely with the Operational Perspective in Chapter 11, as well as facets of Chapters 1, 5, 6 and 8, and is concerned with how IHG can be seen to be consistent, trusted and reliable in all that it does.

- Win with channels and systems.

Almost 70% of total room revenues in 2014 were booked through IHG's channels or direct with the hotels by the 77 million Rewards Club members. Since the launching of the Rewards Club in July 2013, there has been a 10% increase in awareness of IHG as a family of brands. Direct bookings drive the highest rate premium and revenue margin per room night for owners, and the focus on driving system delivery through industry-leading web and mobile channels supports the points made in Chapters 1 and 5 about the importance of technology to service quality and the guest experience.

- Driving operational excellence.

Chapter 8 in particular, and the message in Chapter 11, highlighted the importance to service quality of various tools, systems and models and IHG are also an example of good practice in this respect through:

- *IHG Way of Project Delivery and Hotel Ready* to give their corporate project managers best-practice tools and processes for delivering their initiatives;
- *New Merlin* is a faster, simpler and more social intranet to provide all the tools and information to perform at their best;
- *Hotel Solutions* is the home for Merlin for the hundreds of best-practice tools for improving hotel performance, as well as a community of ideas and exchange of information from more than 4000 hotels;
- *Communications Standards* incorporate a set of guidelines, tools and templates to help all hotels deliver simple, engaging and consistent communications.

Source

Your Guide to 2014: A message from Richard Solomons, Chief Executive of IHG with the notion of internal customers, which was highlighted in Chapter 3, underlining the contribution to this of teamwork. Initiating formal or informal meetings from functional or cross-functional areas would be advantageous (see Chapter 9). This enables the organization to capitalize on a wider range of skills and knowledge.

Returning to the selection of on which business improvement strategy to embark, there are often future milestones that an organization will endeavour to achieve over the next 5 to 10 years' time. These are normally higher than the current performance levels. For example:

- To be world class;
- Reaching a certain size;
- Becoming a role model or leaving a legacy;
- Retaining or gaining new contracts; and
- Gaining advantage over certain competitors.

These goals form the foundations when devising the organization's quality policy. For example, Merlin Entertainments always use the following Vision Statement in relation to beating competitors: 'We are chasing the Mouse or Mickey' – meaning they are continuously striving to beat their leading competitor Disney.

It is imperative for leaders to be aware of, and to understand, the advantages and disadvantages of generic and specific business improvement strategies. This allows them to appraise the vast array of business improvement strategies outlined in Chapters 8, 9 and 10 and relate them to an organization's values, goals and purpose as they formulate quality policy.

It would therefore appear that there are no quick fixes or easy solutions; some organizations have been led to believe that business improvement strategies have a neutral cost because the cost of putting defects right is eliminated. The implementation and maintenance of chosen strategies for delivering this is an unavoidable but necessary cost, and possibly requires process and systems improvements, related registration and inspection fees, staff time and training, and perhaps even the engagement of consultants. This is explained in more detail in the section on operational perspectives later in this chapter.

MULTIDIMENSIONAL STAKEHOLDERS' PERSPECTIVE

The second aspect of strategic planning involves the multidimensional stakeholders' perspective. As Chapter 3 explores, there are a variety of stakeholders with an interest in the sustained success of an organization. Once the stakeholders have been categorized into those that have the most impact on, or value to, an organization, it is imperative that robust data collection methods are used to assess their opinions, satisfaction and engagement. In turn, once analysed, this information needs to be available to form part of the decision-making process. The next section concentrates mainly on customers and employees but other stakeholders are also considered.

Customers

Much has been written in this book and the previous edition of the book on the difficulties of obtaining information from customers about their perceptions of an organization. Some customers will complain when the service or experience provided is below their expectations, but many will not. Some customers are more than likely to place negative comments on social media. Likewise, satisfied or delighted customers may not convey this to an organization and in each of the above scenarios there is no opportunity for the organization to gain valuable information about their customers' needs. It is therefore necessary for organizations to actively solicit and encourage comments, both formal and informal, from their customers as we see in Chapters 9 and 10.

There is no single formula for measuring complaints, but a complaints or service recovery guide should comprise the following metrics:

- Number of complaints over a period of time or per department;
- Trends or frequency of similar complaints;
- Time taken to respond to and resolve the complaint;
- Employee empowerment based on the number of complaints resolved by front-line employees; and
- Cost of complaint – time, money and resources.

Therefore, designing and implementing a single service recovery form for all employees to use is desirable and should track all of the above issues. Empowering employees to design and implement such an instrument so everyone is engaged in the process of managing service recovery will ultimately increase customer engagement. Customers want someone to champion their cause of dissatisfaction and in the LETS operational environment a speedy if not immediate resolution is usually required. Although soliciting and managing customers' complaints is an important way of gaining an insight into service provision, a customer may not give an organization a second chance. Therefore knowing how to meet their needs is a pro-active way of not only reducing complaints but also retaining clients.

SERVQUAL and its LETS derivatives, explained in Chapter 10, go some way towards an organization not only gaining an insight into customers' expectations and perceptions but also employees' views as well. Whilst there are critics of this as a method of measuring customer satisfaction, it goes further than a simplistic questionnaire left in a hotel room or on a table in a restaurant.

Although the authors have argued strongly that measuring customer satisfaction levels is an important indicator of service quality, research has found that customers who are only satisfied with the service offered switch to a competitor. LETS organizations that are measuring customer engagement are ultimately interested in building a loyal customer base that can in turn deliver superior financial returns. Although customer engagement can be measured in a variety of ways, the Human Sigma approach is endorsed (see Chapter 8) as one of the most effective methods. Based on the findings, customer engagement can be categorized according to four levels.

1. Fully engaged customers.
2. Engaged customers.
3. Disengaged customers.
4. Actively disengaged.

Employees

Just as with customer satisfaction, employee satisfaction only goes so far in telling the employees' story and does not consider the effective commitment of the employee. Employee engagement is one of the most vital indicators of business success. The three theories examined in Chapter 3 known as the cycles of failure, success and mediocrity illustrate the interrelationship between customers, employees and the level of organizational success. The impact of staff having a positive attitude to customers is now known as emotional labour and was explored in Chapter 7.

To assess the level of engagement of employees requires an engagement survey that differs from the traditional employee satisfaction survey. The most famous and supported employee engagement survey is that devised as part of the Human Sigma model. The survey consists of only 12 questions but they measure the percentage of employees that are actively engaged, engaged, disengaged and actively disengaged (see also Chapter 8). Low levels of employee engagement are said to equal an absence of customer engagement. Therefore, human resources and operations/customer service should work closely together.

The importance of employees has been a major theme throughout the book and it cannot be stressed enough that it is vital that they are seen as a major resource of an organization, not only to deliver the service or experience but also to promote the organization's core values. The information that all employees gain from interacting with each other and with the external customers is so invaluable that there must be ways for them to disseminate this throughout the organization. If an organizational culture of blame exists, where faults and mistakes are only used to discipline staff, accurate information will not be forthcoming and mistakes may be concealed.

Equally, if suggestions from staff are ignored or seen as inappropriate for their pay grade, this valuable information stream will dry up (see Chapter 9). Whilst it is difficult for some managers to delegate, and to acknowledge that front-line staff have insights they do not have, it is imperative that this is undertaken. It must be stressed that this change of attitude by managers can be very difficult to instigate in the LETS operational environment where employees are temporary or on casual contracts. As always, training is needed for both managers and staff (including temporary staff) to help this change of culture and it also needs to be promoted by senior managers as part of the organization's core values. A case study accompanying Chapter 3 demonstrates this in practice in the Marriott International Inc. Hotels.

Other stakeholders

Customers and employees are said to be primary stakeholders of LETS organizations but, as illustrated in Chapter 8, many other organizations such as suppliers can not only influence the day-to-day management of the service offering but are a necessary part of the decision-making process. The supply chain of a leisure centre or cultural services facility is usually based in the same geographical area, unlike the tourism industry that is regularly reliant on a global supply chain for transportation, accommodation and excursions. The same can be said for e-commerce LETS organizations, where not only their supply chain but also their customer base can be from all over the world.

As mentioned in Chapter 9, feedback should be gathered from all stakeholders in a number of ways, both formal and informal. As suppliers and other strategic partners are paramount in the delivery of the customer service experience, a direct approach is recommended such as in-depth interviews. This is because there is a need to form relationships and promote trust so that all the goals of both parties are met. Although face-to-face interviews are best this is not always possible in a global supply chain. Although technology such as conference calls can be used once trust has been established, it is hard to develop a relationship via this method of communication.

Chapter 8 highlights the notion of 'super vendors', which comes about when an organization uses a formal assessment, via a customized set of criteria, to ascertain the potential performance of a supplier. This process is said to open communication channels, and build partnerships based on organizations with like-minded core values. The supplier or vendor that receives the higher ratings is not only awarded the contract but can become part of the business improvement processes of the organization.

Strategies that can be put into place to reward excellent suppliers include:

- Awards events;
- Away days at a sporting or other LETS events;
- Access to skills and knowledge of the organization, especially training courses; and
- Joint decision-making.

Again the Marriott International Inc. Hotels case study demonstrates this in practice.

OPERATIONAL PERSPECTIVE

The third aspect of strategic planning relates to operational imperatives. There are a number of operational perspectives that are frequently mentioned by practitioners in the LETS industry when asked about awareness or implementation of a range of integrated quality management systems (IMS), quality management systems (QMS) and measuring and monitoring tools:

- Time-consuming;
- Limited knowledge;

- Insufficient resources;
- Financial constraints;
- Not aware of any improvement tools; and
- No perceived benefits (Sutton, 2015: 313).

The six operational perspectives that are listed above are not free standing but are interrelated. For example, organizational financial constraints give rise to the notion that there is a lack of resources to either divert staff from front-line operations to attend training seasons, or to engage additional staff.

The authors would suggest that the 'cost of failure' could be much higher than the cost of introducing business improvement strategies. Failure in the LETS context can lead to a reduction in demand as the service experience does not evolve to reflect changing needs of existing or new market segments or can mean that the quality of service delivery is inconsistent or generally inappropriate for the target market. This failure is highlighted in a number of UK television programmes such as Alex Polizzi's *The Hotel Inspector* and Mary Portas' *Secret Shopper*, where both presenters use their experience of the hospitality and retail industries, respectively, to reposition a number of failing establishments. Most of these establishments are in danger of closing down as they are making little or no profit.

When an organization is considering introducing, and subsequently implementing, a business improvement strategy, a number of operational perspectives will require different approaches, dependent on the size and structure of the organization. The next three sections will examine the introduction, initial implementation and maintenance of IMSs, QMSs and tools in LETS organizations that are owner managed (e.g. small gyms and fitness studios; bed and breakfast accommodation), SMEs (e.g. leisure centres, theme parks and heritage attractions) and multinationals (such as airlines, hotel and fitness chains). The first of the three sections will compare and contrast the introduction of IMSs, QMSs and tools in LETS owner managed SMEs and multinationals, utilizing Sutton's (2015) research findings.

Introduction of IMS, QMS and tools

Sutton (2015) found that a number of respondents were not aware of, or did not understand, the benefits of introducing business improvement strategies. This is prevalent in owner-managed organizations and smaller SMEs where the concentration can be on monitoring and measuring statutory obligations such as health and safety at work, risk management and food hygiene that can attract fines or even imprisonment if the laws and regulations are not adhered to.

Even though national tourist boards provide e-courses, other trade bodies do not help spread the word and inform members, as their quality awards require very little in the way of evidence of improvement. There are many alternative ways of gaining awareness but they can be expensive, from £120 (non-members) for a local Chamber of Commerce half-day Introduction to Continuous Improvement Course to consultants and professional institutes' provision at £750 for a 2-day Implementing QMS Course. This cost, combined with the addition of accommodation and travel expenses, plus leaving the business short-staffed for over 2 days, would be prohibitive for many smaller establishments. Fortunately, the subject matter in this book should give the reader not only awareness but also an in-depth understanding of a variety of business improvement strategies, and how an organization can address the questions above, and formulate and introduce a quality policy into the workplace.

Although a complex IMS such as the Business Excellence model and a QMS such as QUEST would be very difficult for an owner-managed LETS establishment to introduce, a simplistic informal/passive measuring and monitoring tool should be achievable (e.g. engaging customers or feedback monitoring on social media) with minimum resources and cost (see Chapter 10). Unlike SMEs and multinationals, owner-managers and their small workforce are able to engage with their customers at every available opportunity. These 'moments of opportunity' gather vital information such as critical incidents, customer complaints and, sometimes, praise that need to be communicated throughout the workforce. Whilst this may take the form of a formal staff meeting once a week with small numbers of staff, this can also be achieved by informal conversations. The main problem with taking an informal perspective to business improvement when staff are under pressure is that the information gathering and dissemination does not take place. Equally, any on-the-job training needs may not be undertaken.

Another concern is that without a recognized third-party accreditation such as hotel rating systems (see Chapters 8 and 9) there is an over-reliance on information gathered from within the organization. The robustness and accuracy of this information can be questionable depending on whether the organization has a culture that learns from mistakes rather than having a culture of blame. The alternative of external accreditations has financial implications, but the organization will gain another perspective on their service offering.

Changing the culture of an organization is very difficult and it is progressively more so when the number of outlets and branches increases. SMEs and multinationals will have some of the same operational issues when introducing both simplistic QMSs and complex IMSs. When introducing any IMS, QMS or tools in both types of organizations, a series of tasks have to be undertaken – each with its own financial and other resource implications:

- Awareness training for senior managements (enables them to formulate the quality policy);
- Identification of specific business improvement leader/s;*
- Specialist training for business improvement leader/s;*
- Training of permanent staff, including part-time workers;
- Training of casual staff;
- Designing service experience processes, including setting of KPIs;
- Designing measuring and monitoring tools;
- Designing service recovery techniques; and
- IMS and QMS registration fees (if appropriate).

*It must be noted that from an operational perspective, whilst the authors are insistent that staff need to be consulted and committed to the change of culture that the introduction of IMS and QMS requires, it is necessary to have staff members that oversee the introduction and subsequent management of an IMS, QMS and tools known as Quality Champions or Business Improvement leaders.

The above list of requirements can be daunting for an organization but even more so for one that has no staff with experience of IMS, QMS and tools. To overcome this, a number of professional bodies have written specific versions of their IMS and QMS especially for SMEs including BSI ISO 9001 (see Chapter 8), and advice and training is available from many accreditation and awards bodies. Additionally, self-assessed IMSs, QMSs and tools such as Human Sigma and Balanced Scorecard (see Chapter 8) can be an excellent first stage before embarking on an externally third-party assessed IMS or QMS.

As previously stated, it is very hard to change an established organizational culture. Therefore it is necessary to decide whether to introduce an IMS or QMS in 'step changes', implementing a couple of transitional elements at any one time or whether the 'big bang' approach is appropriate with everything introduced at once. As Chapter 8 indicated, the assessment criteria of many complex IMSs can be successfully achieved by incorporating other QMSs and tools. For example, the IMS known as the Business Excellence Model has criteria that the less complex QMS and tools such as QUEST, Customer Service Excellence Model, SERVQUAL and Investors in People will meet (see Chapter 8). Equally, some of the QUEST and Customer Service Excellence criteria can be met by complaint tracking systems and customer surveys (see Chapters 9 and 10). Therefore a step-change strategy of introducing a limited number of monitoring and measuring tools first, before moving on to the more complex IMSs and QMSs may be advantageous.

The 'big bang' introduction of every aspect of proposed business improvement strategies may be possible in SMEs or multinationals if the organization pilots the changes in one branch or functional area before rolling them out company-wide. This allows for the business improvement leader/s to concentrate on one part of the organization at the initial implementation stage. Although it is not envisaged that owner-managed organizations will attempt to adopt one of the complex IMSs or QMSs, the introduction at the same time of a number of monitoring or measuring tools can be easily accommodated within these establishments.

The initial implementation of business improvement strategies will be considered in the next section.

Initial implementation of IMS, QMS and tools

Below is a list of tasks that need to be achieved to ensure a successful, initial implementation of the business improvement strategies. Even though the complexity of the IMS, QMS and tools will dictate the difficulty of each task, that will have to be addressed by all types of organization: owner-managed, SMEs and multinationals. The list includes:

1. Purchase of measuring and monitoring equipment including hardware and software.
2. Additional staff or additional staff hours required.
3. Review and re-design (such as KPIs).
4. Internal audit for a self-assessed and external accredited IMS and QMS.
5. Transition from one set of working practices to another.

It can easily be seen that the first four tasks all have financial and other resource implications that are extra to the normal LETS operational environment. The success of the initial implementation will go some way to reassuring staff that it is worthwhile. Having the benefit of extra staff, or allowing staff to work overtime to help facilitate the initial implementation, demonstrates that senior management is committed to its success.

At this stage it is necessary to review, with all staff, the newly implemented strategies and to re-design processes or give extra training if found to be necessary. Again this could be seen as adding an extra burden on to other staff if adequate resources are not available. A major motivator at this time would be if the internal audits demonstrated that improvements had been achieved. Staff would see this as just rewards for all the hard work undertaken. Although the notion of selecting either 'step change' or 'big bang' change has been discussed in the previous section on introducing business improvement strategies into an organization, it is still necessary to consider this in more detail. The transition from one set of working practices to another has major connotations for the success of the whole culture change and business improvement.

It is necessary to plan for this transition, as it is very rare for an organization suddenly to stop one way of operating and immediately start another. Business improvement leaders need to ascertain which, if any, processes can be instantly changed and which will have a lead time. For example, if a different method is going to be used to solicit customer feedback such as online surveys, what is going to happen to any subsequently returned customer comment cards?

Research carried out by one author found that planning for the transition was one of the critical factors in the success of the initial implementation. It was observed that when the initial implementation of a new business improvement strategy overlapped with an existing one, the boundaries became distorted and staff operationalized a hybrid strategy. Unfortunately it is difficult for these practices to be unravelled, especially when training budgets have already been spent.

Although the initial implementation of business improvement strategies will highlight any problems and concerns with the chosen strategies, it will also enable the service experience to be reviewed. Both of these two operational perspectives need to be considered at appropriate intervals. The next section will examine the ongoing management of not only the service experience but also the actual business improvement strategies known by quality assurance practitioners as 'maintenance'.

Maintaining the quality and uniqueness of the service experience

The maintenance and more importantly the continuous improvement of the service experience for LETS industry consumers and customers require resources. Unfortunately it can be quite difficult to quantify the actual cost savings that can be gained from continuously seeking improvements and delivering appropriate service offerings to offset these necessary expenses; the list of tasks and the resources required for this can seem to outweigh any cost savings, especially for owner-managed establishments, but as mentioned previously the cost of failure can be even higher.

Resources required to continuously improve the service experience are listed below:

- Training for newly appointed permanent staff, including part-time staff;
- Training for new casual staff;
- Staff time for monitoring, measuring and reporting;
- Business improvement leaders' time for collating, analysing data and dissemination of findings;
- Business improvement leaders' time for reviewing findings;
- Staff time – reviewing findings;
- Re-design of processes such as KPIs;
- Re-design of service experience; and
- Business improvement leaders retraining existing staff.

Once the introduction and initial implementation of the business improvement strategies has been completed it is essential that organizational leaders remain committed and support staff and value the research findings. They need to be able to allocate resources to re-designing the service experience in light of the findings and realize that training is still required, especially when new staff are recruited. These are a necessary requirement no matter which of the three types of organization is involved. Owner-managers and senior managers need also to be aware that the actual business improvement strategies need ongoing management. This will be discussed next.

Maintenance of the IMS, QMS and tools

Similarly, the maintenance and ongoing management of the IMS, QMS and tools require resources. Staff sometimes consider this to be diverting resources away from the actual service experience for the customers. Therefore it is imperative at the onset to consider the ongoing resource implication of each business improvement strategy. For example, how frequently should a customer survey be administered? There are cost implications not only for the distribution of the survey but also (at an even higher cost) for the collation and analysis of the data. Another example is how often an internal quality assurance audit should take place. The cost of even once a year is high given the amount of time needed for staff and business improvement leaders to prepare and perform this task in a robust and meaningful manner.

With externally accredited IMSs and QMSs there are requirements to be re-assessed. For example, ISO 9001:2015 requires an organization to be re-certified every 3 years although interim assessments are available if required – with additional cost implications. Unfortunately, it is very difficult to give an example of these costs as they are all based on the size of the organization and the complexity of the scope of the certification.

Below is a list of tasks that are necessary to maintain an IMS, QMS and associated tools:

- Business improvement leaders – preparation for internal and external accreditation/ certification;
- Staff – preparation for internal and external accreditation/certification;
- External accreditation/certification fees; and
- Business improvement leaders – additional training to keep up to date.

Without the commitment from senior staff to make available the necessary funds and personnel for both sets of tasks associated with the ongoing maintenance of IMSs, QMSs and tools, organizations tend to implement improvement strategies that have very little direct costs. These include quality circles/quality improvement teams, suggestion systems and customer comment cards, as we saw in Chapter 10. Although they can have a valid position within a well thought through quality policy, ad hoc monitoring and measuring tools with no quality champion and very little staff commitment are less likely to succeed.

RESEARCH PERSPECTIVE

The final aspect of introducing, initializing and maintaining business improvement strategies in an organization, not considered so far in this chapter, is whether or not to engage the help of a quality management consultant company.

In-house research or engage consultants?

The questions that LETS organizations need to ask in deciding whether to engage a consultant or to conduct in-house research include the following:

- Is there the expertise within the organization?
- Have the staff within their existing workload time to devote to an additional task within the time-frame available?
- Is there money to pay for outside help?
- What level of importance does the organization place on having reliable data about its customers', employees' and other stakeholders' views of the service provided?
- What is the longer-term cycle of needing to repeat the research?

By answering these questions in the context of the complexity of the task to be carried out (from the simplistic task of devising, collecting and collating data to the more complex task of trying to 'win' a business excellence award requiring a major business review), the decision whether or not to engage consultants becomes clearer, particularly if underpinned by listing the pros and cons. The advantages and disadvantages of an organization carrying out its own research or commissioning the work from a specialist organization are shown in Table 11.1.

An example of a LETS organization engaging external consultants is the hotel chain Premier Inn, which has used an independent market research agency to conduct an online survey of guests after their stay. The agency uses Premier Inn's customer database to e-mail departed guests with a URL to follow to complete the survey. Guests are offered a substantial monthly cash prize draw as an incentive to encourage completion.

CONCLUSIONS

The need for resources, especially staff time, is the predominant factor throughout this chapter and it can be very difficult to justify this need, especially when owner-managed establishments are involved. Some organizations find that external accreditation or certification to a specific QMS such as ISO 9001:2015 (see Chapter 8) is a prerequisite for winning and retaining contracts. Therefore there is a direct correlation between the cost of implementation and the return on investment.

Business improvement is sometimes seen as a 'fad' by LETS practitioners who have witnessed their organizations instigating a variety of strategies that seem to have no benefit to the company and only give extra work to front-line staff. Equally, the senior management can sometimes abandon their chosen quality policy too soon, before any benefits to the business can be seen.

Formal methods and approaches therefore provide organizations with the opportunity to progress beyond the serendipitous circumstances that have sometimes determined product and service developments in the past. Quality is a strategic issue and many aspects of service quality involve the operationalizing of strategic thinking within organizations about their customers and their requirements. We have set out throughout the book to update thinking on service quality and its underpinning theories and to apply them to particular contexts and examples across the LETS industry. Managing service quality in leisure, events, tourism and sport requires a distinctive approach because of the nature of the leisure and tourism product, now firmly rooted in the experience economy and an immersive experience for the individual. The service offering is a complex mix of attributes and quality dimensions, including contextual, human, social, environmental and physical factors, with the interaction between customers and staff, the co-creation of value and the frequent role of the customer in the service encounter providing distinctive characteristics. Two significant points immediately emerged, namely that, first, customers and employees are central to the judgement of quality and, second, there is a need for continuous improvement to meet their ever-changing expectations.

Recognizing the social nature or the impact of the employee–customer encounter has on the overall service experience within the LETS industry is critical. For example, it has been argued

Table 11.1. **The advantages and disadvantages of in-house research versus engaging consultants.**

Methods	Advantages	Disadvantages
In-house research	Indirect costs, therefore may seem cheaper.	May interfere with other roles and responsibilities of the staff assigned to the task.
	Good access to colleagues and data in the organization.	Staff may have private agendas to explore and use the process to their own ends.
	Experience in the industry context.	May not have the expertise to use more complex methodologies, etc.
Engaging consultants	Additional staff for a short, fixed period of time.	Direct costs, therefore seems expensive.
		Not experienced in the industry context.
	Have the expertise to carry out the task accurately.	Not responsible for implementing the findings, nor subsequent success or failure.
	Different approach, not related to existing cultures and traditions of the organization or industry.	An existing member of staff needs to be responsible for the project and for liaising with the consultants.
	Catalyst for change.	Large project may need a large in-house liaison team.
	Blaming changes on third-party research recommendations can reduce staff resistance to them.	Conflict may result, which, whilst potentially healthy, will require time to be resolved.
		Consultants may seek to evidence what they think senior managers wish to hear.
		Can be difficult to find a consultancy that is right for the organization.

that service encounters are first and foremost social encounters and must therefore proceed from a conceptualization of these structural and dynamic factors that affect social identification.

The success of LETS organizations is determined by the enhancement of that experience and the emotional responses of the individual, including the employees, to the attributes of the service offering, together with the extent to which organizations understand their customers and are able to utilize the increasingly sophisticated array of quality systems, awards and tools to ensure they consistently meet the needs and wants of customers. In the first edition we posed the question of whether advances in technology and service processes would create more standardized and impersonal experiences or would the interaction between staff and customers continue to be pivotal to many organizations. The evidence is that many LETS organizations recognize this dichotomy, if not always successful in what they do, although the majority of global LETS brands utilize business improvement strategies to distinguish themselves from their competitors, enabling them to achieve business excellence and have loyal and engaged customers and staff. The challenge still remains for much of the LETS industry to marry a systematic and planned approach with the delivery of a personalized, fulfilling and increasingly emotional customer experience, co-created by actively engaged employees and, hopefully, this second edition can make a contribution to achieving this.

REFERENCES

Berry, L.L. (1999) *Discovering the Soul of Service: The Nine Drivers of Sustainable Business Success*. Free Press, New York.
Michelli, J. (2008) *The New Gold Standard*. McGraw-Hill, New York.
Sutton, C. (2015) The human sigma approach to business improvement in tourism SMEs. *Journal of Small Business and Enterprise Development* 22(2) 302–319.

Index

Note: italic page numbers indicate figures and tables.